UNDERSTANDING CHILDREN THROUGH ASTROLOGY

by
Samantha A. Davis

TOP OF THE MOUNTAIN PUBLISHING
Largo, Florida 34643-5117 U.S.A.

TOP OF THE MOUNTAIN PUBLISHING
11701 South Belcher Road, Suite 123
Largo, Florida 34643-5117 U.S.A.
SAN 287-590X
FAX (24 hour) (813) 536-3681
PHONE (813) 530-0110

Copyright 1993 by Samantha A. Davis

1st edition 1992
2nd edition (revised) 1993

Library of Congress Cataloging in Publication Data
Davis, Samantha A., 1940
Understanding children through astrology : a uniquely
new approach
/ by Samantha A. Davis
p.cm.
Includes Index.
ISBN 1-56087-072-9: $16.95
1. Astrology and child rearing. I. Title.
BF1729.C45D39   1993
133.5'86491—dc20   93-14947CIP

Manufactured in the United States of America

DEDICATION

To the molders of our future — the parents,
caregivers, and teachers everywhere... may you gain
better understanding, perception and sensitivity
toward the children of Mother Earth, no matter
what their age.

To the *psychotherapists* who are using astrological
charts to gain accurate information about their
patients' personalities...

And to the *Inner Child* within us all.

Contents

Contents

FOREWORD

There's something remarkable about gaining that extra-special insight into personalities... whether it is your own, your loved ones' or your friends'. We all benefit when we better understand how each person functions — and when we know their likes and dislikes.

Samantha A. Davis' *Understanding Children Through Astrology* takes the basic approach to Astrology and child-rearing. As Samantha's long-time friend, aunt of thirty nephews and nieces, seven grand nephews and nieces, and fellow author, I can relate to her concern for the children of our future.

Although most of us may think that astrology and raising children do not necessarily go hand-in-hand, there's something unique and essential in recognizing that astrology does play a role in how we all develop. From this book, I gained a broad perspective on why children (I even looked up my husband Tag's chart) behave the way they do... why they want what they want... what makes them throw temper tantrums one minute and act like angels the next!

This book is written for people like me... who don't have an in-depth knowledge of what makes up an astrological personality profile... yet are concerned about the welfare of children and their interests. This book is easy-to-read and the tables are simple-to-follow for the parent, caretaker or therapist in understanding the psyche. This work is not difficult to understand, and provides a practical reference for people who want access to how they, their friends and family members tick!

With *Understanding Children Through Astrology*, Samantha takes the guess-work out of raising children. She realizes you may not have all the time in the world to sit and read a lengthy, all-engrossing guide to personality. Because of her experience as a mother of four, Samantha takes into account your time, your knowledge, your experience and your children... she completes a book which is both instrumental in educating yourself and your children.

Building communication is crucial in the early years of childhood development. It is the first steps towards fulfilling and successful relationships. With this book, you can start early with your newborn... or renew already established intimacy with your children... or initiate positive relationships for improvement. Don't wait until it's too late; it's never too early — no matter how old your children are.

This book allowed me a profound look into myself and my loved ones. (I now even use astrology to better understand my employees and my sisters and brothers.) I found that Tag's "Astrological Personality Profile," described in Samantha's book, fits him like a glove! A great work for all parents, teachers and therapists!

Dr. Judith Powell
Author of *Silva Mind Mastery for the '90s*

PREFACE

Parenthood and *Caregiving* are the most important and creative experiences we encounter in life. Unfortunately, most of us have little knowledge and less experience with which to handle this challenge. Where does one go to learn to be a good parent, guardian or caregiver? That's a good question! In previous decades, parenting was not as difficult to handle because children were expected to follow in their parents' footsteps and not as much emphasis was placed on the individual or their possible future potential. Now, with much less restriction in our society and more recognition of individuality, the problems of parenting, teaching, and counseling have grown tremendously. Our children are now exposed to more, are more aware... and have more potential than ever before (to rise or fall!). No wonder it has become even more challenging to be a parent, caregiver and/or therapist in this new decade!

As a mother of four, *astrology* has helped me to understand and guide my children on an individual basis. With a better understanding of how they think, what their emotional makeup is, what they will or won't respond to, and where their talents lie, we have developed more compatible and closer, loving relationships. I have the advantage of knowing their strengths and weaknesses, giving me the ability to guide and direct them from childhood to adulthood with greater understanding. This eliminated frustrations for all of us.

I realize *astrology* is a complicated subject and not all parents have the time or the energy to devote to studying it as I have. This reason is what prompted me to write this book — to give an *un*complicated overview written in a way to best serve the understanding of children. It is my intention to share this small part of the astrological wisdom in an easy, intelligible way... as it specifically applies to raising and guiding children.

Since each being (child or otherwise) is a complete and unique individual, it becomes very clear that each should be treated and handled on an individual basis. We are not sheep, to be herded together and driven down the same path and neither are our children. It has been said that *children are merely small adults in the process of becoming, only with less experience or wisdom upon which to draw.* That's where we come in as parents and teachers. We set the stage and show them the way through example; through love and understanding.

What works and is best for one child may not at all apply to the next. *Astrology stresses individuality.* Let's imagine a picture of the Universe (as much as we know of it) was taken at the exact moment of a child's birth, at that specific location — and that this picture of the heavens becomes their own personal road map to their destiny. This image sounds fatalistic, as if there is no freedom of will, but that's not true... as you will learn in this book. In fact, that is *the purpose of this book — for you to guide, influence and liberate your child's free will!*

Let me compare life to a trip across the country. If you started on your trip without a map, you would sooner or later (mostly later), arrive at your destination. However, along the way you may hit bad roads, detours, take the long way, take the wrong way and even get lost. Life can be the same. Each individual's astrological chart is their own personal road map to their own life's trip. We can choose to use a map for guidance or we can wander along full of only hopes and wishes.

I believe *astrology* is only one of several maps or tools which are here for us to use as we journey through the experience of life. The study of our palms is another, our numerological significance is still another and there are many more. They all collaborate with one another and are merely different approaches to gaining the directions and reading the road signs. Invariably, these routes all follow one basic blueprint — each person is an individual with a specific purpose and path.

The challenges arise only when we lack knowledge or comprehension of how to read these maps and use these tools. This is one time when a little bit of knowledge is not dangerous because every little bit of information will add to a better understanding.

In one's personal astrological chart, what may be considered a negative characteristic (I prefer to call them obstacles to be overcome or non-beneficial expressions) can be changed into a beneficial expression, by understanding and working with that characteristic. Remember, the *planets are just energy — how each of us* chooses to express these energies makes the difference. Once the obstacle is seen and understood, it can then be removed or changed. The lines on our hands can even be seen to change as *we* change. In *astrology*, we say that the non-beneficial effects will no longer be felt, that we *transcend* them. It's up to us to raise our level of consciousness and to help others do the same. As parents, caregivers, therapists and teachers, this education is our primary responsibility to our children and those under our care. The astrological chart is the map, how we individually follow it depends on us.

I hope you find this information enlightening. I know it will give you insight plus some very useful tools. To be covered are the two *luminaries* — the *Sun*, which is the spirit and vital force — the *Moon*, the emotional makeup. Also explained are the three *personal planets* which are: *Mercury*, representing the thought processes and mental attitudes; *Venus*, showing the way love is experienced, as well as the appreciation of beauty and how one relates to other people; and *Mars*, symbolizing the type of energy, aggressiveness, and drive. Also included are the two connecting planets: Jupiter, representing our abundance and good fortune and point of expansion; and Saturn, representing our discipline, limitations and lessons to be learned in this life.

There are easy-to-use tables in each chapter where you will be able to find out what sign these planets fall in for your children... no matter what their age. *Do check your own chart* and see how many roadblocks or obstacles you may or may not have already overcome, and how much of your own potential *you* have developed. Discover too, how your chart relates to each child's and how you can improve these relationships! This process gets a little complicated, so I suggest you see a *professional* astrologer and ask for *comparison charts*.

If you should happen to know what your child's *Ascendant* sign is, read the Sun sign description of that sign and you will have even one more piece of your little angel's intricate personality puzzle.

It is advisable to read the brief description at the beginning of each chapter in order to understand how the energy of the planet functions. As for that extremely important (and usually baffling) subject on how to most effectively discipline the *individual* child, I will give practical methods of discipline which will work well for the different signs. It is important to help children develop positively and not throw roadblocks in their way! The results of using these astrological applications are better than a slap... and there is no damage to the individual child's potential!

The information in this book will help to make your daily life with your children a little more understandable, pleasant, and productive.

Thank you for having the interest and taking the time to help our children to be happier, more secure adults. The future of our world is dependent on it!

Samantha A. Davis

ACKNOWLEDGMENTS

To my daughter Gina Johns and my friend Barbara Friedman (without both of their help, this book would have never materialized).

To Colette Lamphear, for her patience and persistance in entering the tables on the computer.

To my creative editor, Yvonne Fawcett, who made sure I covered all the bases, astrologically speaking.

To Alina Nguyen and John Anderson, who put the finishing touches on my book.

To my good friends Judi and Tag Powell, for publishing my work.

To all my teachers along the way.

And to my husband Bill, whose encouragement and patience were invaluable.

"The stars above us
govern our conditions."
William Shakespeare

INTRODUCTION

Programming — How It All Begins

To better understand how our programming begins, we need to know how our brain/ mind works. To do that, let's start thinking of the brain as a computer (yes, we are all much more than a computer). Visualize or imagine that inside your head is a computer with a screen or monitor, and a keyboard. The brain is the machine part of our being, the command center. Once we understand it, we can function much more effectively. As it is, most people are operating the brain-computer without instructions or guidelines, thereby not obtaining maximum benefit while allowing the computer to run without direction!

Let's imagine you have a brand *new* computer. You have to put programs into the computer in order to have it produce anything. What you get out is a product of what is put in. GIGO, the computer term meaning garbage in—garbage out, explains this concept well. If we put garbage into the computer, that is what we will get back — garbage. So it is the same with the brain. If we put negative or non-beneficial thoughts into our brain for programs, our lives will reflect the results of these programs. Once we realize this relationship, it simply becomes a process of clearing out or *canceling* out the garbage, then *replacing* it with beneficial thoughts or programs.

Programming, to carry on the analogy, is the learned personality developed to fit in and become accepted in the environment and by society (what Freud called the *Superego*). It is easy now to see the importance of early or initial programming! With beneficial programming from the beginning, limitations are lessened and potentials enhanced and accelerated. An important point to remember is — *your life up until now is in many ways a result of the programming you received, whether it was beneficial or not.* And yes, our personalities are a result of *far more* than our programs. We all need to realize this aspect so we can tap into our own innate special selves, as shown in our own special and individual *horoscopes!*

Consider for a moment that we are a fetus in the womb. We have oneness in physical form with another human in physical form, our mother. There is total sharing and unity. As we separate at birth from this oneness to take responsibility for our own functioning, scientific research shows we are operating at a *very slow brainwave frequency*. This slow frequency relates to the *feeling level* of our being. Whatever happens while in this frequency is impressed very strongly on our brain cells; our memory. If these feelings are beneficial impressions such as a harmonious, loving environment, we will feel secure and confident. If it is a hostile environment with much anger, or even anxiety, then we will develop fear and detachment. This factor is the whole basis of our human development and cannot be stressed strongly enough! These early experiences make the difference between feeling accepted and supported... or just the opposite. Is the environment one which stimulates the survival instincts and the need to protect oneself? Or is it one which stimulates unity and is a safe place to develop one's sense of SELF?

Parents and caregivers are the first influences on their babies' biological computers. They continue to have the strongest influence because they are the children's first authority figures. Children are dependent upon adult guidance, protection, and love... for their very survival.

In the beginning, since babies have not developed language skills, they are functioning only from the feeling and thought levels. There is actually a communication that takes place through thought on an inner level we don't yet fully understand, but we all appear to respond to it. We have found that when we attach feelings, emotions, and pictures to the *thought forms*, the message transmission is stronger.

For example: you are tired. You start thinking, the baby might not sleep through the night. The more you think about it and remember the last time you were up all night, or visualize your baby crying, the better chance there is of making that happen. *Where our attention goes, our energy flows!* This means that if we put energy into a fear — we will produce it as a reality, as easily as when we put our energy into a desire to create it as a reality. Thus, we project our fears to our children and the children under our care. They receive these feelings as *programs* and experience their lives accordingly. For instance, if a parent fears illness, they could have a child who often produces illness, or even a chronic problem.

We can resolve this non-beneficial projection to our children by *clearing out our own fears and garbage* — so we are better able to give our children programs which bring them beneficial results. Remember that the programs we received from our parents were the best ones they had with their level of understanding at that time. We can now give our children a head start!

The best way I know to eliminate our personal fear-and-anger-based programs is to understand the true meaning of emotions. *Emotions are the messengers between the inner-self or who we were at birth — and the* programming we have received after we arrived. Since *fears are learned*, any fear-based emotion is the inner-self saying that something in the programming is not serving our best interests. These non-beneficial emotions show us where we need to make changes and reprogram.

Since these programs either came from others or were created from early childhood experiences, it is logical they could be inappropriate now. So work on digging out these old reactions and thoughts — and *cancel*. Now add and continually repeat a new beneficial program to change the attitude. The next time the same program is activated (or someone "pulls your chain") you are better able to respond with conscious control... instead of with unconscious blind fear/anger reaction. As we continue this process of reinforcing the new program, the old one weakens. As we release the old program, we eliminate the negative. When there is no longer any energy being put into a fear or anger... it isn't created... it is *uncreated*!

Unproductive emotions are based on lack of security, lack of control... or even a lack of comfort. When we experience good emotions, it is because we are receiving what we want from the environment... or something or someone is reflecting, sending something which makes us feel good.

Understanding how the brain is programmed and combining it with the new awareness that *astrology* gives us, we can *reprogram ourselves*, and we can start viewing everyone, including our children, in a new light. If others are negative, they are experiencing a lacking in some aspect of their lives. If they are positive and loving, their needs are being satisfied. They feel secure. We can project this security onto our environment... onto our children.

I believe that by *Understanding Children Through Astrology*, the natural inclinations of our very individualistic children will surface... we can begin to reprogram the negative and program in the positive. After reading this book, you will gain a better knowledge on how to develop each child's own creating, producing, serving, responding, loving qualities... to make this a better, safer, happier world for us all.

*"No one should attempt the
practice of healing without first having
a thorough knowledge of astrology."*
Hippocrates, Father of Medicine

CHAPTER 1

Three Master Keys in
the Art of Parenting

*A*side from love, good communication and
the ability to motivate are the two most
important considerations for mastering the *art of
parenting*. Actually, they are important for establishing
any relationship, and are especially crucial in guiding
children. The word *guiding* is the clue here. The role
of parenting or caregiving is to be a proficient facilitator. A facilitator acts as a catalyst to bring out a person's
best, to help them develop and utilize their greatest
potential.

As Kahlil Gibran in his infinite wisdom stated,
"Your children are not your children — they are the
sons and daughters of life longing for itself. They come

through you but not from you, and though they are with you they belong not to you — you may give them your love but not your thoughts for they have their own thoughts."

It is not intended for us to own our children or to mold or shape them into what *we* think they should be. Once this is understood, we can begin to take a more objective approach to parenting and apply our unlimited creativity into handling and guiding our children's development more effectively. In this very sense, astrology is the perfect tool as it enables one to look at a child's makeup objectively, as well as it describes the various individual personality characteristics.

1. The Communication Key

Verbal communication is one of our primary modes of interacting with one another. It is also one of our areas of most difficulty. In verbal communication, words are the tools we use to share concepts. Yet, each of us responds and reacts differently to the same words. We have different meanings for the same words and place different importance and value on them. Some people resonate with words which create feeling and others are activated with words which stimulate thought and objectivity.

We need to understand that we all process very differently, bringing us to the question — "who is responsible for the communication to be understood?"

The answer? — "Responsibility for a mutual understanding is always placed with the person who is presenting the communication!" As parents, it is extremely important that you present your information in a manner in which your child is able to easily receive and understand it. This suggestion means you must understand how *your child* processes his or her information.

For example, the planet Mercury and its placement by each astrological sign will provide you insight into the frequency which each child is attuned. Think of it as a radio station — in order to have clear reception you must be tuned into the right frequency. When Mercury is placed in different signs, our mental processes function differently. Each sign has its own frequency or mode for transmission and reception. By knowing how your child's Mercury or thought process operates, you can adjust your own mode and tune into their frequency. This interaction is called *establishing rapport* — a valuable skill to learn for effective communication in every relationship.

For further comprehension of how this works, let's briefly examine some different placements. When Mercury is placed in the sign of Gemini it expresses itself in its purist form. This child is logical, rational, and is able to think, reason and understand easily. Their thought process is like a computer because it takes information and processes it rapidly. These children thrive on information. They have no interference from emotions or feelings about what they take in —

they simply assimilate it objectively. On the other hand, when Mercury is placed in the sign of Cancer, it is difficult for the child to have a thought without a feeling, or a feeling without a thought. This level of communication is because the sign of Cancer is emotional and sensitive, often lacking in logic. When communicating with the Mercury in Gemini, using the word think (i.e. "I *think* this," or "what do you *think* about") — is most effective. When communicating with the Mercury in Cancer, using the word feel (i.e. "I *feel* this," or what do you *feel* about") — will provide best results. Some signs respond to a practical approach and others need pictures painted with words because they are so visual. As you can see, understanding a child's Mercury placement is a valuable asset for establishing rapport. Refer to the Mercury section in this book for complete descriptions.

Seven Communication Skills

1. Be aware of your tone. Sometimes we say one thing with our words and quite another with our tone. Since children function at a more sensitive brainwave frequency, this discrepancy is very obvious to them and will cause confusion.

2. Listen first. Most people want to talk first. They want you to know their thoughts and feelings, and to be understood first. If you do speak first, most people will not really be listening; they either will be speaking or preparing to speak. The best approach to gaining rapport is to say, "Let me listen to you first." Next start thinking "win-win" to find the best solution for everyone involved.

3. Always validate the other person first before presenting different or opposing information. Since everyone has a built-in survival mechanism that automatically begins to prepare a defense when their rightness is threatened, it is necessary to validate their viewpoint (even if you disagree) to eliminate this automatic process. Simply say, "I understand how you might think that way," or "I can see how you might feel this way." By doing this you, as a parent, stop any defensiveness and can establish rapport with your children. The next step is to ask, "May I *share* my thoughts, feelings, or ideas with you?" The word *share* is important here and asking permission will open them to being receptive. This process is what I call *productive disagreement.*

4. Get feedback for clarity or understanding to be sure you are being understood. Ask questions like, "What did you hear me say?," or "What do you think I mean?" For your own clarification you can ask, "I thought I heard you say — is that what you meant?" Remember that everyone is processing differently. The information is always entering and projecting through a person's own filters. Since no two people can stand in the same exact place, everyone's perceptions are a little different.

5. *Become aware of body language.* It is helpful to watch body postures and facial expressions when communicating with others, especially your child. An awareness of your own body language is also important. For instance, if you tell a child "I love you" in a cool, detached tone of voice with your arms crossed across your chest, you will not convey what you mean because of your body language. The words become insignificant; they are disregarded and the message is lost — distance is gained rather than love. Touching your child while speaking with him or her is another effective tool. Hold your children's hand when explaining things to them. Finally, start talking "with" them instead of "to" them.

6) *Listen... Listen... Listen.* Most of us are not very good at doing this. As parents, we may think we listen, yet I find there is always room for improvement. This listening ability is a learned and developed skill. It is not instinctual and most of us never refine it. When I say "listen," I mean not only to hear WHAT is being said, I also mean to pay attention to HOW it is said. What kind of words are used? Learn to respond most effectively by using the same types of words, such as feel, think, see, hear, etc. This response also aids in establishing rapport. Next, start listening to yourself as well. How do *you* say things? This way you can tune into any negativity within yourself and become aware

of what you are telling yourself and ultimately, your child. How many of us ever *really* listen to ourselves?

7. *Honesty is mandatory!* Lying to children creates insecurity, lack of trust, fear, and leads to lack of faith. Since children function primarily on the Alpha brainwave frequency, and have a very high degree of intuitive awareness, it is next to impossible to fool them. It is better not to try. It is always best to be honest. There is always a way to handle any situation honestly, even if it is something your children don't need to or shouldn't know. You can still be honest by saying, "I don't want to discuss it right now." Finally, I would like to share an idea with you. What if we were all telepathic and everyone knew what everyone else was truly thinking all the time!? How differently do you think life would be? I suggest it would be a good exercise for us all to start living our lives as if this idea were true (on some level I think it is!).

2. The Motivation Key

Knowing how to motivate another person, especially a child, is half the battle of becoming a successful facilitator-parent. The trick is to create the *desire* within the child to want to take an initiative. Most of us will take action when we can see a benefit for ourselves; we will do or act on something for self-gratification and self-gain. Some people are more motivated to do for others, yet the result is still the same — their actions make them feel good about themselves.

Astrologically, Mars is considered the motivating factor since it describes the drive plus *where* and *how* we use our energy. Refer to the Mars section in this book for your clues on how to motivate your child to produce beneficial results.

In addition, we always need to consider the Sun's placement since it is the inner-force and primary essence within us all. The Venus placement describes what makes us feel good, comfortable and loved, plus what we value. The Moon explains the emotional make-up, our fears and compassions.

With all of this information available, we owe it to our future world to use it so that we may help our children to become more self-actualized and fulfilled individuals. Our children are our most valuable assets and our world's future caretakers.

Seven Motivation Skills

1. Create a comfort level or pleasant atmosphere for your child in order to establish rapport. Talk first about a pleasant experience which your child has had in the past—or a pleasant experience which you shared together. This act will create even more comfort and open receptivity.

2. *Be aware of and keep in mind what turns your child on... what sparks their interests.* Awareness will enable you to present your information in a manner most appealing to the youth. Associate what you are presenting to something the subject likes or would like — relate both of your interests to find a common meeting ground. Connect your presentation to things which will bring joy to the youth.

3. *Stimulate interest and create desire.* Find the benefit for the child. Show them you are giving them something they want, and which will make them receive pleasure. Point out the beneficial outcomes. Show them enthusiasm and excitement in your communication. Make them want what you are presenting by showing them the positive results.

4. *Ask motivating questions.* Statements like, "Wouldn't you like to..." or "Wouldn't you feel good about..." will stimulate their thought processes in a positive manner. Give them time to think about your questions, and time to respond. Ask for their ideas on how to solve problems, and give them choices. I have found that by asking for their ideas on solving problems, some very creative and beneficial solutions are discovered. You can also ask your youth what they would do if they were the parent. This position causes them to view the situation very differently than they would have before. Next, letting children make choices

simulates growth and promotes maturity. It also contributes to becoming responsible for their own actions and life. You can present the choices such as, "If you do that — this will happen," and, "If you do this — this will happen; the choice is yours." Not many of us are happy being dictated to. At least your children *do* have a choice this way. Our process of learning is through our mistakes, sometimes it is best to let them make a few.

5. *Point out some of their other accomplishments which corroborate with or validate your presentation.* Praise the qualities they possess which will contribute to their ability to accomplish what you are presenting. For example, recognize the good listening skills in your child, and he or she will continue to listen intently and avidly. Thus, you are emphasizing a quality which will result in the development of positive behavior and trust. Make your youth feel good about him/herself. Build up and strengthen their confidence, and they will look to you for support, strength and guidance.

6. *Eliminate pressure tactics and maintain a level of objectivity.* Present your information in a clear and objective manner, without emotions or expectations involved. Simply present the facts, the pros and cons. You also can give your thoughts and ideas on the subject, and what you would do in a similar situation

without expectation. It is vitally important to always see the circumstances from your youth's point-of-view.

7. Back off and give them the opportunity to process your idea. This final and closing communication process is most important because it will provide space and room for individual decision-making. Your child will have the opportunity to make his or her own choices. Tell them, "It is your choice because, ultimately, everyone has to take responsibility for their own beliefs, actions and selections." Help your youth if he or she asks for it, and always support his or her decision. Even if you don't agree with their choices, it is important to try to understand their point-of-view. Then let them pay their own consequences or reap their own rewards.

3. The Discipline Key

The basis of all discipline is right thinking and beneficial action. How does a person know when he or she is off-track? It is by way of our mistakes—we all make them at one time or another. This process is constant and applies to all areas of life. We make mistakes in our relationships, our emotions, our social life, our finances—even in how we maintain our physical health. From an internal point-of-view, when we are off-track, we begin to feel uncomfortable, unfulfilled, restricted, resentful, angry, depressed, less energetic and even ill.

Since all we think is manifested in our physical world, it is the thinking which will put us back on-track. Any person who has ever overcome any difficulty has taken control of their thinking. Every one of us has the ability to command our thoughts. This capability is the KEY to good discipline.

As parent-facilitators, it is our purpose to assist our young to develop their own ability for self-discipline. It is up to us to teach them the skill of disciplined thinking—we must all learn it, we do not arrive on this planet having it. The sooner we learn how to govern our thoughts, the quicker our lives are enhanced by happiness, productivity and love. How well a person is disciplined is directly related to how much responsibility he or she has been given or has voluntarily assumed.

As you can see, it is important to give our youth as much responsibility as early in life as possible. With this responsibility, they can practice developing *self*-discipline. Helping your child with this skill is one of the most precious gifts you could ever give to them. Inner-control over thoughts, feelings and actions will affect how our youth learn, work, play and deal with the many situations they must, inevitably, confront.

Somehow, most of us have equated discipline with drudgery. It would be to our advantage to associate it with Joy! Some parents try to make life as easy as possible for their children, some even think they are supposed to. In many cases, these parents take total responsibility for their children—leaving them obligation-

free and without a set basis for striving toward achieve-
ment. Believe me, if you think non-responsibility protects our youth, you are not doing them any favors!
This type of behavior only leaves them unprepared for
real-life experiences, and impairs their ability to have
joyful lives. *Good discipline is a habit which produces
beneficial results, and is formed from repetition.* As parent-facilitators, our job is to help our children develop
these beneficial habits. The following skills will aid you
with this education process.

Seven Discipline Skills

1. *Ask for the behavior you want* rather than telling
children what you don't want. Make it a positive statement, not a negative.
Example:
(a) Close the door quietly — rather than — Don't
slam the door.
(b) Drive carefully — rather than — Don't have an
accident.
(c) Please stop doing... — rather than — Don't do...
Always ask for the positive. In this manner you will
be creating the most beneficial results.

2. *Think first before speaking.* When your child
presents a situation to you or asks a question, answer:
"Let me think about it for a minute." Two things happen: you get time to work out any feelings you have

about the subject, and you get time to think through what you want to say. Then you can respond with an objective, logical, unemotional answer or solution.

3. *Modify your reactions.* Use the old saying, "Take a deep breath and count to ten." If you react to anything your children do or say with anger, disgust, shock or horror you will be threatening their survival (and further openness) from an inner-level of consciousness. Any time you invalidate or make *anyone* wrong in any way, you have threatened their survival, and they will immediately prepare a defense. This response is an automatic internal process. It applies even more so to your relationships with your children... if you attack their survival they will develop a defense. Lying becomes an easy way to avoid these unpleasant reactions from you, and you can be sure that your child won't be sharing everything with you. If your child can tell you the truth and come to you with anything... and you respond in a calm, solution-oriented manner... you will have a closer and better relationship. You also can teach them, through your behavior, that it is best to deal with life in a truthful, logical, calm manner.

4. *Start becoming solution-oriented.* Too often we tend to look at new situations concerning our children as problems. Change *problems* to *challenges* and focus on finding *solutions*. By doing this you will change the energy around any given situation.

5. *Use distraction whenever possible,* with young children in particular. Divert their attention away from whatever you don't want them to do, and lead them on to something else. When dealing with or counter-acting negativity, it is best to distract attention rather than fight head-on. By reading the placements of their planets, you can learn what they will respond to best.

6. *Tell them what you are going to do when they misbehave.* Example: "I will not drive the car while there is fighting." Then simply pull to the side of the road, and stop the car whenever there is fighting. Sit there until they stop misbehaving. They will soon get tired of this behavior. And moreover, they will know what to expect by your consistency of word *and* action.

7. Finally and most importantly is to avoid guilt. *Guilt has absolutely no beneficial result.* Not only is it unproductive, it also is a detriment to one's health. Stop using guilt to manipulate. Avoid instilling guilt in your child to gain results or effect change. Instead, find a way to create a desire within them to take action. This method is the highest form of manipulation... and a healthy one!

"Astrology does not offer an explanation of the
laws of the Universe, nor why the Universe exists.
What it does, to put it in simplest terms,
is to show us that there is a correspondence between
macrocosm and microcosm. In short,
that there is a rhythm to the Universe, and
that our own lives partake of the rhythm..."
                                          Henry Miller

CHAPTER 2

ABC's of Astrology

This science of the stars was first "discovered" and recorded by the original astrologers — the *Chaldeans*. So renown was their wisdom of the skys, that they are mentioned as "wise men" in the Bible's *Old Testament*.

Astrology is a tool which enables us to realize the natural inclinations of each *individual* personality... their personal road map. The *astrological chart* provides specific information as to a person's strengths and weaknesses. Each *planet* symbolically represents a *characteristic* of the personality, and the *sign* that the planet is in determines the way in which the characteristic is *expressed*. The number of *degrees* between the planets forms the angle that shows us how the planet's characteristics interact with one another — whether with harmony and ease, or with conflict and tension.

Astrology gives us this knowledge so we can choose to take responsibility and "respond" rather than "react" to these influences. It also prevents us from wasting time, energy, and emotion with unnecessary resistance to another person's planetary configurations. The astrological chart shows us where to put our and our children's energy to accelerate talents and abilities, and where to modify any less-desirable characteristics.

Another use of the astrological tool is as a *timing* device. Carl Jung called timing *synchronicity* meaning coincidence. And since everything in the Universe is energy, including human beings, and all energy is interrelated, astrology shows how our personal clock or timing interacts with the universal clock or timing. (Visualize gears within gears within gears, the same as when looking at the inside of a watch, with each gear interacting with the others.)

Knowing when to move forward and when to wait is invaluable information. Having this information *ahead* of time gives us the ability to direct events in our lives more beneficially, more productively. We can also modify or soften the effects of any undesirable events.

There has been much written about your child's *Sun sign* and I am sure that this alone has given you much insight. This book will go further and define additional personal components of your child's makeup. We will cover the two luminaries — the Sun and the Moon, and the three personal planets — Mercury, Venus, and Mars. Jupiter and Saturn, important connecting planets in themselves, are also covered in this book to a lesser degree, because Mercury, Venus, and Mars are, I believe, more pertinent in dealing with the communication and the interaction between parent/caregiver and child.

The outer planets — Uranus, Neptune, and Pluto — are further away from Earth, causing their cycles to be longer; thus, they stay in one sign for longer periods of time. It has been said that these three planets have influence over generation consciousness and possibly transformations.

There is another important facet in the astrological chart which is called the *Ascendant* or *Rising sign*, and which must be calculated by an astrologer, or an astrology computer program — according to the exact time, place, and date of birth. It is the sign that was coming up on the horizon at the place of birth. The ascendant has *influence over the physical body*, such as its bone structure, its shape, and size — and represents the *personality* which we develop and learn to use as a safe or acceptable way to communicate with and interact with the outer world.

Other considerations in reading the astrological map are what we call the aspects. *Aspects* are the number of degrees that each planet is from one another, or the angles that they may form to each other based on a 360-degree circle. We call this circle a *wheel*. The wheel is then divided into 12 thirty-degree sections which we call *houses*. Each house has the qualities of different sides of life, such as partnerships, money, health, friends, children, love, sex. The house that the planet is in has an influence over that area of life. Think of the *planets* as the *energy*... the *sign* that the planet is in as the way that the energy is *expressed*... and the *house* that it is in as the *life area* in which that particular planet expresses itself.

This information is more complex than what is intended for this book. Not everyone wants to become an astrologer. It is not my purpose to give you a complete analysis of your child, but to help you relate better, to try and be a more effective 'parent-facilitator' — through an understanding of the luminaries and the three personal planets, and how they respond in the different signs. If you desire, the *complete analysis* should be done by a fully-integrated computer program, or by a competent, helpful, positive-thinking, solution-oriented astrologer.

"We are born at a given moment,
in a given place and,
like vintage years of wine,
we have the qualities of the year and
of the season in which we are born."

Carl G. Jung

CHAPTER 3

Retrogrades

Retrogrades is a term that we use to describe a planet's *apparent* backward motion. The fact is all the planets are always moving forward and it is only an illusion that they sometimes seem to be going backwards. We can explain this by using the example of picturing two cars traveling down the street at the same speed. When one increases its speed, the other appears to be going backward when being viewed from the faster car. From the Earth, this is how the planets look to us.

Any planet in a retrograde motion will have its energies flowing in a different direction. Retrogrades give us the opportunity to go back over things, make changes, and eliminate any non-beneficial thoughts and situations in our lives. Retrogrades tend to *stimulate internalization* — we may focus more on our own growth, our needs, and desires. If planets are retrograde in the birth chart, their energies will be of a more internalized nature. We are often quick to make the word "different" mean wrong, because it is unfamiliar, and as long as a retrograde is understood it can be worked with.

A retrograde planet child may have to work harder to achieve their full purpose and potential and it may be a longer time coming, but the strength upon which it is built can be drawn on forever. A retrograde gives the power to go back and redo or undo, and then go on again. It may take a little more discipline to develop the retrograde potential, but it is always well worth the effort.

The retrograde planet usually works on the subjective or inner-conscious level. Retrograde planets are extremely important because their significance is not as easily recognized. Since they are of an internal nature, they are keys to our personal complexities. It is an area where the potential may be delayed, or assets and liabilities may have been overlooked. Examine them closely and gain valuable tips.

The retrogrades will be described separately at the beginning of each planet section for a clearer understanding of how each planet might be acting in an internalized manner. These planets will present to you some interesting challenges.

You will be able to tell when a planet is *retrograde* by an R in the tables, on the day that it turns in the retrograde direction. It will stay that way until a D appears next to the sign in the tables, indicating that it has turned in *direct motion* (the Sun and Moon will always be going forward).

You might want to check how many days *after* your child's birth date a planet changes direction. Take each day to equal one year — you may see a change in your child the year it changes. For example, *ten days* after the child's birthday, Mercury might turn from retrograde to direct motion. So when the child is *ten years* old, he might start to express his thinking more openly and directly... or be more eager or able to learn. If you were to see that eight days after the birthday, the planet Mars changed from direct to retrograde, at age eight the child might internalize his anger instead of expressing it in a healthy, open manner.

The chapters on Mercury, Venus, and Mars will each have a more complete explanation of how these energies change.

Other considerations that might alter the planets' placements in the signs are important enough to bear repeating.

The *aspects* or *angles* in degrees that one planet is from another have a certain effect on each one. Not every angle has the same effect. Some work with more harmony and ease than others, and some have a more difficult effect. (See the Glossary for more on aspects.) The *house position* of the planet in the chart, or the particular area of life in which each planet works, makes a difference too. Aside from these consider-ations, you will find a high degree of accuracy in the following descriptions.

"We and the cosmos are one. The cosmos is a vast living body, of which we are still parts.
The Sun is a great heart whose tremors run through our smallest veins. The Moon is a great gleaming nerve-center from which we quiver forever. Who knows the power that Venus has over us, or Mars? But it is a vital power, rippling exquisitely through us all the time.
D.H. Lawrence, Apocalypse

CHAPTER 4

The Sun — The Vital Force

*T*he Sun, giver of life, is the vital force, *core*, or *inner drive* within us. It is the energizing force of the being! No matter what else the chart says, it will only be an extension, an addition, or modification of what the vital force is. Some of us show this inner self and some of us don't. We are more inclined to be true to ourselves, (our Sun sign) in early childhood and then again in old age. The stronger of us may overcome conditioning, programming, and expectation and remain ourselves always, but not many. No matter how obvious it is or isn't, the core of our being will still be the same. By understanding this inner drive, we will be better equipped to help our children develop themselves and express their inner-selves in a more positive, productive manner.

It is important to understand this inner drive — to not damage, destroy, or inhibit its functions. By knowing the beneficial and non-beneficial sides of this drive, we can encourage discipline over the *non-beneficial* and stimulate strength in the *beneficial*. Environment has an important influence over the expression of the being, and as parents and caregivers we have the first opportunity to nurture the potential. This is a great responsibility... and a great challenge.

First, start by thinking of your child not as a girl or a boy or even a child, but as a small person needing your assistance while growing and learning to mature. All beings are equipped with their own individual set of functions and their own purpose in life. We are all happier when we are expressing ourselves as we really are and fulfilling our own purpose. If more people would or could do this, it would eliminate most frustrations and negativity. Try not to put conditions and expectations on your children, but love them for themselves; love them as they are. The only trick is to help them understand... to help them accept, discipline, and develop themselves. Stop trying to make of these little beings what you want them to be... or think they should be... or what *you* want to be — and start helping them be the best of whom they really are!

The Sun is the energizing force of the character and should be allowed to flow freely, not blocked with restriction or filtered through limitations.

As you read of the different life forces or Sun signs, you will begin to see why each being might act the way they do. It is fascinating and encouraging to note that Jeane Dixon in her book, *Yesterday, Today and Tomorrow*, has shown us how each one of Jesus' twelve disciples may have belonged to one of the twelve astrological signs. Coincidence? Or maybe it was just to show us that each of us belonging to a specific Sun sign is needed to fulfill his or her purpose in the master plan.

How to Use Sun Tables

These Sun tables show the day of the month for each year that the Sun moved into a new sign. The information was taken from the American Ephemeris in which the dates were calculated for midnight, based on universal time, the same as Greenwich mean time.

On occasion, a person whose birthdate is on the day the Sun changes signs, or one which is on the day before, could be either sign based on the time and location of birth. These are called "Cuspal Births," and should be calculated exactly by an astrologer or a computer. For all others the Sun will be in a sign from the date shown until the next date given.

Example: For the year 1900, the sun entered Pisces on Feb 20, and stayed in Pisces until March 22, when it entered Aries. Birthdates from February 20, through March 21, the person would be a Pisces. Birthdates from March 22, through April 20, would be an Aries — and so on.

Hint: Use a ruler to move across the page to avoid mistakes.

SIGNS

ARI	Aries	LIB	Libra
TAU	Taurus	SCO	Scorpio
GEM	Gemini	SAG	Sagittarius
CAN	Cancer	CAP	Capricorn
LEO	Leo	AQU	Aquarius
VIR	Virgo	PIS	Pisces

	1900		1901		1902		1903		1904		1905	
JAN	21	AQU	21	AQU	21	AQU	22	AQU	22	AQU	21	AQU
FEB	20	PIS	20	PIS	20	PIS	20	PIS	21	PIS	20	PIS
MAR	22	ARI	22	ARI	22	ARI	22	ARI	22	ARI	22	ARI
APR	21	TAU	21	TAU	22	TAU	22	TAU	21	TAU	21	TAU
MAY	22	GEM	22	GEM	23	GEM	23	GEM	22	GEM	22	GEM
JUN	22	CAN	23	CAN	23	CAN	23	CAN	22	CAN	23	CAN
JUL	24	LEO	24	LEO	24	LEO	24	LEO	24	LEO	24	LEO
AUG	24	VIR	24	VIR	25	VIR	25	VIR	24	VIR	24	VIR
SEP	24	LIB	24	LIB	24	LIB	25	LIB	24	LIB	24	LIB
OCT	24	SCO	25	SCO	25	SCO	25	SCO	24	SCO	25	SCO
NOV	23	SAG	23	SAG	24	SAG	24	SAG	23	SAG	23	SAG
DEC	23	CAP	23	CAP	23	CAP	24	CAP	23	CAP	23	CAP

	1906		1907		1908		1909		1910		1911	
JAN	21	AQU	22	AQU	22	AQU	21	AQU	21	AQU	22	AQU
FEB	20	PIS	20	PIS	20	PIS	20	PIS	20	PIS	20	PIS
MAR	22	ARI	22	ARI	22	ARI	22	ARI	22	ARI	22	ARI
APR	22	TAU	22	TAU	21	TAU	21	TAU	21	TAU	22	TAU
MAY	23	GEM	23	GEM	22	GEM	22	GEM	22	GEM	23	GEM
JUN	23	CAN	23	CAN	22	CAN	23	CAN	23	CAN	23	CAN
JUL	24	LEO	25	LEO	24	LEO	24	LEO	24	LEO	25	LEO
AUG	25	VIR	25	VIR	24	VIR	24	VIR	25	VIR	25	VIR
SEP	24	LIB	25	LIB	24	LIB	24	LIB	24	LIB	25	LIB
OCT	25	SCO	25	SCO	24	SCO	25	SCO	25	SCO	25	SCO
NOV	24	SAG	24	SAG	23	SAG	23	SAG	24	SAG	24	SAG
DEC	23	CAP	23	CAP	23	CAP	23	CAP	23	CAP	23	CAP

	1912		1913		1914		1915		1916		1917	
JAN	22	AQU	21	AQU	21	AQU	22	AQU	22	AQU	21	AQU
FEB	20	PIS	20	PIS	20	PIS	20	PIS	20	PIS	20	PIS
MAR	21	ARI	22	ARI	22	ARI	22	ARI	21	ARI	22	ARI
APR	21	TAU	21	TAU	21	TAU	22	TAU	21	TAU	21	TAU
MAY	22	GEM	22	GEM	22	GEM	23	GEM	22	GEM	22	GEM
JUN	22	CAN	23	CAN	23	CAN	23	CAN	23	CAN	23	CAN
JUL	24	LEO	24	LEO	24	LEO	24	LEO	24	LEO	24	LEO
AUG	24	VIR	24	VIR	25	VIR	25	VIR	24	VIR	24	VIR
SEP	24	LIB	24	LIB	24	LIB	25	LIB	24	LIB	24	LIB
OCT	24	SCO	25	SCO	25	SCO	25	SCO	24	SCO	24	SCO
NOV	23	SAG	23	SAG	24	SAG	24	SAG	23	SAG	23	SAG
DEC	23	CAP	23	CAP	23	CAP	23	CAP	23	CAP	23	CAP

	1918		1919		1920		1921		1922		1923	
JAN	21	AQU	22	AQU	22	AQU	21	AQU	21	AQU	22	AQU
FEB	20	PIS	20	PIS	20	PIS	20	PIS	20	PIS	20	PIS
MAR	22	ARI	22	ARI	21	ARI	22	ARI	22	ARI	22	ARI
APR	21	TAU	22	TAU	21	TAU	21	TAU	21	TAU	22	TAU
MAY	22	GEM	23	GEM	22	GEM	22	GEM	22	GEM	23	GEM
JUN	23	CAN	23	CAN	22	CAN	22	CAN	23	CAN	23	CAN
JUL	24	LEO	24	LEO	24	LEO	24	LEO	24	LEO	24	LEO
AUG	24	VIR	25	VIR	24	VIR	24	VIR	24	VIR	25	VIR
SEP	24	LIB	25	LIB	24	LIB	24	LIB	24	LIB	25	LIB
OCT	25	SCO	25	SCO	24	SCO	24	SCO	25	SCO	25	SCO
NOV	24	SAG	24	SAG	23	SAG	23	SAG	24	SAG	24	SAG
DEC	23	CAP	23	CAP	23	CAP	23	CAP	23	CAP	23	CAP

Sun Tables

	1924		1925		1926		1927		1928		1929	
JAN	22	AQU	21	AQU	21	AQU	22	AQU	22	AQU	21	AQU
FEB	20	PIS	20	PIS	20	PIS	20	PIS	20	PIS	20	PIS
MAR	21	ARI	22	ARI	22	ARI	22	ARI	21	ARI	22	ARI
APR	21	TAU	21	TAU	21	TAU	22	TAU	21	TAU	21	TAU
MAY	22	GEM	22	GEM	22	GEM	23	GEM	22	GEM	22	GEM
JUN	22	CAN	22	CAN	23	CAN	23	CAN	22	CAN	22	CAN
JUL	24	LEO	24	LEO	24	LEO	24	LEO	24	LEO	24	LEO
AUG	24	VIR	24	VIR	24	VIR	25	VIR	24	VIR	24	VIR
SEP	24	LIB	24	LIB	24	LIB	25	LIB	24	LIB	24	LIB
OCT	24	SCO	24	SCO	25	SCO	25	SCO	24	SCO	24	SCO
NOV	23	SAG	23	SAG	24	SAG	24	SAG	23	SAG	23	SAG
DEC	23	CAP	23	CAP	23	CAP	23	CAP	23	CAP	23	CAP

	1930		1931		1932		1933		1934		1935	
JAN	21	AQU	21	AQU	22	AQU	21	AQU	21	AQU	21	AQU
FEB	20	PIS	20	PIS	20	PIS	19	PIS	20	PIS	20	PIS
MAR	22	ARI	22	ARI	21	ARI	21	ARI	22	ARI	2	ARI
APR	21	TAU	21	TAU	21	TAU	21	TAU	21	TAU	21	TAU
MAY	22	GEM	22	GEM	22	GEM	22	GEM	22	GEM	22	GEM
JUN	22	CAN	23	CAN	22	CAN	22	CAN	22	CAN	23	CAN
JUL	24	LEO	24	LEO	23	LEO	24	LEO	24	LEO	24	LEO
AUG	24	VIR	24	VIR	24	VIR	24	VIR	24	VIR	24	VIR
SEP	24	LIB	24	LIB	24	LIB	24	LIB	24	LIB	24	LIB
OCT	24	SCO	25	SCO	24	SCO	24	SCO	24	SCO	25	SCO
NOV	23	SAG	24	SAG	23	SAG	23	SAG	23	SAG	24	SAG
DEC	23	CAP	23	CAP	22	CAP	23	CAP	23	CAP	23	CAP

	1936		1937		1938		1939		1940		1941	
JAN	22	AQU	21	AQU	21	AQU	21	AQU	21	AQU	21	AQU
FEB	20	PIS	19	PIS	20	PIS	20	PIS	20	PIS	19	PIS
MAR	21	ARI	21	ARI	22	ARI	22	ARI	21	ARI	21	ARI
APR	21	TAU	21	TAU	21	TAU	21	TAU	21	TAU	21	TAU
MAY	22	GEM	22	GEM	22	GEM	22	GEM	22	GEM	2	GEM
JUN	22	CAN	22	CAN	22	CAN	23	CAN	22	CAN	22	CAN
JUL	23	LEO	24	LEO	24	LEO	24	LEO	3	LEO	24	LEO
AUG	24	VIR	24	VIR	24	VIR	24	VIR	24	VIR	24	VIR
SEP	24	LIB	24	LIB	24	LIB	24	LIB	23	LIB	24	LIB
OCT	24	SCO	24	SCO	24	SCO	25	SCO	24	SCO	24	SCO
NOV	23	SAG	23	SAG	23	SAG	23	SAG	23	SAG	23	SAG
DEC	22	CAP	23	CAP	23	CAP	23	CAP	22	CAP	23	CAP

	1942		1943		1944		1945		1946		1947	
JAN	21	AQU	21	AQU	21	AQU	21	AQU	21	AQU	21	AQU
FEB	20	PIS	20	PIS	20	PIS	19	PIS	20	PIS	20	PIS
MAR	22	ARI	22	ARI	21	ARI	21	ARI	22	ARI	22	ARI
APR	21	TAU	21	TAU	21	TAU	21	TAU	21	TAU	21	TAU
MAY	22	GEM	22	GEM	21	GEM	22	GEM	22	GEM	22	GEM
JUN	22	CAN	23	CAN	22	CAN	22	CAN	22	CAN	23	CAN
JUL	24	LEO	24	LEO	23	LEO	24	LEO	24	LEO	24	LEO
AUG	24	VIR	24	VIR	24	VIR	24	VIR	24	VIR	24	VIR
SEP	24	LIB	24	LIB	23	LIB	24	LIB	24	LIB	24	LIB
OCT	24	SCO	25	SCO	24	SCO	24	SCO	24	SCO	25	SCO
NOV	23	SAG	23	SAG	23	SAG	23	SAG	23	SAG	23	SAG
DEC	23	CAP	23	CAP	22	CAP	22	CAP	23	CAP	23	CAP

	1948		1949		1950		1951		1952		1953	
JAN	21	AQU	21	AQU	21	AQU	21	AQU	21	AQU	21	AQU
FEB	20	PIS	19	PIS	20	PIS	20	PIS	20	PIS	19	PIS
MAR	21	ARI	21	ARI	21	ARI	22	ARI	21	ARI	21	ARI
APR	20	TAU	21	TAU	21	TAU	21	TAU	20	TAU	21	TAU
MAY	21	GEM	22	GEM	22	GEM	22	GEM	21	GEM	22	GEM
JUN	22	CAN	22	CAN	22	CAN	23	CAN	22	CAN	22	CAN
JUL	23	LEO	23	LEO	24	LEO	24	LEO	23	LEO	23	LEO
AUG	24	VIR	24	VIR	24	VIR	24	VIR	23	VIR	24	VIR
SEP	23	LIB	24	LIB	24	LIB	24	LIB	23	LIB	24	LIB
OCT	24	SCO	24	SCO	24	SCO	25	SCO	24	SCO	24	SCO
NOV	23	SAG	23	SAG	23	SAG	23	SAG	23	SAG	23	SAG
DEC	22	CAP	22	CAP	23	CAP	23	CAP	22	CAP	22	CAP

	1954		1955		1956		1957		1958		1959	
JAN	21	AQU	21	AQU	21	AQU	21	AQU	21	AQU	21	AQU
FEB	19	PIS	20	PIS	20	PIS	19	PIS	19	PIS	20	PIS
MAR	21	ARI	22	ARI	21	ARI	21	ARI	21	ARI	22	ARI
APR	21	TAU	21	TAU	21	TAU	21	TAU	21	TAU	21	TAU
MAY	22	GEM	22	GEM	21	GEM	22	GEM	22	GEM	22	GEM
JUN	22	CAN	22	CAN	22	CAN	22	CAN	22	CAN	22	CAN
JUL	24	LEO	24	LEO	23	LEO	23	LEO	24	LEO	24	LEO
AUG	24	VIR	24	VIR	23	VIR	24	VIR	24	VIR	24	VIR
SEP	24	LIB	24	LIB	23	LIB	24	LIB	24	LIB	24	LIB
OCT	24	SCO	24	SCO	24	SCO	24	SCO	23	SCO	24	SCO
NOV	23	SAG	23	SAG	23	SAG	23	SAG	23	SAG	23	SAG
DEC	23	CAP	23	CAP	22	CAP	22	CAP	23	CAP	23	CAP

	1960		1961		1962		1963		1964		1965	
JAN	21	AQU	21	AQU	21	AQU	21	AQU	21	AQU	21	AQU
FEB	20	PIS	19	PIS	19	PIS	20	PIS	20	PIS	19	PIS
MAR	21	ARI	21	ARI	21	ARI	22	ARI	21	ARI	21	ARI
APR	20	TAU	21	TAU	21	TAU	21	TAU	20	TAU	21	TAU
MAY	21	GEM	22	GEM	22	GEM	22	GEM	21	GEM	22	GEM
JUN	22	CAN	22	CAN	22	CAN	22	CAN	22	CAN	22	CAN
JUL	23	LEO	23	LEO	24	LEO	24	LEO	23	LEO	23	LEO
AUG	23	VIR	24	VIR	24	VIR	24	VIR	23	VIR	24	VIR
SEP	23	LIB	24	LIB	24	LIB	24	LIB	23	LIB	24	LIB
OCT	24	SCO	24	SCO	24	SCO	24	SCO	24	SCO	24	SCO
NOV	23	SAG	23	SAG	23	SAG	23	SAG	23	SAG	23	SAG
DEC	22	CAP	22	CAP	23	CAP	23	CAP	22	CAP	22	CAP

	1966		1967		1968		1969		1970		1971	
JAN	21	AQU	21	AQU	21	AQU	21	AQU	21	AQU	21	AQU
FEB	19	PIS	20	PIS	20	PIS	19	PIS	19	PIS	20	PIS
MAR	21	ARI	22	ARI	21	ARI	21	ARI	21	ARI	21	ARI
APR	21	TAU	21	TAU	20	TAU	21	TAU	21	TAU	22	TAU
MAY	22	GEM	22	GEM	21	GEM	22	GEM	22	GEM	22	GEM
JUN	22	CAN	22	CAN	22	CAN	22	CAN	22	CAN	22	CAN
JUL	24	LEO	24	LEO	23	LEO	23	LEO	24	LEO	24	LEO
AUG	24	VIR	24	VIR	23	VIR	24	VIR	24	VIR	24	VIR
SEP	24	LIB	24	LIB	23	LIB	24	LIB	24	LIB	24	LIB
OCT	24	SCO	24	SCO	24	SCO	24	SCO	24	SCO	24	SCO
NOV	23	SAG	23	SAG	23	SAG	23	SAG	23	SAG	23	SAG
DEC	23	CAP	23	CAP	22	CAP	22	CAP	23	CAP	23	CAP

Sun Tables

	1972	1973	1974	1975	1976	1977
JAN	21 AQU	20 AQU	21 AQU	21 AQU	21 AQU	20 AQU
FEB	20 PIS	19 PIS	19 PIS	20 PIS	20 PIS	19 PIS
MAR	21 ARI	21 ARI	21 ARI	22 ARI	21 ARI	21 ARI
APR	21 TAU	21 TAU	21 TAU	22 TAU	21 TAU	20 TAU
MAY	21 GEM	21 GEM	22 GEM	22 GEM	21 GEM	21 GEM
JUN	22 CAN	22 CAN	22 CAN	22 CAN	22 CAN	22 CAN
JUL	23 LEO	23 LEO	24 LEO	24 LEO	23 LEO	23 LEO
AUG	23 VIR	24 VIR	24 VIR	24 VIR	23 VIR	24 VIR
SEP	23 LIB	23 LIB	24 LIB	24 LIB	23 LIB	23 LIB
OCT	24 SCO	24 SCO	24 SCO	24 SCO	24 SCO	24 SCO
NOV	22 SAG	23 SAG	23 SAG	23 SAG	22 SAG	23 SAG
DEC	22 CAP	22 CAP	23 CAP	23 CAP	22 CAP	22 CAP

	1978	1979	1980	1981	1982	1983
JAN	21 AQU	21 AQU	21 AQU	20 AQU	21 AQU	21 AQU
FEB	19 PIS	20 PIS	20 PIS	19 PIS	19 PIS	20 PIS
MAR	21 ARI	22 ARI	21 ARI	21 ARI	21 ARI	21 ARI
APR	21 TAU	21 TAU	21 TAU	20 TAU	21 TAU	21 TAU
MAY	22 GEM	22 GEM	21 GEM	21 GEM	22 GEM	22 GEM
JUN	22 CAN	22 CAN	22 CAN	22 CAN	22 CAN	22 CAN
JUL	23 LEO	24 LEO	23 LEO	23 LEO	23 LEO	24 LEO
AUG	24 VIR	24 VIR	23 VIR	24 VIR	24 VIR	24 VIR
SEP	24 LIB	24 LIB	23 LIB	23 LIB	24 LIB	24 LIB
OCT	24 SCO	24 SCO	24 SCO	24 SCO	24 SCO	24 SCO
NOV	23 SAG	23 SAG	22 SAG	23 SAG	23 SAG	23 SAG
DEC	23 CAP	23 CAP	22 CAP	22 CAP	22 CAP	23 CAP

	1984	1985	1986	1987	1988	1989
JAN	21 AQU	20 AQU	21 AQU	21 AQU	21 AQU	20 AQU
FEB	20 PIS	19 PIS	19 PIS	19 PIS	20 PIS	19 PIS
MAR	21 ARI	21 ARI	21 ARI	21 ARI	21 ARI	21 ARI
APR	20 TAU	20 TAU	21 TAU	21 TAU	20 TAU	20 TAU
MAY	21 GEM	21 GEM	22 GEM	22 GEM	21 GEM	21 GEM
JUN	21 CAN	22 CAN	22 CAN	22 CAN	21 CAN	22 CAN
JUL	23 LEO	23 LEO	23 LEO	24 LEO	23 LEO	23 LEO
AUG	23 VIR	23 VIR	24 VIR	24 VIR	23 VIR	23 VIR
SEP	23 LIB	23 LIB	24 LIB	24 LIB	23 LIB	23 LIB
OCT	24 SCO	24 SCO	24 SCO	24 SCO	23 SCO	24 SCO
NOV	22 SAG	23 SAG	23 SAG	23 SAG	22 SAG	23 SAG
DEC	22 CAP	22 CAP	22 CAP	23 CAP	22 CAP	22 CAP

	1990	1991	1992	1993	1994	1995
JAN	21 AQU	21 AQU	21 AQU	20 AQU	21 AQU	21 AQU
FEB	19 PIS	19 PIS	20 PIS	19 PIS	19 PIS	19 PIS
MAR	21 ARI	21 ARI	21 ARI	21 ARI	21 ARI	21 ARI
APR	21 TAU	21 TAU	20 TAU	20 TAU	21 TAU	21 TAU
MAY	22 GEM	22 GEM	21 GEM	21 GEM	22 GEM	22 GEM
JUN	22 CAN	22 CAN	21 CAN	22 CAN	22 CAN	22 CAN
JUL	23 LEO	24 LEO	23 LEO	23 LEO	23 LEO	24 LEO
AUG	24 VIR	24 VIR	23 VIR	23 VIR	24 VIR	24 VIR
SEP	24 LIB	24 LIB	23 LIB	23 LIB	24 LIB	24 LIB
OCT	24 SCO	24 SCO	23 SCO	24 SCO	24 SCO	24 SCO
NOV	23 SAG	23 SAG	22 SAG	23 SAG	23 SAG	23 SAG
DEC	22 CAP	23 CAP	22 CAP	22 CAP	22 CAP	23 CAP

	1996	1997	1998	1999	2000	2001
JAN	21 AQU	20 AQU	21 AQU	21 AQU	21 AQU	20 AQU
FEB	20 PIS	19 PIS	19 PIS	19 PIS	20 PIS	19 PIS
MAR	21 ARI	21 ARI	21 ARI	21 ARI	21 ARI	21 ARI
APR	20 TAU	20 TAU	21 TAU	21 TAU	20 TAU	20 TAU
MAY	21 GEM	21 GEM	22 GEM	22 GEM	21 GEM	21 GEM
JUN	21 CAN	22 CAN	22 CAN	22 CAN	21 CAN	22 CAN
JUL	23 LEO	23 LEO	23 LEO	24 LEO	23 LEO	23 LEO
AUG	23 VIR	23 VIR	24 VIR	24 VIR	23 VIR	23 VIR
SEP	23 LIB	23 LIB	24 LIB	24 LIB	23 LIB	23 LIB
OCT	23 SCO	24 SCO	24 SCO	24 SCO	23 SCO	24 SCO
NOV	22 SAG	23 SAG	23 SAG	23 SAG	22 SAG	23 SAG
DEC	22 CAP	22 CAP	22 CAP	23 CAP	22 CAP	22 CAP

	2002	2003	2004	2005	2006	2007
JAN	21 AQU	21 AQU	21 AQU	20 AQU	20 AQU	2⌐ AQU
FEB	19 PIS	19 PIS	20 PIS	19 PIS	19 PIS	19 PIS
MAR	21 ARI	21 ARI	21 ARI	21 ARI	21 ARI	21 ARI
APR	21 TAU	21 TAU	20 TAU	20 TAU	21 TAU	21 TAU
MAY	22 GEM	22 GEM	21 GEM	21 GEM	21 GEM	22 GEM
JUN	22 CAN	22 CAN	21 CAN	22 CAN	22 CAN	22 CAN
JUL	23 LEO	24 LEO	23 LEO	23 LEO	23 LEO	23 LEO
AUG	24 VIR	24 VIR	23 VIR	23 VIR	24 VIR	24 VIR
SEP	23 LIB	24 LIB	23 LIB	23 LIB	23 LIB	24 LIB
OCT	24 SCO	24 SCO	23 SCO	24 SCO	24 SCO	24 SCO
NOV	23 SAG	23 SAG	22 SAG	23 SAG	23 SAG	23 SAG
DEC	22 CAP	23 CAP	22 CAP	22 CAP	22 CAP	23 CAP

	2008	2009	2010	2011	2012	2013
JAN	21 AQU	20 AQU	20 AQU	21 AQU	21 AQU	20 AQU
FEB	20 PIS	19 PIS	19 PIS	19 PIS	20 PIS	19 PIS
MAR	21 ARI	21 ARI	21 ARI	21 ARI	20 ARI	21 ARI
APR	20 TAU	20 TAU	20 TAU	21 TAU	20 TAU	20 TAU
MAY	21 GEM	21 GEM	21 GEM	22 GEM	21 GEM	21 GEM
JUN	21 CAN	22 CAN	22 CAN	22 CAN	21 CAN	21 CAN
JUL	23 LEO	23 LEO	23 LEO	23 LEO	23 LEO	23 LEO
AUG	23 VIR	23 VIR	24 VIR	24 VIR	23 VIR	23 VIR
SEP	23 LIB	23 LIB	23 LIB	24 LIB	23 LIB	23 LIB
OCT	23 SCO	24 SCO	24 SCO	24 SCO	23 SCO	24 SCO
NOV	22 SAG	22 SAG	23 SAG	23 SAG	22 SAG	22 SAG
DEC	22 CAP	22 CAP	22 CAP	23 CAP	22 CAP	22 CAP

	2014	2015	2016	2017	2018	2019
JAN	20 AQU	21 AQU	21 AQU	20 AQU	20 AQU	21 AQU
FEB	19 PIS	19 PIS	20 PIS	19 PIS	19 PIS	19 PIS
MAR	21 ARI	21 ARI	20 ARI	21 ARI	21 ARI	21 ARI
APR	20 TAU	21 TAU	20 TAU	20 TAU	20 TAU	21 TAU
MAY	21 GEM	22 GEM	21 GEM	21 GEM	21 GEM	22 GEM
JUN	22 CAN	22 CAN	21 CAN	21 CAN	22 CAN	22 CAN
JUL	23 LEO	23 LEO	23 LEO	23 LEO	23 LEO	23 LEO
AUG	23 VIR	24 VIR	23 VIR	23 VIR	23 VIR	24 VIR
SEP	23 LIB	24 LIB	23 LIB	23 LIB	23 LIB	24 LIB
OCT	24 SCO	24 SCO	23 SCO	24 SCO	24 SCO	24 SCO
NOV	23 SAG	23 SAG	22 SAG	22 SAG	23 SAG	23 SAG
DEC	22 CAP	22 CAP	22 CAP	22 CAP	22 CAP	22 CAP

Sun Tables

	2020		2021		2022		2023		2024		2025	
JAN	21	AQU	20	AQU	20	AQU	21	AQU	21	AQU	20	AQU
FEB	19	PIS	19	PIS	19	PIS	19	PIS	19	PIS	19	PIS
MAR	20	ARI	21	ARI	21	ARI	21	ARI	20	ARI	21	ARI
APR	20	TAU	20	TAU	20	TAU	21	TAU	20	TAU	20	TAU
MAY	21	GEM	21	GEM	21	GEM	22	GEM	21	GEM	21	GEM
JUN	21	CAN	21	CAN	22	CAN	22	CAN	21	CAN	21	CAN
JUL	23	LEO	23	LEO	23	LEO	23	LEO	23	LEO	23	LEO
AUG	23	VIR	23	VIR	23	VIR	24	VIR	23	VIR	23	VIR
SEP	23	LIB	23	LIB	23	LIB	24	LIB	23	LIB	23	LIB
OCT	23	SCO	23	SCO	24	SCO	24	SCO	23	SCO	23	SCO
NOV	22	SAG	22	SAG	23	SAG	23	SAG	22	SAG	22	SAG
DEC	22	CAP	22	CAP	22	CAP	22	CAP	22	CAP	22	CAP

Children with Sun in Aries

Peter was the *Aries* apostle. He was the one who Christ chose first and *Aries* is the first sign of the zodiac. Because of being the first, and representing the early part of life, we call Aries *the Child of the Zodiac.* Symbolized by the *ram*, it rules the *head* of the body. Words like *headlong* and *headstrong* are used to describe this sign.

Your Aries child may have many head injuries, headaches, or be born with a birthmark on the head or face. Most older Aries have acquired a scar in those areas. Aries hair is usually curly and their teeth may be slightly elongated. *Eyes* are piercingly direct. The ruler of Aries is *Mars*, the warrior.

The Aries nature is impatient, courageous, and aggressive. Your Aries child will be direct, outspoken, and blunt. Teaching them to be considerate of other people's feelings will help your Aries in a positive way. Aries will have a tendency to charge into things impulsively, and should be taught to look before leaping; to use a small amount of caution to assure more success. Their enthusiasm is great, which stimulates others who are less initiating or courageous. They are very inventive, have a quick mind, and are wonderful at pioneering and initiating new projects and concepts.

One problem is that they are easily distracted and may turn that enthusiasm to something new before they have followed through or finished the previous undertakings. Discipline in the area of "persistence" would be a valuable attribute.

Give Aries the opportunity for many new challenges and they will be happy. They need more freedom than most to explore untrodden areas and conquer these new vistas for themselves. If this freedom is curtailed, they will start butting their heads in some way against the restriction — or the restrictor!

Stimulate this curious Aries with a challenge when presenting anything. For instance, say to them, "See if you can pour the milk without spilling a drop," and you've immediately sparked a challenge! Don't say or order, "You must pour the milk without spilling it," or negatively say, "You can't pour the milk because you will probably spill it." Wrong! When the challenge is conquered it strengthens the natural flow of the Aries ability and directs them toward positive actions. Success with these challenges is important, so be sure to help them select realistic objectives.

Fire is their element, giving them much energy and a bit of an explosive temper. This fire may rage fiercely but it starts and stops quickly... and when it's out, it is out and forgotten. The words are not remembered and certainly not meant — it is fire being released like steam through a safety valve. If this child has plenty of physical activity, much of this energy can be expended for positive benefit. There must be some outlet for them, the more physical and active the better.

Aries children can be quite rambunctious when they have energy which is stored up inside. To help them release this energy constructively, put a march on and let them march around the house, or take them out and run them around the block. They enjoy lively music and are quick to respond when they are encouraged to dance. Moving their bodies to music is a wonderful way for them to release any frustrations. Anything you can think of to constructively put them into physical action will be good for them.

These children are naturally attracted to the *color red* since it is the color assigned to Aries, not to mention the red planet — Mars which is its ruler. You should take note that they seem to have even more energy when they wear red or when it is prominent in their environment. Since they have an abundance of energy anyway, you may want to consider calming them down by dressing them in blue, green, yellow, or white. Also choose the colors for their bedrooms with thought and care. These children are often inclined to run high fevers so be sure to dress them in these cooler, calmer colors when this occurs.

Since an Aries will dislike routine or any kind of monotony, discovering new ways of doing things will have to be developed continually. The best *disciplinary* methods for Aries are *restriction* or *confinement*. For an Aries child, sitting still in a chair for ten whole minutes is a dreadful chore. Be careful that the length of time is thoughtfully considered because they still need to have ample physical activity to function properly. Start with ten minutes and then tell them that the next time you will have to add ten more, and so on. This warning will make them think twice. The Aries child does need to think more and act less!

For young Aries children, distraction works particularly well when you wish to change their mood or behavior. The Aries is one of the signs whose attention can be diverted with almost anything, especially if action is involved. Start a new project or take a walk — their whole mood will change and you will have transformed unproductive into productive. As parent or caregiver, help them to control their impatience and to apply persistence in order to finish tasks they have started. Teach them that finishing is as important as starting. They should be allowed to develop their natural initiative; and be encouraged to be logical and *think* before acting with blind courage. Your Aries is strong and vital — do not push them or you'll have much resistance, even a young rebel.

They are energetic, courageous, inventive, and bright. Help them to know it, and to use it for good.

Refer to Mercury in Aries for *key words* to use in your communications with your Aries child.

Aries Birthday Poem

Aries my child,
come let me dust you
with the power of
patience.
Let me put love
behind your courage
so you might lead in
exaltation.
Feel the power of the Sun,
then know the need for
humbleness,
lest you burn that which
you desire to nurture
and bless.
Come my Aries warrior –
protector of the needy,
let me bathe you
in the waters of your own
valor and strength.
I'll place in these waters
the fragrance of flowers
to add softness to your ways,
and soothe you
with the coolness of mint
to keep your fires temperate.
Your mind is like

a bursting sky rocket,
ever reaching out
to spread more light
with energy of only a few,
but keep your sights lofty
and skyward flowing
to illuminate – that's the clue.
You're truly a diamond in the rough,
with more of everything than enough.
Hope your year is filled
with lots of good stuff,
Happy Birthday – Best Wishes –
and the Best of Luck!

Children with Sun in Taurus

The apostle whose Sun was in Taurus was *Simon.* As a young man he was uncompromising, determined, and stubborn, much like the *bull* which is the symbol for *Taurus.* Simon was slow to accept the concept of unity, slow to change his attitude from preaching war to preaching peace and bringing all people together. It is the same with most Taureans: they are slow to make changes, because they are stubborn.

The part of the body governed by Taurus is the *throat,* and the planet that rules it is *Venus.* It is no wonder that we have so many famous singers born with the Sun in Taurus. Keep in mind that *the part of the body which a sign rules or governs may have weakness as well as strength.* It may be wise to protect these children's necks, and by all means keep them warm in cold weather... they may have a predisposition toward sore throats. Sometimes these are caused because these children have an inclination to hold feelings in and not say what they think or feel. Teach them that holding back or trying to endure something is not helpful to any situation.

These children are attracted to *pastel colors* and soft hues. They enjoy gentle, sensual music. When they are ill or just generally out of sorts, put them in soft plushy clothes, soften the lights, and put on Nat King Cole, or a soft rock station. They will soon be soothed.

Through the use of speech they can accomplish almost anything as they are convincing as well as persistent. Arguing with them can present quite a challenge. The best way to win with them is through indirect action — back off and give them time. They can't be pushed. If you do — watch out! They are generally peaceful, but if you try to force them or anger them they have a fierce volcanic temper, and you will be well advised to wait until they cool down. You will get nowhere until then.

The element for Taurus is *earth* and since it is a *fixed sign* we are dealing with "rock." Taurus can be the rock of Gibraltar and have the same endurance. They are *strong and steady.* They are not easily discouraged and will stay with things that they believe have value.

They can brave the challenge, no matter how difficult. They usually accomplish more than most — but need to learn the difference between persistence and stubbornness. Taureans hate to change, so your best approach is to show them the value of the change and how it will serve their purpose. Gain their cooperation because they are tough competitors. Your Taurus will have great powers of persuasion, persistence, and determination. They can resist and persist with a vengeance.

The Taurean can be jealous, *possessive*, and greedy. They are *materialistic*, and they are sensual, and are attached to having their comforts satisfied. They will be attracted to and enjoy all of the finer things in life. They have a tendency to overindulge and need to learn discipline with their eating and drinking to avoid being overweight and unhealthy. Sauces and rich foods can be a weakness. Teach them to enjoy healthier foods that taste good. *Taste is* an important sense to a Taurean, as sight is to an Aries.

You will win points by loving, touching or anything that gives them pleasure. Stroking or hugging them when you are eliciting their cooperation will help.

An important lesson for Taureans to learn is detachment. *They are too possessive.* They are attached to everything and everyone. They will want to hold on to and own people and things. Teach them that the true values in life are not in possessions, but in one's self and in one another. Once they value themselves and value the unity of us all, they will be a strong force in motivating others. Teach them that principle and purpose are more important than all the material possessions in the world.

The best *disciplinary* method to use if you have been unsuccessful getting their cooperation is to *deny them their comforts and pleasures.* Taking away their dessert, television, back rubs, or anything else which is pleasurable to them will have an effect. By the same token, rewarding them with the same for good behavior will give Taureans incentive to cooperate. But do not, I repeat, do *not* use corporal punishment on a Taurean! It only makes them more stubborn and also unforgiving — for they deeply feel physical pain along with the emotional pain.

Help your Taureans to know their strengths and weaknesses, develop patience yourself, and enjoy an affectionate, loving relationship.

Refer to Mercury in Taurus for *key words* to use in your communication with your Taurus child.

Taurus Birthday Poem

A greeting of friendship to the
sign of the bull,
standing firm with strength
you are stable and reliable.
You're persistent, reliant,

and determined
but slow to adjust
so learning not to push you
 for us is a must.
We see gentle kindness so long
as you're not poked,
but an unyielding opponent when
furiously provoked.
A lover of comfort often
overindulged,
learn how greediness makes the
wrong kind of bulge.
It's very important to be
somewhat detached,
and your sense of true values
cannot be matched.
We know you can do it but
stop fearing loss,
know you are reliable and
God is the boss.
You are devoted as anyone –
having more patience than most,
deliberate and steadfast, after you
begin you can coast.
It's nice to know you are
clever with money,
someone who isn't, it wouldn't
be funny.
You're needed and respected, we're

glad you're here,
a toast to your Birthday and to
a productive year.

Children with Sun in Gemini

The apostle born with the Sun in Gemini was *James (The Less)*. He was called The Less only because of his physical structure, so don't think less in any other aspect for *Gemini*.

Gemini is ruled by the planet *Mercury* and is associated with the *arms, shoulders, nervous system, and lungs.* Its element is *air.* When we think about air we realize that it is all around us and it moves as we move through it. All air signs are mental and intellectual in quality, and since Gemini is *mutable* in its *Mode of Action*, their thoughts are all over the place! *Mutable* means flexible, changeable, adaptable, flowing, and spontaneous. Therefore, Gemini children are bright, quick, mercurial and full of action — probably too much action at times to suit most parents. They are also quite capable of doing more than one thing at a time. There is never with them a dull moment. In fact, for these children boredom is truly horrendous. They are very quick to learn anything, being the mimic of the zodiac so watch your own bad habits — theirs is a mind that never stops. They must be fed constantly with positive material or they will find their own material, and that can be dangerous.

Geminis are fond of humor and have a natural quick wit. Their remarks at times may be considered by some as being smart alecky or flippant, but to them it is just humor and a natural loquaciousness.

Talking is one of their long suits. Speaking of long suits, sharing could be another. They are not possessive in anything. They enjoy having new things as much as anyone but once they have something, if it breaks or is lost, it won't be important. Chances are that something newer has caught their eye anyway. Their attention span is rather short but they absorb so quickly, it just means that they are ready for more material. They may have trouble doing or learning anything with which they have no interest. Help them to develop good reading habits and your biggest problem of keeping them occupied will be solved. Their thirst for knowledge then can be satisfied. They are ambidextrous and very good at doing anything with their hands. Challenge them with crafts.

The astrological symbol for Gemini is the *twins*, representing a duality, and they *are* definitely changeable... often confusing and maddening everyone and seeming like two very different people indeed. Because of this characteristic a Gemini can espouse an idea on one occasion and have the opposite idea on another. They can change as quickly as you can change a TV channel. It is wise for the Gemini to become aware that this extreme flexibility can often be perceived by others as inconsistent, not dependable, or fickle.

With all this quickness and manual dexterity, a lot of Geminis are quite good at sports (particularly golf and tennis). Maybe this is because they like games. At times, life may even appear to be a game to these free spirits, always moving on to the next experience. When it comes to *discipline*, this very mental child will respond best if you give an *explanation of why* an action is taken. Just be sure that you have good, sound logical reasons if you expect results. For the young Gemini, distraction works very well, as they are intrigued with anything new. Because they want to learn and experience everything, their attention is easily diverted. Another effective disciplinary measure would be *isolation*. Communication is primary to them so they are not good loners. They need to have someone to talk to and will not be comfortable when shut off by themselves. (Now *that* would be the proper punishment!)

Speaking of communication, Geminis are not always the best listeners — they are more interested in doing the talking themselves. In fact, sometimes they are not even aware of whether others are listening or not... at times, they don't even care! Teach them that communication is a two-way street. Let them know that it is important for others to share ideas as well.

Geminis are very adaptable and will easily adjust to change. A new residence or a new school will not be traumatic. In fact, it's stimulating — new friends! Obviously, they are not attracted to tradition or ritual. They relate and respond on a mental level rather than an emotional one. In fact, they may even have difficulty understanding people who display great emotion. These children are usually wondering why. Teach them to become aware of others' sensitivities whether they are understood or not.

Feed this airy mental computer with plenty of positive material and have fun with your Gemini.

Refer to Mercury in Gemini for *key words* to use in your communications with your Gemini child.

Gemini Birthday Poem

Hello, playful Gemini, you
bright quick-witted youth,
if you learn perseverance,
reality is your truth.
We love to see your active
energy directed in so many
different ways,
let us help you learn to
follow through to bring all the result
that positively pays.
You are adaptable and versatile,
not to mention dexterous and duel,
with a fine logic and a mind
of reason that provides the fuel.
Limit your expressiveness

to the things that count the most,
lest you become quite restless,
scattered and even verbose.
I see you always inquiring,
curious and diverse,
a very short attention span that
absorbs quickly and at first.
You always love surprises and
learning things new, so
this is a part of change that is
often good for you.
Acquiring understanding is a
necessary part,
for you who are a thinker to the
end from the start.
So knuckle down and concentrate,
let's now see things through.
Good luck with best wishes and
have a Happy Birthyear too!

Children with Sun in Cancer

We find the lovable apostle, *Andrew,* born with his Sun in *Cancer.* He was a fisherman and Peter's older brother. Since Cancers have such strong natural needs for spirituality to help eliminate their fears, Andrew was already working closely with John the Baptist. He had no doubts about his purpose of serving others in self-sacrificing humility. He had no need to be the leader or to have a position of great importance; he only had to be a part of the family and to serve to the best of his ability.

The symbol for Cancer is the *crab*. When we think of the crab we remember that it moves sideways to avoid anything approaching it. Cancer people are much the same — they are not direct with their approach. When threatened, they withdraw and retract like the crab, hiding and pulling into its shell. The crab actually carries its home, or shell, with it wherever it goes. This may be why *home* is so important to Cancerians, and why wherever they go, they set about making it home-like.

Cancer is a *water* sign and is ruled by the *Moon*. This gives them qualities of being receptive and responsive. They feel everything... and will be especially affected by the cycle of the Moon. The new Moon and the full Moon can cause them to be more emotional and sensitive. Teach them to be aware of this monthly cycle so they can be prepared and armor themselves.

Although Cancer is a water sign, notice that the crab is comfortable on both land and in the water. A good way to calm and soothe your Cancer is with a bath or playing in water. The sea also has a great calming effect upon the Cancerian. Teach them early to swim and they will always have a way to work out any frustrations. Some of the great amateur sailors of the world are born in this sign.

The sign of Cancer has influence over the *stomach, breast, and solar plexus.* Cancer children might have a tendency to have a *nervous stomach* and should be careful about what and when they eat. In extreme cases, they could get an ulcer. They should avoid eating when emotionally upset or highly excited, and should never be forced to eat! The *breast* is symbolic of their need to be nurtured and to nurture others. Moon children have a strong need to feel protected in their environment. They must feel secure in the love from those close to them... secure that their environment is safe and stable... and secure that they will be taken care of.

Since the *solar plexus* is a strong area of psychic reception, this may explain why the Cancerian is so sensitive to everyone and everything around them. They have highly developed intuitive and psychic abilities, and are operating almost totally on the feeling level. These strong feelings and psychic experiences can be frightening to them so it is important to teach your Cancer child that it is a gift and to not be afraid of it!

These children need to be taught to affirm on a daily basis that they are protected from all negative input. This will build belief and become fact. They are psychic sponges and will absorb whatever energy and feelings are in the environment. They will feel what other people are feeling. If there is sadness, they will be sad; if there is happiness, they will be happy. Obviously one of the most important things that a parent can do is to keep the environment as tranquil, peaceful, and as happy as possible. Help them select positive "up" people for friends.

These children like old familiar things, and can become too attached to objects and people. They are inclined to collect things and will enjoy any hobby that includes collecting. But if they don't learn to let go of some possessions, their life will be filled with clutter. Teach them the very necessary art of organization. And teach them the value of change — of letting go of things, people, and unworthy concepts. Most importantly, teach them that placing their security in anything outside of themselves is an insecure position — security has to come from within. Amassing great quantities of things to surround themselves with won't help. If this is not learned, Cancer can be quite selfish, quite unturned... always trying to protect themselves. On the other hand, when they are secure in their own minds they can be outgoing, affectionate, and generous.

Family is important to Cancer, so planning family activities and doing things together is a must. Let them help you plan and they will love it.

When you want their cooperation with anything, tell them how you feel when they do something wrong and ask them how they would feel if they were in your place. Usually they will come around. Use a lot of feeling words in your communication. They are devastated with any harsh or brash *disciplining. Sharing feelings* works best.

Be sure to give these Cancer children lots of hugs and always be aware of their sensitivities.

Refer to Mercury in Cancer for *key words* to use in your communications with your Cancer child.

Cancer Birthday Poem

To the sign of Cancer ruled by our Moon,
we wish all your needs be fulfilled really soon.
You may be a worrier and frugal about worth –
too attached to the familiar that you have
on this Earth.
It's good to be diligent and
somewhat reserved,
but let loose the material, let God
give the deserved.
Then temper with reason and perception,
know that security comes with self-integration.
It's true you're domestic and maternal to the end,
you nurture and protect –
a good kind of friend.
But try not to be smothering
when you mother us all,
or attached and over-sensitive
whenever you fall.
Your feeling is necessary from
which we can learn,
so don't be tenacious, insistent,

or stern.
You are psychic and perceptive,
gifts worth more than most,
we'll give you reassurance
as long as you don't coast.
We love you for you without
being told,
and wish you the best that this
year can hold.

Children with Sun in Leo

The apostle *John* best represents the Sun in Leo. He was the youngest and joined with Peter, an Aries, another fire sign, to spread the word throughout Asia Minor. He was still writing and teaching until his death which demonstrates the persistence of *Leo*.

Leo is the *heart* and *spine* in the physical body. The *heart* shows us the powerful love and warmth of which Leos are capable. All energy needs proper expression so even love needs direction. The Leo needs to understand how to balance the love of self and love given to others. Leos usually have *positive self-esteem*; unfortunately, when it is overdone they can be egotistical and arrogant. Learning to send the power of their love out to the world will empower others to be loving too. They are *natural leaders* and like to be looked up to, and they will best fulfill their role by incorporating some humility into their personalities.

The *spine* is what gives Leo a strong backbone. They will accept a challenge no matter how difficult, and will stand tall with their heads high. When Leos enter a room, they command attention by the way they carry themselves, as their symbol is the regal *lion*. They walk erectly, with dignity, and demand respect as if they were royalty. They have been called regal and lofty yet should be advised to stay in touch with their "subjects" if they expect cooperation. Thinking that they are better than anyone else should be kept to themselves. They must learn to control their words and actions, or it will cause resentment in others. A good leader needs to focus on being of service to all.

Ruled by the *Sun*, Leo is a *fixed fire sign*. The Sun shows the power and radiance, and is the giver of life. The fixed fire can be either contained fire as in a fireplace which keeps us warm, or it can be a welder's torch which can be very dangerous and harmful. Leos need to learn that other people don't have the same high energy and that their fire might get too hot for others or prove exhausting, causing others to move away. Leos *want approval* and applause more than most people but they will benefit their purpose if made aware to *occasionally* share the spotlight. A little moderation will go a long way.

Leo the actor always wants center stage, and demands recognition. If they don't get enough loving attention in childhood, they could become the unstoppable show-off. It is best to inspire them to participate in plays or any productive way of performing. They are *very dramatic* and have great flair. It is always better when they use these attributes on stage or in some other beneficial way.

Respect is important to Leos and they yearn to achieve some importance in life. Being a fire sign, they are usually direct and honest. They are not likely to lie and will not treat others kindly who do. They are demanding of themselves and will also be demanding of those whom they love and are close to. Everything these children do they feel is a reflection of themselves so they will work harder than most to do their best, always reaching for perfection. They will expect the same from others and will be amazed that others can be happy with less. Because of this, they have a hard time delegating authority... when they are to be held *personally responsible* for the work. (Their motto is: When you want something done right, do it yourself!) Otherwise, they will be great at delegating and giving directions — because they need the detail people to plan the nitty gritty and carry out the grand scheme.

Leo's lesson to learn is that perfection is seen differently through each person's eyes. Life is too short and they may even be hurting their own health (heart) with this attitude. When they can depersonalize allowing their thinking to become more objective, they will be able to see that others have needs too! Then they can give their great abundance of warmth and love that brings them and those around them such joy.

In *disciplining* a Leo always try to do it *with respect and dignity*. Never threaten their integrity or you may arouse a temper with the force of Mount St. Helens. The best way to get cooperation is to *praise them* for their accomplishments. If you tell them that they did a great job, you will get an even better one next time. Even if it wasn't the best, it will get better. If they seem to be frustrated about something or unusually pushy and aggressive, take them for a brisk walk in nature. This will usually calm them down.

It is Leo who roars and scares the enemy. It is Leo who protects (at any sacrifice, even life) its loved ones! who stands tall in the face of adversity, inspires the faltering, and puts spunk into the timid.

Without Leo this would be a world with less color, less courage... less conviction. They believe supremely in themselves, and inspire others to take heart (a symbol of Leo). In short, Leo is bigger than life! And oh how a grimy, petty, frightened earth-world does need them!

But one caution. A little Leo, with difficult, frustrating, non-beneficial aspects in their chart could be the Cowardly Lion... who cries out, and mews like a kitten, for your help. You, as did Dorothy, can give them heart, courage... through your love and belief in them.

Your Leo will look for the good in situations, and is creative, loyal, forgiving, even magnanimous in mind and purse, sometimes to a fault (a true Leo is always an "easy touch"). Help them to use their strengths to empower the world.

Refer to Mercury in Leo for *key words* to use in your communications with your Leo child.

Leo Birthday Poem

Leo – Lord of the jungle, king of kings,
a salute from your subjects
who wish you all things.
We're loyal to you 'cause
you're loyal to us.
We'll submit to your will
without any fuss.
You're blessed with leader-
ship brave and direct,
done with affection which
brings the right effect.
You're honest, reliant and beat too,
you show your confidence with dignity,
so determined are you.
Who cares if you're dramatic and
a showman at heart,
it's part of your vitality that's

seen from the start.
Besides, you're magnetic with
passion we can't resist,
and none are more generous of
themselves and their gifts.
With all of this talent beware
of extremes,
things overdone can soon change
the whole theme.
Your power turns dictatorial
not pleasant to feel
an overbearing arrogance is
not a good deal.
So – just step out of your ego and
try on humility,
and you'll shine like the Sun
at the beginning of dawn.
This year should be yours from
now to the end –
here's all the luck and the love
that we have to send.

Children with Sun in Virgo

Phillip was the apostle who best fit the description
for the sign of Virgo. He was the business manager
who took care of *practical* things, such as where they all

would stay and where they would eat. Like other Virgos, he had no need for recognition, and, in fact, isn't mentioned that often in the scriptures. Most Virgos are like that — they quietly go about their work knowing what is most important is to do the job to the best of their ability. The fame and even the money is not as important as doing the job well. Success to them is based on *performance*. They are methodical and meticulous. They are analytical and neat, using both their head and their hands. They are always an asset because they present the facts, and put form and organization into life. It makes sense that Virgo is an *earth* sign and is ruled by *Mercury*.

Virgo symbolically represents the assimilation process in the physical body, and is symbolized by *the Virgin*. A vİrgin represents purity and perfection, two characteristics that are strong in Virgos. The statement "cleanliness is next to Godliness" comes to mind, and maybe we all need a little more Virgo in our lives. They certainly like having themselves clean and groomed, and most of them want their environment clean, organized, and neat. They will think better when their surroundings are orderly. The problem is that if they set their standards too high, they become nitpicks and nervous, the typical type "A" personality. When they set the same *high standards* for others (and they do), not only are they disappointed, but others will see them as too critical and impossible to please or satisfy. Since they really are happiest when they are helping someone else, learning to be nonjudgemental will be the quality which will bring results. Being less critical and more loving will make their service to others more effective. Helping Virgo to accept other people as they are gives your child a better starting point to really help others.

The Virgo child has wonderful *mental* powers. They have great concentration and a retentive *memory*. Their brain is like a masterful computer, always taking in information, categorizing it, detailing it, organizing it, and then *using* it. They are great with *detail*, when they're working with their hands or their brain. They like to work with projects which are practical and will develop skills in these areas. They also like to handle routine jobs. They are much more realistic than most.

Virgos are very interested in *health* and *diet*. They can be hypochondriacs always worrying about their own health, or they will study nutrition and attempt to lead healthy lives. They are not only concerned with the quality of the food, but they will also want it to look appealing. Some Virgos become vegetarians; some are just finicky eaters. They will have definite ideas about what they will and won't eat. If you keep their diet simple, plain, with no sauces, and only a few combinations, they will be happier. If you tell them the health benefits of the food you are serving them, they are more apt to eat what you present. Just be sure that you have your facts straight because they will probably check them out. Many Virgos end up in the field of nutrition. Many make wonderful surgeons because they not only are concerned about the body, but are so level-headed, unemotional and exact.

One area in which they have difficulty is being able to express their personal feelings. They are not very gregarious and can appear distant and aloof. This is the reason why they need love, assurance, and acceptance. They appear aloof because they are shy and uncertain of themselves. Be sure to make the effort to approach them and give them plenty of affection even if you have to initiate it most of the time. One of their lessons is to learn to be more open and loving... and by your doing this, you will help them.

To *discipline* a Virgo you might *ask them* what they would do if they were you or ask what they think is the best way to handle the situation. You just might be surprised at what they come up with. Usually if you keep them busy with new things to learn, little jobs to do, and plenty of craft projects, they won't get into any trouble.

Refer to Mercury in Virgo for *key words* to use in your communications with your Virgo child.

Virgo Birthday Poem

To the sign of the Virgin
a part of our wheel,
all the best wishes that
our poem can reveal.

And how does one share with
our Virgo friends?
With logic and reason –
that's how this mind extends.
We'll meet on a chord
that's efficient and reserved,
we'll serve and be served with
the balance deserved.
And with the methods
you've refined to be precise,
they are so practical, and you are
so skilled to give articulate advice.
To have caution and discriminate
is a part of the whole,
but to leave out feeling
inhibits the soul.
So don't be a skeptic or
pick at perfection,
accept what you have – for it
is your selection.
You are our worker –
fastidious and clean,
a need to be neat and useful
is certainly seen.
Let's analyze it now
and carefully join forces,
all must be pure,
we come from the same sources.
We know that you're shy

*to you we extend
an invitation to the best
of all we can send.*

Children with Sun in Libra

Bartholomew fits the sign of *Libra* well because Libra is an *air* sign which means that it is strongly influenced by the *intellect*. Bartholomew appears to have been the best educated of all the apostles, having a strong love of knowledge. He was observed as handling all difficulties and hostilities with a calm, logical approach. As a Libra, he was able to see both sides of a situation and attempted to administer assistance to all with fairness. He is sometimes called Nathanael in the scriptures, which points to the duality so characteristic of Libra. At times, Libran natives appear fickle because they seem to vacillate and can be so evasive. The main reason for this behavior is because they are always weighing both sides of everything. This sign can see, understand, and sympathize with each point of view. No wonder the symbol for Libra is *the scales*, always looking for and trying to balance... as well as being the symbol for justice. This sign is continually weighing and evaluating.

The children who are born under Libra are *charming and diplomatic. They will want to have a very active social life and are sometimes called social butterflies. They are friendly, outgoing*, generally good natured, and will work hard at being liked. It is very important to them to be liked by everyone. The problem is that they have a tendency to try to be all things to all people. This can be overwhelming and may bring out some of the non-beneficial characteristics such as appeasing, pacifying, and settling for peace at any price — since they basically dislike discord and are always striving for harmony. They can become non-committal, seem *indecisive*, or be easily influenced. They also are inclined to be *gullible*, especially while they are young. Because popularity is so important to them, be sure to teach Libra children to avoid sacrificing their principles to obtain it, because they have all the natural abilities to be liked without doing so.

These children will want to help everyone and are strong catalysts in inspiring others. They are sometimes called the *peacemakers of the zodiac*. No wonder so many choose professions as lawyers and counselors. They generally enjoy and work well with most people. You will find large numbers of them on any list of *Who's Who*.

If all this sweetness doesn't sound like your little Libra, be aware that there is another side to this sign. They can be dominating and strong-willed. These children sometimes enjoy the contest of argument for argument's sake; they enjoy all one-on-one encounters as long as it is kept on a high intellectual level! Many generals and strategists were born in this sign.

Libras have been known to be great perfectionists with high personal standards, sometimes making them difficult to live with. On the plus side, they are fastidious, modest, neat, and refined. These children appreciate, even *need* beautiful surroundings. They will feel best and be far more cooperative when their environment is peaceful, harmonious, and beautifully arranged.

They have an eye for quality and are attracted to culture and all forms of the fine arts. These children can be very creative and artistic. They have a developed sense of color and balance, and love all beautiful things. But help them develop a practical sense too.

Since Libra is *the relationship sign*, it is not unusual for them to always want to do everything with someone... they dislike doing anything alone. It is as though they need the reflection of someone else to know who they are. It is important to help them learn the discipline of working alone. And most importantly — the discipline of getting started, and then completing it! I is also *important* to give them some tests or responsibilities — or they can grow up "spoiled" and have great difficulty adjusting to the real world.

You will get their best cooperation by working with them or assigning them to work with someone else. Since they dislike any type of work that is dirty, put your efforts into selecting jobs where they will be able to use their talents of beautifying.

In the physical body, Libra rules the *kidneys*, the *purifying* system of the body. The planet of love, *Venus*, is the planet which rules Libra and so it is *love that purifies the soul*. Children of this sign are very affection- ate and have a lot of love to give. They also need the love returned. They are generous and sharing and want to be appreciated for that. They are very "other-people" oriented. They will love to entertain so mothers, be prepared to have the neighborhood at your house. You may find your home the meeting place for clubs and party planning, and usually the place where the parties are held.

Since friends are so important to them, be sure to teach them to choose their friends with care. They need models who are positive and loving, with high prin- ciples and integrity... just as they have... so they won't later suffer the agonies of disillusionment from those who don't have high standards.

If it is necessary to *discipline* these children they will respond best when you go about it in a calm, logical and reasoning way. Be sure they understand. Be as tactful as you can and be sure you are *fair* — for the concept of fairness is a fetish with Librans. These chil- dren react poorly to harshness and dislike anything ugly, vulgar, or unjust. *Ask for their cooperation*, discuss the matter together, elicit their suggestions. Compro- mise if you can, then they will feel that together you both have created a win-win situation. A devastating punishment for these children would be to have phone privileges removed, or being told they will be unable to attend the next party or social event. Remember, if you choose to attack or confront them you will likely get the same behavior in return. Mirror to them what you want. They will prefer pleasant interaction when cooperating with you.

The children of this sign are *romantic* by nature, and are inclined to be *idealistic* at times. They are liberal, broadminded, and tolerant. They are willing to fight for justice and are fairminded. Help them to choose worthwhile causes so that their energy and time can be beneficially utilized and not spent on futile causes. They can sometimes remind one of Don Quixote! They usually have good judgment on their own but can sometimes, in their zeal to please, be taken in by others who will use and misuse them. These children have high principles — when given a choice between two undesirable options they will refuse to compromise these principles and will choose neither option.

As you can see, you have a fascinating combination here. They are easy to work with once you understand them. These children will want to live life to the fullest so I am sure it will be an exciting experience for all whom they share it with. Have fun, they will insist on it!

Refer to Mercury in Libra for *key words* to use in your communications with your Libra child.

Libra Birthday Poem

How thankful are we for Libra,
a sign of beauty in our zodiac,
the one who speaks of justice,
and displays refinement with
charm and tact.
Our airy social butterfly adds
color and grace to our world,
who touches everything with gentle
love that makes flowers uncurl.
Pursuing harmony with understanding,
you show us the way to peace
that cooperating and compromise
make feelings of separateness cease.
You are creative and liberal,
appreciation for all forms of art
no need to vacillate or be evasive
in matters of the heart.
You have the skill to expose us to
beauty and things of taste,
let's open our hearts and
join together around our zodiac wheel.
Being part of the oneness
is a wonderful way to feel.
We'll sing from outer spaces of love
a tribute to you and your worth,
and wish you the best of gifts,
from the Universe and from our Earth.

Children with Sun in Scorpio

Dear *Thomas*, our doubting Thomas! Truly our *Scorpio* apostle... remembering that he was the one who would not believe that Christ had risen without first seeing him and touching his wounds. So typical of Scorpio who says, "Prove it to me." Always the *skeptic*, wanting personal experience before believing and accepting. However, once they have been convinced and decide to commit themselves they show passionate *determination* and great *loyalty*. Scorpios are real fighters and live the motto: "When the going get's tough — the tough get going." These are the children who won't cry when they are hurt or spanked, because they don't want to show weakness. Instead they will clench their teeth or look back at the inflicter with their penetrating defiant eyes, often thinking, "Just wait — I'll get you back some day." They have a tendency to be *vindictive* so it is most important for them to learn at a young age to forgive and forget. Help them realize it is unhealthy in every way to hold grudges and keep negative thoughts.

Scorpios are among the strong-minded signs of the zodiac, if not *the* strongest sign. How they use their power, for benefit or not, will be determined by the type of guidance these children receive in their early years. It is extremely important for them to establish strong spiritual values as young as possible. When these children use their power in a positive way their influence can help others make transformational changes. It is critical that they be directed wisely.

There is no halfway or in-between with these children. It is either black or white, devil or angel, due to their *fixed watery sign*. To give an example: Jonas Salk is a Scorpio using his power with positive expression; Charles Manson is a Scorpio using his power in the most negative expression.

The symbols that are given to Scorpio explain very clearly the choices they have. *Scorpio is the only sign that has three different symbols!* First, the *scorpion* which is the lowest expression with strong self-preservation and survival instincts, yet it will sting itself for lack of something else to sting. Second, is the *eagle* showing the heights to which these children can soar. Third is the *Phoenix Bird* rising out of the ashes having died and then being transformed. *Transformation* is a keyword for Scorpio and each person in this sign must undergo this process in order to fulfill their destiny. They must surrender the ego or personality to the spirit and use their strength in service to the world. These children need to learn about the powerful leaders throughout history, both the good and the destructive. This will help to stress the importance of the choices they make through life and guide them to follow the high path. The negative side unfortunately has given us some of the most clever and brutal criminals ever known. However, examples of famous Scorpios are Theodore Roosevelt, Charles Atlas, Picasso, John Phillip Sousa,

Marie Curie, George Patton, Nehru, Martin Luther and Daniel Boone!

In the body, Scorpio rules the *reproductive organs*, which explains why these children have such dynamic and creative energy. They also have strong regenerative powers, both physically and psychically, and will recover from even the most devastating experiences, becoming even stronger as a result. They are filled with courage and conviction and lack understanding or patience with those who are timid or weak. These children will approach situations with single-minded enthusiasm, accepting them as stimulating challenges. Most Scorpios are destined to become famous through great accomplishments.

Many people find Scorpios hard to know because they are so secretive. On the other hand, because *they* have such highly developed psychic abilities and are able to see beneath the surface, it is difficult to keep a secret *from* them! As their parent, trying to hide a truth will be useless. They will expect and need honest answers to their questions and are usually able to handle the truth of any situation. When *disciplining* them, be sure to think the situation through before taking action and be sure to make the *punishment fair*. In projects always remember to ask for their assistance rather than telling them what to do. Don't demand for their cooperation. This action only would bring out the streak of perversity in them — making them do just the opposite!

These children have *strong emotions* and experience life with extreme intensity. One of the greatest lessons you can teach them is to learn how to separate from their feelings by objectively observing themselves. This lesson will be a lifelong challenge but well worth the effort. The danger is that when the emotions are not controlled or used positively, the intensity involved can cause unbelievable destruction to themselves (like the scorpion stinging itself) as well as to others. These children have sharp tongues, stinging wit, and are prone to sarcasm. They must be made aware that their words can do great and lasting harm. Once they develop compassion and humility, their passions can rise to a higher level and be used to benefit others. It will be wise to *teach them the law of cause and effect* — meaning, what one puts out, one gets back... or what goes around comes around. This will be a good incentive to get them to act in kinder, more beneficial ways. Learning to turn the other cheek will curb their vindictiveness. The earlier they are helped to see this, to work on purifying themselves of Scorpio venom, the better for all.

Finally, these children, like the scorpion, seem to be always on the defensive, so you might as well give up trying to deceive or mislead them, or manipulate them in any way. Treat them openly, and honestly. Enlist them as an ally and you will be protected by their strength, and have their loyalty for life.

Refer to Mercury in Scorpio for *key words* to use in your communications with your Scorpio child.

Scorpio Birthday Poem

Here's an offering to Scorpio
the power of our signs,
sent with love and respect
from our soul, heart, and mind.
Your fierce determination
is a wonder to see,
a quality you use well
as you show us how to be.
As with the apostle Thomas
your doubting is strong,
it keeps you reserved
and slow to join the throng.
You perceive with under-
standing of things not easily seen,
you know the depths of wisdom
and show us what they mean.
We know that secrets are
an instinctive part of you,
but when you choose to share
the things you give are truth.
We love you for your strength
and hope you'll love yourself,

*we want to send you happiness
peace and good health.
Have a year filled with beauty
with all the gifts a world can give,
Happy Birthday for now
and for each birthday that you live.*

Children with Sun in Sagittarius

James the Greater, called the "son of thunder" by
Christ, demonstrates the qualities of *Sagittarius*. The
Greater was added to his name to distinguish him from
the other James who was shorter. His responses were
optimistic and *enthusiastic*, and he was always ready to
gallop off to a new adventure. His comments were
brutally frank like a clap of thunder, often unnerving
those exposed. Expect the same from these children
born in the sign of Sagittarius. One of your most important challenges as their parent or caregiver will be
to teach them the art of diplomacy, and how to pause
and think and then choose their words carefully. They
never mean harm... there is nothing vicious in the Sag
nature – only unthinking spontaneity!

Sagittarius is a *mutable fire* sign, causing these
children to be outgoing, and impulsive. It also causes
a quick fiery temper that burns furiously... and then
out. To assist in extinguishing this blast, don't feed it
any response and the blaze will quickly dissipate. Simply observe the outrage and then calmly redirect their
attention to something else. Taking them for a walk is

an excellent way to diffuse any lingering hostility (and this sign does *not* store up negative feelings). Walking will always be the best way for these children to release any anxieties or frustrations.

There are two reasons which explain why a walk works so well at dissipating emotions. The first is because Sagittarius has influence over the *hips* and *thighs* in the physical body, therefore the freedom and movement that walking creates releases any pent-up energy. Secondly, the symbol for Sagittarius is the *centaur*, half horse and half man. When the children of this sign get to expend the physical energy charging through the animal part of their symbol, then they are free to utilize their human ability of logic and wisdom and can more clearly think through situations.

These children's approach to life is direct like the centaur archer's arrows. You will always know where you stand, and they don't hesitate to tell you what is on their minds. Unless you are prepared for the blunt truth, don't ask for their opinions. They are seldom shy or timid about telling you exactly what you think. They dislike beating around the bush and will let everyone know it. They are *honest* and will tell the truth as *they* see it. One caution is that they can be *careless* with details and may not have all the facts. Another is that they may have a tendency to be reckless or rash, so teach them to think before speaking or taking any action.

Freedom is mandatory for Sagittarius. Their theme is "Don't fence me in!" When these children feel penned in too tightly they will kick and carry on like a mustang held in a confined area. That's the centaur showing itself again. The best way to handle this need for freedom is to allow them to take the lead whenever feasible, and give them many opportunities to make their own choices. Explain to these children that if they make wise choices and act in a responsible manner they can continue to choose for themselves. Let them know that this *is* the way to the freedom they crave. If you should find your young Sagittarian child cranky or irritable, check to see if you have dressed them in something too tight. These children will even need freedom with their clothing!

You will discover that the children of this sign are very *independent* and they find it difficult to stay within any boundaries. They will even end a friendship or any relationship rather than be restricted by it. For young children, anyone telling them who they can or can't have as a friend is fatal. For older children who have begun to date, anyone of the opposite sex expecting to possess them should be prepared to have the relationship be of short duration.

These children are *easily bored*, going from one thing to another. This mental scatterdness can also move into the physical — with them being a bit messy and disorganized. They are always looking to the future, thinking up new things to do and new places to go. They like continuous activity so be prepared. The natives of this sign *love sports and travel.* They are good with animals, especially large ones, and will feel at home in the forest. These suggestions should give you some ideas of how to keep them busy. Keeping their days filled with activities which they enjoy will create happy children who will require little or no discipline. However, when *discipline* is required the worst punishment for these children is any form of *restriction* or *confinement.* It is always wise to be truthful with them to retain their respect. It is also important to be fair and just. They will respond better with discussions that are direct and to the point. These are children who will give you some interesting feedback if you ask for their suggestions and opinions — many times they will give you the solutions!

Your Sag will be lucky and no matter how close to the wire they may come, something will save their day at the eleventh hour. It is almost as if they know this deep inside. This luck is also why they are such big *gamblers,* and will gallop forth where others fear to tread. They have a natural ability to see the whole picture rather than any particular part. They look at the whole of society rather than individuals. They expand their interest to all nationalities and are not prejudiced or biased. Their philosophies are far reaching and futuristic. They are comfortable with abstract ideas... and I'm sure these children will present you with many new ways of looking at life. They like to be acknowledged for their abilities so I suggest that you compliment them, love them — and give them plenty of space to be themselves.

Refer to Mercury in Sagittarius for *key words* to use in your communications with your Sagittarius child.

Sagittarius Birthday Poem

What would the world be without
the truth of a Sagittarian,
but pay heed my friend and
let me remind you once again.
Your words can come like flying arrows,
shot direct and straight with a pierce,
so painful without loving tact.
Now nobody's perfect and
we need people like you,
who are frank, optimistic,
and sincerely honest too.
At dinner you charm us with
philosophy and such,
it's your outgoing nature
that we love so much.
For who knows one more jovial or
brighter than you,
or who lives a life of freedom
more than you do.

You spread yourself generously,
as does the Sun,
please tell us what you know
for you hold wisdom.
Thank you for daring just to be you—
here's sending a HAPPY BIRTHDAY and
wishes that come true...

Children with Sun in Capricorn

The apostle who aligns with the sign of *Capricorn* is *Matthew*, the tax collector. When we realize that the natural instincts of a Capricorn are to be in a position of authority, and that they need to be respected by others, it is clear to see why Matthew had chosen his profession. Capricorns do make wonderful administrators. They are *serious* and *responsible*. They take time to assess the situation, which makes them *able to respond* with practical, useful solutions.

The symbol for Capricorn is the *goat* who surefootedly and very carefully places each foot, always looking for solid ground before moving on. They are *persistent*, *determined*, and will climb to great heights. Professionally, Capricorns aspire to high positions no matter what arena they choose, but, usually they choose to work within the status quo in fields that are socially acceptable and well-respected. This obviously is a sign which clings to customs and is comfortable with tradition. They have a strong appreciation for money and will usually focus on obtaining financial success. They are achievement-oriented and will strive to accomplish in areas that have strong purpose.

Most of the time these children are so serious they appear old for their years. They seem to be born as adults and will act in very *mature* ways. You can count on them to behave well in situations where adult contact is required. Even as young children, Capricorns are *easy to discipline* and can be trusted with responsibility. They are almost overly *conscientious*. They thrive on others taking them seriously, and on receiving praise for performing well. They will want to please you, to gain your respect. They are wonderfully *self-disciplined*.

These children are *ambitious* and are *hard workers*. In fact, they feel that work is virtuous and that everyone should work for whatever they get. These are the children who will want to have a job at an early age or will always be thinking up ways to earn money. They may even start their own little business. They are very *persistent* and will still be plugging along after most would have given up.

Capricorn is an *earth* sign which causes the children of this sign to gravitate toward the material side of life. They are *realistic* and place little value in fantasy or intangibles. They are interested in accumulating material substances, both money and possessions. They are often good at using materials to build with, many even become contractors. In fact, they excel at *building* structures of any nature. And figuratively, they are al-

ways building their lives... and climbing like the mountain goat.

It is not surprising to discover that Capricorn
rules the *skeletal system* and the *skin* in the physical
body; one is the structure and the other is the form.
This sign also rules *teeth* and the *knees*. Since the knee
is one of the most complex joints in the body and is
necessary for good mobility, it is important for these
natives to take care of their knees. Teach them the value
of life-long, daily-done exercise — to keep them flexible
and to avoid becoming rigid, mentally as well as physically. Remember, one is apt to develop a weakness in
that area of the body that a sign rules. Since Capricorn
rules knees and skeletal system, they often develop
arthritis later — all the more reason for exercise and
flexibility!

These children are *collectors*, and like to hold on
to everything they accumulate. The caution here is that
in extreme cases accumulating too much around oneself can be immobilizing, giving them no room to move
or grow! Also holding on too tightly can cause a rigidity, and without movement *psychic* atrophy sets in. The
same problem exists with *patience*, a characteristic of
this sign — if carried to it's extreme and they wait too
long, an opportunity could be missed.

When these children reach school age, don't be
surprised if they show little or no interest in subjects
which they consider to have no practical application.
They are primarily interested in learning about what

can be useful to them. Since they tend to be focused on the past and are establishment-oriented, you will be able to teach them wisdom through reading and learning about the people throughout history who reached positions of great authority and respect. These children will work very hard in school and usually make excellent students. They are *organized* and will respect teachers who are. They are concerned about their reputation and will do everything to acquire a good one; woe to him who sullies their reputation, or embarrasses them in any way!

Two of the worst things anyone can do to a Capricorn is to imply that they are incompetent, or to treat them with disrespect. If they are commended for their accomplishments they will eagerly take on more responsibility. But be sure to watch they don't take on so much that their lives are filled only with work and duty. They need to be encouraged to play and sometimes have fun. Help them to develop a sense of humor. These children appear to be *pessimistic* because they have a tendency to look first at the down side of situations. For them it is a form of self-protection. They feel that by looking for the pitfalls they can more easily avoid them. Help them to become aware of how others might react to this "downer" approach so that they won't be considered a wet blanket, or the one who rains on other people's parades! The best advice I can think of is for you to teach them to *always* keep one thought in mind — lighten up!

Refer to Mercury in Capricorn for *key words* to use in your communications with your Capricorn child.

Capricorn Birthday Poem

To our responsible Capricorn Brothers
here and out there,
a few words of tribute
to show that we care.
We know your sense of self-
preservation is important,
both here and above,
but don't be so fearful —
let down your defenses,
and taste of love.
Being ruled by Saturn the tester,
is definitely stiff your life will be filled
with lessons of patience and thrift.
Your serious self-discipline and
perfection is most admirable to see,
but we wouldn't be here on Earth if we
compared to the one called thee.
We need your caution to
lead us to safety,
we count on you to be practical
and productive.
We call on your dependability

and your endurance.
It's your persistence and diplomacy
that give us comfort and reassurance.
Just remember for yourself—
there is strength in humility,
simply drop your pessimism—
for you have the ability.
We hope this year and
all the rest too,
bring the happiest of Birthdays
always for you...

Children with Sun in Aquarius

Thaddaeus, nicknamed *Jude*, is our apostle for the sign of *Aquarius*. He was one of the least known of the apostles, supposedly the brother of James the Less. It is so typical of Aquarius to work behind the scenes and to shun the spotlight. Their need seems only to be able to fight for the cause rather than to be the center of attention. Thaddaeus or Jude is known as the apostle of the impossible and is prayed to as a last resort when all seems hopeless. It makes sense when we know that the planet *Uranus* with its *unpredictable* nature rules the sign of Aquarius. The key phrase for Uranus is — *expect the unexpected!* These natives are capable of a powerful love for all mankind and they possess a strong desire for *humanitarian* service. If needed, they will

stand alone against the status quo to eliminate suffering, and will fight for any worthwhile cause.

The symbol for Aquarius is *the water bearer*. Since
water is a necessity to live, it is thought that he is
pouring forth in abundance the substance of life. This
thougt may be the mission of Aquarius — *to bring new
life to us all.* Although he is pouring water, it should be
remembered that Aquarius is an *air* sign. Sometimes
this gets confused.

Like all air signs these children will operate in a
logical, and *intellectual* manner. They are *objective*, and
experience life using a mental approach. Because of a
lack of emotional display, to some they may *seem impersonal* and aloof. They are definitely *independent* and
have *no* need for approval. This characteristic causes
them to be comfortable going their own way without
becoming concerned about what others may think.
They are quite self-sufficient and march to their own
drummer. These children are the entrepreneurs of the
world. They are individuals in every sense of the word.
They are often unconventional and always unique, to
say the least. Freedom is extremely important to the
children born under this sign. *They need the freedom to
be who they are and to do their own thing.* Their approach
may be unorthodox, and sometimes they are defiant of
established customs and tradition. This behavior may
take some getting used to, but how would we ever find
new ways to live life and make improvements if we
never tried something different?

These children are *non-conformists* and totally in-
different to their environment, especially in the sense
of how they dress. They are not likely to get caught up
in the latest fad or even know what they should wear
to a particular event. They will need your guidance in
this area, but I suggest that you insist only when it is
absolutely necessary. They still need their individual
freedom to be themselves, plus they can be quite stubborn and can NOT be pushed. They have their own
ideas about most everything so you will need to be
creative and discover ways to motivate them to make
necessary changes or concessions. Sometimes presenting what you want in the form of a suggestion and then
backing away, will give them the needed space to make
the change on their own. Remember, they must decide
for themselves so present your ideas in a calm, logical
way and give them space and time to come around.

Your main challenge with these children will be to
keep enough variety in their lives. They will always
want to be learning new things, especially subjects
pertaining to science, exploration, and new technology
— especially computers, and they love science fiction!

Aquarian children are very curious about everything. Generally they like to study and they have good
retentive memories. You will find that they will need a
minimum amount of supervision when it comes to
schoolwork. They can also be very creative and innovative in the areas of art, music, and literature — they
will produce very original and unusual material. They
will always pursue a broad range of interests, activities,

and people. In reference to the latter, be prepared because they may choose some very different, unusual types for friends. These choices may not make sense to you but please be patient with them since your Aquarian probably has a reason. Know that these children of Aquarius are their own persons, so the company they keep does *not* have that great an influence over them. Besides, they will have many friends who are all very different.

These children are sometimes viewed as the *rebels* because they are often seen as fighting for reform. They look for causes as they are true humanitarians. They will join groups who work for social and political reform. After all, a *key word* for Uranus, their ruler, is *liberation*. Sometimes these natives seem radical in their approach; however, they are intellectually rational. Although they are progressive *free thinkers* and the revolutionaries of the world, appeal to that rational side if they go overboard and become fanatic — and there is that danger, being a free-thinking *fixed* sign! They will often want to participate in marches and protests for they are real crusaders. Direct them to worthwhile causes so that they won't simply become a renegade and a rioter. Show them how to use their enthusiasm in peaceful, constructive, nondestructive ways.

Before Uranus was discovered, the old rulership of Aquarius was the planet Saturn. You may remember that Saturn rules Capricorn so you know it represents responsibility, order, and perseverance — therefore these children do have some of those qualities. I see older Aquarians more inclined to demonstrate the Saturn side, and younger Aquarians demonstrating the experimental, futuristic, unconventional side. It is natural for Aquarians to have keen intuitions and good psychic powers... so they may see and know things that others are as yet unaware.

One problem this sign has is that they are so focused on the masses that sometimes they neglect their families. Teach them that charity begins at home. A detached attitude is not as appropriate in family matters as it is in dealing with worldly matters. They can be very warmhearted — they just need you to help them work on expressing it at home with the family!

Aquarius has influence over the *ankles* and *circulation* in the physical body. The ankles are part of the foundational structure, therefore they need to be strong. Encourage these children to walk, to do up-and-down ankle exercises, and to choose activities which will create strength in this area... like dancing! And these same activities will help the circulation. Aquarians have a tendency to be more mental than physical, so do see to it that they add some physical activities to their *daily* routine.

I am sure that by now you have a pretty good idea of the fun in store for you with your interesting little Aquarian, so I will leave you with this — do NOT try to control or force them. Keep daily life filled with as many new experiences as possible, and you will enjoy an exciting life together. Remember — they *are* the Age of Aquarius!

Refer to Mercury in Aquarius for *key words* to use in your communications with your Aquarius child.

Aquarius Birthday Poem

What a pleasure to know you, and
how you do add to our group
you point our eyes to the
future, and find new ways to
lead the troops.
Your intuitive intellect,
unconventional as it is
creates ingenious
originality the rest of us
might miss.
You bring with you the
 philosophy of individual pursuit
you teach us independence and
freedom to boot.
A spirited reformer geared to humanity
and universal truth
resourceful and determined, we understand
when you are aloof.
But, please don't detach,
be impersonal, or rebel

*we know you're self-sufficient and a
non-conformist as well.
Besides, who is more progressively
inventive and practical too,
we need this discerning genius
that comes only from you.
Here's hoping your days are
extraordinary all year through,
and wish you success forever in
whatever you do.*

Children with Sun in Pisces

Last but definitely not least is *Pisces*. Here we find individuals who have amazing abilities and are very complex. Those born under this sign are often *misunderstood* as was the apostle *Judas Iscariot*. He is often thought of as the traitor, but when we re-examine the events to understand his motives and intentions, the picture changes. His motive was to end the oppression and suffering which the people endured under the cruel and brutal rulership of the Romans. His intention was to bring Jesus together with this political power believing that Jesus would confront them and bring the wrath of God upon them. Then Jesus could become emperor of Rome, thereby ending suffering and restoring decency. Judas was so desperate for social and political reform that he completely missed the point that Jesus wasn't here to rule the Earth, but that His mission was to leave a message which would change it for all time. This factor makes it seem very probable why Jesus chose Judas... *because* of his zeal for the people... and knowing full well what was going to happen.

In retrospect, the part Judas played was most important, since singularly his actions birthed the beginning of Christianity... which was all part of the divine plan. Judas didn't want to hurt Jesus — he wanted to empower Him and when his plan didn't work he became despondent and committed suicide. The other apostles then chose Matthew to take his place.

The symbol for Pisces is *the two fish* swimming in different directions. This indicates that the children born under this sign have *a choice of two directions*. One of their problems is that they are too susceptible to external influences, so whatever the greatest force in their environment determines which way they swim. As their parent or caregiver, it is most important that you stimulate them in the best direction, and help them develop their spiritual nature. Once this becomes their main direction, they will be able to accomplish much in this too realistic world.

Without a strong spiritual background and solid foundation, they can be misled into squander and deception. These children may have a tendency to want to escape the world of reality and to spend their time daydreaming and in fantasy land. Sometimes the world is too harsh, cruel, and hurts too much for them to endure. This is because they "feel" everything so personally. Pisces children need to learn to view the world and other people more objectively. When they can do this, everything that happens around them will affect them less. Otherwise they will always feel like the victim... vulnerable, and at the mercy of their environment.

Pisces is a *water* sign so we find these children *emotional*, *sensitive*, and *intuitive*. They can be like sponges, soaking up everyone's feelings. This, of course, causes them to be not only sympathetic, but also empathetic. They literally can feel the pain and the joy of others — even while watching a play or the evening news. That is why they must be very careful not to become moody or sink into the problems of others. So you can see how important it is to surround them with as much positivity as possible. When you do this they can blossom and develop all of their artistic and creative abilities.

These children are very imaginative and will show great inspiration. Teach them to work at and to follow through with their ideas... and to produce the results for this the material world. They sometimes lack persistence and need lots of encouragement in this area. To start with, help them to set and complete short-term goals. As they succeed with these, it will become easier to complete long-term goals. These children are susceptible to *procrastination* and are sometimes 'afraid' to take that first step... so gently guide them in the direction that is needed. They are *adaptable* and *flexible* so this shouldn't be too hard.

Children of this sign are very visual, so when you are teaching them, paint pictures with your words and they will better remember. For example: if you are giving them directions to reach a certain destination, rather than saying, "Turn right at the third street down," say, "Turn right at the street that has the yellow house on the corner... with a marble birdbath by the big fur tree... and a red-white-and-blue mailbox by the road." They are quick to "see" mental pictures and in this way will learn rapidly. Also, when they are school age the more visual aids you can use the better. They will enjoy television so utilize any video aids you can. But don't let them become TV-addicted — or addicted to any escape, or fantasy world. Later in life, without early guidance into the real world, they could escape into alcohol or worse. But do allow them some time alone to imagine and dream up something wonderful for the rest of us earthbound creatures.

It is very important to be affectionate and give these children of Pisces a lot of reassurance, because they are inclined to feel unworthy or experience some feeling of inferiority (because they don't feel at home on Earth!). They are easily hurt and can cry readily. Be *gentle* about *discipline* and always be aware of how sensitive they are — *never* use corporal punishment on them!

The part of the physical body that Pisces rules is the *feet*. Since the feet are the support for the rest of the body, it is necessary to have strong, well-formed feet for good mobility. When the foundations of your Pisces children is built on the strength of the spiritual, their physical world can stand tall.

This sign of the fish is known for its accomplishments in the worlds of art and music, as well as in religion and medicine. They have great compassion and are capable of great sacrifice. They serve with devotion and can truly be the healers of us all, in mind and body. As they develop the perseverance of the disciple Matthew, they will become determined to excel in the world.

Because these children have such highly developed psychic sensitivity, teach them to see a spiritual white light surrounding them and protecting them at all times from any negativity. Help them to develop their natural intuitive ability and to use *it* to make decisions. Let them know that it is a gift and that it should be used wisely.

These children need your attention and your encouragement. Reward them with doing things together — and reward them often. Be sure to give them lots of love and reassurance, and be considerate of their sensitivity. This will ensure a joyful and rewarding life together.

Refer to Mercury in Pisces for *key words* to use in your communications with your Pisces child.

Pisces Birthday Poem

Hail to Pisces, the last and
most needed of our zodiac friends,
for how can we have a beginning until we have an end?
You show us we must to leave
Earth in order to ascend,
and do it by dreaming of
things beyond now and then.
Your visions will take us
 there with inspiration too,
if you'll utilize your genius
and show us what to do.
Take us to fantasy land
where dreams are more true.
You know the way past the darkness,
please help us get through.
How we need your perception
creative as it is,
God shared with you the secrets
that were only His.
You are sensitive and caring
and filled with compassion,
serving the masses in your
charitable fashion.
As masquerader or poet,
your gifts of emotion,

you bring imagination and
intuitive devotion.
Is it illusion–confusion–delusion
or what?
Show us the way through a door
that is shut.
How can you feel unworthy and
martyr yourself,
with all this talent–the
best kind of wealth.
To you–Happy Birthday
Success and Good Health!

*"An estimated 32 million people,
according to a recent "Gallup Poll," believe that
the movement of the planets affect their lives."
Sydney Omarr, national columnist on astrology*

CHAPTER 5

The Moon — The Tug on Emotions

The Moon is the fastest moving celestial body in our solar system. It travels through the entire zodiac, each one of the twelve signs, every month. It stays in each sign for approximately two and a half days which is the average of 28 days, the lunar cycle. The Moon is the activator, or trigger which causes events to happen, and mood changes to occur. As it moves through the different signs each month, *it makes contact with and activates each planet* in everyone's individual horoscope. This is why we have highs and lows and is what causes our feelings and reactions to change from day-to-day. When we understand this, we become less apt to expect anyone, including ourselves, to feel or act consistently the same all of the time!

Symbolically the Moon represents the *emotions* — our feelings about and our reactions to our environment. The sign that our Moon is in describes how we experience the emotions and how they will be expressed. The Moon also represents *security*. It denotes how comfortable we are with our environment. It shows whether we feel like an important necessary part of our society, with a purpose in this world. It shows whether we are needed and whether the world fills our needs. By understanding what your child's needs are, we as parents and caregivers can begin to provide what is necessary.

When you read the description for each child's Moon placement, you will understand how his or her emotional nature functions. This will *help clarify how you should develop your child's security and fulfill his or her needs.*

How to Use Moon Tables

The Moon moves very quickly through the signs each month, staying in a sign approximately two and a half days. These tables will show the date that the Moon moved into a new sign for each month.

If you are checking a birthdate which was on a day that the Moon moved into a new sign, unless you know what time the Moon changed signs, you will have to read the description of the previous sign as well. After reading both profiles, you should know what sign the Moon was in for the person in question.

Find the year and month in which you were born. Use a ruler to move down the page to the day.

SIGNS

ARI	Aries		LIB	Libra
TAU	Taurus		SCO	Scorpio
GEM	Gemini		SAG	Sagittarius
CAN	Cancer		CAP	Capricorn
LEO	Leo		AQU	Aquarius
VIR	Virgo		PIS	Pisces

Moon Tables

1900

JAN		FEB		MAR		APR		MAY		JUN	
1	CAP	1	PIS	1	PIS	1	TAU	1	GEM	2	LEO
3	AQU	3	ARI	3	GEM	3	GEM	3	CAN	4	VIR
5	PIS	5	TAU	5	TAU	6	CAN	5	LEO	7	LIB
7	ARI	8	GEM	7	GEM	8	LEO	8	VIR	9	SCO
9	TAU	10	CAN	9	CAN	10	VIR	10	LIB	12	SAG
11	GEM	12	LEO	12	LEO	13	LIB	13	SCO	14	CAP
14	CAN	15	VIR	14	VIR	15	SCO	15	SAG	16	AQU
16	LEO	17	LIB	17	LIB	18	SAG	17	CAP	18	PIS
19	VIR	20	SCO	19	SCO	20	CAP	20	AQU	20	ARI
21	LIB	22	SAG	22	SAG	22	AQU	22	PIS	22	TAU
24	SCO	25	CAP	24	CAP	25	PIS	24	ARI	24	GEM
26	SAG	27	AQU	26	AQU	27	ARI	26	TAU	27	CAN
28	CAP			28	PIS	29	TAU	28	GEM	29	LEO
30	AQU			30	ARI			30	CAN		

JUL		AUG		SEP		OCT		NOV		DEC	
1	VIR	1	LIB	2	SAG	1	CAP	2	PIS	1	ARI
4	LIB	3	SCO	4	CAP	4	AQU	4	ARI	3	TAU
6	SCO	5	SAG	6	AQU	6	PIS	6	TAU	5	GEM
9	SAG	8	CAP	8	PIS	8	ARI	8	GEM	8	CAN
11	CAP	10	AQU	10	ARI	10	TAU	10	CAN	10	LEO
13	AQU	12	PIS	12	TAU	12	GEM	12	LEO	12	VIR
15	PIS	14	ARI	14	GEM	14	CAN	15	VIR	15	LIB
17	ARI	16	TAU	16	CAN	16	LEO	17	LIB	17	SCO
20	TAU	18	GEM	19	LEO	19	VIR	20	SCO	20	SAG
22	GEM	20	CAN	21	VIR	21	LIB	22	SAG	22	CAP
24	CAN	23	LEO	24	LIB	24	SCO	25	CAP	24	AQU
26	LEO	25	VIR	26	SCO	26	SAG	27	AQU	26	PIS
29	VIR	28	LIB	29	SAG	28	CAP	29	PIS	29	ARI
31	LIB	30	SCO			31	AQU			31	TAU

1901

JAN		FEB		MAR		APR		MAY		JUN	
2	GEM	3	LEO	2	LEO	3	LIB	3	SCO	1	SAG
4	CAN	5	VIR	4	VIR	5	SCO	5	SAG	4	CAP
6	LEO	7	LIB	7	LIB	8	SAG	8	CAP	6	AQU
9	VIR	10	SCO	9	SCO	10	CAP	10	AQU	9	PIS
11	LIB	12	SAG	12	SAG	13	AQU	12	PIS	11	ARI
14	SCO	15	CAP	14	CAP	15	PIS	14	ARI	13	TAU
16	SAG	17	AQU	16	AQU	17	ARI	16	TAU	15	GEM
18	CAP	19	PIS	19	PIS	19	TAU	18	GEM	17	CAN
21	AQU	21	ARI	21	ARI	21	GEM	21	CAN	19	LEO
23	PIS	23	TAU	23	TAU	23	CAN	23	LEO	21	VIR
25	ARI	25	GEM	25	GEM	25	LEO	25	VIR	24	LIB
27	TAU	28	CAN	27	CAN	28	VIR	27	LIB	26	SCO
29	GEM			29	LEO	30	LIB	30	SCO	29	SAG
31	CAN			31	VIR						

JUL		AUG		SEP		OCT		NOV		DEC	
1	CAP	2	PIS	1	ARI	2	GEM	3	LEO	2	VIR
4	AQU	4	ARI	3	TAU	4	CAN	5	VIR	5	LIB
6	PIS	6	TAU	5	GEM	6	LEO	7	LIB	7	SCO
8	ARI	8	GEM	7	CAN	9	VIR	10	SCO	10	SAG
10	TAU	11	CAN	9	LEO	11	LIB	12	SAG	12	CAP
12	GEM	13	LEO	11	VIR	14	SCO	15	CAP	15	AQU
14	CAN	15	VIR	14	LIB	16	SAG	17	AQU	17	PIS
16	LEO	17	LIB	16	SCO	19	CAP	20	PIS	19	ARI
19	VIR	20	SCO	19	SAG	21	AQU	22	ARI	21	TAU
21	LIB	22	SAG	21	CAP	23	PIS	24	TAU	23	GEM
24	SCO	25	CAP	24	AQU	25	ARI	26	GEM	25	CAN
26	SAG	27	AQU	26	PIS	27	TAU	28	CAN	27	LEO
29	CAP	29	PIS	28	ARI	29	GEM	30	LEO	30	VIR
31	AQU			30	TAU	31	CAN				

1902

	JAN		FEB		MAR		APR		MAY		JUN
1	LIB	2	SAG	2	SAG	3	AQU	3	PIS	1	ARI
3	SCO	5	CAP	4	CAP	5	PIS	5	ARI	3	TAU
6	SAG	7	AQU	6	AQU	7	ARI	7	TAU	5	GEM
8	CAP	9	PIS	9	PIS	9	TAU	9	GEM	7	CAN
11	AQU	12	ARI	11	ARI	11	GEM	11	CAN	9	LEO
13	PIS	14	TAU	13	TAU	14	CAN	13	LEO	11	VIR
15	ARI	16	GEM	15	GEM	16	LEO	15	VIR	14	LIB
18	TAU	18	CAN	17	CAN	18	VIR	17	LIB	16	SCO
20	GEM	20	LEO	19	LEO	20	LIB	20	SCO	19	SAG
22	CAN	22	VIR	22	VIR	23	SCO	22	SAG	21	CAP
24	LEO	25	LIB	24	LIB	25	SAG	25	CAP	24	AQU
26	VIR	27	SCO	26	SCO	28	CAP	27	AQU	26	PIS
28	LIB			29	SAG	30	AQU	30	PIS	28	ARI
31	SCO			31	CAP						

	JUL		AUG		SEP		OCT		NOV		DEC
1	TAU	1	CAN	2	VIR	1	LIB	2	SAG	2	CAP
3	GEM	3	LEO	4	LIB	3	SCO	5	CAP	5	AQU
5	CAN	5	VIR	6	SCO	6	SAG	7	AQU	7	PIS
7	LEO	7	LIB	9	SAG	8	CAP	10	PIS	9	ARI
9	VIR	10	SCO	11	CAP	11	AQU	12	ARI	12	TAU
11	LIB	12	SAG	14	AQU	13	PIS	14	TAU	14	GEM
13	SCO	15	CAP	16	PIS	16	ARI	16	GEM	16	CAN
16	SAG	17	AQU	18	ARI	18	TAU	18	CAN	18	LEO
18	CAP	20	PIS	20	TAU	20	GEM	20	LEO	20	VIR
21	AQU	22	ARI	23	GEM	22	CAN	22	VIR	22	LIB
23	PIS	24	TAU	25	CAN	24	LEO	25	LIB	24	SCO
26	ARI	26	GEM	27	LEO	26	VIR	27	SCO	27	SAG
28	TAU	28	CAN	29	VIR	28	LIB	30	SAG	29	CAP
30	GEM	30	LEO			31	SCO				

1903

	JAN		FEB		MAR		APR		MAY		JUN
1	AQU	2	ARI	1	ARI	2	GEM	1	CAN	2	VIR
3	TAU	4	TAU	4	TAU	4	CAN	3	LEO	4	LIB
6	GEM	6	GEM	6	GEM	6	LEO	6	VIR	6	SCO
8	CAN	9	CAN	8	CAN	8	VIR	8	LIB	9	SAG
10	LEO	11	LEO	10	LEO	10	LIB	10	SCO	11	CAP
12	VIR	13	VIR	12	VIR	13	SCO	12	SAG	14	AQU
14	LIB	15	LIB	14	LIB	15	SAG	15	CAP	16	PIS
16	SCO	17	SCO	16	SCO	17	CAP	17	AQU	19	ARI
18	SAG	19	SAG	19	SAG	20	AQU	20	PIS	21	TAU
21	CAP	22	CAP	21	CAP	23	PIS	22	ARI	23	GEM
23	AQU	24	AQU	24	AQU	25	ARI	25	TAU	25	CAN
26	PIS	27	PIS	26	PIS	27	TAU	27	GEM	27	LEO
28	ARI			29	ARI	29	GEM	29	CAN	29	VIR
31	TAU			31	TAU			31	LEO		

	JUL		AUG		SEP		OCT		NOV		DEC
1	LIB	2	SAG	1	CAP	1	AQU	2	ARI	2	TAU
3	SCO	5	CAP	3	AQU	3	PIS	4	TAU	4	GEM
6	SAG	7	AQU	6	PIS	6	ARI	7	GEM	6	CAN
8	CAP	10	PIS	8	ARI	8	TAU	9	CAN	8	LEO
11	AQU	12	ARI	11	TAU	10	GEM	11	LEO	10	VIR
13	PIS	15	TAU	13	GEM	12	CAN	13	VIR	12	LIB
16	ARI	17	GEM	15	CAN	15	LEO	15	LIB	15	SCO
18	TAU	19	CAN	17	LEO	17	VIR	17	SCO	17	SAG
20	GEM	21	LEO	19	VIR	19	SCO	20	SAG	19	CAP
23	CAN	23	VIR	21	LIB	21	SAG	22	CAP	22	AQU
25	LEO	25	LIB	24	SCO	23	CAP	24	AQU	24	PIS
27	VIR	27	SCO	26	SAG	26	AQU	27	PIS	27	ARI
29	LIB	29	SAG	28	CAP	28	PIS	29	ARI	29	TAU
31	SCO					31	ARI			31	GEM

1904

JAN		FEB		MAR		APR		MAY		JUN	
2	CAN	1	LEO	1	VIR	2	SCO	1	SAG	2	AQU
4	LEO	3	VIR	3	LIB	4	SAG	4	CAP	5	PIS
6	VIR	5	LIB	5	SCO	6	CAP	6	AQU	8	ARI
9	LIB	7	SCO	8	SAG	9	AQU	9	PIS	10	TAU
11	SCO	9	SAG	10	CAP	11	PIS	11	ARI	12	GEM
13	SAG	12	CAP	12	AQU	14	ARI	14	TAU	14	CAN
15	CAP	14	AQU	15	PIS	16	TAU	16	GEM	17	LEO
18	AQU	17	PIS	18	ARI	19	GEM	18	CAN	19	VIR
21	PIS	19	ARI	20	TAU	21	CAN	20	LEO	21	LIB
23	ARI	22	TAU	22	GEM	23	LEO	22	VIR	23	SCO
26	TAU	24	GEM	25	CAN	25	VIR	24	LIB	25	SAG
28	GEM	26	CAN	27	LEO	27	LIB	27	SCO	27	CAP
30	CAN	28	LEO	29	VIR	29	SCO	29	SAG	30	AQU
				31	LIB			31	CAP		

JUL		AUG		SEP		OCT		NOV		DEC	
2	PIS	1	ARI	2	GEM	2	CAN	3	VIR	2	LIB
5	ARI	4	TAU	5	CAN	4	LEO	5	LIB	4	SCO
7	TAU	6	GEM	7	LEO	6	VIR	7	SCO	6	SAG
10	GEM	8	CAN	9	VIR	8	LIB	9	SAG	8	CAP
12	CAN	10	LEO	11	LIB	10	SCO	11	CAP	11	AQU
14	LEO	12	VIR	13	SCO	12	SAG	13	AQU	13	PIS
16	VIR	14	LIB	15	SAG	14	CAP	16	PIS	16	ARI
18	LIB	16	SCO	17	CAP	17	AQU	18	ARI	18	TAU
20	SCO	19	SAG	20	AQU	19	PIS	21	TAU	20	GEM
22	SAG	21	CAP	22	PIS	22	ARI	23	GEM	23	CAN
25	CAP	23	AQU	25	ARI	24	TAU	25	CAN	25	LEO
27	AQU	25	PIS	27	TAU	27	GEM	28	LEO	27	VIR
30	PIS	28	ARI	30	GEM	29	CAN	30	VIR	29	LIB
		31	TAU			31	LEO			31	SCO

1905

JAN		FEB		MAR		APR		MAY		JUN	
2	SAG	1	CAP	3	AQU	1	PIS	1	ARI	2	GEM
5	CAP	3	AQU	5	PIS	4	ARI	4	TAU	5	CAN
7	AQU	6	PIS	7	ARI	6	TAU	6	GEM	7	LEO
9	PIS	8	ARI	10	TAU	9	GEM	8	CAN	9	VIR
12	ARI	11	TAU	13	GEM	11	CAN	11	LEO	11	LIB
14	TAU	13	GEM	15	CAN	13	LEO	13	VIR	13	SCO
17	GEM	16	CAN	17	LEO	16	VIR	15	LIB	15	SAG
19	CAN	18	LEO	19	VIR	18	LIB	17	SCO	18	CAP
21	LEO	20	VIR	21	LIB	20	SCO	19	SAG	20	AQU
23	VIR	22	LIB	23	SCO	22	SAG	21	CAP	22	PIS
25	LIB	24	SCO	25	SAG	24	CAP	23	AQU	25	ARI
27	SCO	26	SAG	27	CAP	26	AQU	26	PIS	27	TAU
30	SAG	28	CAP	30	AQU	28	PIS	28	ARI	30	GEM
								31	TAU		

JUL		AUG		SEP		OCT		NOV		DEC	
2	CAN	1	LEO	1	LIB	1	SCO	1	CAP	1	AQU
4	LEO	3	VIR	3	SCO	3	SAG	3	AQU	3	PIS
6	VIR	5	LIB	5	SAG	5	CAP	6	PIS	5	ARI
9	LIB	7	SCO	7	CAP	7	AQU	8	ARI	8	TAU
11	SCO	9	SAG	10	AQU	9	PIS	11	TAU	10	GEM
13	SAG	11	CAP	12·	PIS	12	ARI	13	GEM	13	CAN
15	CAP	13	AQU	15	ARI	14	TAU	16	CAN	15	LEO
17	AQU	16	PIS	17	TAU	17	GEM	18	LEO	18	VIR
19	PIS	18	ARI	20	GEM	19	CAN	20	VIR	20	LIB
22	ARI	21	TAU	22	CAN	22	LEO	22	LIB	22	SCO
24	TAU	23	GEM	24	LEO	24	VIR	24	SCO	24	SAG
27	GEM	26	CAN	27	VIR	26	LIB	26	SAG	26	CAP
29	CAN	28	LEO	29	LIB	28	SCO	28	CAP	28	AQU
		30	VIR			30	SAG			30	PIS

1906

JAN		FEB		MAR		APR		MAY		JUN	
2	ARI	1	TAU	2	GEM	1	CAN	1	LEO	2	LIB
4	TAU	3	GEM	5	CAN	4	LEO	3	VIR	4	SCO
7	GEM	6	CAN	7	LEO	6	VIR	5	LIB	6	SAG
9	CAN	8	LEO	9	VIR	8	LIB	7	SCO	8	CAP
11	LEO	10	VIR	12	LIB	10	SCO	9	SAG	10	AQU
14	VIR	12	LIB	14	SCO	12	SAG	11	CAP	12	PIS
16	LIB	14	SCO	16	SAG	14	CAP	14	AQU	14	ARI
18	SCO	16	SAG	18	CAP	16	AQU	16	PIS	17	TAU
20	SAG	19	CAP	20	AQU	19	PIS	18	ARI	19	GEM
22	CAP	21	AQU	22	PIS	21	ARI	21	TAU	22	CAN
24	AQU	23	PIS	25	ARI	23	TAU	23	GEM	24	LEO
27	PIS	25	ARI	27	TAU	26	GEM	26	CAN	27	VIR
29	ARI	28	TAU	30	GEM	29	CAN	28	LEO	29	LIB
								31	VIR		

JUL		AUG		SEP		OCT		NOV		DEC	
1	SCO	2	CAP	2	PIS	2	ARI	1	TAU	3	CAN
3	SAG	4	AQU	5	ARI	4	TAU	3	GEM	5	LEO
5	CAP	6	PIS	7	TAU	7	GEM	6	CAN	8	VIR
7	AQU	8	ARI	9	GEM	9	CAN	8	LEO	10	LIB
9	PIS	11	TAU	12	CAN	12	LEO	11	VIR	12	SCO
12	ARI	13	GEM	14	LEO	14	VIR	13	LIB	14	SAG
14	TAU	16	CAN	17	VIR	16	LIB	15	SCO	16	CAP
17	GEM	18	LEO	19	LIB	18	SCO	17	SAG	18	AQU
19	CAN	20	VIR	21	SCO	20	SAG	19	CAP	20	PIS
22	LEO	23	LIB	23	SAG	22	CAP	21	AQU	23	ARI
24	VIR	25	SCO	25	CAP	25	AQU	23	PIS	25	TAU
26	LIB	27	SAG	27	AQU	27	PIS	25	ARI	28	GEM
28	SCO	29	CAP	30	PIS	29	ARI	28	TAU	30	CAN
31	SAG	31	AQU					30	GEM		

1907

JAN		FEB		MAR		APR		MAY		JUN	
2	LEO	3	LIB	2	LIB	2	SAG	2	CAP	2	PIS
4	VIR	5	SCO	4	SCO	5	CAP	4	AQU	5	ARI
6	LIB	7	SAG	6	SAG	7	AQU	6	PIS	7	TAU
9	SCO	9	CAP	8	CAP	9	PIS	8	ARI	9	GEM
11	SAG	11	AQU	10	AQU	11	ARI	11	TAU	12	CAN
13	CAP	13	PIS	13	PIS	13	TAU	13	GEM	14	LEO
15	AQU	15	ARI	15	ARI	16	GEM	16	CAN	17	VIR
17	PIS	18	TAU	17	TAU	18	CAN	18	LEO	19	LIB
19	ARI	20	GEM	20	GEM	21	LEO	21	VIR	22	SCO
21	TAU	23	CAN	22	CAN	23	VIR	23	LIB	24	SAG
24	GEM	25	LEO	25	LEO	26	LIB	25	SCO	26	CAP
26	CAN	28	VIR	27	VIR	28	SCO	27	SAG	28	AQU
29	LEO			29	LIB	30	SAG	29	CAP	30	PIS
31	VIR			31	SCO			31	AQU		

JUL		AUG		SEP		OCT		NOV		DEC	
2	ARI	3	GEM	2	CAN	2	LEO	3	LIB	2	SCO
4	TAU	5	CAN	4	LEO	4	VIR	5	SCO	5	SAG
7	GEM	8	LEO	7	VIR	6	LIB	7	SAG	7	CAP
9	CAN	10	VIR	9	LIB	9	SCO	9	CAP	9	AQU
12	LEO	13	LIB	11	SCO	11	SAG	11	AQU	11	PIS
14	VIR	15	SCO	14	SAG	13	CAP	13	PIS	13	ARI
17	LIB	17	SAG	16	CAP	15	AQU	16	ARI	15	TAU
19	SCO	20	CAP	18	AQU	17	PIS	18	TAU	18	GEM
21	SAG	22	AQU	20	PIS	19	ARI	20	GEM	20	CAN
23	CAP	24	PIS	22	ARI	22	TAU	23	CAN	23	LEO
25	AQU	26	ARI	24	TAU	24	GEM	25	LEO	25	VIR
27	PIS	28	TAU	27	GEM	26	CAN	28	VIR	28	LIB
29	ARI	30	GEM	29	CAN	29	LEO	30	LIB	30	SCO
31	TAU					31	VIR				

1908

JAN		FEB		MAR		APR		MAY		JUN	
1	SAG	2	AQU	2	PIS	3	TAU	2	GEM	1	CAN
3	CAP	4	PIS	4	ARI	5	GEM	5	CAN	3	LEO
5	AQU	6	ARI	6	TAU	7	CAN	7	LEO	6	VIR
7	PIS	8	TAU	8	GEM	10	LEO	10	VIR	8	LIB
9	ARI	10	GEM	11	CAN	12	VIR	12	LIB	11	SCO
11	TAU	13	CAN	13	LEO	15	LIB	14	SCO	13	SAG
14	GEM	15	LEO	16	VIR	17	SCO	17	SAG	15	CAP
16	CAN	18	VIR	18	LIB	19	SAG	19	CAP	17	AQU
19	LEO	20	LIB	21	SCO	21	CAP	21	AQU	19	PIS
21	VIR	22	SCO	23	SAG	24	AQU	23	PIS	21	ARI
24	LIB	25	SAG	25	CAP	26	PIS	25	ARI	23	TAU
26	SCO	27	CAP	27	AQU	28	ARI	27	TAU	26	GEM
28	SAG	29	AQU	29	PIS	30	TAU	29	GEM	28	CAN
31	CAP			31	ARI						

JUL		AUG		SEP		OCT		NOV		DEC	
1	LEO	2	LIB	1	SCO	3	CAP	1	AQU	2	ARI
3	VIR	4	SCO	3	SAG	5	AQU	3	PIS	5	TAU
6	LIB	7	SAG	5	CAP	7	PIS	5	ARI	7	GEM
8	SCO	9	CAP	7	AQU	9	ARI	7	TAU	9	CAN
10	SAG	11	AQU	9	PIS	11	TAU	9	GEM	11	LEO
12	CAP	13	PIS	11	ARI	13	GEM	12	CAN	14	VIR
15	AQU	15	ARI	13	TAU	15	CAN	14	LEO	16	LIB
17	PIS	17	TAU	16	GEM	18	LEO	17	VIR	19	SCO
19	ARI	19	GEM	18	CAN	20	VIR	19	LIB	21	SAG
21	TAU	22	CAN	20	LEO	23	LIB	22	SCO	23	CAP
23	GEM	24	LEO	23	VIR	25	SCO	24	SAG	26	AQU
25	CAN	27	VIR	25	LIB	28	SAG	26	CAP	28	PIS
28	LEO	29	LIB	28	SCO	30	CAP	28	AQU	30	ARI
30	VIR			30	SAG			30	PIS		

1909

JAN		FEB		MAR		APR		MAY		JUN	
1	TAU	2	CAN	1	CAN	2	VIR	2	LIB	1	SCO
3	GEM	4	LEO	3	LEO	5	LIB	4	SCO	3	SAG
5	CAN	7	VIR	6	VIR	7	SCO	7	SAG	5	CAP
8	LEO	9	LIB	8	LIB	10	SAG	9	CAP	8	AQU
10	VIR	12	SCO	11	SCO	12	CAP	11	AQU	10	PIS
13	LIB	14	SAG	13	SAG	14	AQU	14	PIS	12	ARI
15	SCO	16	CAP	16	CAP	16	PIS	16	ARI	14	TAU
18	SAG	18	AQU	18	AQU	18	ARI	18	TAU	16	GEM
20	CAP	20	PIS	20	PIS	20	TAU	20	GEM	18	CAN
22	AQU	22	ARI	22	ARI	22	GEM	22	CAN	21	LEO
24	PIS	24	TAU	24	TAU	24	CAN	24	LEO	23	VIR
26	ARI	27	GEM	26	GEM	27	LEO	27	VIR	25	LIB
28	TAU			28	CAN	29	VIR	29	LIB	28	SCO
30	GEM			31	LEO					30	SAG

JUL		AUG		SEP		OCT		NOV		DEC	
3	CAP	1	AQU	2	ARI	1	TAU	2	CAN	1	LEO
5	AQU	3	PIS	4	TAU	3	GEM	4	LEO	4	VIR
7	PIS	5	ARI	6	GEM	5	CAN	6	VIR	6	LIB
9	ARI	7	TAU	8	CAN	8	LEO	9	LIB	9	SCO
11	TAU	10	GEM	10	LEO	10	VIR	11	SCO	11	SAG
13	GEM	12	CAN	13	VIR	13	LIB	14	SAG	14	CAP
16	CAN	14	LEO	15	LIB	15	SCO	16	CAP	16	AQU
18	LEO	17	VIR	18	SCO	18	SAG	19	AQU	18	PIS
20	VIR	19	LIB	20	SAG	20	CAP	21	PIS	20	ARI
23	LIB	22	SCO	23	CAP	22	AQU	23	ARI	22	TAU
25	SCO	24	SAG	25	AQU	25	PIS	25	TAU	24	GEM
28	SAG	27	CAP	27	PIS	27	ARI	27	GEM	29	CAN
30	CAP	29	AQU	29	ARI	29	TAU	29	CAN	31	VIR
		31	PIS			31	GEM				

1910

JAN		FEB		MAR		APR		MAY		JUN	
3	LIB	1	SCO	1	SCO	2	CAP	2	AQU	2	ARI
5	SCO	4	SAG	3	SAG	4	AQU	4	PIS	4	TAU
8	SAG	6	CAP	6	CAP	7	PIS	6	ARI	6	GEM
10	CAP	9	AQU	8	AQU	9	ARI	8	TAU	9	CAN
12	AQU	11	PIS	10	PIS	11	TAU	10	GEM	11	LEO
14	PIS	13	ARI	12	ARI	13	GEM	12	CAN	13	VIR
16	ARI	15	TAU	14	TAU	15	CAN	14	LEO	15	LIB
19	TAU	17	GEM	16	GEM	17	LEO	17	VIR	18	SCO
21	GEM	19	CAN	18	CAN	19	VIR	19	LIB	20	SAG
23	CAN	21	LEO	21	LEO	22	LIB	22	SCO	23	CAP
25	LEO	24	VIR	23	VIR	24	SCO	24	SAG	25	AQU
27	VIR	26	LIB	25	LIB	27	SAG	27	CAP	27	PIS
30	LIB			28	SCO	29	CAP	29	AQU	30	ARI
				31	SAG			31	PIS		

JUL		AUG		SEP		OCT		NOV		DEC	
2	TAU	2	CAN	1	LEO	3	LIB	1	SCO	1	SAG
4	GEM	4	LEO	3	VIR	5	SCO	4	SAG	4	CAP
6	CAN	7	VIR	5	LIB	8	SAG	6	CAP	6	AQU
8	LEO	9	LIB	8	SCO	10	CAP	9	AQU	9	PIS
10	VIR	11	SCO	10	SAG	13	AQU	11	PIS	11	ARI
13	LIB	14	SAG	13	CAP	15	PIS	13	ARI	13	TAU
15	SCO	16	CAP	15	AQU	17	ARI	15	TAU	15	GEM
18	SAG	19	AQU	17	PIS	19	TAU	17	GEM	17	CAN
20	CAP	21	PIS	20	ARI	21	GEM	19	CAN	19	LEO
22	AQU	23	ARI	22	TAU	23	CAN	21	LEO	21	VIR
25	PIS	25	TAU	24	GEM	25	LEO	24	VIR	23	LIB
27	ARI	27	GEM	26	CAN	27	VIR	26	LIB	26	SCO
29	TAU	30	CAN	28	LEO	30	LIB	29	SCO	28	SAG
31	GEM			30	VIR					31	CAP

1911

JAN		FEB		MAR		APR		MAY		JUN	
2	AQU	1	PIS	3	ARI	1	TAU	2	CAN	1	LEO
5	PIS	3	ARI	5	TAU	3	GEM	5	LEO	3	VIR
7	ARI	5	TAU	7	GEM	5	CAN	7	VIR	5	LIB
9	TAU	8	GEM	9	CAN	7	LEO	9	LIB	8	SCO
11	GEM	10	CAN	11	LEO	10	VIR	11	SCO	10	SAG
13	CAN	12	LEO	13	VIR	12	LIB	14	SAG	13	CAP
15	LEO	14	VIR	16	LIB	14	SCO	17	CAP	15	AQU
17	VIR	16	LIB	18	SCO	17	SAG	19	AQU	18	PIS
20	LIB	19	SCO	20	SAG	19	CAP	21	PIS	20	ARI
22	SCO	21	SAG	23	CAP	22	AQU	24	ARI	22	TAU
25	SAG	24	CAP	25	AQU	24	PIS	26	TAU	24	GEM
27	CAP	26	AQU	28	PIS	26	ARI	28	GEM	26	CAN
30	AQU	28	PIS	30	ARI	28	TAU	30	CAN	28	LEO
						30	GEM			30	VIR

JUL		AUG		SEP		OCT		NOV		DEC	
3	LIB	1	SCO	3	CAP	2	AQU	1	PIS	1	ARI
5	SCO	4	SAG	5	AQU	5	PIS	4	ARI	3	TAU
7	SAG	6	CAP	8	PIS	7	ARI	6	TAU	5	GEM
10	CAP	9	AQU	10	ARI	9	TAU	8	GEM	7	CAN
13	AQU	11	PIS	12	TAU	11	GEM	10	CAN	9	LEO
15	PIS	14	ARI	14	GEM	14	CAN	12	LEO	11	VIR
17	ARI	16	TAU	16	CAN	16	LEO	14	VIR	14	LIB
20	TAU	18	GEM	18	LEO	18	VIR	16	LIB	16	SCO
22	GEM	20	CAN	21	VIR	20	LIB	19	SCO	18	SAG
24	CAN	22	LEO	23	LIB	22	SCO	21	SAG	21	CAP
26	LEO	24	VIR	25	SCO	25	SAG	24	CAP	23	AQU
28	VIR	26	LIB	27	SAG	27	CAP	26	AQU	26	PIS
30	LIB	29	SCO	30	CAP	30	AQU	29	PIS	28	ARI
		31	SAG							31	TAU

1912

	JAN		FEB		MAR		APR		MAY		JUN
2	GEM	2	LEO	1	LEO	1	LIB	1	SCO	2	CAP
4	CAN	4	VIR	3	SCO	3	SCO	3	SAG	4	AQU
6	LEO	6	LIB	5	LIB	6	SAG	5	CAP	7	PIS
8	VIR	8	SCO	7	SCO	8	CAP	8	AQU	9	ARI
10	LIB	11	SAG	9	SAG	11	AQU	10	PIS	11	TAU
12	SCO	13	CAP	12	CAP	13	PIS	13	ARI	14	GEM
15	SAG	16	AQU	14	AQU	15	ARI	15	TAU	16	CAN
17	CAP	18	PIS	17	PIS	18	TAU	17	GEM	18	LEO
20	AQU	21	ARI	19	ARI	20	GEM	19	CAN	20	VIR
22	PIS	23	TAU	21	TAU	22	CAN	21	LEO	22	LIB
25	ARI	25	GEM	24	GEM	24	LEO	23	VIR	24	SCO
27	TAU	28	CAN	26	CAN	26	VIR	26	LIB	26	SAG
29	GEM			28	LEO	28	LIB	28	SCO	29	CAP
31	CAN			30	VIR			30	SAG		

	JUL		AUG		SEP		OCT		NOV		DEC
1	AQU	3	ARI	1	TAU	1	GEM	1	LEO	1	VIR
4	PIS	5	TAU	4	GEM	3	CAN	4	VIR	3	LIB
6	ARI	7	GEM	6	CAN	5	LEO	6	LIB	5	SCO
9	TAU	10	CAN	8	LEO	7	VIR	8	SCO	7	SAG
11	GEM	12	LEO	10	VIR	9	LIB	10	SAG	10	CAP
13	CAN	14	VIR	12	LIB	12	SCO	12	CAP	12	AQU
15	LEO	16	LIB	14	SCO	14	SAG	15	AQU	15	PIS
17	VIR	18	SCO	16	SAG	16	CAP	17	PIS	17	ARI
19	LIB	20	SAG	19	CAP	19	AQU	20	ARI	20	TAU
21	SCO	22	CAP	21	AQU	21	PIS	22	TAU	22	GEM
24	SAG	25	AQU	24	PIS	24	ARI	25	GEM	24	CAN
26	CAP	27	PIS	26	ARI	26	TAU	27	CAN	26	LEO
29	AQU	30	ARI	29	TAU	28	GEM	29	LEO	28	VIR
31	PIS					30	CAN			30	LIB

1913

	JAN		FEB		MAR		APR		MAY		JUN
1	SCO	2	CAP	2	CAP	3	PIS	3	ARI	1	TAU
4	SAG	5	AQU	4	AQU	5	ARI	5	TAU	4	GEM
6	CAP	7	PIS	7	PIS	8	TAU	7	GEM	6	CAN
9	AQU	10	ARI	9	ARI	11	GEM	10	CAN	8	LEO
11	PIS	12	TAU	12	TAU	13	CAN	12	LEO	10	VIR
14	ARI	15	GEM	14	GEM	15	LEO	14	VIR	12	LIB
16	TAU	17	CAN	16	CAN	17	VIR	16	LIB	15	SCO
18	GEM	19	LEO	18	LEO	19	LIB	18	SCO	17	SAG
21	CAN	21	VIR	20	VIR	21	SCO	20	SAG	19	CAP
23	LEO	23	LIB	22	LIB	23	SAG	23	CAP	21	AQU
25	VIR	25	SCO	24	SCO	25	CAP	25	AQU	24	PIS
27	LIB	27	SAG	27	SAG	28	AQU	27	PIS	26	ARI
29	SCO			29	CAP	30	PIS	30	ARI	29	TAU
31	SAG			31	AQU						

	JUL		AUG		SEP		OCT		NOV		DEC
1	GEM	2	LEO	2	LIB	2	SCO	2	CAP	2	AQU
3	CAN	4	VIR	4	SCO	4	SAG	5	AQU	5	PIS
5	LEO	6	LIB	6	SAG	6	CAP	7	PIS	7	ARI
8	VIR	8	SCO	9	CAP	8	AQU	10	ARI	10	TAU
10	LIB	10	SAG	11	AQU	11	PIS	12	TAU	12	GEM
12	SCO	13	CAP	14	PIS	13	ARI	15	GEM	14	CAN
14	SAG	15	AQU	16	ARI	16	TAU	17	CAN	17	LEO
16	CAP	17	PIS	19	TAU	18	GEM	19	LEO	19	VIR
19	AQU	20	ARI	21	GEM	21	CAN	21	VIR	21	LIB
21	PIS	22	TAU	24	CAN	23	LEO	24	LIB	23	SCO
24	ARI	25	GEM	26	LEO	25	VIR	26	SCO	25	SAG
26	TAU	27	CAN	28	VIR	27	LIB	28	SAG	27	CAP
29	GEM	29	LEO	30	LIB	29	SCO	30	CAP	30	AQU
31	CAN	31	VIR			31	SAG				

1914

JAN		FEB		MAR		APR		MAY		JUN	
1	PIS	2	TAU	2	TAU	3	CAN	2	LEO	1	VIR
3	ARI	5	GEM	4	GEM	5	LEO	5	VIR	3	LIB
6	TAU	7	CAN	6	CAN	7	VIR	7	LIB	5	SCO
8	GEM	9	LEO	9	LEO	9	LIB	9	SCO	7	SAG
11	CAN	11	VIR	11	VIR	11	SCO	11	SAG	9	CAP
13	LEO	13	LIB	13	LIB	13	SAG	13	CAP	11	AQU
15	VIR	15	SCO	15	SCO	15	CAP	15	AQU	14	PIS
17	LIB	18	SAG	17	SAG	18	AQU	17	PIS	16	ARI
19	SCO	20	CAP	19	CAP	20	PIS	20	ARI	19	TAU
21	SAG	22	AQU	21	AQU	23	ARI	22	TAU	21	GEM
24	CAP	25	PIS	24	PIS	25	TAU	25	GEM	24	CAN
26	AQU	27	ARI	26	ARI	28	GEM	27	CAN	26	LEO
28	PIS			29	TAU	30	CAN	30	LEO	28	VIR
31	ARI			30	GEM					30	LIB

JUL		AUG		SEP		OCT		NOV		DEC	
2	SCO	1	SAG	1	AQU	1	PIS	2	TAU	2	GEM
4	SAG	3	CAP	4	PIS	3	ARI	5	GEM	4	CAN
7	CAP	5	AQU	6	ARI	6	TAU	7	CAN	7	LEO
9	AQU	7	PIS	9	TAU	8	GEM	10	LEO	9	VIR
11	PIS	10	ARI	11	GEM	11	CAN	12	VIR	11	LIB
13	ARI	12	TAU	14	CAN	13	LEO	14	LIB	13	SCO
16	TAU	15	GEM	16	LEO	16	VIR	16	SCO	15	SAG
18	GEM	17	CAN	18	VIR	18	LIB	18	SAG	17	CAP
21	CAN	20	LEO	20	LIB	20	SCO	20	CAP	20	AQU
23	LEO	22	VIR	22	SCO	22	SAG	22	AQU	22	PIS
25	VIR	24	LIB	24	SAG	24	CAP	24	PIS	24	ARI
27	LIB	26	SCO	26	CAP	26	AQU	27	ARI	27	TAU
30	SCO	28	SAG	29	AQU	28	PIS	29	TAU	29	GEM
		30	CAP			31	ARI				

1915

JAN		FEB		MAR		APR		MAY		JUN	
1	CAN	2	VIR	1	VIR	2	SCO	1	SAG	1	AQU
3	LEO	4	LIB	3	LIB	4	SAG	3	CAP	4	PIS
5	VIR	6	SCO	5	SCO	6	CAP	5	AQU	6	ARI
8	LIB	8	SAG	7	SAG	8	AQU	7	PIS	8	TAU
10	SCO	10	CAP	9	CAP	10	PIS	10	ARI	11	GEM
12	SAG	12	AQU	12	AQU	13	ARI	12	TAU	14	CAN
14	CAP	15	PIS	14	PIS	15	TAU	15	GEM	16	LEO
16	AQU	17	ARI	16	ARI	18	GEM	17	CAN	18	VIR
18	PIS	19	TAU	19	TAU	20	CAN	20	LEO	21	LIB
21	ARI	22	GEM	21	GEM	23	LEO	22	VIR	23	SCO
23	TAU	24	CAN	24	CAN	25	VIR	24	LIB	25	SAG
26	GEM	27	LEO	26	LEO	27	LIB	27	SCO	27	CAP
28	CAN			28	VIR	29	SCO	28	SAG	29	AQU
30	LEO			31	LIB			30	CAP		

JUL		AUG		SEP		OCT		NOV		DEC	
1	PIS	2	TAU	1	GEM	1	CAN	2	LIB	2	LIB
3	ARI	5	GEM	3	CAN	3	LEO	4	SCO	4	SCO
6	TAU	7	CAN	6	LEO	6	VIR	6	SAG	6	SAG
8	GEM	10	LEO	8	VIR	8	LIB	8	CAP	8	CAP
11	CAN	12	VIR	10	LIB	10	SCO	10	AQU	10	AQU
13	LEO	14	LIB	13	SCO	12	SAG	12	PIS	12	PIS
16	VIR	16	SCO	15	SAG	14	CAP	15	ARI	14	ARI
18	LIB	19	SAG	17	CAP	16	AQU	17	TAU	17	TAU
20	SCO	21	CAP	19	AQU	18	PIS	19	GEM	19	GEM
22	SAG	23	AQU	21	PIS	21	ARI	22	CAN	22	CAN
24	CAP	25	PIS	23	ARI	23	TAU	24	LEO	24	LEO
26	AQU	27	ARI	26	TAU	26	GEM	27	VIR	27	VIR
28	PIS	29	TAU	28	GEM	28	CAN	29	LIB	29	LIB
31	ARI					31	LEO			31	SCO

Moon Tables

1916

JAN		FEB		MAR		APR		MAY		JUN	
2	SAG	1	CAP	1	AQU	2	ARI	1	TAU	2	CAN
4	CAP	3	AQU	3	PIS	4	TAU	4	GEM	5	LEO
6	AQU	5	PIS	5	ARI	6	GEM	6	CAN	8	VIR
8	PIS	7	ARI	8	TAU	9	CAN	9	LEO	10	LIB
11	ARI	9	TAU	10	GEM	11	LEO	11	VIR	12	SCO
13	TAU	12	GEM	13	CAN	14	VIR	14	LIB	14	SAG
15	GEM	14	CAN	15	LEO	16	LIB	16	SCO	16	CAP
18	CAN	17	LEO	18	VIR	18	SCO	18	SAG	18	AQU
20	LEO	19	VIR	20	LIB	20	SAG	20	CAP	20	PIS
23	VIR	22	LIB	22	SCO	23	CAP	22	AQU	22	ARI
25	LIB	24	SCO	24	SAG	25	AQU	24	PIS	25	TAU
28	SCO	26	SAG	26	CAP	27	PIS	26	ARI	27	GEM
30	SAG	28	CAP	28	AQU	29	ARI	29	TAU	30	CAN
				31	PIS			31	GEM		

JUL		AUG		SEP		OCT		NOV		DEC	
2	LEO	1	VIR	2	SCO	2	SAG	2	AQU	1	PIS
5	VIR	3	LIB	4	SAG	4	CAP	4	PIS	4	ARI
7	LIB	6	SCO	6	CAP	6	AQU	6	ARI	6	TAU
10	SCO	8	SAG	8	AQU	8	PIS	9	TAU	8	GEM
12	SAG	10	CAP	11	PIS	10	ARI	11	GEM	11	CAN
14	CAP	12	AQU	13	ARI	12	TAU	13	CAN	13	LEO
16	AQU	14	PIS	15	TAU	14	GEM	16	LEO	16	VIR
18	PIS	16	ARI	17	GEM	17	CAN	18	VIR	18	LIB
20	ARI	18	TAU	20	CAN	19	LEO	21	LIB	20	SCO
22	TAU	21	GEM	22	LEO	22	VIR	23	SCO	23	SAG
24	GEM	23	CAN	25	VIR	24	LIB	25	SAG	25	CAP
27	CAN	26	LEO	27	LIB	27	SCO	27	CAP	27	AQU
30	LEO	28	VIR	29	SCO	29	SAG	29	AQU	29	PIS
		31	LIB			31	CAP			31	ARI

1917

JAN		FEB		MAR		APR		MAY		JUN	
2	TAU	1	GEM	2	CAN	1	LEO	1	VIR	2	SCO
4	GEM	3	CAN	5	LEO	4	VIR	4	LIB	5	SAG
7	CAN	6	LEO	7	VIR	6	LIB	6	SCO	7	CAP
9	LEO	8	VIR	10	LIB	9	SCO	8	SAG	9	AQU
12	VIR	11	LIB	12	SCO	11	SAG	10	CAP	11	PIS
14	LIB	13	SCO	15	SAG	13	CAP	12	AQU	13	ARI
17	SCO	15	SAG	17	CAP	15	AQU	15	PIS	15	TAU
19	SAG	18	CAP	19	AQU	17	PIS	17	ARI	17	GEM
21	CAP	20	AQU	21	PIS	19	ARI	19	TAU	20	CAN
23	AQU	22	PIS	23	ARI	21	TAU	21	GEM	22	LEO
25	PIS	24	ARI	25	TAU	24	GEM	23	CAN	25	VIR
27	ARI	26	TAU	27	GEM	26	CAN	26	LEO	27	LIB
29	TAU	28	GEM	30	CAN	29	LEO	28	VIR	30	SCO
								31	LIB		

JUL		AUG		SEP		OCT		NOV		DEC	
2	SAG	3	AQU	1	PIS	2	TAU	1	GEM	1	CAN
4	CAP	5	PIS	3	ARI	5	GEM	3	CAN	3	LEO
6	AQU	7	ARI	5	TAU	7	CAN	6	LEO	5	VIR
8	PIS	9	TAU	7	GEM	9	LEO	8	VIR	8	LIB
10	ARI	11	GEM	9	CAN	12	VIR	11	LIB	10	SCO
12	TAU	13	CAN	12	LEO	14	LIB	13	SCO	13	SAG
15	GEM	16	LEO	15	VIR	17	SCO	15	SAG	15	CAP
17	CAN	18	VIR	17	LIB	19	SAG	18	CAP	17	AQU
19	LEO	21	LIB	19	SCO	21	CAP	20	AQU	19	PIS
22	VIR	23	SCO	22	SAG	24	AQU	22	PIS	21	ARI
25	LIB	26	SAG	24	CAP	26	PIS	24	ARI	23	TAU
27	SCO	28	CAP	26	AQU	28	ARI	26	TAU	26	GEM
29	SAG	30	AQU	28	PIS	30	TAU	28	GEM	28	CAN
31	CAP			30	ARI					30	LEO

1918

JAN		FEB		MAR		APR		MAY		JUN	
2	VIR	1	LIB	2	SCO	1	SAG	1	CAP	1	PIS
4	LIB	3	SCO	5	SAG	3	CAP	3	AQU	4	ARI
7	SCO	6	SAG	7	CAP	6	AQU	5	PIS	6	TAU
9	SAG	8	CAP	9	AQU	8	PIS	7	ARI	8	GEM
11	CAP	10	AQU	11	PIS	10	ARI	9	TAU	10	CAN
13	AQU	12	PIS	13	ARI	12	TAU	11	GEM	12	LEO
16	PIS	14	ARI	15	TAU	14	GEM	13	CAN	15	VIR
18	ARI	16	TAU	17	GEM	16	CAN	16	LEO	17	LIB
20	TAU	18	GEM	20	CAN	18	LEO	18	VIR	20	SCO
22	GEM	20	CAN	22	LEO	21	VIR	21	LIB	22	SAG
24	CAN	23	LEO	25	VIR	23	LIB	23	SCO	24	CAP
27	LEO	25	VIR	27	LIB	26	SCO	26	SAG	27	AQU
29	VIR	28	LIB	30	SCO	28	SAG	28	CAP	29	PIS
								30	AQU		

JUL		AUG		SEP		OCT		NOV		DEC	
1	ARI	1	GEM	2	LEO	2	VIR	3	SCO	3	SAG
3	TAU	3	CAN	4	VIR	4	LIB	5	SAG	5	CAP
5	GEM	6	LEO	7	LIB	7	SCO	8	CAP	8	AQU
7	CAN	8	VIR	9	SCO	9	SAG	10	AQU	10	PIS
9	LEO	11	LIB	12	SAG	12	CAP	13	PIS	12	ARI
12	VIR	13	SCO	14	CAP	14	AQU	15	ARI	14	TAU
14	LIB	16	SAG	17	AQU	16	PIS	17	TAU	16	GEM
17	SCO	18	CAP	19	PIS	18	ARI	19	GEM	18	CAN
19	SAG	20	AQU	21	ARI	20	TAU	21	CAN	20	LEO
22	CAP	22	PIS	23	TAU	22	GEM	23	LEO	23	VIR
24	AQU	24	ARI	25	GEM	24	CAN	25	VIR	25	LIB
26	PIS	26	TAU	27	CAN	27	LEO	28	LIB	28	SCO
28	ARI	28	GEM	29	LEO	29	VIR	30	SCO	30	SAG
30	TAU	31	CAN			31	LIB				

1919

JAN		FEB		MAR		APR		MAY		JUN	
2	CAP	2	PIS	2	PIS	2	TAU	2	GEM	2	LEO
4	AQU	4	ARI	4	ARI	4	GEM	4	CAN	4	VIR
6	PIS	7	TAU	6	TAU	6	CAN	6	LEO	7	LIB
8	ARI	9	GEM	8	GEM	9	LEO	8	VIR	9	SCO
10	TAU	11	CAN	10	CAN	11	VIR	11	LIB	12	SAG
12	GEM	13	LEO	12	LEO	13	LIB	13	SCO	14	CAP
15	CAN	15	VIR	15	VIR	16	SCO	16	SAG	17	AQU
17	LEO	18	LIB	17	LIB	18	SAG	18	CAP	19	PIS
19	VIR	20	SCO	20	SCO	21	CAP	21	AQU	21	ARI
21	LIB	23	SAG	22	SAG	23	AQU	23	PIS	23	TAU
24	SCO	25	CAP	25	CAP	26	PIS	25	ARI	25	GEM
26	SAG	28	AQU	27	AQU	28	ARI	27	TAU	28	CAN
29	CAP			29	PIS	30	TAU	29	GEM	30	LEO
31	AQU			31	ARI			31	CAN		

JUL		AUG		SEP		OCT		NOV		DEC	
2	VIR	1	LIB	2	SAG	2	CAP	3	PIS	2	ARI
4	LIB	3	SCO	4	CAP	4	AQU	5	ARI	4	TAU
7	SCO	5	SAG	7	AQU	6	PIS	7	TAU	6	GEM
9	SAG	8	CAP	9	PIS	9	ARI	9	GEM	8	CAN
12	CAP	10	AQU	11	ARI	11	TAU	11	CAN	10	LEO
14	AQU	13	PIS	13	TAU	13	GEM	13	LEO	13	VIR
16	PIS	15	ARI	15	GEM	15	CAN	15	VIR	15	LIB
19	ARI	17	TAU	17	CAN	17	LEO	18	LIB	17	SCO
21	TAU	19	GEM	20	LEO	19	VIR	20	SCO	20	SAG
23	GEM	21	CAN	22	VIR	21	LIB	23	SAG	22	CAP
25	CAN	23	LEO	24	LIB	24	SCO	25	CAP	25	AQU
27	LEO	26	VIR	27	SCO	26	SAG	28	AQU	27	PIS
29	VIR	28	LIB	29	SAG	28	CAP	30	PIS	30	ARI
		30	SCO			31	AQU				

133

1920

JAN		FEB		MAR		APR		MAY		JUN	
1	TAU	1	CAN	2	LEO	2	LIB	2	SCO	1	SAG
3	GEM	3	LEO	4	VIR	5	SCO	5	SAG	3	CAP
5	CAN	5	VIR	6	LIB	7	SAG	7	CAP	6	AQU
7	LEO	8	LIB	8	SCO	10	CAP	10	AQU	8	PIS
9	VIR	10	SCO	11	SAG	12	AQU	12	PIS	11	ARI
11	LIB	13	SAG	13	CAP	15	PIS	14	ARI	13	TAU
14	SCO	16	CAP	16	AQU	17	ARI	16	TAU	15	GEM
16	SAG	18	AQU	18	PIS	19	TAU	18	GEM	17	CAN
19	CAP	20	PIS	20	ARI	21	GEM	20	CAN	19	LEO
21	AQU	23	ARI	23	TAU	23	CAN	22	LEO	21	VIR
24	PIS	25	TAU	25	GEM	25	LEO	25	VIR	23	LIB
26	ARI	27	GEM	27	CAN	27	VIR	27	LIB	26	SCO
28	TAU	29	CAN	29	LEO	30	LIB	29	SCO	28	SAG
30	GEM			31	VIR						

JUL		AUG		SEP		OCT		NOV		DEC	
1	CAP	2	PIS	3	TAU	2	GEM	3	LEO	2	VIR
3	AQU	4	ARI	5	GEM	4	CAN	5	VIR	4	LIB
6	PIS	6	TAU	7	CAN	6	LEO	7	LIB	6	SCO
8	ARI	9	GEM	9	LEO	8	VIR	9	SCO	9	SAG
10	TAU	11	CAN	11	VIR	11	LIB	12	SAG	11	CAP
12	GEM	13	LEO	13	LIB	13	SCO	14	CAP	14	AQU
14	CAN	15	VIR	16	SCO	15	SAG	17	AQU	16	PIS
16	LEO	17	LIB	18	SAG	18	CAP	19	PIS	19	ARI
18	VIR	19	SCO	20	CAP	20	AQU	22	ARI	21	TAU
21	LIB	22	SAG	23	AQU	23	PIS	24	TAU	23	GEM
23	SCO	24	CAP	25	PIS	25	ARI	26	GEM	25	CAN
25	SAG	27	AQU	28	ARI	27	TAU	28	CAN	27	LEO
28	CAP	29	PIS	30	TAU	29	GEM	30	LEO	29	VIR
30	AQU	31	ARI			31	CAN			31	LIB

1921

JAN		FEB		MAR		APR		MAY		JUN	
3	SCO	1	SAG	1	SAG	2	AQU	2	PIS	1	ARI
5	SAG	4	CAP	3	CAP	5	PIS	4	ARI	3	TAU
8	CAP	6	AQU	6	AQU	7	ARI	7	TAU	5	GEM
10	AQU	9	PIS	8	PIS	9	TAU	9	GEM	7	CAN
13	PIS	11	ARI	11	ARI	12	GEM	11	CAN	9	LEO
15	ARI	14	TAU	13	TAU	14	CAN	13	LEO	11	VIR
18	TAU	16	GEM	15	GEM	16	LEO	15	VIR	14	LIB
20	GEM	18	CAN	17	CAN	18	VIR	17	LIB	16	SCO
22	CAN	20	LEO	20	LEO	20	LIB	20	SCO	18	SAG
24	LEO	22	VIR	22	VIR	22	SCO	22	SAG	21	CAP
26	VIR	24	LIB	24	LIB	24	SAG	24	CAP	23	AQU
28	LIB	26	SCO	26	SCO	27	CAP	27	AQU	26	PIS
30	SCO			28	SAG	29	AQU	29	PIS	28	ARI
				31	CAP					30	TAU

JUL		AUG		SEP		OCT		NOV		DEC	
3	GEM	1	CAN	2	VIR	1	LIB	2	SAG	1	CAP
5	CAN	3	LEO	4	LIB	3	SCO	4	CAP	4	AQU
7	LEO	5	VIR	6	SCO	5	SAG	6	AQU	6	PIS
9	VIR	7	LIB	8	SAG	8	CAP	9	PIS	9	ARI
11	LIB	9	SCO	10	CAP	10	AQU	11	ARI	11	TAU
13	SCO	12	SAG	13	AQU	13	PIS	14	TAU	14	GEM
15	SAG	14	CAP	15	PIS	15	ARI	16	GEM	16	CAN
18	CAP	17	AQU	18	ARI	18	TAU	18	CAN	18	LEO
20	AQU	19	PIS	20	TAU	20	GEM	20	LEO	20	VIR
23	PIS	22	ARI	23	GEM	22	CAN	23	VIR	22	LIB
25	ARI	24	TAU	25	CAN	24	LEO	25	LIB	24	SCO
28	TAU	26	GEM	27	LEO	26	VIR	27	SCO	26	SAG
30	GEM	29	CAN	29	VIR	28	LIB	29	SAG	29	CAP
		31	LEO			30	SCO			31	AQU

1922

JAN		FEB		MAR		APR		MAY		JUN	
3	PIS	1	ARI	1	ARI	2	GEM	1	CAN	2	VIR
5	ARI	4	TAU	3	TAU	4	CAN	4	LEO	4	LIB
8	TAU	6	GEM	6	GEM	6	LEO	6	VIR	6	SCO
10	GEM	9	CAN	8	CAN	8	VIR	8	LIB	8	SAG
12	CAN	11	LEO	10	LEO	10	LIB	10	SCO	11	CAP
14	LEO	13	VIR	12	VIR	12	SCO	12	SAG	13	AQU
16	VIR	15	LIB	14	LIB	15	SAG	14	CAP	15	PIS
18	LIB	17	SCO	16	SCO	17	CAP	17	AQU	18	ARI
20	SCO	19	SAG	18	SAG	19	AQU	19	PIS	20	TAU
23	SAG	21	CAP	20	CAP	22	PIS	22	ARI	23	GEM
25	CAP	24	AQU	23	AQU	24	ARI	24	TAU	25	CAN
27	AQU	26	PIS	25	PIS	27	TAU	26	GEM	27	LEO
30	PIS			28	ARI	29	GEM	29	CAN	29	VIR
				30	TAU			31	LEO		

JUL		AUG		SEP		OCT		NOV		DEC	
1	LIB	2	SAG	3	AQU	2	PIS	1	ARI	1	TAU
3	SCO	4	CAP	5	PIS	5	ARI	4	TAU	4	GEM
6	SAG	7	AQU	8	ARI	8	TAU	6	GEM	6	CAN
8	CAP	9	PIS	10	TAU	10	GEM	9	CAN	8	LEO
10	AQU	12	ARI	13	GEM	12	CAN	11	LEO	10	VIR
13	PIS	14	TAU	15	CAN	15	LEO	13	VIR	12	LIB
15	ARI	16	GEM	17	LEO	17	VIR	15	LIB	15	SCO
18	TAU	19	CAN	19	VIR	19	LIB	17	SCO	17	SAG
20	GEM	21	LEO	21	LIB	21	SCO	19	SAG	19	CAP
22	CAN	23	VIR	23	SCO	23	SAG	21	CAP	21	AQU
24	LEO	25	LIB	25	SAG	25	CAP	24	AQU	23	PIS
27	VIR	27	SCO	28	CAP	27	AQU	26	PIS	26	ARI
29	LIB	29	SAG	30	AQU	30	PIS	29	ARI	28	TAU
31	SCO	31	CAP							31	GEM

1923

JAN		FEB		MAR		APR		MAY		JUN	
2	CAN	1	LEO	2	VIR	1	LIB	2	SAG	1	CAP
4	LEO	3	VIR	4	LIB	3	SCO	4	CAP	3	AQU
7	VIR	5	LIB	6	SCO	5	SAG	7	AQU	5	PIS
9	LIB	7	SCO	8	SAG	7	CAP	9	PIS	8	ARI
11	SCO	9	SAG	11	CAP	9	AQU	11	ARI	10	TAU
13	SAG	11	CAP	13	AQU	12	PIS	14	TAU	13	GEM
15	CAP	14	AQU	15	PIS	14	ARI	16	GEM	15	CAN
17	AQU	16	PIS	18	ARI	17	TAU	19	CAN	17	LEO
20	PIS	19	ARI	20	TAU	19	GEM	21	LEO	20	VIR
22	ARI	21	TAU	23	GEM	22	CAN	23	VIR	22	LIB
25	TAU	24	GEM	25	CAN	24	LEO	26	LIB	24	SCO
27	GEM	26	CAN	28	LEO	26	VIR	28	SCO	26	SAG
30	CAN	28	LEO	30	VIR	28	LIB	30	SAG	28	CAP
						30	SCO			30	AQU

JUL		AUG		SEP		OCT		NOV		DEC	
3	PIS	1	ARI	3	GEM	3	CAN	1	LEO	1	VIR
5	ARI	4	TAU	5	CAN	5	LEO	4	VIR	3	LIB
8	TAU	6	GEM	7	LEO	7	VIR	6	LIB	5	SCO
10	GEM	9	CAN	10	VIR	9	LIB	8	SCO	7	SAG
12	CAN	11	LEO	12	LIB	11	SCO	10	SAG	9	CAP
15	LEO	13	VIR	14	SCO	13	SAG	12	CAP	11	AQU
17	VIR	15	LIB	16	SAG	15	CAP	14	AQU	13	PIS
19	LIB	17	SCO	18	CAP	17	AQU	16	PIS	16	ARI
21	SCO	20	SAG	20	AQU	20	PIS	18	ARI	18	TAU
23	SAG	22	CAP	23	PIS	22	ARI	21	TAU	21	GEM
25	CAP	24	AQU	25	ARI	25	TAU	24	GEM	23	CAN
28	AQU	26	PIS	27	TAU	27	GEM	26	CAN	26	LEO
30	PIS	29	ARI	30	GEM	30	CAN	28	LEO	28	VIR
		31	TAU							30	LIB

Moon Tables

1924

JAN		FEB		MAR		APR		MAY		JUN	
1	SCO	2	CAP	2	AQU	1	PIS	3	TAU	2	GEM
3	SAG	4	AQU	5	PIS	3	ARI	5	GEM	4	CAN
6	CAP	6	PIS	7	ARI	6	TAU	8	CAN	7	LEO
8	AQU	8	ARI	9	TAU	8	GEM	10	LEO	9	VIR
10	PIS	11	TAU	12	GEM	11	CAN	13	VIR	11	LIB
12	ARI	13	GEM	14	CAN	13	LEO	15	LIB	13	SCO
15	TAU	16	CAN	17	LEO	15	VIR	17	SCO	15	SAG
17	GEM	18	LEO	19	VIR	18	LIB	19	SAG	17	CAP
20	CAN	21	VIR	21	LIB	20	SCO	21	CAP	19	AQU
22	LEO	23	LIB	23	SCO	22	SAG	23	AQU	22	PIS
24	VIR	25	SCO	25	SAG	24	CAP	25	PIS	24	ARI
27	LIB	27	SAG	27	CAP	26	AQU	28	ARI	26	TAU
29	SCO	29	CAP	30	AQU	28	PIS	30	TAU	29	GEM
31	SAG					30	ARI				

JUL		AUG		SEP		OCT		NOV		DEC	
1	CAN	3	VIR	1	LIB	1	SCO	1	CAP	3	PIS
4	LEO	5	LIB	3	SCO	3	SAG	3	AQU	5	ARI
6	VIR	7	SCO	5	SAG	5	CAP	5	PIS	7	TAU
9	LIB	9	SAG	8	CAP	7	AQU	8	ARI	10	GEM
11	SCO	11	CAP	10	AQU	9	PIS	10	TAU	12	CAN
13	SAG	13	AQU	12	PIS	11	ARI	12	GEM	15	LEO
15	CAP	15	PIS	14	ARI	14	TAU	15	CAN	17	VIR
17	AQU	18	ARI	16	TAU	16	GEM	17	LEO	20	LIB
19	PIS	20	TAU	19	GEM	19	CAN	20	VIR	22	SCO
21	ARI	22	GEM	21	CAN	21	LEO	22	LIB	24	SAG
24	TAU	25	CAN	24	LEO	24	VIR	24	SCO	26	CAP
26	GEM	27	LEO	26	VIR	26	LIB	26	SAG	28	AQU
29	CAN	30	VIR	28	LIB	28	SCO	28	CAP	30	PIS
31	LEO					30	SAG	30	AQU		

1925

JAN		FEB		MAR		APR		MAY		JUN	
1	ARI	2	GEM	2	GEM	3	LEO	3	VIR	2	LIB
3	TAU	5	CAN	4	CAN	5	VIR	5	LIB	4	SCO
6	GEM	7	LEO	7	LEO	8	LIB	7	SCO	6	SAG
8	CAN	10	VIR	9	VIR	10	SCO	9	SAG	8	CAP
11	LEO	12	LIB	11	LIB	12	SAG	11	CAP	10	AQU
13	VIR	14	SCO	14	SCO	14	CAP	14	AQU	12	PIS
16	LIB	17	SAG	16	SAG	16	AQU	16	PIS	14	ARI
18	SCO	19	CAP	18	CAP	18	PIS	18	ARI	16	TAU
20	SAG	21	AQU	20	AQU	21	ARI	20	TAU	19	GEM
22	CAP	23	PIS	22	PIS	23	TAU	23	GEM	21	CAN
24	AQU	25	ARI	24	ARI	25	GEM	25	CAN	24	LEO
26	PIS	27	TAU	27	TAU	28	CAN	28	LEO	26	VIR
28	ARI			29	GEM	30	LEO	30	VIR	29	LIB
31	TAU			31	CAN						

JUL		AUG		SEP		OCT		NOV		DEC	
1	SCO	2	CAP	2	PIS	2	ARI	2	GEM	2	CAN
3	SAG	4	AQU	4	ARI	4	TAU	5	CAN	5	LEO
5	CAP	6	PIS	6	TAU	6	GEM	7	LEO	7	VIR
7	AQU	8	ARI	9	GEM	8	CAN	10	VIR	10	LIB
9	PIS	10	TAU	11	CAN	11	LEO	12	LIB	12	SCO
11	ARI	12	GEM	14	LEO	13	VIR	15	SCO	14	SAG
14	TAU	15	CAN	16	VIR	16	LIB	17	SAG	16	CAP
16	GEM	17	LEO	19	LIB	18	SCO	19	CAP	18	AQU
19	CAN	20	VIR	21	SCO	20	SAG	21	AQU	20	PIS
21	LEO	22	LIB	23	SAG	23	CAP	23	PIS	22	ARI
24	VIR	25	SCO	25	CAP	25	AQU	25	ARI	25	TAU
26	LIB	27	SAG	27	AQU	27	PIS	27	TAU	27	GEM
28	SCO	29	CAP	30	PIS	29	ARI	30	GEM	29	CAN
31	SAG	31	AQU			31	TAU				

1926

JAN		FEB		MAR		APR		MAY		JUN	
1	LEO	2	LIB	2	LIB	3	SAG	2	CAP	2	PIS
3	VIR	5	SCO	4	SCO	5	CAP	4	AQU	5	ARI
6	LIB	7	SAG	6	SAG	7	AQU	6	PIS	7	TAU
8	SCO	9	CAP	9	CAP	9	PIS	8	ARI	9	GEM
11	SAG	11	AQU	11	AQU	11	ARI	10	TAU	11	CAN
13	CAP	13	PIS	13	PIS	13	TAU	13	GEM	14	LEO
15	AQU	15	ARI	15	ARI	15	GEM	15	CAN	16	VIR
17	PIS	17	TAU	17	TAU	18	CAN	17	LEO	19	LIB
19	ARI	20	GEM	19	GEM	20	LEO	20	VIR	21	SCO
21	TAU	22	CAN	21	CAN	23	VIR	22	LIB	23	SAG
23	GEM	24	LEO	24	LEO	25	LIB	25	SCO	26	CAP
26	CAN	27	VIR	26	VIR	27	SCO	27	SAG	28	AQU
28	LEO			29	LIB	30	SAG	29	CAP	30	PIS
31	VIR			31	SCO			31	AQU		

JUL		AUG		SEP		OCT		NOV		DEC	
2	ARI	2	GEM	1	CAN	1	LEO	2	LIB	2	SCO
4	TAU	5	CAN	4	LEO	3	VIR	5	SCO	4	SAG
6	GEM	7	LEO	6	VIR	6	LIB	7	SAG	7	CAP
9	CAN	10	VIR	9	LIB	8	SCO	9	CAP	9	AQU
11	LEO	12	LIB	11	SCO	11	SAG	12	AQU	11	PIS
14	VIR	15	SCO	14	SAG	13	CAP	14	PIS	13	ARI
16	LIB	17	SAG	16	CAP	15	AQU	16	ARI	15	TAU
19	SCO	19	CAP	18	AQU	17	PIS	18	TAU	17	GEM
21	SAG	22	AQU	20	PIS	19	ARI	20	GEM	20	CAN
23	CAP	24	PIS	22	ARI	21	TAU	22	CAN	22	LEO
25	AQU	26	ARI	24	TAU	23	GEM	24	LEO	24	VIR
27	PIS	28	TAU	26	GEM	26	CAN	27	VIR	27	LIB
29	ARI	30	GEM	28	CAN	28	LEO	29	LIB	29	SCO
31	TAU					31	VIR				

1927

JAN		FEB		MAR		APR		MAY		JUN	
1	SAG	2	AQU	1	AQU	1	ARI	1	TAU	1	CAN
3	CAP	4	PIS	3	PIS	3	TAU	3	GEM	4	LEO
5	AQU	6	ARI	5	ARI	5	GEM	5	CAN	6	VIR
7	PIS	8	TAU	7	TAU	8	CAN	7	LEO	9	LIB
9	ARI	10	GEM	9	GEM	10	LEO	10	VIR	11	SCO
11	TAU	12	CAN	11	CAN	12	VIR	12	LIB	14	SAG
14	GEM	14	LEO	14	LEO	15	LIB	15	SCO	16	CAP
16	CAN	17	VIR	16	VIR	17	SCO	17	SAG	18	AQU
18	LEO	19	LIB	19	LIB	20	SAG	20	CAP	20	PIS
21	VIR	22	SCO	21	SCO	22	CAP	22	AQU	22	ARI
23	LIB	24	SAG	24	SAG	25	AQU	24	PIS	25	TAU
26	SCO	27	CAP	26	CAP	27	PIS	26	ARI	27	GEM
28	SAG			28	AQU	29	ARI	28	TAU	29	CAN
30	CAP			30	PIS			30	GEM		

JUL		AUG		SEP		OCT		NOV		DEC	
1	LEO	2	LIB	1	SCO	1	SAG	2	AQU	1	PIS
3	VIR	5	SCO	4	SAG	3	CAP	4	PIS	4	ARI
6	LIB	7	SAG	6	CAP	6	AQU	6	ARI	6	TAU
8	SCO	10	CAP	8	AQU	8	PIS	8	TAU	8	GEM
11	SAG	12	AQU	10	PIS	10	ARI	10	GEM	10	CAN
13	CAP	14	PIS	12	ARI	12	TAU	12	CAN	12	LEO
15	AQU	16	ARI	14	TAU	14	GEM	14	LEO	14	VIR
18	PIS	18	TAU	16	GEM	16	CAN	17	VIR	17	LIB
20	ARI	20	GEM	19	CAN	18	LEO	19	LIB	19	SCO
22	TAU	22	CAN	21	LEO	21	VIR	22	SCO	22	SAG
24	GEM	25	LEO	23	VIR	23	LIB	24	SAG	24	CAP
26	CAN	27	VIR	26	LIB	26	SCO	27	CAP	26	AQU
28	LEO	30	LIB	28	SCO	28	SAG	29	AQU	29	PIS
31	VIR					31	CAP			31	ARI

1928

JAN		FEB		MAR		APR		MAY		JUN	
2	TAU	2	CAN	1	CAN	1	VIR	1	LIB	2	SAG
4	GEM	5	LEO	3	LEO	4	LIB	4	SCO	5	CAP
6	CAN	7	VIR	5	VIR	6	SCO	6	SAG	7	AQU
8	LEO	9	LIB	8	LIB	9	SAG	9	CAP	10	PIS
11	VIR	12	SCO	10	SCO	11	CAP	11	AQU	12	ARI
13	LIB	14	SAG	13	SAG	14	AQU	13	PIS	14	TAU
15	SCO	17	CAP	15	CAP	16	PIS	16	ARI	16	GEM
18	SAG	19	AQU	18	AQU	18	ARI	18	TAU	18	CAN
20	CAP	21	PIS	20	PIS	20	TAU	20	GEM	20	LEO
23	AQU	23	ARI	22	ARI	22	GEM	22	CAN	22	VIR
25	PIS	25	TAU	24	TAU	24	CAN	24	LEO	25	LIB
27	ARI	28	GEM	26	GEM	26	LEO	26	VIR	27	SCO
29	TAU			28	CAN	29	VIR	28	LIB	30	SAG
31	GEM			30	LEO			31	SCO		

JUL		AUG		SEP		OCT		NOV		DEC	
2	CAP	1	AQU	2	ARI	1	TAU	2	CAN	1	LEO
5	AQU	3	PIS	4	TAU	3	GEM	4	LEO	3	VIR
7	PIS	5	ARI	6	GEM	5	CAN	6	VIR	6	LIB
9	ARI	8	TAU	8	CAN	7	LEO	8	LIB	8	SCO
11	TAU	10	GEM	10	LEO	10	VIR	11	SCO	11	SAG
13	GEM	12	CAN	12	VIR	12	LIB	13	SAG	13	CAP
16	CAN	14	LEO	15	LIB	14	SCO	16	CAP	16	AQU
18	LEO	16	VIR	17	SCO	17	SAG	18	AQU	18	PIS
20	VIR	18	LIB	20	SAG	20	CAP	21	PIS	20	ARI
22	LIB	21	SCO	22	CAP	22	AQU	23	ARI	22	TAU
24	SCO	23	SAG	25	AQU	24	PIS	25	TAU	25	GEM
27	SAG	26	CAP	27	PIS	27	ARI	27	GEM	27	CAN
30	CAP	28	AQU	29	ARI	29	TAU	29	CAN	29	LEO
		31	PIS			31	GEM			31	VIR

1929

JAN		FEB		MAR		APR		MAY		JUN	
2	LIB	1	SCO	2	SAG	1	CAP	1	AQU	2	ARI
4	SCO	3	SAG	5	CAP	4	AQU	4	PIS	4	TAU
7	SAG	6	CAP	7	AQU	6	PIS	6	ARI	6	GEM
9	CAP	8	AQU	10	PIS	8	ARI	8	TAU	8	CAN
12	AQU	10	PIS	12	ARI	11	TAU	10	GEM	10	LEO
14	PIS	13	ARI	14	TAU	13	GEM	12	CAN	13	VIR
17	ARI	15	TAU	16	GEM	15	CAN	14	LEO	15	LIB
19	TAU	17	GEM	19	CAN	17	LEO	16	VIR	17	SCO
21	GEM	19	CAN	21	LEO	19	VIR	19	LIB	20	SAG
23	CAN	21	LEO	23	VIR	21	LIB	21	SCO	22	CAP
25	LEO	23	VIR	25	LIB	24	SCO	23	SAG	25	AQU
27	VIR	26	LIB	27	SCO	26	SAG	26	CAP	27	PIS
29	LIB	28	SCO	30	SAG	29	CAP	28	AQU	30	ARI
								31	PIS		

JUL		AUG		SEP		OCT		NOV		DEC	
2	TAU	2	CAN	1	LEO	2	LIB	1	SCO	1	SAG
4	GEM	4	LEO	3	VIR	4	SCO	3	SAG	3	CAP
6	CAN	6	VIR	5	LIB	7	SAG	6	CAP	5	AQU
8	LEO	8	LIB	7	SCO	9	CAP	8	AQU	8	PIS
10	VIR	11	SCO	9	SAG	12	AQU	11	PIS	10	ARI
12	LIB	13	SAG	12	CAP	14	PIS	13	ARI	13	TAU
14	SCO	16	CAP	15	AQU	17	ARI	15	TAU	15	GEM
17	SAG	18	AQU	17	PIS	19	TAU	17	GEM	17	CAN
19	CAP	21	PIS	19	ARI	21	GEM	19	CAN	19	LEO
22	AQU	23	ARI	22	TAU	23	CAN	21	LEO	21	VIR
24	PIS	25	TAU	24	GEM	25	LEO	24	VIR	23	LIB
27	ARI	28	GEM	26	CAN	27	VIR	26	LIB	25	SCO
29	TAU	30	CAN	28	LEO	30	LIB	28	SCO	28	SAG
31	GEM			30	VIR					30	CAP

1930

JAN		FEB		MAR		APR		MAY		JUN	
1	AQU	2	ARI	2	ARI	2	GEM	2	CAN	2	VIR
4	PIS	5	TAU	4	TAU	5	CAN	4	LEO	4	LIB
6	ARI	7	GEM	6	GEM	7	LEO	6	VIR	7	SCO
8	TAU	9	CAN	8	CAN	9	VIR	8	LIB	9	SAG
11	GEM	11	LEO	10	LEO	11	LIB	10	SCO	11	CAP
13	CAN	13	VIR	12	VIR	13	SCO	13	SAG	14	AQU
15	LEO	15	LIB	15	LIB	15	SAG	15	CAP	16	PIS
17	VIR	17	SCO	17	SCO	18	CAP	18	AQU	19	ARI
19	LIB	20	SAG	19	SAG	20	AQU	20	PIS	21	TAU
21	SCO	22	CAP	21	CAP	23	PIS	23	ARI	24	GEM
23	SAG	25	AQU	24	AQU	25	ARI	25	TAU	26	CAN
26	CAP	27	PIS	26	PIS	28	TAU	27	GEM	28	LEO
28	AQU			29	ARI	30	GEM	29	CAN	30	VIR
31	PIS			31	TAU			31	LEO		

JUL		AUG		SEP		OCT		NOV		DEC	
2	LIB	2	SAG	1	CAP	1	AQU	2	ARI	2	TAU
4	SCO	5	CAP	4	AQU	3	PIS	5	TAU	4	GEM
6	SAG	7	AQU	6	PIS	6	ARI	7	GEM	7	CAN
9	CAP	10	PIS	9	ARI	8	TAU	9	CAN	9	LEO
11	AQU	11	ARI	11	TAU	11	GEM	11	LEO	11	VIR
14	PIS	15	TAU	14	GEM	13	CAN	13	VIR	13	LIB
16	ARI	17	GEM	16	CAN	16	LEO	16	LIB	15	SCO
19	TAU	19	CAN	18	LEO	17	VIR	18	SCO	17	SAG
21	GEM	21	LEO	20	VIR	19	LIB	20	SAG	20	CAP
23	CAN	23	VIR	22	SCO	21	SCO	22	CAP	22	AQU
25	LEO	25	LIB	24	SCO	24	SAG	25	AQU	24	PIS
27	VIR	28	SCO	26	SAG	26	CAP	27	PIS	27	ARI
29	LIB	30	SAG	28	CAP	28	AQU	30	ARI	29	TAU
31	SCO					31	PIS				

1931

JAN		FEB		MAR		APR		MAY		JUN	
1	GEM	1	LEO	1	LEO	1	LIB	1	SCO	1	CAP
3	CAN	3	VIR	3	VIR	3	SCO	3	SAG	4	AQU
5	LEO	5	LIB	5	LIB	5	SAG	5	CAP	6	PIS
7	VIR	8	SCO	7	SCO	8	CAP	7	AQU	9	ARI
9	LIB	10	SAG	9	SAG	10	AQU	10	PIS	11	TAU
11	SCO	12	CAP	11	CAP	13	PIS	12	ARI	14	GEM
13	SAG	15	AQU	14	AQU	15	ARI	15	TAU	16	CAN
16	CAP	17	PIS	16	PIS	18	TAU	17	GEM	18	LEO
18	AQU	20	ARI	19	ARI	20	GEM	20	CAN	20	VIR
21	PIS	22	TAU	21	TAU	22	CAN	22	LEO	22	LIB
23	ARI	25	GEM	24	GEM	25	LEO	24	VIR	24	SCO
26	TAU	27	CAN	26	CAN	27	VIR	26	LIB	27	SAG
28	GEM			28	LEO	29	LIB	28	SCO	29	CAP
30	CAN			30	VIR			30	SAG		

JUL		AUG		SEP		OCT		NOV		DEC	
1	AQU	2	ARI	1	TAU	1	GEM	2	LEO	1	VIR
4	PIS	5	TAU	4	GEM	3	CAN	4	VIR	3	LIB
6	ARI	7	GEM	6	CAN	6	LEO	6	LIB	6	SCO
9	TAU	10	CAN	8	LEO	8	VIR	8	SCO	8	SAG
11	GEM	12	LEO	10	VIR	10	LIB	10	SAG	10	CAP
13	CAN	14	VIR	12	LIB	12	SCO	12	CAP	12	AQU
15	LEO	16	LIB	14	SCO	14	SAG	14	AQU	14	PIS
17	VIR	18	SCO	16	SAG	16	CAP	17	PIS	17	ARI
20	LIB	20	SAG	19	CAP	18	AQU	19	ARI	19	TAU
22	SCO	22	CAP	21	AQU	21	PIS	22	TAU	22	GEM
24	SAG	25	AQU	23	PIS	23	ARI	24	GEM	24	CAN
26	CAP	27	PIS	26	ARI	26	TAU	27	CAN	26	LEO
28	AQU	30	ARI	28	TAU	28	GEM	29	LEO	29	VIR
31	PIS					31	CAN			31	LIB

1932

	JAN		FEB		MAR		APR		MAY		JUN
2	SCO	2	CAP	1	CAP	2	PIS	1	ARI	3	GEM
4	SAG	5	AQU	3	AQU	4	ARI	4	TAU	5	CAN
6	CAP	7	PIS	5	PIS	7	TAU	6	GEM	7	LEO
8	AQU	9	ARI	8	ARI	9	GEM	9	CAN	10	VIR
11	PIS	12	TAU	10	TAU	12	CAN	11	LEO	12	LIB
13	ARI	14	GEM	13	GEM	14	LEO	13	VIR	14	SCO
16	TAU	17	CAN	15	CAN	16	VIR	16	LIB	16	SAG
18	GEM	19	LEO	18	LEO	18	LIB	18	SCO	18	CAP
20	CAN	21	VIR	20	VIR	20	SCO	20	SAG	20	AQU
23	LEO	23	LIB	22	LIB	22	SAG	22	CAP	22	PIS
25	VIR	25	SCO	24	SCO	24	CAP	24	AQU	25	ARI
27	LIB	27	SAG	26	SAG	26	AQU	26	PIS	27	TAU
29	SCO			28	CAP	29	PIS	29	ARI	30	GEM
31	SAG			30	AQU			31	TAU		

	JUL		AUG		SEP		OCT		NOV		DEC
2	CAN	1	LEO	2	LIB	1	SCO	2	CAP	1	AQU
5	LEO	3	VIR	4	SCO	3	SAG	4	AQU	3	PIS
7	VIR	5	LIB	6	SAG	5	CAP	6	PIS	6	ARI
9	LIB	7	SCO	8	CAP	7	AQU	8	ARI	8	TAU
11	SCO	10	SAG	10	AQU	10	PIS	11	TAU	11	GEM
13	SAG	12	CAP	12	PIS	12	ARI	13	GEM	13	CAN
15	CAP	14	AQU	15	ARI	15	TAU	16	CAN	16	LEO
18	AQU	16	PIS	17	TAU	17	GEM	18	LEO	18	VIR
20	PIS	19	ARI	20	GEM	20	CAN	21	VIR	20	LIB
22	ARI	21	TAU	22	CAN	22	LEO	23	LIB	22	SCO
25	TAU	24	GEM	25	LEO	24	VIR	25	SCO	24	SAG
27	GEM	26	CAN	27	VIR	27	LIB	27	SAG	26	CAP
30	CAN	28	LEO	29	LIB	29	SCO	29	CAP	28	AQU
		31	VIR			31	SAG			31	PIS

1933

	JAN		FEB		MAR		APR		MAY		JUN
2	ARI	1	TAU	3	GEM	1	CAN	1	LEO	2	LIB
4	TAU	3	GEM	5	CAN	4	LEO	4	VIR	4	SCO
7	GEM	6	CAN	8	LEO	6	VIR	6	LIB	6	SAG
9	CAN	8	LEO	10	VIR	8	LIB	8	SCO	8	CAP
12	LEO	10	VIR	12	LIB	11	SCO	10	SAG	10	AQU
14	VIR	13	LIB	14	SCO	13	SAG	12	CAP	12	PIS
16	LIB	15	SCO	16	SAG	15	CAP	14	AQU	15	ARI
19	SCO	17	SAG	18	CAP	17	AQU	16	PIS	17	TAU
21	SAG	19	CAP	20	AQU	19	PIS	19	ARI	20	GEM
23	CAP	21	AQU	23	PIS	21	ARI	21	TAU	22	CAN
25	AQU	23	PIS	25	ARI	24	TAU	23	GEM	25	LEO
27	PIS	26	ARI	27	TAU	26	GEM	26	CAN	27	VIR
29	ARI	28	TAU	30	GEM	29	CAN	29	LEO	30	LIB
								31	VIR		

	JUL		AUG		SEP		OCT		NOV		DEC
2	SCO	2	CAP	1	AQU	2	ARI	1	TAU	1	GEM
4	SAG	4	AQU	3	PIS	5	TAU	3	GEM	3	CAN
6	CAP	6	PIS	5	ARI	7	GEM	6	CAN	6	LEO
8	AQU	8	ARI	7	TAU	9	CAN	8	LEO	8	VIR
10	PIS	11	TAU	10	GEM	12	LEO	11	VIR	11	LIB
12	ARI	13	GEM	12	CAN	14	VIR	13	LIB	13	SCO
14	TAU	16	CAN	15	LEO	17	LIB	15	SCO	15	SAG
17	GEM	18	LEO	17	VIR	19	SCO	17	SAG	17	CAP
20	CAN	21	VIR	19	LIB	21	SAG	19	CAP	19	AQU
22	LEO	23	LIB	21	SCO	23	CAP	21	AQU	21	PIS
24	VIR	25	SCO	24	SAG	25	AQU	23	PIS	23	ARI
27	LIB	27	SAG	26	CAP	27	PIS	26	ARI	25	TAU
29	SCO	29	CAP	28	AQU	30	ARI	28	TAU	28	GEM
31	SAG			30	PIS					30	CAN

1934

JAN	FEB	MAR	APR	MAY	JUN
2 LEO	1 VIR	2 LIB	1 SCO	2 CAP	1 AQU
4 VIR	3 LIB	5 SCO	3 SAG	5 AQU	3 PIS
7 LIB	5 SCO	7 SAG	5 CAP	7 PIS	5 ARI
9 SCO	8 SAG	9 CAP	7 AQU	9 ARI	7 TAU
11 SAG	10 CAP	11 AQU	9 PIS	11 TAU	10 GEM
13 CAP	12 AQU	13 PIS	12 ARI	13 GEM	12 CAN
15 AQU	14 PIS	15 ARI	14 TAU	16 CAN	15 LEO
17 PIS	16 ARI	17 TAU	16 GEM	18 LEO	17 VIR
19 ARI	18 TAU	20 GEM	19 CAN	21 VIR	20 LIB
22 TAU	20 GEM	22 CAN	21 LEO	23 LIB	22 SCO
24 GEM	23 CAN	25 LEO	24 VIR	26 SCO	24 SAG
27 CAN	25 LEO	27 VIR	26 LIB	28 SAG	26 CAP
29 LEO	28 VIR	30 LIB	28 SCO	30 CAP	28 AQU
			30 SAG		30 PIS

JUL	AUG	SEP	OCT	NOV	DEC
2 ARI	1 TAU	2 CAN	2 LEO	1 VIR	3 SCO
5 TAU	3 GEM	4 LEO	4 VIR	3 LIB	5 SAG
7 GEM	6 CAN	7 VIR	7 LIB	5 SCO	7 CAP
9 CAN	8 LEO	9 LIB	9 SCO	8 SAG	9 AQU
12 LEO	11 VIR	12 SCO	11 SAG	10 CAP	11 PIS
15 VIR	13 LIB	14 SAG	14 CAP	12 AQU	13 ARI
17 LIB	16 SCO	16 CAP	16 AQU	14 PIS	16 TAU
19 SCO	18 SAG	18 AQU	18 PIS	16 ARI	18 GEM
22 SAG	20 CAP	20 PIS	20 ARI	18 TAU	20 CAN
24 CAP	22 AQU	23 ARI	22 TAU	21 GEM	23 LEO
26 AQU	24 PIS	25 TAU	24 GEM	23 CAN	25 VIR
28 PIS	26 ARI	27 GEM	27 CAN	25 LEO	28 LIB
30 ARI	28 TAU	29 CAN	29 LEO	28 VIR	30 SCO
	30 GEM			30 LIB	

1935

JAN	FEB	MAR	APR	MAY	JUN
1 SAG	2 AQU	2 AQU	2 ARI	1 TAU	2 CAN
4 CAP	4 PIS	4 PIS	4 TAU	4 GEM	5 LEO
6 AQU	6 ARI	6 ARI	6 GEM	6 CAN	7 VIR
8 PIS	8 TAU	8 TAU	8 CAN	8 LEO	10 LIB
10 ARI	10 GEM	10 GEM	11 LEO	11 VIR	12 SCO
12 TAU	13 CAN	12 CAN	13 VIR	13 LIB	14 SAG
14 GEM	15 LEO	15 LEO	16 LIB	16 SCO	17 CAP
17 CAN	18 VIR	17 VIR	18 SCO	18 SAG	19 AQU
19 LEO	20 LIB	20 LIB	21 SAG	20 CAP	21 PIS
22 VIR	23 SCO	22 SCO	23 CAP	22 AQU	23 ARI
24 LIB	25 SAG	24 SAG	25 AQU	24 PIS	25 TAU
27 SCO	27 CAP	27 CAP	27 PIS	27 ARI	27 GEM
29 SAG		29 AQU	29 ARI	29 TAU	29 CAN
31 CAP		31 PIS		31 GEM	

JUL	AUG	SEP	OCT	NOV	DEC
2 LEO	1 VIR	2 SCO	2 SAG	2 AQU	2 PIS
4 VIR	3 LIB	4 SAG	4 CAP	5 PIS	4 ARI
7 LIB	6 SCO	7 CAP	6 AQU	7 ARI	6 TAU
9 SCO	8 SAG	9 AQU	8 PIS	9 TAU	8 GEM
12 SAG	10 CAP	11 PIS	10 ARI	11 GEM	10 CAN
14 CAP	12 AQU	13 ARI	12 TAU	13 CAN	13 LEO
16 AQU	14 PIS	15 TAU	14 GEM	15 LEO	15 VIR
18 PIS	16 ARI	17 GEM	17 CAN	18 VIR	18 LIB
20 ARI	18 TAU	19 CAN	19 LEO	20 LIB	20 SCO
22 TAU	21 GEM	22 LEO	21 VIR	23 SCO	23 SAG
24 GEM	23 CAN	24 VIR	24 LIB	25 SAG	25 CAP
27 CAN	25 LEO	27 LIB	26 SCO	27 CAP	27 AQU
29 LEO	28 VIR	29 SCO	29 SAG	30 AQU	29 PIS
	30 LIB		31 CAP		31 ARI

1936

	JAN		FEB		MAR		APR		MAY		JUN
2	TAU	1	GEM	1	CAN	2	VIR	2	LIB	1	SCO
5	GEM	3	CAN	4	LEO	5	LIB	5	SCO	3	SAG
7	CAN	5	LEO	6	VIR	7	SCO	7	SAG	6	CAP
9	LEO	8	VIR	9	LIB	10	SAG	9	CAP	8	AQU
11	VIR	10	LIB	11	SCO	12	CAP	12	AQU	10	PIS
14	LIB	13	SCO	14	SAG	15	AQU	14	PIS	12	ARI
16	SCO	15	SAG	16	CAP	17	PIS	16	ARI	14	TAU
19	SAG	18	CAP	18	AQU	19	ARI	18	TAU	17	GEM
21	CAP	20	AQU	20	PIS	20	TAU	20	GEM	19	CAN
23	AQU	22	PIS	22	ARI	23	GEM	22	CAN	21	LEO
25	PIS	24	ARI	24	TAU	25	CAN	24	LEO	23	VIR
27	ARI	26	TAU	26	GEM	27	LEO	27	VIR	26	LIB
30	TAU	28	GEM	28	CAN	30	VIR	29	LIB	28	SCO
				31	LEO						

	JUL		AUG		SEP		OCT		NOV		DEC
1	SAG	2	AQU	2	ARI	2	TAU	2	CAN	2	LEO
3	CAP	4	PIS	4	TAU	4	GEM	4	LEO	4	VIR
5	AQU	6	ARI	6	GEM	6	CAN	7	VIR	6	LIB
8	PIS	8	TAU	9	CAN	8	LEO	9	LIB	9	SCO
10	ARI	10	GEM	11	LEO	10	VIR	12	SCO	11	SAG
12	TAU	12	CAN	13	VIR	13	LIB	14	SAG	14	CAP
14	GEM	15	LEO	16	LIB	15	SCO	17	CAP	16	AQU
16	CAN	17	VIR	18	SCO	18	SAG	19	AQU	19	PIS
18	LEO	19	LIB	21	SAG	20	CAP	21	PIS	21	ARI
21	VIR	22	SCO	23	CAP	23	AQU	24	ARI	23	TAU
23	LIB	24	SAG	25	AQU	25	PIS	26	TAU	25	GEM
26	SCO	27	CAP	28	PIS	27	ARI	28	GEM	27	CAN
28	SAG	29	AQU	30	ARI	29	TAU	30	CAN	29	LEO
30	CAP	31	PIS			31	GEM			31	VIR

1937

	JAN		FEB		MAR		APR		MAY		JUN
3	LIB	2	SCO	1	SCI	2	CAP	2	AQU	1	PIS
5	SCO	4	SAG	3	SAG	5	AQU	4	PIS	3	ARI
8	SAG	7	CAP	6	CAP	7	PIS	7	ARI	5	TAU
10	CAP	9	AQU	8	AQU	9	ARI	9	TAU	7	GEM
13	AQU	11	PIS	11	PIS	11	TAU	11	GEM	9	CAN
15	PIS	13	ARI	13	ARI	13	GEM	13	CAN	11	LEO
17	ARI	15	TAU	15	TAU	15	CAN	15	LEO	13	VIR
19	TAU	18	GEM	17	GEM	17	LEO	17	VIR	16	LIB
21	GEM	20	CAN	19	CAN	20	VIR	19	LIB	18	SCO
23	CAN	22	LEO	21	LEO	22	LIB	22	SCO	20	SAG
26	LEO	24	VIR	23	VIR	25	SCO	24	SAG	23	CAP
28	VIR	26	LIB	26	LIB	27	SAG	27	CAP	26	AQU
30	LIB			28	SCO	30	CAP	29	AQU	28	PIS
				31	SAG					30	ARI

	JUL		AUG		SEP		OCT		NOV		DEC
2	TAU	1	GEM	1	LEO	1	VIR	2	SCO	1	SAG
4	GEM	3	CAN	3	VIR	3	LIB	4	SAG	4	CAP
6	CAN	5	LEO	6	LIB	5	SCO	7	CAP	6	AQU
8	LEO	7	VIR	8	SCO	8	SAG	9	AQU	9	PIS
11	VIR	9	LIB	11	SAG	10	CAP	12	PIS	11	ARI
13	LIB	12	SCO	13	CAP	13	AQU	14	ARI	13	TAU
15	SCO	14	SAG	15	AQU	15	PIS	16	TAU	15	GEM
18	SAG	17	CAP	18	PIS	17	ARI	18	GEM	17	CAN
20	CAP	19	AQU	20	ARI	19	TAU	20	CAN	19	LEO
23	AQU	21	PIS·	22	TAU	21	GEM	22	LEO	21	VIR
25	PIS	24	ARI	24	GEM	24	CAN	24	VIR	24	LIB
27	ARI	26	TAU	26	CAN	26	LEO	26	LIB	26	SCO
30	TAU	28	GEM	28	LEO	28	VIR	29	SCO	29	SAG
		30	CAN			30	LIB			31	CAP

1938

JAN		FEB		MAR		APR		MAY		JUN	
3	AQU	1	PIS	1	PIS	1	TAU	1	GEM	1	LEO
5	PIS	4	ARI	3	ARI	4	GEM	3	CAN	3	VIR
7	ARI	6	TAU	5	TAU	6	CAN	5	LEO	6	LIB
10	TAU	8	GEM	7	GEM	8	LEO	7	VIR	8	SCO
12	GEM	10	CAN	9	CAN	10	VIR	9	LIB	10	SAG
14	CAN	12	LEO	12	LEO	12	LIB	12	SCO	13	CAP
16	LEO	14	VIR	14	VIR	15	SCO	14	SAG	16	AQU
18	VIR	16	LIB	16	LIB	17	SAG	17	CAP	18	PIS
20	LIB	19	SCO	18	SCO	19	CAP	19	AQU	20	ARI
22	SCO	21	SAG	21	SAG	22	AQU	22	PIS	23	TAU
25	SAG	24	CAP	23	CAP	24	PIS	24	ARI	25	GEM
27	CAP	26	AQU	26	AQU	27	ARI	26	TAU	27	CAN
30	AQU			28	PIS	29	TAU	28	GEM	29	LEO
				30	ARI			30	CAN		

JUL		AUG		SEP		OCT		NOV		DEC	
1	VIR	2	SCO	3	CAP	3	AQU	2	PIS	1	ARI
3	LIB	4	SAG	5	AQU	5	PIS	4	ARI	4	TAU
5	SCO	7	CAP	8	PIS	8	ARI	6	TAU	6	GEM
8	SAG	9	AQU	10	ARI	10	TAU	8	GEM	8	CAN
10	CAP	12	PIS	12	TAU	12	GEM	10	CAN	10	LEO
13	AQU	14	ARI	15	GEM	14	CAN	12	LEO	12	VIR
15	PIS	16	TAU	17	CAN	16	LEO	15	VIR	14	LIB
18	ARI	18	GEM	19	LEO	18	VIR	17	LIB	16	SCO
20	TAU	21	CAN	21	VIR	20	LIB	19	SCO	19	SAG
22	GEM	23	LEO	23	LIB	23	SCO	21	SAG	21	CAP
24	CAN	25	VIR	25	SCO	25	SAG	24	CAP	24	AQU
26	LEO	27	LIB	28	SAG	27	CAP	26	AQU	26	PIS
28	VIR	29	SCO	30	CAP	30	AQU	29	PIS	29	ARI
30	LIB	31	SAG							31	TAU

1939

JAN		FEB		MAR		APR		MAY		JUN	
2	GEM	1	CAN	2	LEO	3	LIB	2	SCO	1	SAG
4	CAN	3	LEO	4	VIR	5	SCO	4	SAG	3	CAP
6	LEO	5	VIR	6	LIB	7	SAG	7	CAP	5	AQU
8	VIR	7	LIB	8	SCO	9	CAP	9	AQU	8	PIS
10	LIB	9	SCO	10	SAG	12	AQU	12	PIS	10	ARI
12	SCO	11	SAG	13	CAP	14	PIS	14	ARI	13	TAU
15	SAG	14	CAP	15	AQU	17	ARI	16	TAU	15	GEM
17	CAP	16	AQU	18	PIS	19	TAU	19	GEM	17	CAN
20	AQU	19	PIS	20	ARI	21	GEM	21	CAN	19	LEO
22	PIS	21	ARI	23	TAU	24	CAN	23	LEO	21	VIR
25	ARI	24	TAU	25	GEM	26	LEO	25	VIR	23	LIB
27	TAU	26	GEM	27	CAN	28	VIR	27	LIB	26	SCO
30	GEM	28	CAN	29	LEO	30	LIB	29	SCO	28	SAG
				31	VIR					30	CAP

JUL		AUG		SEP		OCT		NOV		DEC	
3	AQU	1	PIS	3	TAU	2	GEM	1	CAN	2	VIR
5	PIS	4	ARI	5	GEM	5	CAN	3	LEO	5	LIB
8	ARI	6	TAU	7	CAN	7	LEO	5	VIR	7	SCO
10	TAU	9	GEM	9	LEO	9	VIR	7	LIB	9	SAG
12	GEM	11	CAN	11	VIR	11	LIB	9	SCO	11	CAP
15	CAN	13	LEO	13	LIB	13	SCO	11	SAG	13	AQU
17	LEO	15	VIR	15	SCO	15	SAG	14	CAP	16	PIS
19	VIR	17	LIB	18	SAG	17	CAP	16	AQU	19	ARI
21	LIB	19	SCO	20	CAP	20	AQU	19	PIS	21	TAU
23	SCO	21	SAG	22	AQU	22	PIS	21	ARI	23	GEM
25	SAG	24	CAP	25	PIS	25	ARI	24	TAU	26	CAN
27	CAP	26	AQU	28	ARI	27	TAU	26	GEM	28	LEO
30	AQU	29	PIS	30	TAU	30	GEM	28	CAN	30	VIR
		31	ARI					30	LEO		

Moon Tables

1940

	JAN		FEB		MAR		APR		MAY		JUN
1	LIB	1	SAG	2	CAP	1	AQU	3	ARI	2	TAU
3	SCO	4	CAP	4	AQU	3	PIS	5	TAU	4	GEM
5	SAG	6	AQU	7	PIS	6	ARI	8	GEM	6	CAN
7	CAP	9	PIS	9	ARI	8	TAU	10	CAN	9	LEO
10	AQU	11	ARI	12	TAU	11	GEM	12	LEO	11	VIR
12	PIS	14	TAU	14	GEM	13	CAN	15	VIR	13	LIB
15	ARI	16	GEM	17	CAN	15	LEO	17	LIB	15	SCO
17	TAU	18	CAN	19	LEO	17	VIR	19	SCO	17	SAG
20	GEM	20	LEO	21	VIR	19	LIB	21	SAG	19	CAP
22	CAN	22	VIR	23	LIB	21	SCO	23	CAP	22	AQU
24	LEO	24	LIB	25	SCO	23	SAG	25	AQU	24	PIS
26	VIR	26	SCO	27	SAG	26	CAP	28	PIS	27	ARI
28	LIB	29	SAG	29	CAP	28	AQU	30	ARI	29	TAU
30	SCO					30	PIS				

	JUL		AUG		SEP		OCT		NOV		DEC
2	GEM	2	LEO	1	VIR	2	SCO	1	SAG	2	AQU
4	CAN	4	VIR	3	LIB	4	SAG	3	CAP	5	PIS
6	LEO	6	LIB	5	SCO	6	CAP	5	AQU	7	ARI
8	VIR	9	SCO	7	SAG	9	AQU	7	PIS	10	TAU
10	LIB	11	SAG	9	CAP	11	PIS	10	ARI	12	GEM
12	SCO	13	CAP	11	AQU	14	ARI	13	TAU	15	CAN
14	SAG	15	AQU	14	PIS	16	TAU	15	GEM	17	LEO
17	CAP	18	PIS	16	ARI	19	GEM	17	CAN	19	VIR
19	AQU	20	ARI	19	TAU	21	CAN	20	LEO	21	LIB
21	PIS	23	TAU	22	GEM	23	LEO	22	VIR	23	SCO
24	ARI	25	GEM	24	CAN	26	VIR	24	LIB	26	SAG
26	TAU	28	CAN	26	LEO	28	LIB	26	SCO	28	CAP
29	GEM	30	LEO	28	VIR	30	SCO	28	SAG	30	AQU
31	CAN			30	LIB			30	CAP		

1941

	JAN		FEB		MAR		APR		MAY		JUN
1	PIS	2	TAU	2	TAU	1	GEM	3	LEO	1	VIR
4	ARI	5	GEM	4	GEM	3	CAN	5	VIR	4	LIB
6	TAU	7	CAN	7	CAN	5	LEO	7	LIB	6	SCO
9	GEM	10	LEO	9	LEO	8	VIR	9	SCO	8	SAG
11	CAN	12	VIR	11	VIR	10	LIB	11	SAG	10	CAP
13	LEO	14	LIB	13	LIB	12	SCO	13	CAP	12	AQU
15	VIR	16	SCO	15	SCO	14	SAG	15	AQU	14	PIS
18	LIB	18	SAG	17	SAG	16	CAP	18	PIS	16	ARI
20	SCO	20	CAP	19	CAP	18	AQU	20	ARI	19	TAU
22	SAG	23	AQU	22	AQU	20	PIS	23	TAU	21	GEM
24	CAP	25	PIS	24	PIS	23	ARI	25	GEM	24	CAN
26	AQU	27	ARI	27	ARI	25	TAU	28	CAN	26	LEO
29	PIS			29	TAU	28	GEM	30	LEO	29	VIR
31	ARI					30	CAN				

	JUL		AUG		SEP		OCT		NOV		DEC
1	LIB	1	SAG	2	AQU	1	PIS	2	TAU	2	GEM
3	SCO	3	CAP	4	PIS	4	ARI	5	GEM	5	CAN
5	SAG	5	AQU	6	ARI	6	TAU	7	CAN	7	LEO
7	CAP	8	PIS	9	TAU	9	GEM	10	LEO	10	VIR
9	AQU	10	ARI	11	GEM	11	CAN	12	VIR	12	LIB
11	PIS	13	TAU	14	CAN	14	LEO	15	LIB	14	SCO
14	ARI	15	GEM	16	LEO	16	VIR	17	SCO	16	SAG
16	TAU	18	CAN	19	VIR	18	LIB	19	SAG	18	CAP
19	GEM	20	LEO	21	LIB	20	SCO	21	CAP	20	AQU
21	CAN	22	VIR	23	SCO	22	SAG	23	AQU	22	PIS
24	LEO	24	LIB	25	SAG	24	CAP	25	PIS	24	ARI
26	VIR	26	SCO	27	CAP	26	AQU	27	ARI	27	TAU
28	LIB	28	SAG	29	AQU	29	PIS	30	TAU	29	GEM
30	SCO	31	CAP			31	ARI				

1942

JAN		FEB		MAR		APR		MAY		JUN	
1	CAN	2	VIR	1	VIR	2	SCO	2	SAG	2	AQU
3	LEO	4	LIB	4	LIB	4	SAG	4	CAP	4	PIS
6	VIR	7	SCO	6	SCO	6	CAP	6	AQU	6	ARI
8	LIB	9	SAG	8	SAG	8	AQU	8	PIS	9	TAU
10	SCO	11	CAP	10	CAP	11	PIS	10	ARI	11	GEM
12	SAG	13	AQU	12	AQU	13	ARI	13	TAU	14	CAN
14	CAP	15	PIS	14	PIS	15	TAU	15	GEM	16	LEO
16	AQU	17	ARI	17	ARI	18	GEM	18	CAN	19	VIR
19	PIS	20	TAU	19	TAU	20	CAN	20	LEO	21	LIB
21	ARI	22	GEM	21	GEM	23	LEO	23	VIR	23	SCO
23	TAU	25	CAN	24	CAN	25	VIR	25	LIB	25	SAG
26	GEM	27	LEO	26	LEO	27	LIB	27	SCO	27	CAP
28	CAN			29	VIR	30	SCO	29	SAG	29	AQU
31	LEO			31	LIB			31	CAP		

JUL		AUG		SEP		OCT		NOV		DEC	
1	PIS	2	TAU	1	GEM	1	CAN	2	VIR	2	LIB
4	ARI	5	GEM	4	CAN	4	LEO	5	LIB	4	SCO
6	TAU	7	CAN	6	LEO	6	VIR	7	SCO	6	SAG
9	GEM	10	LEO	9	VIR	8	LIB	9	SAG	8	CAP
11	CAN	12	VIR	11	LIB	10	SCO	11	CAP	10	AQU
14	LEO	15	LIB	13	SCO	13	SAG	13	AQU	12	PIS
16	VIR	17	SCO	15	SAG	15	CAP	15	PIS	15	ARI
18	LIB	19	SAG	17	CAP	17	AQU	17	ARI	17	TAU
21	SCO	21	CAP	20	AQU	19	PIS	20	TAU	19	GEM
23	SAG	23	AQU	22	PIS	21	ARI	22	GEM	22	CAN
25	CAP	25	PIS	24	ARI	23	TAU	25	CAN	24	LEO
27	AQU	27	ARI	26	TAU	26	GEM	27	LEO	27	VIR
29	PIS	30	TAU	29	GEM	28	CAN	30	VIR	29	LIB
31	ARI					31	LEO				

1943

JAN		FEB		MAR		APR		MAY		JUN	
1	SCO	1	CAP	1	CAP	1	PIS	3	TAU	1	GEM
3	SAG	3	AQU	3	AQU	3	ARI	5	GEM	4	CAN
5	CAP	5	PIS	5	PIS	5	TAU	7	CAN	6	LEO
7	AQU	7	ARI	7	ARI	8	GEM	10	LEO	9	VIR
9	PIS	10	TAU	9	TAU	10	CAN	12	VIR	11	LIB
11	ARI	12	GEM	11	GEM	13	LEO	15	LIB	14	SCO
13	TAU	14	CAN	14	CAN	15	VIR	17	SCO	16	SAG
16	GEM	17	LEO	16	LEO	18	LIB	19	SAG	18	CAP
18	CAN	19	VIR	19	VIR	20	SCO	21	CAP	20	AQU
21	LEO	22	LIB	21	LIB	22	SAG	23	AQU	22	PIS
23	VIR	24	SCO	23	SCO	24	CAP	26	PIS	24	ARI
26	LIB	26	SAG	26	SAG	26	AQU	28	ARI	26	TAU
28	SCO			28	CAP	28	PIS	30	TAU	29	GEM
30	SAG			30	AQU	30	ARI				

JUL		AUG		SEP		OCT		NOV		DEC	
1	CAN	2	VIR	1	LIB	1	SCO	1	CAP	1	AQU
4	LEO	5	LIB	3	SCO	3	SAG	4	AQU	3	PIS
6	VIR	7	SCO	6	SAG	5	CAP	6	PIS	5	ARI
9	LIB	10	SAG	8	CAP	7	AQU	8	ARI	7	TAU
11	SCO	12	CAP	10	AQU	9	PIS	10	TAU	10	GEM
13	SAG	14	AQU	12	PIS	12	ARI	12	GEM	12	CAN
15	CAP	16	PIS	14	ARI	14	TAU	15	CAN	14	LEO
17	AQU	18	ARI	16	TAU	16	GEM	17	LEO	17	VIR
19	PIS	20	TAU	18	GEM	18	CAN	20	VIR	19	LIB
21	ARI	22	GEM	21	CAN	21	LEO	22	LIB	22	SCO
23	TAU	25	CAN	23	LEO	23	VIR	24	SCO	24	SAG
26	GEM	27	LEO	26	VIR	26	LIB	27	SAG	26	CAP
28	CAN	30	VIR	28	LIB	28	SCO	29	CAP	28	AQU
31	LEO					30	SAG			30	PIS

1944

JAN	FEB	MAR	APR	MAY	JUN
1 ARI	2 GEM	3 CAN	1 LEO	1 VIR	3 SCO
3 TAU	4 CAN	5 LEO	4 VIR	4 LIB	5 SAG
6 GEM	7 LEO	8 VIR	6 LIB	6 SCO	7 CAP
8 CAN	9 VIR	10 LIB	9 SCO	9 SAG	9 AQU
11 LEO	12 LIB	13 SCO	11 SAG	11 CAP	11 PIS
13 VIR	14 SCO	15 SAG	14 CAP	13 AQU	13 ARI
16 LIB	17 SAG	17 CAP	16 AQU	15 PIS	16 TAU
18 SCO	19 CAP	19 AQU	18 PIS	17 ARI	18 GEM
20 SAG	21 AQU	22 PIS	20 ARI	19 TAU	20 CAN
23 CAP	23 PIS	24 ARI	22 TAU	21 GEM	22 LEO
25 AQU	25 ARI	26 TAU	24 GEM	24 CAN	25 VIR
27 PIS	27 TAU	28 GEM	26 CAN	26 LEO	27 LIB
29 ARI	29 GEM	30 CAN	29 LEO	29 VIR	30 SCO
31 TAU				31 LIB	

JUL	AUG	SEP	OCT	NOV	DEC
2 SAG	1 CAP	1 PIS	1 ARI	1 GEM	1 CAN
4 CAP	3 AQU	3 ARI	3 TAU	4 CAN	3 LEO
7 AQU	5 PIS	5 TAU	5 GEM	6 LEO	6 VIR
9 PIS	7 ARI	8 GEM	7 CAN	8 VIR	8 LIB
11 ARI	9 TAU	10 CAN	10 LEO	11 LIB	11 SCO
13 TAU	11 GEM	12 LEO	12 VIR	13 SCO	13 SAG
15 GEM	14 CAN	15 VIR	15 LIB	16 SAG	15 CAP
17 CAN	16 LEO	17 LIB	17 SCO	18 CAP	18 AQU
20 LEO	18 VIR	20 SCO	19 SAG	20 AQU	20 PIS
22 VIR	21 LIB	22 SAG	22 CAP	23 PIS	22 ARI
25 LIB	24 SCO	25 CAP	24 AQU	25 ARI	24 TAU
27 SCO	26 SAG	27 AQU	26 PIS	27 TAU	26 GEM
30 SAG	28 CAP	29 PIS	28 ARI	29 GEM	28 CAN
	30 AQU		30 TAU		31 LEO

1945

JAN	FEB	MAR	APR	MAY	JUN
2 VIR	1 LIB	3 SCO	1 SAG	1 CAP	2 PIS
4 LIB	3 SCO	5 SAG	4 CAP	3 AQU	4 ARI
7 SCO	6 SAG	8 CAP	6 AQU	6 PIS	6 TAU
9 SAG	8 CAP	10 AQU	8 PIS	8 ARI	8 GEM
12 CAP	10 AQU	12 PIS	10 ARI	10 TAU	10 CAN
14 AQU	12 PIS	14 ARI	12 TAU	12 GEM	12 LEO
16 PIS	14 ARI	16 TAU	14 GEM	14 CAN	15 VIR
18 ARI	17 TAU	18 GEM	16 CAN	16 LEO	17 LIB
20 TAU	19 GEM	20 CAN	19 LEO	18 VIR	20 SCO
22 GEM	21 CAN	22 LEO	21 VIR	21 LIB	22 SAG
25 CAN	23 LEO	25 VIR	24 LIB	23 SCO	25 CAP
27 LEO	26 VIR	27 LIB	26 SCO	26 SAG	27 AQU
29 VIR	28 LIB	30 SCO	29 SAG	28 CAP	29 PIS
				31 AQU	

JUL	AUG	SEP	OCT	NOV	DEC
1 ARI	2 GEM	2 LEO	2 VIR	1 LIB	3 SAG
3 TAU	4 CAN	5 VIR	4 LIB	3 SCO	6 CAP
6 GEM	6 LEO	7 LIB	7 SCO	6 SAG	8 AQU
8 CAN	8 VIR	10 SCO	10 SAG	8 CAP	10 PIS
10 LEO	11 LIB	12 SAG	12 CAP	11 AQU	12 ARI
12 VIR	13 SCO	15 CAP	14 AQU	13 PIS	15 TAU
15 LIB	16 SAG	17 AQU	17 PIS	15 ARI	17 GEM
17 SCO	18 CAP	19 PIS	19 ARI	17 TAU	19 CAN
20 SAG	21 AQU	21 ARI	21 TAU	19 GEM	21 LEO
22 CAP	23 PIS	23 TAU	23 GEM	21 CAN	23 VIR
24 AQU	25 ARI	25 GEM	25 CAN	23 LEO	25 LIB
26 PIS	27 TAU	27 CAN	27 LEO	26 VIR	28 SCO
29 ARI	29 GEM	30 LEO	29 VIR	28 LIB	30 SAG
31 TAU	31 CAN			30 SCO	

1946

	JAN		FEB		MAR		APR		MAY		JUN
2	CAP	1	AQU	2	PIS	1	ARI	2	GEM	1	CAN
4	AQU	3	PIS	4	ARI	3	TAU	4	CAN	3	LEO
6	PIS	5	ARI	6	TAU	5	GEM	6	LEO	5	VIR
9	ARI	7	TAU	8	GEM	7	CAN	8	VIR	7	LIB
11	TAU	9	GEM	11	CAN	9	LEO	11	LIB	10	SCO
13	GEM	11	CAN	13	LEO	11	VIR	13	SCO	12	SAG
15	CAN	13	LEO	15	VIR	14	LIB	16	SAG	15	CAP
17	LEO	16	VIR	17	LIB	16	SCO	18	CAP	17	AQU
19	VIR	18	LIB	20	SCO	19	SAG	21	AQU	20	PIS
22	LIB	20	SCO	22	SAG	21	CAP	23	PIS	22	ARI
24	SCO	23	SAG	25	CAP	24	AQU	26	ARI	24	TAU
27	SAG	26	CAP	27	AQU	26	PIS	28	TAU	26	GEM
29	CAP	28	AQU	30	PIS	28	ARI	30	GEM	28	CAN
						30	TAU			30	LEO

	JUL		AUG		SEP		OCT		NOV		DEC
2	VIR	1	LIB	2	SAG	2	CAP	1	AQU	3	ARI
4	LIB	3	SCO	5	CAP	4	AQU	3	PIS	5	TAU
7	SCO	6	SAG	7	AQU	7	PIS	5	ARI	7	GEM
9	SAG	8	CAP	9	PIS	9	ARI	7	TAU	9	CAN
12	CAP	11	AQU	12	ARI	11	TAU	10	GEM	11	LEO
14	AQU	13	PIS	14	TAU	13	GEM	12	CAN	13	VIR
17	PIS	15	ARI	16	GEM	15	CAN	14	LEO	15	LIB
19	ARI	17	TAU	18	CAN	17	LEO	16	VIR	18	SCO
21	TAU	20	GEM	20	LEO	20	VIR	18	LIB	20	SAG
23	GEM	22	CAN	22	VIR	22	LIB	20	SCO	23	CAP
25	CAN	24	LEO	25	LIB	24	SCO	23	SAG	25	AQU
27	LEO	26	VIR	27	SCO	27	SAG	25	CAP	28	PIS
30	VIR	28	LIB	29	SAG	29	CAP	28	AQU	30	ARI
		31	SCO					30	PIS		

1947

	JAN		FEB		MAR		APR		MAY		JUN
1	TAU	2	CAN	1	CAN	2	VIR	1	LIB	2	SAG
3	GEM	4	LEO	3	LEO	4	LIB	3	SCO	5	CAP
5	CAN	6	VIR	5	VIR	6	SCO	6	SAG	7	AQU
7	LEO	8	LIB	7	LIB	8	SAG	8	CAP	10	PIS
9	VIR	10	SCO	10	SCO	11	CAP	11	AQU	12	ARI
12	LIB	13	SAG	12	SAG	13	AQU	13	PIS	14	TAU
14	SCO	15	CAP	15	CAP	16	PIS	16	ARI	16	GEM
16	SAG	18	AQU	17	AQU	18	ARI	18	TAU	18	CAN
19	CAP	20	PIS	20	PIS	20	TAU	20	GEM	20	LEO
22	AQU	23	ARI	22	ARI	23	GEM	22	CAN	22	VIR
24	PIS	25	TAU	24	TAU	25	CAN	24	LEO	25	LIB
26	ARI	27	GEM	26	GEM	27	LEO	26	VIR	27	SCO
29	TAU			28	CAN	29	VIR	28	LIB	29	SAG
31	GEM			31	LEO			31	SCO		

	JUL		AUG		SEP		OCT		NOV		DEC
2	CAP	1	AQU	2	ARI	1	TAU	2	CAN	1	LEO
4	AQU	3	PIS	4	TAU	4	GEM	4	LEO	3	VIR
7	PIS	6	ARI	6	GEM	6	CAN	6	VIR	6	LIB
9	ARI	8	TAU	9	CAN	8	LEO	8	LIB	8	SCO
12	TAU	10	GEM	11	LEO	10	VIR	11	SCO	10	SAG
14	GEM	12	CAN	13	VIR	12	LIB	13	SAG	13	CAP
16	CAN	14	LEO	15	LIB	15	SCO	15	CAP	15	AQU
18	LEO	16	VIR	17	SCO	17	SAG	18	AQU	18	PIS
20	VIR	18	LIB	19	SAG	19	CAP	20	PIS	20	ARI
22	LIB	20	SCO	22	CAP	22	AQU	23	ARI	23	TAU
24	SCO	23	SAG	24	AQU	24	PIS	25	TAU	25	GEM
27	SAG	25	CAP	27	PIS	26	ARI	27	GEM	27	CAN
29	CAP	28	AQU	29	ARI	29	TAU	29	CAN	29	LEO
		30	PIS			31	GEM			31	VIR

Moon Tables

1948

JAN		FEB		MAR		APR		MAY		JUN	
2	LIB	3	SAG	1	SAG	2	AQU	2	PIS	1	ARI
4	SCO	5	CAP	3	CAP	5	PIS	5	ARI	3	TAU
6	SAG	8	AQU	6	AQU	7	ARI	7	TAU	6	GEM
9	CAP	10	PIS	8	PIS	10	TAU	9	GEM	9	CAN
11	AQU	13	ARI	11	ARI	12	GEM	11	CAN	10	LEO
14	PIS	15	TAU	13	TAU	14	CAn	14	LEO	12	VIR
16	ARI	17	GEM	16	GEM	16	LEO	16	VIR	14	LIB
19	TAU	20	CAN	18	CAN	18	VIR	18	LIB	16	SCO
21	GEM	22	LEO	20	LEO	21	LIB	20	SCO	18	SAG
23	CAN	24	VIR	22	VIR	23	SCO	22	SAG	21	CAP
25	LEO	26	LIB	24	LIB	25	SAG	25	CAP	23	AQU
27	VIR	28	SCO	26	SCO	27	CAP	27	AQU	26	PIS
29	LIB			28	SAG	30	AQU	29	PIS	28	ARI
31	SCO			31	CAP						

JUL		AUG		SEP		OCT		NOV		DEC	
1	TAU	2	CAN	2	VIR	1	LIB	2	SAG	2	CAP
3	GEM	4	LEO	4	LIB	3	SCO	4	CAP	4	AQU
5	CAN	6	VIR	6	SCO	6	SAG	7	AQU	6	PIS
7	LEO	8	LIB	8	SAG	8	CAP	9	PIS	9	ARI
9	VIR	10	SCO	11	CAP	10	AQU	12	ARI	12	TAU
11	LIB	12	SAG	13	AQU	13	PIS	14	TAU	14	GEM
13	SCO	14	CAP	16	PIS	15	ARI	17	GEM	16	CAN
16	SAG	17	AQU	18	ARI	18	TAU	19	CAN	18	LEO
18	CAP	19	PIS	21	TAU	20	GEM	21	LEO	20	VIR
21	AQU	22	ARI	23	GEM	23	CAN	23	VIR	22	LIB
23	PIS	24	TAU	25	CAN	25	LEO	25	LIB	25	SCO
26	ARI	27	GEM	27	LEO	27	VIR	27	SCO	27	SAG
28	TAU	29	CAN	29	VIR	29	LIB	29	SAG	29	CAP
30	GEM	31	LEO			31	SCO			31	AQU

1949

JAN		FEB		MAR		APR		MAY		JUN	
3	PIS	2	ARI	1	ARI	2	GEM	2	CAN	2	VIR
5	ARI	4	TAU	3	TAU	5	CAN	4	LEO	5	LIB
8	TAU	7	GEM	6	GEM	7	LEO	6	VIR	7	SCO
10	GEM	9	CAN	8	CAN	9	VIR	8	LIB	9	SAG
12	CAN	11	LEO	10	LEO	11	LIB	10	SCO	11	CAP
15	LEO	13	VIR	13	VIR	13	SCO	12	SAG	13	AQU
17	VIR	15	LIB	15	LIB	15	SAG	15	CAP	16	PIS
19	LIB	17	SCO	17	SCO	17	CAP	17	AQU	18	ARI
21	SCO	19	SAG	19	SAG	19	AQU	19	PIS	21	TAU
23	SAG	22	CAP	21	CAP	22	PIS	22	ARI	23	GEM
25	CAP	24	AQU	23	AQU	24	ARI	24	TAU	25	CAN
28	AQU	26	PIS	26	PIS	27	TAU	27	GEM	28	LEO
30	PIS			28	ARI	29	GEM	29	CAN	30	VIR
				31	TAU			31	LEO		

JUL		AUG		SEP		OCT		NOV		DEC	
2	LIB	2	SAG	1	CAP	3	PIS	2	ARI	1	TAU
4	SCO	5	CAP	3	AQU	5	ARI	4	TAU	4	GEM
6	SAG	7	AQU	6	PIS	8	TAU	7	GEM	6	CAN
8	CAP	9	PIS	8	ARI	10	GEM	9	CAN	9	LEO
11	AQU	12	ARI	11	TAU	13	CAN	11	LEO	11	VIR
13	PIS	14	TAU	13	GEM	15	LEO	14	VIR	13	LIB
15	ARI	17	GEM	15	CAN	17	VIR	16	LIB	15	SCO
18	TAU	19	CAN	18	LEO	19	LIB	18	SCO	17	SAG
20	GEM	21	LEO	20	VIR	21	SCO	20	SAG	19	CAP
23	CAN	23	VIR	22	LIB	23	SAG	22	CAP	21	AQU
25	LEO	25	LIB	24	SCO	25	CAP	24	AQU	24	PIS
27	VIR	27	SCO	26	SAG	28	AQU	26	PIS	26	ARI
29	LIB	30	SAG	28	CAP	30	PIS	29	ARI	29	TAU
31	SCO			30	AQU					31	GEM

1950

JAN		FEB		MAR		APR		MAY		JUN	
3	CAN	1	LEO	1	LEO	1	LIB	1	SCO	1	CAP
5	LEO	3	VIR	3	VIR	3	SCO	3	SAG	3	AQU
7	VIR	6	LIB	5	LIB	5	SAG	5	CAP	5	PIS
9	LIB	8	SCO	7	SCO	7	CAP	7	AQU	8	ARI
11	SCO	10	SAG	9	SAG	10	AQU	9	PIS	10	TAU
14	SAG	12	CAP	11	CAP	12	PIS	12	ARI	13	GEM
16	CAP	14	AQU	13	AQU	14	ARI	14	TAU	15	CAN
18	AQU	16	PIS	16	PIS	17	TAU	17	GEM	18	LEO
20	PIS	19	ARI	18	ARI	19	GEM	19	CAN	20	VIR
22	ARI	21	TAU	21	TAU	22	CAN	22	LEO	22	LIB
25	TAU	24	GEM	23	GEM	24	LEO	24	VIR	25	SCO
28	GEM	26	CAN	26	CAN	27	VIR	26	LIB	27	SAG
30	CAN			28	LEO	29	LIB	28	SCO	29	CAP
				30	VIR			30	SAG		

JUL		AUG		SEP		OCT		NOV		DEC	
1	AQU	2	ARI	2	GEM	3	CAN	2	LEO	1	VIR
3	PIS	4	TAU	5	CAN	5	LEO	4	VIR	3	LIB
5	ARI	7	GEM	8	LEO	7	VIR	6	LIB	6	SCO
8	TAU	9	CAN	10	VIR	10	LIB	8	SCO	8	SAG
10	GEM	11	LEO	12	LIB	12	SCO	10	SAG	10	CAP
13	CAN	14	VIR	14	SCO	14	SAG	12	CAP	12	AQU
15	LEO	16	LIB	16	SAG	16	CAP	14	AQU	14	PIS
17	VIR	18	SCO	18	CAP	18	AQU	16	PIS	16	ARI
20	LIB	20	SAG	21	AQU	20	PIS	19	ARI	19	TAU
22	SCO	22	CAP	23	PIS	23	ARI	21	TAU	21	GEM
24	SAG	24	AQU	25	ARI	25	TAU	24	GEM	24	CAN
26	CAP	27	PIS	28	TAU	28	GEM	26	CAN	26	LEO
28	AQU	29	ARI	30	GEM	30	CAN	29	LEO	28	VIR
30	PIS	31	TAU							31	LIB

1951

JAN		FEB		MAR		APR		MAY		JUN	
2	SCO	2	CAP	2	CAP	2	PIS	2	ARI	3	GEM
4	SAG	4	AQU	4	AQU	5	ARI	4	TAU	5	CAN
6	CAP	7	PIS	6	PIS	7	TAU	7	GEM	8	LEO
8	AQU	9	ARI	8	ARI	9	GEM	9	CAN	10	VIR
10	PIS	11	TAU	11	TAU	12	CAN	12	LEO	13	LIB
12	ARI	14	GEM	13	GEM	14	LEO	14	VIR	15	SCO
15	TAU	16	CAN	16	CAN	17	VIR	16	LIB	17	SAG
17	GEM	19	LEO	18	LEO	19	LIB	19	SCO	19	CAP
20	CAN	21	VIR	20	VIR	21	SCO	21	SAG	21	AQU
22	LEO	23	LIB	23	LIB	23	SAG	23	CAP	23	PIS
25	VIR	25	SCO	25	SCO	25	CAP	25	AQU	25	ARI
27	LIB	28	SAG	27	SAG	27	AQU	27	PIS	28	TAU
29	SCO			29	CAP	29	PIS	29	ARI	30	GEM
31	SAG			31	AQU			31	TAU		

JUL		AUG		SEP		OCT		NOV		DEC	
3	CAN	1	LEO	3	LIB	2	SCO	1	SAG	2	AQU
5	LEO	4	VIR	5	SCO	4	SAG	3	CAP	4	PIS
8	VIR	6	LIB	7	SAG	6	CAP	5	AQU	6	ARI
10	LIB	9	SCO	9	CAP	8	AQU	7	PIS	9	TAU
12	SCO	11	SAG	11	AQU	11	PIS	9	ARI	11	GEM
14	SAG	13	CAP	13	PIS	13	ARI	11	TAU	13	CAN
16	CAP	15	AQU	15	ARI	15	TAU	14	GEM	16	LEO
18	AQU	17	PIS	18	TAU	17	GEM	16	CAN	19	VIR
20	PIS	19	ARI	20	GEM	20	CAN	19	LEO	21	LIB
23	ARI	21	TAU	23	CAN	22	LEO	21	VIR	23	SCO
25	TAU	24	GEM	25	LEO	25	VIR	24	LIB	25	SAG
27	GEM	26	CAN	28	VIR	27	LIB	26	SCO	27	CAP
30	CAN	29	LEO	30	LIB	29	SCO	28	SAG	29	AQU
		31	VIR					30	CAP	31	PIS

Moon Tables

1952

JAN		FEB		MAR		APR		MAY		JUN	
3	ARI	1	TAU	2	GEM	1	CAN	3	VIR	2	LIB
5	TAU	3	GEM	4	CAN	3	LEO	5	LIB	4	SCO
7	GEM	6	CAN	7	LEO	6	VIR	8	SCO	6	SAG
10	CAN	9	LEO	9	VIR	8	LIB	10	SAG	8	CAP
12	LEO	11	VIR	12	LIB	10	SCO	12	CAP	10	AQU
15	VIR	14	LIB	14	SCO	13	SAG	14	AQU	12	PIS
17	LIB	16	SCO	16	SAG	15	CAP	16	PIS	15	ARI
20	SCO	18	SAG	19	CAP	17	AQU	18	ARI	17	TAU
22	SAG	20	CAP	21	AQU	19	PIS	21	TAU	19	GEM
24	CAP	22	AQU	23	PIS	21	ARI	23	GEM	22	CAN
26	AQU	24	PIS	25	ARI	23	TAU	25	CAN	24	LEO
28	PIS	26	ARI	27	TAU	26	GEM	28	LEO	27	VIR
30	ARI	29	TAU	29	GEM	28	CAN	30	VIR	29	LIB
						30	LEO				

JUL		AUG		SEP		OCT		NOV		DEC	
2	SCO	2	CAP	1	AQU	2	ARI	1	TAU	2	CAN
4	SAG	4	AQU	3	PIS	4	TAU	3	GEM	5	LEO
6	CAP	6	PIS	5	ARI	6	GEM	5	CAN	7	VIR
8	AQU	8	ARI	7	TAU	9	CAN	7	LEO	10	LIB
10	PIS	10	TAU	9	GEM	11	LEO	10	VIR	12	SCO
12	ARI	13	GEM	11	CAN	14	VIR	13	LIB	15	SAG
14	TAU	15	CAN	14	LEO	16	LIB	15	SCO	17	CAP
16	GEM	18	LEO	16	VIR	19	SCO	17	SAG	19	AQU
19	CAN	20	VIR	19	LIB	21	SAG	19	CAP	21	PIS
21	LEO	23	LIB	21	SCO	23	CAP	21	AQU	23	ARI
24	VIR	25	SCO	24	SAG	25	AQU	24	PIS	25	TAU
26	LIB	27	SAG	26	CAP	27	PIS	26	ARI	27	GEM
29	SCO	30	CAP	28	AQU	29	ARI	28	TAU	30	CAN
31	SAG			30	PIS			30	GEM		

1953

JAN		FEB		MAR		APR		MAY		JUN	
1	LEO	3	LIB	2	LIB	1	SCO	2	CAP	1	AQU
4	VIR	5	SCO	4	SCO	3	SAG	5	AQU	3	PIS
6	LIB	7	SAG	7	SAG	5	CAP	7	PIS	5	ARI
9	SCO	10	CAP	9	CAP	7	AQU	9	ARI	7	TAU
11	SAG	12	AQU	11	AQU	10	PIS	11	TAU	9	GEM
13	CAP	14	PIS	13	PIS	12	ARI	13	GEM	12	CAN
15	AQU	16	ARI	15	ARI	14	TAU	15	CAN	14	LEO
17	PIS	18	TAU	17	TAU	16	GEM	18	LEO	16	VIR
19	ARI	20	GEM	19	GEM	18	CAN	20	VIR	19	LIB
21	TAU	22	CAN	22	CAN	20	LEO	23	LIB	21	SCO
24	GEM	25	LEO	24	LEO	23	VIR	25	SCO	24	SAG
26	CAN	27	VIR	27	VIR	25	LIB	27	SAG	26	CAP
28	LEO			29	LIB	28	SCO	30	CAP	28	AQU
31	VIR					30	SAG			30	PIS

JUL		AUG		SEP		OCT		NOV		DEC	
2	ARI	1	TAU	1	CAN	1	LEO	2	LIB	2	SCO
5	TAU	3	GEM	4	LEO	4	VIR	5	SCO	5	SAG
7	GEM	5	CAN	6	VIR	6	LIB	7	SAG	7	CAP
9	CAN	8	LEO	9	LIB	9	SCO	10	CAP	9	AQU
11	LEO	10	VIR	11	SCO	11	SAG	12	AQU	11	PIS
14	VIR	13	LIB	14	SAG	13	CAP	14	PIS	14	ARI
16	LIB	15	SCO	16	CAP	16	AQU	16	ARI	16	TAU
19	SCO	18	SAG	18	AQU	18	PIS	18	TAU	18	GEM
21	SAG	20	CAP	21	PIS	20	ARI	20	GEM	20	CAN
23	CAP	22	AQU	23	ARI	22	TAU	22	CAN	22	LEO
26	AQU	24	PIS	25	TAU	24	GEM	25	LEO	25	VIR
28	PIS	26	ARI	27	GEM	26	CAN	27	VIR	27	LIB
30	ARI	28	TAU	29	CAN	28	LEO	30	LIB	30	SCO
		30	GEM			31	VIR				

1954

JAN		FEB		MAR		APR		MAY		JUN	
1	SAG	2	AQU	1	AQU	2	ARI	1	TAU	2	CAN
3	CAP	4	PIS	3	PIS	4	TAU	3	GEM	4	LEO
6	AQU	6	ARI	5	ARI	6	GEM	5	CAN	6	VIR
8	PIS	8	TAU	7	TAU	8	CAN	8	LEO	9	LIB
10	ARI	10	GEM	10	GEM	10	LEO	10	VIR	11	SCO
12	TAU	13	CAN	12	CAN	13	VIR	12	LIB	14	SAG
14	GEM	15	LEO	14	LEO	15	LIB	15	SCO	16	CAP
16	CAN	17	VIR	16	VIR	18	SCO	17	SAG	19	AQU
19	LEO	20	LIB	19	LIB	20	SAG	20	CAP	21	PIS
21	VIR	22	SCO	21	SCO	23	CAP	22	AQU	23	ARI
23	LIB	25	SAG	24	SAG	25	AQU	25	PIS	25	TAU
26	SCO	27	CAP	26	CAP	27	PIS	27	ARI	27	GEM
28	SAG			29	AQU	29	ARI	29	TAU	29	CAN
31	CAP			31	PIS			31	GEM		

JUL		AUG		SEP		OCT		NOV		DEC	
1	LEO	2	LIB	1	SCO	1	SAG	2	AQU	2	PIS
4	VIR	5	SCO	4	SAG	4	CAP	5	PIS	4	ARI
6	LIB	7	SAG	6	CAP	6	AQU	7	ARI	6	TAU
9	SCO	10	CAP	9	AQU	8	PIS	9	TAU	8	GEM
11	SAG	12	AQU	11	PIS	10	ARI	11	GEM	10	CAN
14	CAP	14	PIS	13	ARI	12	TAU	13	CAN	12	LEO
16	AQU	16	ARI	15	TAU	14	GEM	15	LEO	14	VIR
18	PIS	19	TAU	17	GEM	16	CAN	17	VIR	17	LIB
20	ARI	21	GEM	19	CAN	19	LEO	20	LIB	19	SCO
22	TAU	23	CAN	21	LEO	21	VIR	22	SCO	22	SAG
24	GEM	25	LEO	24	VIR	23	LIB	25	SAG	24	CAP
27	CAN	27	VIR	26	LIB	26	SCO	27	CAP	27	AQU
29	LEO	30	LIB	29	SCO	28	SAG	30	AQU	29	PIS
31	VIR					31	CAP			31	ARI

1955

JAN		FEB		MAR		APR		MAY		JUN	
3	TAU	1	GEM	2	CAN	1	LEO	2	LIB	1	SCO
5	GEM	3	CAN	4	LEO	3	VIR	5	SCO	4	SAG
7	CAN	5	LEO	7	VIR	5	LIB	7	SAG	6	CAP
9	LEO	7	VIR	9	LIB	8	SCO	10	CAP	9	AQU
11	VIR	10	LIB	11	SCO	10	SAG	12	AQU	11	PIS
13	LIB	12	SCO	14	SAG	13	CAP	15	PIS	13	ARI
16	SCO	15	SAG	16	CAP	15	AQU	17	ARI	16	TAU
18	SAG	17	CAP	19	AQU	18	PIS	19	TAU	18	GEM
21	CAP	19	AQU	21	PIS	20	ARI	21	GEM	20	CAN
23	AQU	22	PIS	23	ARI	22	TAU	23	CAN	22	LEO
25	PIS	24	ARI	25	TAU	24	GEM	25	LEO	24	VIR
28	ARI	26	TAU	27	GEM	26	CAN	27	VIR	26	LIB
30	TAU	28	GEM	29	CAN	28	LEO	30	LIB	28	SCO
						30	VIR				

JUL		AUG		SEP		OCT		NOV		DEC	
1	SAG	2	AQU	1	PIS	1	ARI	1	GEM	1	CAN
3	CAP	5	PIS	3	ARI	3	TAU	3	CAN	3	LEO
6	AQU	7	ARI	5	TAU	5	GEM	5	LEO	5	VIR
8	PIS	9	TAU	8	GEM	7	CAN	7	VIR	7	LIB
11	ARI	11	GEM	10	CAN	9	LEO	10	LIB	9	SCO
13	TAU	13	CAN	12	LEO	11	VIR	12	SCO	12	SAG
15	GEM	15	LEO	14	VIR	13	LIB	15	SAG	14	CAP
17	CAN	18	VIR	16	LIB	16	SCO	17	CAP	17	AQU
19	LEO	20	LIB	18	SCO	18	SAG	20	AQU	19	PIS
21	VIR	22	SCO	21	SAG	21	CAP	22	PIS	22	ARI
23	LIB	25	SAG	23	CAP	23	AQU	24	ARI	24	TAU
26	SCO	27	CAP	26	AQU	26	PIS	27	TAU	26	GEM
28	SAG	30	AQU	28	PIS	28	ARI	29	GEM	28	CAN
31	CAP					30	TAU			30	LEO

1956

	JAN		FEB		MAR		APR		MAY		JUN
1	VIR	2	SCO	3	SAG	1	CAP	1	AQU	3	ARI
3	LIB	4	SAG	5	CAP	4	AQU	4	PIS	5	TAU
6	SCO	7	CAP	8	AQU	6	PIS	6	ARI	7	GEM
8	SAG	9	AQU	10	PIS	9	ARI	8	TAU	9	CAN
11	CAP	12	PIS	12	ARI	11	TAU	11	GEM	11	LEO
13	AQU	14	ARI	15	TAU	13	GEM	13	CAN	13	VIR
16	PIS	16	TAU	17	GEM	15	CAN	15	LEO	15	LIB
18	ARI	19	GEM	19	CAN	17	LEO	17	VIR	18	SCO
20	TAU	21	CAN	21	LEO	20	VIR	19	LIB	20	SAG
22	GEM	23	LEO	23	VIR	22	LIB	21	SCO	22	CAP
24	CAN	25	VIR	25	LIB	24	SCO	24	SAG	25	AQU
26	LEO	27	LIB	28	SCO	26	SAG	26	CAP	27	PIS
28	VIR	29	SCO	30	SAG	29	CAP	29	AQU	30	ARI
31	LIB							31	PIS		

	JUL		AUG		SEP		OCT		NOV		DEC
2	TAU	1	GEM	1	LEO	1	VIR	1	SCO	1	SAG
4	GEM	3	CAN	3	VIR	3	LIB	3	SAG	3	CAP
6	CAN	5	LEO	5	LIB	5	SCO	6	CAP	6	AQU
8	LEO	7	VIR	7	SCO	7	SAG	8	AQU	8	PIS
10	VIR	9	LIB	10	SAG	10	CAP	11	PIS	11	ARI
12	LIB	11	SCO	12	CAP	12	AQU	13	ARI	13	TAU
15	SCO	13	SAG	15	AQU	15	PIS	16	TAU	15	GEM
17	SAG	16	CAP	17	PIS	17	ARI	18	GEM	17	CAN
20	CAP	18	AQU	20	ARI	19	TAU	20	CAN	19	LEO
22	AQU	21	PIS	22	TAU	22	GEM	22	LEO	21	VIR
25	PIS	23	ARI	24	GEM	24	CAN	24	VIR	24	LIB
27	ARI	26	TAU	26	CAN	26	LEO	26	LIB	26	SCO
30	TAU	28	GEM	29	LEO	28	VIR	29	SCO	28	SAG
		30	CAN			30	LIB			31	CAP

1957

	JAN		FEB		MAR		APR		MAY		JUN
2	AQU	1	PIS	3	ARI	1	TAU	1	GEM	1	LEO
5	PIS	3	ARI	5	TAU	4	GEM	3	CAN	4	VIR
7	ARI	6	TAU	7	GEM	6	CAN	5	LEO	6	LIB
9	TAU	8	GEM	10	CAN	8	LEO	7	VIR	8	SCO
12	GEM	10	CAN	12	LEO	10	VIR	9	LIB	10	SAG
14	CAN	12	LEO	14	VIR	12	LIB	12	SCO	12	CAP
16	LEO	14	VIR	16	LIB	14	SCO	14	SAG	15	AQU
18	VIR	16	LIB	18	SCO	16	SAG	16	CAP	17	PIS
20	LIB	18	SCO	20	SAG	19	CAP	18	AQU	20	ARI
22	SCO	21	SAG	22	CAP	21	AQU	21	PIS	22	TAU
24	SAG	23	CAP	25	AQU	24	PIS	23	ARI	25	GEM
27	CAP	26	AQU	27	PIS	26	ARI	26	TAU	27	CAN
29	AQU	28	PIS	30	ARI	29	TAU	28	GEM	29	LEO
								30	CAN		

	JUL		AUG		SEP		OCT		NOV		DEC
1	VIR	1	SCO	2	CAP	2	AQU	1	PIS	1	ARI
3	LIB	4	SAG	5	AQU	4	PIS	3	ARI	3	TAU
5	SCO	6	CAP	7	PIS	7	ARI	6	TAU	5	GEM
7	SAG	8	AQU	10	ARI	9	TAU	8	GEM	8	CAN
10	CAP	11	PIS	12	TAU	12	GEM	10	CAN	10	LEO
12	AQU	13	ARI	15	GEM	14	CAN	13	LEO	12	VIR
15	PIS	16	TAU	17	CAN	16	LEO	15	VIR	14	LIB
17	ARI	18	GEM	19	LEO	18	VIR	17	LIB	16	SCO
20	TAU	21	CAN	21	VIR	21	LIB	19	SCO	18	SAG
22	GEM	23	LEO	23	LIB	23	SCO	21	SAG	21	CAP
24	CAN	25	VIR	25	SCO	25	SAG	23	CAP	23	AQU
26	LEO	27	LIB	27	SAG	27	CAP	26	AQU	25	PIS
28	VIR	29	SCO	29	CAP	29	AQU	28	PIS	28	ARI
30	LIB	31	SAG							30	TAU

1958

JAN		FEB		MAR		APR		MAY		JUN	
2	GEM	3	LEO	2	LEO	1	VIR	2	SCO	3	CAP
4	CAN	5	VIR	4	VIR	3	LIB	4	SAG	5	AQU
6	LEO	7	LIB	6	LIB	5	SCO	6	CAP	7	PIS
8	VIR	9	SCO	8	SCO	7	SAG	8	AQU	10	ARI
10	LIB	11	SAG	10	SAG	9	CAP	11	PIS	12	TAU
12	SCO	13	CAP	12	CAP	11	AQU	13	ARI	15	GEM
15	SAG	16	AQU	15	AQU	13	PIS	16	TAU	17	CAN
17	CAP	18	PIS	17	PIS	16	ARI	18	GEM	19	LEO
19	AQU	21	ARI	20	ARI	19	RAU	21	CAN	21	VIR
22	PIS	23	TAU	22	TAU	21	GEM	23	LEO	24	LIB
24	ARI	26	GEM	25	GEM	23	CAN	25	VIR	26	SCO
27	TAU	28	CAN	27	CAN	26	LEO	27	LIB	28	SAG
29	GEM			29	LEO	28	VIR	29	SCO	30	CAP
31	CAN					30	LIB	31	SAG		

JUL		AUG		SEP		OCT		NOV		DEC	
2	AQU	1	PIS	2	TAU	2	GEM	1	CAN	3	VIR
4	PIS	3	ARI	5	GEM	4	CAN	3	LEO	5	LIB
7	ARI	6	TAU	7	CAN	7	LEO	5	VIR	7	SCO
9	TAU	8	GEM	9	LEO	9	VIR	7	LIB	9	SAG
12	GEM	11	CAN	11	VIR	11	LIB	9	SCO	11	CAP
14	CAN	13	LEO	13	LIB	13	SCO	11	SAG	13	AQU
17	LEO	15	VIR	15	SCO	15	SAG	13	CAP	15	PIS
19	VIR	17	LIB	18	SAG	17	CAP	16	AQU	18	ARI
21	LIB	19	SCO	20	CAP	19	AQU	18	PIS	20	TAU
23	SCO	21	SAG	22	AQU	22	PIS	20	ARI	23	GEM
25	SAG	23	CAP	24	PIS	24	ARI	23	TAU	25	CAN
27	CAP	26	AQU	27	ARI	27	TAU	25	GEM	27	LEO
29	AQU	28	PIS	29	TAU	29	GEM	28	CAN	30	VIR
		31	ARI					30	LEO		

1959

JAN		FEB		MAR		APR		MAY		JUN	
1	LIB	1	SAG	1	SAG	1	AQU	1	PIS	2	TAU
3	SCO	4	CAP	3	CAP	4	PIS	3	ARI	5	GEM
5	SAG	6	AQU	5	AQU	6	ARI	6	TAU	7	CAN
7	CAP	8	PIS	7	PIS	8	TAU	8	GEM	9	LEO
9	AQU	10	ARI	10	ARI	11	GEM	11	CAN	12	VIR
12	PIS	13	TAU	12	TAU	14	CAN	13	LEO	14	LIB
14	ARI	15	GEM	15	GEM	16	LEO	16	VIR	16	SCO
17	TAU	18	CAN	17	CAN	18	VIR	18	LIB	18	SAG
19	GEM	20	LEO	20	LEO	20	LIB	20	SCO	20	CAP
21	CAN	22	VIR	22	VIR	22	SCO	22	SAG	22	AQU
24	LEO	24	LIB	24	LIB	24	SAG	24	CAP	24	PIS
26	VIR	27	SCO	26	SCO	26	CAP	26	AQU	27	ARI
28	LIB			28	SAG	28	AQU	28	PIS	29	TAU
30	SCO			30	CAP			30	ARI		

JUL		AUG		SEP		OCT		NOV		DEC	
2	GEM	1	CAN	2	VIR	1	LIB	2	SAG	1	CAP
4	CAN	3	LEO	4	LIB	3	SCO	4	CAP	3	AQU
7	LEO	5	VIR	6	SCO	5	SAG	6	AQU	5	PIS
9	VIR	8	LIB	8	SAG	7	CAP	8	PIS	8	ARI
11	LIB	10	SCO	10	CAP	10	AQU	10	ARI	10	TAU
13	SCO	12	SAG	12	AQU	12	PIS	13	TAU	13	GEM
16	SAG	14	CAP	15	PIS	14	ARI	15	GEM	15	CAN
18	CAP	16	AQU	17	ARI	17	TAU	18	CAN	18	LEO
20	AQU	18	PIS	19	TAU	19	GEM	20	LEO	20	VIR
22	PIS	20	ARI	22	GEM	22	CAN	23	VIR	22	LIB
24	ARI	23	TAU	24	CAN	24	LEO	25	LIB	25	SCO
27	TAU	25	GEM	27	LEO	26	VIR	27	SCO	27	SAG
29	GEM	28	CAN	29	VIR	29	LIB	29	SAG	29	CAP
		30	LEO			31	SCO			31	AQU

1960

	JAN		FEB		MAR		APR		MAY		JUN
2	PIS	3	TAU	1	TAU	2	CAN	2	LEO	1	VIR
4	ARI	5	GEM	4	GEM	5	LEO	5	VIR	3	LIB
6	TAU	8	CAN	6	CAN	7	VIR	7	LIB	6	SCO
9	GEM	10	LEO	9	LEO	10	LIB	9	SCO	8	SAG
11	CAN	13	VIR	11	VIR	12	SCO	11	SAG	10	CAP
14	LEO	15	LIB	13	LIB	14	SAG	13	CAP	12	AQU
16	VIR	17	SCO	15	SCO	16	CAP	15	AQU	14	PIS
19	LIB	19	SAG	17	SAG	18	AQU	17	PIS	16	ARI
21	SCO	21	CAP	20	CAP	20	PIS	20	ARI	18	TAU
23	SAG	23	AQU	22	AQU	22	ARI	22	TAU	21	GEM
25	CAP	26	PIS	24	PIS	25	TAU	24	GEM	23	CAN
27	AQU	28	ARI	26	ARI	27	GEM	27	CAN	26	LEO
29	PIS			28	TAU	30	CAN	29	LEO	28	VIR
31	ARI			31	GEM						

	JUL		AUG		SEP		OCT		NOV		DEC
1	LIB	1	SAG	2	AQU	1	PIS	2	TAU	2	GEM
3	SCO	3	CAP	4	PIS	3	ARI	4	GEM	4	CAN
5	SAG	5	AQU	6	ARI	6	TAU	7	CAN	7	LEO
7	CAP	7	PIS	8	TAU	8	GEM	9	LEO	9	VIR
9	AQU	10	ARI	11	GEM	10	CAN	12	VIR	12	LIB
11	PIS	12	TAU	13	CAN	13	LEO	14	LIB	14	SCO
13	ARI	14	GEM	16	LEO	15	VIR	16	SCO	16	SAG
15	TAU	17	CAN	18	VIR	18	LIB	19	SAG	18	CAP
18	GEM	19	LEO	20	LIB	20	SCO	21	CAP	20	AQU
20	CAN	22	VIR	23	SCO	22	SAG	23	AQU	22	PIS
23	LEO	24	LIB	25	SAG	24	CAP	25	PIS	24	ARI
25	VIR	26	SCO	27	CAP	26	AQU	27	ARI	26	TAU
28	LIB	29	SAG	29	AQU	28	PIS	29	TAU	29	GEM
30	SCO	31	CAP			31	ARI			31	CAN

1961

	JAN		FEB		MAR		APR		MAY		JUN
3	LEO	2	VIR	1	VIR	2	SCO	2	SAG	2	AQU
5	VIR	4	LIB	3	LIB	4	SAG	4	CAP	4	PIS
8	LIB	6	SCO	6	SCO	6	CAP	6	AQU	6	ARI
10	SCO	9	SAG	8	SAG	9	AQU	8	PIS	8	TAU
12	SAG	11	CAP	10	CAP	11	PIS	10	ARI	11	GEM
14	CAP	13	AQU	12	AQU	13	ARI	12	TAU	13	CAN
16	AQU	15	PIS	14	PIS	15	TAU	14	GEM	16	LEO
18	PIS	17	ARI	16	ARI	17	GEM	17	CAN	18	VIR
20	ARI	19	TAU	18	TAU	19	CAN	19	LEO	21	LIB
23	TAU	21	GEM	21	GEM	22	LEO	22	VIR	23	SCO
25	GEM	24	CAN	23	CAN	25	VIR	24	LIB	25	SAG
28	CAN	26	LEO	26	LEO	27	LIB	27	SCO	27	CAP
30	LEO			28	VIR	29	SCO	29	SAG	29	AQU
				31	LIB			31	CAP		

	JUL		AUG		SEP		OCT		NOV		DEC
1	PIS	2	TAU	1	GEM	3	LEO	2	VIR	1	LIB
4	ARI	4	GEM	3	CAN	5	VIR	4	LIB	4	SCO
6	TAU	7	CAN	5	LEO	8	LIB	6	SCO	6	SAG
8	GEM	9	LEO	8	VIR	10	SCO	9	SAG	8	CAP
10	CAN	12	VIR	10	LIB	13	SAG	11	CAP	10	AQU
13	LEO	14	LIB	13	SCO	15	CAP	13	AQU	13	PIS
15	VIR	17	SCO	15	SAG	17	AQU	15	PIS	15	ARI
18	LIB	19	SAG	18	CAP	19	PIS	17	ARI	17	TAU
20	SCO	21	CAP	20	AQU	21	ARI	20	TAU	19	GEM
23	SAG	23	AQU	22	PIS	23	TAU	22	GEM	21	CAN
25	CAP	25	PIS	24	ARI	25	GEM	24	CAN	24	LEO
27	AQU	27	ARI	26	TAU	28	CAN	26	LEO	26	VIR
29	PIS	29	TAU	28	GEM	30	LEO	29	VIR	29	LIB
31	ARI			30	CAN					31	SCO

1962

JAN		FEB		MAR		APR		MAY		JUN	
3	SAG	1	CAP	1	CAP	1	PIS	1	ARI	1	GEM
5	CAP	3	AQU	3	AQU	3	ARI	3	TAU	3	CAN
7	AQU	5	PIS	5	PIS	5	TAU	5	GEM	6	LEO
9	PIS	7	ARI	7	ARI	7	GEM	7	CAN	8	VIR
11	ARI	9	TAU	9	TAU	9	CAN	9	LEO	10	LIB
13	TAU	12	GEM	11	GEM	12	LEO	12	VIR	13	SCO
15	GEM	14	CAN	13	CAN	14	VIR	14	LIB	15	SAG
18	CAN	16	LEO	16	LEO	17	LIB	17	SCO	18	CAP
20	LEO	19	VIR	18	VIR	19	SCO	19	SAG	20	AQU
23	VIR	21	LIB	21	LIB	22	SAG	21	CAP	22	PIS
25	LIB	24	SCO	23	SCO	24	CAP	24	AQU	24	ARI
28	SCO	26	SAG	26	SAG	26	AQU	26	PIS	26	TAU
30	SAG			28	CAP	28	PIS	28	ARI	28	GEM

JUL		AUG		SEP		OCT		NOV		DEC	
1	CAN	2	VIR	3	SCO	3	SAG	1	CAP	1	AQU
3	LEO	4	LIB	5	SAG	5	CAP	4	AQU	3	PIS
5	VIR	7	SCO	8	CAP	7	AQU	6	PIS	5	ARI
8	LIB	9	SAG	10	AQU	10	PIS	8	ARI	7	TAU
10	SCO	11	CAP	12	PIS	12	ARI	10	TAU	9	GEM
13	SAG	14	AQU	14	ARI	14	TAU	12	GEM	11	CAN
15	CAP	16	PIS	16	TAU	16	GEM	14	CAN	14	LEO
17	AQU	18	ARI	18	GEM	18	CAN	16	LEO	16	VIR
19	PIS	20	TAU	20	CAN	20	LEO	19	VIR	19	LIB
21	ARI	22	GEM	23	LEO	22	VIR	21	LIB	21	SCO
23	TAU	24	CAN	25	VIR	25	LIB	24	SCO	24	SAG
26	GEM	26	LEO	28	LIB	27	SCO	26	SAG	26	CAP
28	CAN	29	VIR	30	SCO	30	SAG	29	CAP	28	AQU
30	LEO	31	LIB							30	PIS

1963

JAN		FEB		MAR		APR		MAY		JUN	
1	ARI	2	GEM	1	GEM	2	LEO	2	VIR	3	SCO
4	TAU	4	CAN	3	CAN	4	VIR	4	LIB	5	SAG
6	GEM	6	LEO	6	LEO	7	LIB	7	SCO	8	CAP
8	CAN	9	VIR	8	VIR	9	SCO	9	SAG	10	AQU
10	LEO	11	LIB	11	LIB	12	SAG	12	CAP	12	PIS
12	VIR	14	SCO	13	SCO	14	CAP	14	AQU	15	ARI
15	LIB	16	SAG	16	SAG	17	AQU	16	PIS	17	TAU
17	SCO	19	CAP	18	CAP	19	PIS	18	ARI	19	GEM
20	SAG	21	AQU	20	AQU	21	ARI	20	TAU	21	CAN
22	CAP	23	PIS	23	PIS	23	TAU	22	GEM	23	LEO
25	AQU	25	ARI	25	ARI	25	GEM	24	CAN	25	VIR
27	PIS	27	TAU	27	TAU	27	CAN	27	LEO	28	LIB
29	ARI			29	GEM	29	LEO	29	VIR	30	SCO
31	TAU			31	CAN			31	LIB		

JUL		AUG		SEP		OCT		NOV		DEC	
3	SAG	1	CAP	2	PIS	2	ARI	2	GEM	2	CAN
5	CAP	4	AQU	4	ARI	4	TAU	4	CAN	4	LEO
7	AQU	6	PIS	7	TAU	6	GEM	6	LEO	6	VIR
10	PIS	8	ARI	9	GEM	8	CAN	9	VIR	8	LIB
12	ARI	10	TAU	11	CAN	10	LEO	11	LIB	11	SCO
14	TAU	12	GEM	13	LEO	12	VIR	14	SCO	13	SAG
16	GEM	14	CAN	15	VIR	15	LIB	16	SAG	16	CAP
18	CAN	17	LEO	18	LIB	17	SCO	19	CAP	18	AQU
20	LEO	19	VIR	20	SCO	20	SAG	21	AQU	21	PIS
23	VIR	21	LIB	23	SAG	22	CAP	24	PIS	23	ARI
25	LIB	24	SCO	25	CAP	25	AQU	26	ARI	25	TAU
27	SCO	26	SAG	28	AQU	27	PIS	28	TAU	27	GEM
30	SAG	29	CAP	30	PIS	29	ARI	30	GEM	29	CAN
		31	AQU			31	TAU				

1964

	JAN		FEB		MAR		APR		MAY		JUN
2	VIR	1	LIB	2	SCO	1	SAG	1	CAP	2	PIS
5	LIB	4	SCO	4	SAG	3	CAP	3	AQU	4	ARI
7	SCO	6	SAG	7	CAP	6	AQU	5	PIS	6	TAU
10	SAG	9	CAP	9	AQU	8	PIS	8	ARI	8	GEM
12	CAP	11	AQU	12	PIS	10	ARI	10	TAU	10	CAN
15	AQU	13	PIS	14	ARI	12	TAU	12	GEM	12	LEO
17	PIS	16	ARI	16	TAU	14	GEM	14	CAN	14	VIR
19	ARI	18	TAU	18	GEM	16	CAN	16	LEO	17	LIB
21	TAU	20	GEM	20	CAN	19	LEO	18	VIR	19	SCO
24	GEM	22	CAN	22	LEO	21	VIR	20	LIB	22	SAG
26	CAN	24	LEO	25	VIR	23	LIB	23	SCO	24	CAP
28	LEO	26	VIR	27	LIB	26	SCO	25	SAG	27	AQU
30	VIR	28	LIB	29	SCO	28	SAG	28	CAP	29	PIS
								30	AQU		

	JUL		AUG		SEP		OCT		NOV		DEC
1	ARI	2	GEM	2	LEO	2	VIR	3	SCO	2	SAG
4	TAU	4	CAN	5	VIR	4	LIB	5	SAG	5	CAP
6	GEM	6	LEO	7	LIB	6	SCO	8	CAP	7	AQU
8	CAN	8	VIR	9	SCO	9	SAG	10	AQU	10	PIS
10	LEO	10	LIB	11	SAG	11	CAP	13	PIS	12	ARI
12	VIR	13	SCO	14	CAP	14	AQU	15	ARI	15	TAU
14	LIB	15	SAG	16	AQU	16	PIS	17	TAU	17	GEM
16	SCO	18	CAP	19	PIS	19	ARI	19	GEM	19	CAN
19	SAG	20	AQU	21	ARI	21	TAU	21	CAN	21	LEO
21	CAP	23	PIS	23	TAU	23	GEM	23	LEO	23	VIR
24	AQU	25	ARI	25	GEM	25	CAN	25	VIR	25	LIB
26	PIS	27	TAU	28	CAN	27	LEO	28	LIB	27	SCO
29	ARI	29	GEM	30	LEO	29	VIR	30	SCO	30	SAG
31	TAU	31	CAN			31	LIB				

1965

	JAN		FEB		MAR		APR		MAY		JUN
1	CAP	2	PIS	2	PIS	3	TAU	2	GEM	1	CAN
4	AQU	5	ARI	4	ARI	5	GEM	4	CAN	3	LEO
6	PIS	7	TAU	6	TAU	7	CAN	6	LEO	5	VIR
9	ARI	9	GEM	9	GEM	9	LEO	8	VIR	7	LIB
11	TAU	11	CAN	11	CAN	11	VIR	11	LIB	9	SCO
13	GEM	13	LEO	13	LEO	13	LIB	13	SCO	12	SAG
15	CAN	16	VIR	15	VIR	16	SCO	15	SAG	14	CAP
17	LEO	18	LIB	17	LIB	18	SAG	18	CAP	16	AQU
19	VIR	20	SCO	19	SCO	20	CAP	20	AQU	19	PIS
21	LIB	22	SAG	22	SAG	23	AQU	23	PIS	21	ARI
23	SCO	25	CAP	24	CAP	25	PIS	25	ARI	24	TAU
26	SAG	27	AQU	27	AQU	28	ARI	27	TAU	26	GEM
28	CAP			29	PIS	30	TAU	30	GEM	28	CAN
31	AQU			31	ARI					30	LEO

	JUL		AUG		SEP		OCT		NOV		DEC
2	VIR	3	SCO	1	SAG	1	CAP	2	PIS	2	ARI
4	LIB	5	SAG	4	CAP	4	AQU	5	ARI	5	TAU
6	SCO	7	CAP	6	AQU	6	PIS	7	TAU	7	GEM
9	SAG	10	AQU	9	PIS	9	ARI	9	GEM	9	CAN
11	CAP	13	PIS	11	ARI	11	TAU	12	CAN	11	LEO
14	AQU	15	ARI	14	TAU	13	GEM	14	LEO	13	VIR
16	PIS	17	TAU	16	GEM	15	CAN	16	VIR	15	LIB
19	ARI	20	GEM	18	CAN	17	LEO	18	LIB	17	SCO
21	TAU	22	CAN	20	LEO	20	VIR	20	SCO	20	SAG
23	GEM	24	LEO	22	VIR	22	LIB	22	SAG	22	CAP
25	CAN	26	VIR	24	LIB	24	SCO	25	CAP	25	AQU
27	LEO	28	LIB	26	SCO	26	SAG	27	AQU	27	PIS
29	VIR	30	SCO	29	SAG	28	CAP	30	PIS	30	ARI
31	LIB					31	AQU				

1966

	JAN		FEB		MAR		APR		MAY		JUN
1	TAU	2	CAN	1	CAN	2	VIR	1	LIB	2	SAG
3	GEM	4	LEO	3	LEO	4	LIB	3	SCO	4	CAP
5	CAN	6	VIR	5	VIR	6	SCO	5	SAG	6	AQU
7	LEO	8	LIB	7	LIB	8	SAG	8	CAP	9	PIS
9	VIR	10	SCO	9	SCO	10	CAP	10	AQU	11	ARI
11	LIB	12	SAG	12	SAG	13	AQU	12	PIS	14	TAU
14	SCO	15	CAP	14	CAP	15	PIS	15	ARI	16	GEM
16	SAG	17	AQU	16	AQU	18	ARI	17	TAU	18	CAN
18	CAP	20	PIS	19	PIS	20	TAU	20	GEM	20	LEO
21	AQU	22	ARI	21	ARI	22	GEM	22	CAN	23	VIR
23	PIS	25	TAU	24	TAU	25	CAN	24	LEO	25	LIB
26	ARI	27	GEM	26	GEM	27	LEO	26	VIR	27	SCO
28	TAU			29	CAN	29	VIR	28	LIB	29	SAG
31	GEM			31	LEO			31	SCO		

	JUL		AUG		SEP		OCT		NOV		DEC
1	CAP	2	PIS	1	ARI	1	TAU	2	CAN	2	LEO
4	AQU	5	ARI	4	TAU	3	GEM	4	LEO	4	VIR
6	PIS	7	TAU	6	GEM	6	CAN	6	VIR	6	LIB
9	ARI	10	GEM	9	CAN	8	LEO	8	LIB	8	SCO
11	TAU	12	CAN	11	LEO	10	VIR	11	SCO	10	SAG
14	GEM	14	LEO	13	VIR	12	LIB	13	SAG	12	CAP
16	CAN	16	VIR	15	LIB	14	SCO	15	CAP	14	AQU
18	LEO	18	LIB	17	SCO	16	SAG	17	AQU	17	PIS
20	VIR	20	SCO	19	SAG	18	CAP	20	PIS	19	ARI
22	LIB	22	SAG	21	CAP	21	AQU	22	ARI	22	TAU
24	SCO	25	CAP	23	AQU	23	PIS	25	TAU	24	GEM
26	SAG	27	AQU	26	PIS	26	ARI	27	GEM	27	CAN
29	CAP	30	PIS	28	ARI	28	TAU	29	CAN	29	LEO
31	AQU					31	GEM			31	VIR

1967

	JAN		FEB		MAR		APR		MAY		JUN
2	LIB	3	SAG	2	SAG	3	AQU	2	PIS	1	ARI
4	SCO	5	CAP	4	CAP	5	PIS	5	ARI	4	TAU
6	SAG	7	AQU	6	AQU	8	ARI	7	TAU	6	GEM
9	CAP	10	PIS	9	PIS	10	TAU	10	GEM	9	CAN
11	AQU	12	ARI	11	ARI	13	GEM	12	CAN	11	LEO
13	PIS	15	TAU	14	TAU	15	CAN	15	LEO	13	VIR
16	ARI	17	GEM	16	GEM	17	LEO	17	VIR	15	LIB
18	TAU	19	CAN	19	CAN	20	VIR	19	LIB	17	SCO
21	GEM	22	LEO	21	LEO	22	LIB	21	SCO	19	SAG
23	CAN	24	VIR	23	VIR	24	SCO	23	SAG	21	CAP
25	LEO	26	LIB	25	LIB	26	SAG	25	CAP	24	AQU
27	VIR	28	SCO	27	SCO	28	CAP	27	AQU	26	PIS
29	LIB			29	SAG	30	AQU	30	PIS	28	ARI
31	SCO			31	CAP						

	JUL		AUG		SEP		OCT		NOV		DEC
1	TAU	2	CAN	1	LEO	2	LIB	1	SCO	2	CAP
3	GEM	4	LEO	3	VIR	3	SCO	3	SAG	4	AQU
6	CAN	7	VIR	5	LIB	6	SAG	5	CAP	7	PIS
8	LEO	9	LIB	7	SCO	9	CAP	7	AQU	9	ARI
10	VIR	11	SCO	9	SAG	11	AQU	9	PIS	12	TAU
12	LIB	13	SAG	11	CAP	13	PIS	12	ARI	14	GEM
15	SCO	15	CAP	14	AQU	16	ARI	14	TAU	17	CAN
17	SAG	17	AQU	16	PIS	18	TAU	17	GEM	19	LEO
19	CAP	20	PIS	18	ARI	21	GEM	19	CAN	21	VIR
21	AQU	22	ARI	21	TAU	23	CAN	22	LEO	24	LIB
23	PIS	25	TAU	23	GEM	26	LEO	24	VIR	26	SCO
26	ARI	27	GEM	26	CAN	28	VIR	26	LIB	28	SAG
28	TAU	30	CAN	28	LEO	30	LIB	28	SCO	30	CAP
31	GEM			30	VIR			30	SAG		

1968

JAN		FEB		MAR		APR		MAY		JUN	
1	AQU	2	ARI	3	TAU	2	GEM	1	CAN	2	VIR
3	PIS	4	TAU	5	GEM	4	CAN	4	LEO	5	LIB
6	ARI	7	GEM	8	CAN	7	LEO	6	VIR	7	SCO
8	TAU	9	CAN	10	LEO	9	VIR	8	LIB	9	SAG
11	GEM	12	LEO	12	VIR	11	LIB	10	SCO	11	CAP
13	CAN	14	VIR	14	LIB	13	SCO	12	SAG	13	AQU
15	LEO	16	LIB	17	SCO	15	SAG	14	CAP	15	PIS
18	VIR	18	SCO	19	SAG	17	CAP	16	AQU	17	ARI
20	LIB	20	SAG	21	CAP	19	AQU	19	PIS	20	TAU
22	SCO	22	CAP	23	AQU	21	PIS	21	ARI	22	GEM
24	SAG	25	AQU	25	PIS	24	ARI	24	TAU	25	CAN
26	CAP	27	PIS	28	ARI	26	TAU	26	GEM	27	LEO
28	AQU	29	ARI	30	TAU	29	GEM	29	CAN	30	VIR
31	PIS							31	LEO		

JUL		AUG		SEP		OCT		NOV		DEC	
2	LIB	3	SAG	1	CAP	2	PIS	1	ARI	1	TAU
4	SCO	5	CAP	3	AQU	5	ARI	3	TAU	3	GEM
6	SAG	7	AQU	5	PIS	7	TAU	6	GEM	6	CAN
8	CAP	9	PIS	7	ARI	10	GEM	8	CAN	8	LEO
10	AQU	11	ARI	10	TAU	12	CAN	11	LEO	11	VIR
12	PIS	13	TAU	12	GEM	15	LEO	13	VIR	13	LIB
15	ARI	16	GEM	15	CAN	17	VIR	16	LIB	15	SCO
17	TAU	18	CAN	17	LEO	19	LIB	18	SCO	17	SAG
20	GEM	21	LEO	20	VIR	21	SCO	20	SAG	19	CAP
22	CAN	23	VIR	22	LIB	23	SAG	22	CAP	21	AQU
25	LEO	25	LIB	24	SCO	25	CAP	24	AQU	23	PIS
27	VIR	28	SCO	26	SAG	27	AQU	26	PIS	26	ARI
29	LIB	30	SAG	28	CAP	30	PIS	28	ARI	28	TAU
31	SCO			30	AQU					30	GEM

1969

JAN		FEB		MAR		APR		MAY		JUN	
2	CAN	1	LEO	2	VIR	1	LIB	1	SCO	1	CAP
4	LEO	3	VIR	5	LIB	3	SCO	3	SAG	3	AQU
7	VIR	6	LIB	7	SCO	5	SAG	5	CAP	5	PIS
9	LIB	8	SCO	9	SAG	8	CAP	7	AQU	7	ARI
12	SCO	10	SAG	11	CAP	10	AQU	9	PIS	10	TAU
14	SAG	12	CAP	13	AQU	12	PIS	11	ARI	12	GEM
16	CAP	14	AQU	16	PIS	14	ARI	14	TAU	15	CAN
18	AQU	16	PIS	18	ARI	16	TAU	16	GEM	17	LEO
20	PIS	18	ARI	20	TAU	19	GEM	19	CAN	20	VIR
22	ARI	21	TAU	22	GEM	21	CAN	21	LEO	22	LIB
24	TAU	23	GEM	25	CAN	24	LEO	24	VIR	25	SCO
27	GEM	26	CAN	27	LEO	26	VIR	26	LIB	27	SAG
29	CAN	28	LEO	30	VIR	29	LIB	28	SCO	29	CAP
								30	SAG		

JUL		AUG		SEP		OCT		NOV		DEC	
1	AQU	1	ARI	2	GEM	2	CAN	1	LEO	1	VIR
3	PIS	3	TAU	5	CAN	4	LEO	3	VIR	3	LIB
5	ARI	6	GEM	7	LEO	7	VIR	6	LIB	5	SCO
7	TAU	8	CAN	10	VIR	9	LIB	8	SCO	8	SAG
10	GEM	11	LEO	12	LIB	12	SCO	10	SAG	10	CAP
12	CAN	13	VIR	14	SCO	14	SAG	12	CAP	12	AQU
15	LEO	16	LIB	17	SAG	16	CAP	14	AQU	14	PIS
17	VIR	18	SCO	19	CAP	18	AQU	16	PIS	16	ARI
20	LIB	20	SAG	21	AQU	20	PIS	19	ARI	18	TAU
22	SCO	22	CAP	23	PIS	22	ARI	21	TAU	20	GEM
24	SAG	24	AQU	25	ARI	25	TAU	23	GEM	23	CAN
26	CAP	26	PIS	27	TAU	27	GEM	26	CAN	25	LEO
28	AQU	29	ARI	29	GEM	29	CAN	28	LEO	28	VIR
30	PIS	31	TAU							30	LIB

1970

	JAN		FEB		MAR		APR		MAY		JUN
2	SCO	2	CAP	2	CAP	2	PIS	2	ARI	2	GEM
4	SAG	4	AQU	4	ARI	4	ARI	4	TAU	5	CAN
6	CAP	6	PIS	6	PIS	6	TAU	6	GEM	7	LEO
8	AQU	8	ARI	8	ARI	9	GEM	8	CAN	10	VIR
10	PIS	11	TAU	10	TAU	11	CAN	11	LEO	12	LIB
12	ARI	13	GEM	12	GEM	14	LEO	13	VIR	15	SCO
14	TAU	15	CAN	15	CAN	16	VIR	16	LIB	17	SAG
17	GEM	18	LEO	17	LEO	19	LIB	18	SCO	19	CAP
19	CAN	20	VIR	20	VIR	21	SCO	20	SAG	21	AQU
22	LEO	23	LIB	22	LIB	23	SAG	23	CAP	23	PIS
24	VIR	25	SCO	25	SCO	25	CAP	25	AQU	25	ARI
27	LIB	28	SAG	27	SAG	27	AQU	27	PIS	27	TAU
29	SCO			29	CAP	30	PIS	29	ARI	30	GEM
31	SAG			31	AQU			31	TAU		

	JUL		AUG		SEP		OCT		NOV		DEC
2	CAN	1	LEO	2	LIB	2	SCO	3	CAP	2	AQU
4	LEO	3	VIR	5	SCO	4	SAG	5	AQU	4	PIS
7	VIR	6	LIB	7	SAG	6	CAP	7	PIS	6	ARI
10	LIB	8	SCO	9	CAP	9	AQU	9	ARI	8	TAU
12	SCO	11	SAG	11	AQU	11	PIS	11	TAU	11	GEM
14	SAG	13	CAP	13	PIS	13	ARI	13	GEM	13	CAN
16	CAP	15	AQU	15	ARI	15	TAU	16	CAN	15	LEO
18	AQU	17	PIS	17	TAU	17	GEM	18	LEO	18	VIR
20	PIS	19	ARI	19	GEM	19	CAN	20	VIR	20	LIB
22	ARI	21	TAU	22	CAN	22	LEO	23	LIB	23	SCO
25	TAU	23	GEM	24	LEO	24	VIR	25	SCO	25	SAG
27	GEM	26	CAN	27	VIR	27	LIB	28	SAG	27	CAP
29	CAN	28	LEO	29	LIB	29	SCO	30	CAP	29	AQU
		31	VIR			31	SAG			31	PIS

1971

	JAN		FEB		MAR		APR		MAY		JUN
3	ARI	1	TAU	2	GEM	1	CAN	1	LEO	2	LIB
5	TAU	3	GEM	5	CAN	3	LEO	3	VIR	5	SCO
7	GEM	5	CAN	7	LEO	6	VIR	6	LIB	7	SAG
9	CAN	8	LEO	10	VIR	8	LIB	8	SCO	9	CAP
12	LEO	10	VIR	12	LIB	11	SCO	11	SAG	11	AQU
14	VIR	13	LIB	15	SCO	13	SAG	13	CAP	14	PIS
17	LIB	15	SCO	17	SAG	16	CAP	15	AQU	16	ARI
19	SCO	18	SAG	19	CAP	18	AQU	17	PIS	18	TAU
22	SAG	20	CAP	22	AQU	20	PIS	20	ARI	20	GEM
24	CAP	22	AQU	24	PIS	22	ARI	22	TAU	22	CAN
26	AQU	24	PIS	26	ARI	24	TAU	24	GEM	24	LEO
28	PIS	26	ARI	28	TAU	26	GEM	26	CAN	27	VIR
30	ARI	28	TAU	30	GEM	28	CAN	28	LEO	29	LIB
								30	VIR		

	JUL		AUG		SEP		OCT		NOV		DEC
2	SCO	1	SAG	2	AQU	1	PIS	2	TAU	1	GEM
4	SAG	3	CAP	4	PIS	3	ARI	4	GEM	3	CAN
7	CAP	5	AQU	6	ARI	5	TAU	6	CAN	5	LEO
9	AQU	7	PIS	8	TAU	7	GEM	8	LEO	8	VIR
11	PIS	9	ARI	10	GEM	9	CAN	10	VIR	10	LIB
13	ARI	11	TAU	12	CAN	12	LEO	13	LIB	13	SCO
15	TAU	13	GEM	14	LEO	14	VIR	15	SCO	15	SAG
17	GEM	16	CAN	17	VIR	16	LIB	18	SAG	17	CAP
19	CAN	18	LEO	19	LIB	19	SCO	20	CAP	20	AQU
22	LEO	20	VIR	22	SCO	22	SAG	23	AQU	22	PIS
24	VIR	23	LIB	24	SAG	24	CAP	25	PIS	24	ARI
27	LIB	26	SCO	27	CAP	26	AQU	27	ARI	26	TAU
29	SCO	28	SAG	29	AQU	29	PIS	29	TAU	28	GEM
		30	CAP			31	ARI			30	CAN

Moon Tables

1972

	JAN		FEB		MAR		APR		MAY		JUN
2	LEO	3	LIB	1	LIB	2	SAG	2	CAP	1	AQU
4	VIR	5	SCO	4	SCO	5	CAP	5	AQU	3	PIS
6	LIB	8	SAG	6	SAG	7	AQU	7	PIS	5	ARI
9	SCO	10	CAP	9	CAP	10	PIS	9	ARI	7	TAU
11	SAG	12	AQU	11	AQU	12	ARI	11	TAU	9	GEM
14	CAP	15	PIS	13	PIS	14	TAU	13	GEM	11	CAN
16	AQU	17	ARI	15	ARI	16	GEM	15	CAN	14	LEO
18	PIS	19	TAU	17	TAU	18	CAN	17	LEO	16	VIR
20	ARI	21	GEM	19	GEM	20	LEO	19	VIR	18	LIB
23	TAU	23	CAN	21	CAN	22	VIR	22	LIB	21	SCO
25	GEM	25	LEO	24	LEO	25	LIB	24	SCO	23	SAG
27	CAN	28	VIR	26	VIR	27	SCO	27	SAG	26	CAP
29	LEO			28	LIB	30	SAG	29	CAP	28	AQU
31	VIR			31	SCO					30	PIS

	JUL		AUG		SEP		OCT		NOV		DEC
3	ARI	1	TAU	1	CAN	1	LEO	2	LIB	1	SCO
5	TAU	3	GEM	4	LEO	3	VIR	4	SCO	4	SAG
7	GEM	5	CAN	6	VIR	5	LIB	7	SAG	7	CAP
9	CAN	7	LEO	8	LIB	8	SCO	9	CAP	9	AQU
11	LEO	10	VIR	11	SCO	10	SAG	12	AQU	11	PIS
13	VIR	12	LIB	13	SAG	13	CAP	14	PIS	14	ARI
15	LIB	14	SCO	16	CAP	15	AQU	16	ARI	16	TAU
18	SCO	17	SAG	18	AQU	18	PIS	18	TAU	18	GEM
20	SAG	19	CAP	20	PIS	20	ARI	20	GEM	20	CAN
23	CAP	22	AQU	22	ARI	22	TAU	22	CAN	22	LEO
25	AQU	24	PIS	24	TAU	24	GEM	24	LEO	24	VIR
28	PIS	26	ARI	27	GEM	26	CAN	27	VIR	26	LIB
30	ARI	28	TAU	29	CAN	28	LEO	29	LIB	29	SCO
		30	GEM			30	VIR				

1973

	JAN		FEB		MAR		APR		MAY		JUN
3	CAP	2	AQU	1	AQU	2	ARI	1	TAU	2	CAN
5	AQU	4	PIS	3	PIS	4	TAU	3	GEM	4	LEO
8	PIS	6	ARI	5	ARI	6	GEM	5	CAN	6	VIR
10	ARI	8	TAU	8	TAU	8	CAN	7	LEO	8	LIB
12	TAU	10	GEM	10	GEM	10	LEO	10	VIR	11	SCO
14	GEM	13	CAN	12	CAN	12	VIR	12	LIB	13	SAG
16	CAN	15	LEO	14	LEO	15	LIB	14	SCO	16	CAP
18	LEO	17	VIR	16	VIR	17	SCO	17	SAG	18	AQU
20	VIR	19	LIB	18	LIB	20	SAG	19	CAP	21	PIS
23	LIB	21	SCO	21	SCO	22	CAP	22	AQU	23	ARI
25	SCO	24	SAG	23	SAG	25	AQU	24	PIS	25	TAU
28	SAG	26	CAP	26	CAP	27	PIS	27	ARI	27	GEM
30	CAP			28	AQU	29	ARI	29	TAU	29	CAN
				31	PIS			31	GEM		

	JUL		AUG		SEP		OCT		NOV		DEC
1	LEO	2	LIB	1	SCO	3	CAP	2	AQU	1	PIS
3	VIR	4	SCO	3	SAG	5	AQU	4	PIS	4	ARI
5	LIB	7	SAG	5	CAP	8	PIS	6	ARI	6	TAU
8	SCO	9	CAP	8	AQU	10	ARI	9	TAU	8	GEM
10	SAG	12	AQU	10	PIS	12	TAU	11	GEM	10	CAN
13	CAP	14	PIS	13	ARI	14	GEM	13	CAN	12	LEO
15	AQU	16	ARI	15	TAU	16	CAN	15	LEO	14	VIR
18	PIS	19	TAU	17	GEM	19	LEO	17	VIR	16	LIB
20	ARI	21	GEM	19	CAN	21	VIR	19	LIB	19	SCO
22	TAU	23	CAN	21	LEO	23	LIB	22	SCO	21	SAG
25	GEM	25	LEO	23	VIR	25	SCO	24	SAG	24	CAP
27	CAN	27	VIR	26	LIB	28	SAG	26	CAP	26	AQU
29	LEO	29	LIB	28	SCO	30	CAP	29	AQU	29	PIS
31	VIR			30	SAG					31	ARI

1974

JAN		FEB		MAR		APR		MAY		JUN	
2	TAU	1	GEM	2	CAN	1	LEO	2	LIB	1	SCO
5	GEM	3	CAN	4	LEO	3	VIR	4	SCO	3	SAG
7	CAN	5	LEO	7	VIR	5	LIB	7	SAG	6	CAP
9	LEO	7	VIR	9	LIB	7	SCO	9	CAP	8	AQU
11	VIR	9	LIB	11	SCO	9	SAG	12	AQU	11	PIS
13	LIB	11	SCO	13	SAG	12	CAP	14	PIS	13	ARI
15	SCO	14	SAG	16	CAP	14	AQU	17	ARI	15	TAU
17	SAG	16	CAP	18	AQU	17	PIS	19	TAU	18	GEM
20	CAP	19	AQU	21	PIS	19	ARI	21	GEM	20	CAN
22	AQU	21	PIS	23	ARI	22	TAU	23	CAN	22	LEO
25	PIS	24	ARI	25	TAU	24	GEM	25	LEO	24	VIR
27	ARI	26	TAU	27	GEM	26	CAN	27	VIR	26	LIB
30	TAU	28	GEM	30	CAN	28	LEO	30	LIB	28	SCO
						30	VIR			30	SAG

JUL		AUG		SEP		OCT		NOV		DEC	
3	CAP	2	AQU	3	ARI	2	TAU	1	GEM	1	CAN
5	AQU	4	PIS	5	TAU	5	GEM	3	CAN	3	LEO
8	PIS	7	ARI	8	GEM	7	CAN	5	LEO	5	VIR
10	ARI	9	TAU	10	CAN	9	LEO	8	VIR	7	LIB
13	TAU	11	GEM	12	LEO	11	VIR	10	LIB	9	SCO
15	GEM	13	CAN	14	VIR	13	LIB	12	SCO	11	SAG
17	CAN	15	LEO	16	LIB	15	SCO	14	SAG	14	CAP
19	LEO	17	VIR	18	SCO	18	SAG	16	CAP	16	AQU
21	VIR	19	LIB	20	SAG	20	CAP	19	AQU	19	PIS
23	LIB	22	SCO	23	CAP	22	AQU	21	PIS	21	ARI
25	SCO	24	SAG	25	AQU	25	PIS	24	ARI	24	TAU
28	SAG	26	CAP	28	PIS	27	ARI	26	TAU	26	GEM
30	CAP	29	AQU	30	ARI	30	TAU	28	GEM	28	CAN
		31	PIS							30	LEO

1975

JAN		FEB		MAR		APR		MAY		JUN	
1	VIR	2	SCO	1	SCO	2	CAP	2	AQU	3	ARI
3	LIB	4	SAG	3	SAG	4	AQU	4	PIS	5	TAU
5	SCO	6	CAP	5	CAP	7	PIS	7	ARI	8	GEM
8	SAG	9	AQU	8	AQU	9	ARI	9	TAU	10	CAN
10	CAP	11	PIS	10	PIS	12	TAU	11	GEM	12	LEO
12	AQU	14	ARI	13	ARI	14	GEM	14	CAN	14	VIR
15	PIS	16	TAU	15	TAU	16	CAN	16	LEO	16	LIB
17	ARI	19	GEM	18	GEM	19	LEO	18	VIR	18	SCO
20	TAU	21	CAN	20	CAN	21	VIR	20	LIB	21	SAG
22	GEM	23	LEO	22	LEO	23	LIB	22	SCO	23	CAP
24	CAN	25	VIR	24	VIR	25	SCO	24	SAG	25	AQU
26	LEO	27	LIB	26	LIB	27	SAG	27	CAP	28	PIS
28	VIR			28	SCO	29	CAP	29	AQU	30	ARI
30	LIB			30	SAG			31	PIS		

JUL		AUG		SEP		OCT		NOV		DEC	
3	TAU	1	GEM	2	LEO	2	VIR	2	SCO	2	SAG
5	GEM	4	CAN	4	VIR	4	LIB	4	SAG	4	CAP
7	CAN	6	LEO	6	LIB	6	SCO	6	CAP	6	AQU
9	LEO	8	VIR	8	SCO	8	SAG	9	AQU	8	PIS
11	VIR	10	LIB	10	SAG	10	CAP	11	PIS	11	ARI
14	LIB	12	SCO	13	CAP	12	AQU	14	ARI	13	TAU
16	SCO	14	SAG	15	AQU	15	PIS	16	TAU	16	GEM
18	SAG	16	CAP	18	PIS	17	ARI	19	GEM	18	CAN
20	CAP	19	AQU	20	ARI	20	TAU	21	CAN	20	LEO
23	AQU	21	PIS	23	TAU	22	GEM	23	LEO	23	VIR
25	PIS	24	ARI	25	GEM	25	CAN	25	VIR	25	LIB
28	ARI	26	TAU	27	CAN	27	LEO	27	LIB	27	SCO
30	TAU	29	GEM	30	LEO	29	VIR	30	SCO	29	SAG
		31	CAN			31	LIB			31	CAP

Moon Tables

1976

JAN		FEB		MAR		APR		MAY		JUN	
2	AQU	1	PIS	2	ARI	1	TAU	3	CAN	1	LEO
5	PIS	4	ARI	4	TAU	3	GEM	5	LEO	4	VIR
7	ARI	6	TAU	7	GEM	6	CAN	7	VIR	6	LIB
10	TAU	9	GEM	9	CAN	8	LEO	10	LIB	8	SCO
12	GEM	11	CAN	12	LEO	10	VIR	12	SCO	10	SAG
15	CAN	13	LEO	14	VIR	12	LIB	14	SAG	12	CAP
17	LEO	15	VIR	16	LIB	14	SCO	16	CAP	14	AQU
19	VIR	17	LIB	18	SCO	16	SAG	18	AQU	17	PIS
21	LIB	19	SCO	20	SAG	18	CAP	20	PIS	19	ARI
23	SCO	21	SAG	22	CAP	20	AQU	23	ARI	22	TAU
25	SAG	24	CAP	24	AQU	23	PIS	25	TAU	24	GEM
27	CAP	26	AQU	27	PIS	25	ARI	28	GEM	26	CAN
30	AQU	28	PIS	29	ARI	28	TAU	30	CAN	29	LEO
						30	GEM				

JUL		AUG		SEP		OCT		NOV		DEC	
1	VIR	1	SCO	2	CAP	1	AQU	2	ARI	2	TAU
3	LIB	4	SAG	4	AQU	4	PIS	5	TAU	5	GEM
5	SCO	6	CAP	7	PIS	6	ARI	8	GEM	7	CAN
7	SAG	8	AQU	9	ARI	9	TAU	10	CAN	10	LEO
9	CAP	10	PIS	11	TAU	11	GEM	12	LEO	12	VIR
12	AQU	13	ARI	14	GEM	14	CAN	15	VIR	14	LIB
14	PIS	15	TAU	17	CAN	16	LEO	17	LIB	16	SCO
16	ARI	18	GEM	19	LEO	18	VIR	19	SCO	18	SAG
19	TAU	20	CAN	21	VIR	21	LIB	21	SAG	20	CAP
21	GEM	22	LEO	23	LIB	23	SCO	23	CAP	22	AQU
24	CAN	25	VIR	25	SCO	25	SAG	25	AQU	25	PIS
26	LEO	27	LIB	27	SAG	27	CAP	27	PIS	27	ARI
28	VIR	29	SCO	29	CAP	29	AQU	30	ARI	30	TAU
30	LIB	31	SAG			31	PIS				

1977

JAN		FEB		MAR		APR		MAY		JUN	
1	GEM	2	LEO	2	LEO	2	LIB	2	SCO	2	CAP
4	CAN	5	VIR	4	VIR	5	SCO	4	SAG	4	AQU
6	LEO	7	LIB	6	LIB	7	SAG	6	CAP	7	PIS
8	VIR	9	SCO	8	SCO	9	CAP	8	AQU	9	ARI
10	LIB	11	SAG	10	SAG	11	AQU	10	PIS	11	TAU
13	SCO	13	CAP	12	CAP	13	PIS	13	ARI	14	GEM
15	SAG	15	AQU	15	AQU	15	ARI	15	TAU	16	CAN
17	CAP	17	PIS	17	PIS	18	TAU	18	GEM	19	LEO
19	AQU	20	ARI	19	ARI	20	GEM	20	CAN	21	VIR
21	PIS	22	TAU	22	TAU	23	CAN	23	LEO	24	LIB
23	ARI	25	GEM	24	GEM	25	LEO	25	VIR	26	SCO
26	TAU	27	CAN	27	CAN	28	VIR	27	LIB	28	SAG
28	GEM			29	LEO	30	LIB	29	SCO	30	CAP
31	CAN			31	VIR			31	SAG		

JUL		AUG		SEP		OCT		NOV		DEC	
2	AQU	3	ARI	1	TAU	1	GEM	3	LEO	2	VIR
4	PIS	5	TAU	4	GEM	4	CAN	5	VIR	5	LIB
6	ARI	7	GEM	6	CAN	6	LEO	7	LIB	7	SCO
9	TAU	10	CAN	9	LEO	9	VIR	9	SCO	9	SAG
11	GEM	12	LEO	11	VIR	11	LIB	11	SAG	11	CAP
14	CAN	15	VIR	13	LIB	13	SCO	13	CAP	13	AQU
16	LEO	17	LIB	16	SCO	15	SAG	15	AQU	15	PIS
19	VIR	19	SCO	18	SAG	17	CAP	18	PIS	17	ARI
21	LIB	21	SAG	20	CAP	19	AQU	20	ARI	19	TAU
23	SCO	24	CAP	22	AQU	21	PIS	22	TAU	22	GEM
25	SAG	26	AQU	24	PIS	24	ARI	25	GEM	25	CAN
27	CAP	28	PIS	26	ARI	26	TAU	27	CAN	27	LEO
29	AQU	30	ARI	29	TAU	28	GEM	30	LEO	30	VIR
31	PIS					31	CAN				

1978

JAN		FEB		MAR		APR		MAY		JUN	
1	LIB	2	SAG	1	SAG	1	AQU	1	PIS	1	TAU
3	SCO	4	CAP	3	CAP	3	PIS	3	ARI	4	GEM
5	SAG	6	AQU	5	AQU	6	ARI	5	TAU	6	CAN
7	CAP	8	PIS	7	PIS	8	TAU	8	GEM	9	LEO
9	AQU	10	ARI	9	ARI	10	GEM	10	CAN	11	VIR
11	PIS	12	TAU	12	TAU	13	CAN	13	LEO	14	LIB
13	ARI	15	GEM	14	GEM	15	LEO	15	VIR	16	SCO
16	TAU	17	CAN	16	CAN	18	VIR	17	LIB	18	SAG
18	GEM	20	LEO	19	LEO	20	LIB	20	SCO	20	CAP
21	CAN	22	VIR	21	VIR	22	SCO	22	SAG	22	AQU
23	LEO	24	LIB	24	LIB	24	SAG	24	CAP	24	PIS
26	VIR	27	SCO	26	SCO	26	CAP	26	AQU	26	ARI
28	LIB			28	SAG	29	AQU	28	PIS	29	TAU
30	SCO			30	CAP			30	ARI		

JUL		AUG		SEP		OCT		NOV		DEC	
1	GEM	2	LEO	1	VIR	1	LIB	2	SAG	1	CAP
4	CAN	5	VIR	4	LIB	3	SCO	4	CAP	3	AQU
6	LEO	7	LIB	6	SCO	5	SAG	6	AQU	5	PIS
9	VIR	10	SCO	8	SAG	8	CAP	8	PIS	7	ARI
11	LIB	12	SAG	10	CAP	10	AQU	10	ARI	10	TAU
13	SCO	14	CAP	12	AQU	12	PIS	12	TAU	12	GEM
16	SAG	16	AQU	14	PIS	14	ARI	15	GEM	14	CAN
18	CAP	18	PIS	17	ARI	16	TAU	17	CAN	17	LEO
20	AQU	20	ARI	19	TAU	18	GEM	20	LEO	19	VIR
22	PIS	22	TAU	21	GEM	21	CAN	22	VIR	22	LIB
24	ARI	25	GEM	23	CAN	23	LEO	25	LIB	24	SCO
26	TAU	27	CAN	26	LEO	26	VIR	27	SCO	27	SAG
28	GEM	30	LEO	28	VIR	28	LIB	29	SAG	29	CAP
31	CAN					31	SCO			31	AQU

1979

JAN		FEB		MAR		APR		MAY		JUN	
2	PIS	2	TAU	2	TAU	3	CAN	2	LEO	1	VIR
4	ARI	5	GEM	4	GEM	5	LEO	5	VIR	4	LIB
6	TAU	7	CAN	6	CAN	8	VIR	7	LIB	6	SCO
8	GEM	9	LEO	9	LEO	10	LIB	10	SCO	8	SAG
11	CAN	12	VIR	11	VIR	12	SCO	12	SAG	11	CAP
13	LEO	15	LIB	14	LIB	15	SAG	14	CAP	13	AQU
16	VIR	17	SCO	16	SCO	17	CAP	16	AQU	15	PIS
18	LIB	19	SAG	19	SAG	19	AQU	18	PIS	17	ARI
21	SCO	21	CAP	21	CAP	21	PIS	21	ARI	19	TAU
23	SAG	24	AQU	23	AQU	23	ARI	23	TAU	22	GEM
25	CAP	26	PIS	25	PIS	25	TAU	25	GEM	24	CAN
27	AQU	28	ARI	27	ARI	28	GEM	27	CAN	26	LEO
29	PIS			29	TAU	30	CAN	30	LEO	29	VIR
31	ARI			31	GEM						

JUL		AUG		SEP		OCT		NOV		DEC	
1	LIB	2	SAG	1	CAP	2	PIS	1	ARI	2	GEM
4	SCO	4	CAP	3	AQU	4	ARI	3	TAU	4	CAN
6	SAG	6	AQU	5	PIS	6	TAU	5	GEM	7	LEO
8	CAP	8	PIS	7	ARI	8	GEM	7	CAN	9	VIR
10	AQU	10	ARI	9	TAU	11	CAN	9	LEO	12	LIB
12	PIS	13	TAU	11	GEM	13	LEO	12	VIR	14	SCO
14	ARI	15	GEM	13	CAN	16	VIR	14	LIB	17	SAG
16	TAU	17	CAN	16	LEO	18	LIB	17	SCO	19	CAP
19	GEM	20	LEO	18	VIR	21	SCO	19	SAG	21	AQU
21	CAN	22	VIR	21	LIB	23	SAG	22	CAP	23	PIS
23	LEO	25	LIB	23	SCO	25	CAP	24	AQU	25	ARI
26	VIR	27	SCO	26	SAG	28	AQU	26	PIS	27	TAU
28	LIB	30	SAG	28	CAP	30	PIS	28	ARI	30	GEM
31	SCO			30	AQU			30	TAU		

163

Moon Tables

1980

JAN		FEB		MAR		APR		MAY		JUN	
1	CAN	2	VIR	3	LIB	2	SCO	1	SAG	2	AQU
3	LEO	4	LIB	5	SCO	4	SAG	4	CAP	4	PIS
6	VIR	7	SCO	8	SAG	6	CAP	6	AQU	6	ARI
8	LIB	9	SAG	10	CAP	9	AQU	8	PIS	9	TAU
11	SCO	12	CAP	12	AQU	11	PIS	10	ARI	11	GEM
13	SAG	14	AQU	14	PIS	13	ARI	12	TAU	13	CAN
15	CAP	16	PIS	16	ARI	15	TAU	14	GEM	15	LEO
17	AQU	18	ARI	18	TAU	17	GEM	16	CAN	17	VIR
19	PIS	20	TAU	20	GEM	19	CAN	19	LEO	20	LIB
21	ARI	22	GEM	23	CAN	21	LEO	21	VIR	22	SCO
24	TAU	24	CAN	25	LEO	24	VIR	24	LIB	25	SAG
26	GEM	27	LEO	27	VIR	26	LIB	26	SCO	27	CAP
28	CAN	29	VIR	30	LIB	29	SCO	29	SAG	29	AQU
30	LEO							31	CAP		

JUL		AUG		SEP		OCT		NOV		DEC	
2	PIS	2	TAU	3	CAN	2	LEO	1	VIR	1	LIB
4	ARI	4	GEM	5	LEO	5	VIR	3	LIB	3	SCO
6	TAU	6	CAN	7	VIR	7	LIB	6	SCO	6	SAG
8	GEM	9	LEO	10	LIB	10	SCO	8	SAG	8	CAP
10	CAN	11	VIR	12	SCO	12	SAG	11	CAP	10	AQU
12	LEO	14	LIB	15	SAG	15	CAP	13	AQU	13	PIS
15	VIR	16	SCO	17	CAP	17	AQU	15	PIS	15	ARI
17	LIB	19	SAG	20	AQU	19	PIS	18	ARI	17	TAU
20	SCO	21	CAP	22	PIS	21	ARI	20	TAU	19	GEM
22	SAG	23	AQU	24	ARI	23	TAU	22	GEM	21	CAN
25	CAP	25	PIS	26	TAU	25	GEM	24	CAN	23	LEO
27	AQU	27	ARI	28	GEM	27	CAN	26	LEO	25	VIR
29	PIS	29	TAU	30	CAN	29	LEO	28	VIR	28	LIB
31	ARI	31	GEM							30	SCO

1981

JAN		FEB		MAR		APR		MAY		JUN	
2	SAG	1	CAP	2	AQU	1	PIS	1	ARI	1	GEM
4	CAP	3	AQU	5	PIS	3	ARI	3	TAU	3	CAN
7	AQU	5	PIS	7	ARI	5	TAU	5	GEM	5	LEO
9	PIS	7	ARI	9	TAU	7	GEM	7	CAN	7	VIR
11	ARI	9	TAU	11	GEM	9	CAN	9	LEO	10	LIB
13	TAU	12	GEM	13	CAN	11	LEO	11	VIR	12	SCO
15	GEM	14	CAN	15	LEO	14	VIR	13	LIB	15	SAG
17	CAN	16	LEO	18	VIR	16	LIB	16	SCO	17	CAP
20	LEO	18	VIR	20	LIB	19	SCO	18	SAG	20	AQU
22	VIR	21	LIB	22	SCO	21	SAG	21	CAP	22	PIS
24	LIB	23	SCO	25	SAG	24	CAP	23	AQU	24	ARI
27	SCO	26	SAG	27	CAP	26	AQU	26	PIS	26	TAU
29	SAG	28	CAP	30	AQU	28	PIS	28	ARI	28	GEM
								30	TAU	30	CAN

JUL		AUG		SEP		OCT		NOV		DEC	
2	LEO	1	VIR	2	SCO	2	SAG	1	CAP	1	AQU
5	VIR	3	LIB	5	SAG	5	CAP	3	AQU	3	PIS
7	LIB	6	SCO	7	CAP	7	AQU	6	PIS	5	ARI
10	SCO	8	SAG	10	AQU	9	PIS	8	ARI	7	TAU
12	SAG	11	CAP	12	PIS	11	ARI	10	TAU	9	GEM
15	CAP	13	AQU	14	ARI	13	TAU	12	GEM	11	CAN
17	AQU	16	PIS	16	TAU	15	GEM	14	CAN	13	LEO
19	PIS	18	ARI	18	GEM	18	CAN	16	LEO	16	VIR
21	ARI	20	TAU	20	CAN	20	LEO	18	VIR	18	LIB
24	TAU	22	GEM	22	LEO	22	VIR	21	LIB	20	SCO
26	GEM	24	CAN	25	VIR	24	LIB	23	SCO	23	SAG
28	CAN	26	LEO	27	LIB	27	SCO	25	SAG	25	CAP
30	LEO	28	VIR	29	SCO	29	SAG	28	CAP	28	AQU
		31	LIB							30	PIS

Moon Tables

1982

	JAN		FEB		MAR		APR		MAY		JUN
2	ARI	2	GEM	1	GEM	2	LEO	1	VIR	2	SCO
4	TAU	4	CAN	3	CAN	4	VIR	4	LIB	5	SAG
6	GEM	6	LEO	6	LEO	6	LIB	6	SCO	7	CAP
8	CAN	8	VIR	8	VIR	9	SCO	8	SAG	10	AQU
10	LEO	11	LIB	10	LIB	11	SAG	11	CAP	12	PIS
12	VIR	13	SCO	12	SCO	14	CAP	13	AQU	15	ARI
14	LIB	15	SAG	15	SAG	16	AQU	16	PIS	17	TAU
17	SCO	18	CAP	17	CAP	19	PIS	18	ARI	19	GEM
19	SAG	20	AQU	20	AQU	21	ARI	20	TAU	21	CAN
22	CAP	23	PIS	22	PIS	23	TAU	22	GEM	23	LEO
24	AQU	25	ARI	24	ARI	25	GEM	24	CAN	25	VIR
26	PIS	27	TAU	27	TAU	27	CAN	26	LEO	27	LIB
29	ARI			29	GEM	29	LEO	29	VIR	29	SCO
31	TAU			31	CAN			31	LIB		

	JUL		AUG		SEP		OCT		NOV		DEC
2	SAG	1	CAP	2	PIS	2	ARI	2	GEM	2	CAN
4	CAP	3	AQU	4	ARI	4	TAU	4	CAN	4	LEO
7	AQU	6	PIS	7	TAU	6	GEM	6	LEO	6	VIR
9	PIS	8	ARI	9	GEM	8	CAN	9	VIR	8	LIB
12	ARI	10	TAU	11	CAN	10	LEO	11	LIB	10	SCO
14	TAU	13	GEM	13	LEO	12	VIR	13	SCO	13	SAG
16	GEM	15	CAN	15	VIR	15	LIB	15	SAG	15	CAP
18	CAN	17	LEO	17	LIB	17	SCO	18	CAP	18	AQU
20	LEO	19	VIR	19	SCO	19	SAG	21	AQU	20	PIS
22	VIR	21	LIB	22	SAG	22	CAP	23	PIS	23	ARI
24	LIB	23	SCO	24	CAP	24	AQU	25	ARI	25	TAU
27	SCO	25	SAG	27	AQU	27	PIS	28	TAU	27	GEM
29	SAG	28	CAP	29	PIS	29	ARI	30	GEM	29	CAN
		31	AQU			31	TAU			31	LEO

1983

	JAN		FEB		MAR		APR		MAY		JUN
2	VIR	1	LIB	2	SCO	1	SAG	1	CAP	2	PIS
4	LIB	3	SCO	5	SAG	3	CAP	3	AQU	5	ARI
7	SCO	5	SAG	7	CAP	6	AQU	6	PIS	7	TAU
9	SAG	8	CAP	10	AQU	8	PIS	8	ARI	9	GEM
12	CAP	10	AQU	12	PIS	11	ARI	11	TAU	11	CAN
14	AQU	13	PIS	15	ARI	13	TAU	13	GEM	13	LEO
17	PIS	15	ARI	17	TAU	15	GEM	15	CAN	15	VIR
19	ARI	18	TAU	19	GEM	18	CAN	17	LEO	17	LIB
21	TAU	20	GEM	21	CAN	20	LEO	19	VIR	20	SCO
24	GEM	22	CAN	23	LEO	22	VIR	21	LIB	22	SAG
26	CAN	24	LEO	26	VIR	24	LIB	23	SCO	24	CAP
28	LEO	26	VIR	28	LIB	26	SCO	26	SAG	27	AQU
30	VIR	28	LIB	30	SCO	28	SAG	28	CAP	29	PIS
								31	AQU		

	JUL		AUG		SEP		OCT		NOV		DEC
2	ARI	1	TAU	1	CAN	1	LEO	1	LIB	1	SCO
4	TAU	3	GEM	3	LEO	3	VIR	3	SCO	3	SAG
7	GEM	5	CAN	5	VIR	5	LIB	6	SAG	5	CAP
9	CAN	7	LEO	7	LIB	7	SCO	8	CAP	8	AQU
11	LEO	9	VIR	10	SCO	9	SAG	10	AQU	10	PIS
13	VIR	11	LIB	12	SAG	11	CAP	13	PIS	13	ARI
15	LIB	13	SCO	14	CAP	14	AQU	15	ARI	15	TAU
17	SCO	15	SAG	17	AQU	16	PIS	18	TAU	17	GEM
19	SAG	18	CAP	19	PIS	19	ARI	20	GEM	20	CAN
22	CAP	20	AQU	22	ARI	21	TAU	22	CAN	22	LEO
24	AQU	23	PIS	24	TAU	24	GEM	24	LEO	24	VIR
27	PIS	25	ARI	26	GEM	26	CAN	26	VIR	26	LIB
29	ARI	28	TAU	29	CAN	28	LEO	29	LIB	28	SCO
		30	GEM			30	VIR			30	SAG

1984

JAN		FEB		MAR		APR		MAY		JUN	
2	CAP	3	PIS	1	PIS	2	TAU	2	GEM	1	CAN
4	AQU	5	ARI	4	ARI	5	GEM	4	CAN	3	LEO
6	PIS	8	TAU	6	TAU	7	CAN	6	LEO	5	VIR
9	ARI	10	GEM	8	GEM	9	LEO	9	VIR	7	LIB
11	TAU	12	CAN	11	CAN	11	VIR	11	LIB	9	SCO
14	GEM	15	LEO	13	LEO	13	LIB	13	SCO	11	SAG
16	CAN	17	VIR	15	VIR	15	SCO	15	SAG	13	CAP
18	LEO	19	LIB	17	LIB	17	SAG	17	CAP	16	AQU
20	VIR	21	SCO	19	SCO	20	CAP	19	AQU	18	PIS
22	LIB	23	SAG	21	SAG	22	AQU	22	PIS	21	ARI
24	SCO	25	CAP	23	CAP	25	PIS	24	ARI	23	TAU
26	SAG	28	AQU	26	AQU	27	ARI	27	TAU	26	GEM
29	CAP			28	PIS	30	TAU	29	GEM	28	CAN
31	AQU			31	ARI					30	LEO

JUL		AUG		SEP		OCT		NOV		DEC	
2	VIR	3	SCO	1	SAG	1	CAP	2	PIS	1	ARI
4	LIB	5	SAG	3	CAP	3	AQU	4	ARI	4	TAU
6	SCO	7	CAP	6	AQU	5	PIS	7	TAU	6	GEM
9	SAG	9	AQU	8	PIS	8	ARI	9	GEM	9	CAN
11	CAP	12	PIS	11	ARI	10	TAU	12	CAN	11	LEO
13	AQU	14	ARI	13	TAU	13	GEM	14	LEO	13	VIR
16	PIS	17	TAU	16	GEM	15	CAN	16	VIR	15	LIB
18	ARI	19	GEM	18	CAN	18	LEO	18	LIB	17	SCO
21	TAU	22	CAN	20	LEO	20	VIR	20	SCO	20	SAG
23	GEM	24	LEO	22	VIR	22	LIB	22	SAG	22	CAP
25	CAN	26	VIR	24	LIB	24	SCO	24	CAP	24	AQU
27	LEO	28	LIB	26	SCO	26	SAG	27	AQU	26	PIS
29	VIR	30	SCO	28	SAG	28	CAP	29	PIS	29	ARI
31	LIB					30	AQU			31	TAU

1985

JAN		FEB		MAR		APR		MAY		JUN	
3	GEM	2	CAN	1	CAN	2	VIR	1	LIB	2	SAG
5	CAN	4	LEO	3	LEO	4	LIB	3	SCO	4	CAP
7	LEO	6	VIR	5	VIR	6	SCO	5	SAG	6	AQU
9	VIR	8	LIB	7	LIB	8	SAG	7	CAP	8	PIS
12	LIB	10	SCO	9	SCO	10	CAP	9	AQU	11	ARI
14	SCO	12	SAG	11	SAG	12	AQU	12	PIS	13	TAU
16	SAG	14	CAP	14	CAP	14	PIS	14	ARI	16	GEM
18	CAP	17	AQU	16	AQU	17	ARI	17	TAU	18	CAN
20	AQU	19	PIS	18	PIS	20	TAU	19	GEM	20	LEO
23	PIS	21	ARI	21	ARI	22	GEM	22	CAN	23	VIR
25	ARI	24	TAU	23	TAU	25	CAN	24	LEO	25	LIB
28	TAU	27	GEM	26	GEM	27	LEO	26	VIR	27	SCO
30	GEM			28	CAN	29	VIR	29	LIB	29	SAG
				31	LEO			31	SCO		

JUL		AUG		SEP		OCT		NOV		DEC	
1	CAP	2	PIS	1	ARI	3	GEM	2	CAN	1	LEO
3	AQU	4	ARI	3	TAU	5	CAN	4	LEO	4	VIR
5	PIS	7	TAU	6	GEM	8	LEO	6	VIR	6	LIB
8	ARI	9	GEM	8	CAN	10	VIR	9	LIB	8	SCO
10	TAU	12	CAN	10	LEO	12	LIB	11	SCO	10	SAG
13	GEM	14	LEO	13	VIR	14	SCO	13	SAG	12	CAP
15	CAN	16	VIR	15	LIB	16	SAG	15	CAP	14	AQU
18	LEO	18	LIB	17	SCO	18	CAP	17	AQU	16	PIS
20	VIR	20	SCO	19	SAG	20	AQU	19	PIS	19	ARI
22	LIB	22	SAG	21	CAP	23	PIS	21	ARI	21	TAU
24	SCO	25	CAP	23	AQU	25	ARI	24	TAU	24	GEM
26	SAG	27	AQU	25	PIS	28	TAU	26	GEM	26	CAN
28	CAP	29	PIS	28	ARI	30	GEM	29	CAN	29	LEO
31	AQU			30	TAU					31	VIR

1986

	JAN		FEB		MAR		APR		MAY		JUN
2	LIB	1	SCO	2	SAG	2	AQU	2	PIS	3	TAU
4	SCO	3	SAG	4	CAP	5	PIS	4	ARI	5	GEM
6	SAG	5	CAP	6	AQU	7	ARI	7	TAU	8	CAN
8	CAP	7	AQU	8	PIS	9	TAU	9	GEM	11	LEO
11	AQU	9	PIS	11	ARI	12	GEM	12	CAN	13	VIR
13	PIS	11	ARI	13	TAU	14	CAN	14	LEO	15	LIB
15	ARI	14	TAU	16	GEM	17	LEO	17	VIR	17	SCO
17	TAU	16	GEM	18	CAN	19	VIR	19	LIB	19	SAG
20	GEM	19	CAN	21	LEO	21	LIB	21	SCO	21	CAP
22	CAN	21	LEO	23	VIR	24	SCO	23	SAG	23	AQU
25	LEO	24	VIR	25	LIB	26	SAG	25	CAP	26	PIS
27	VIR	26	LIB	27	SCO	28	CAP	27	AQU	28	ARI
29	LIB	28	SCO	29	SAG	30	AQU	29	PIS	30	TAU
				31	CAP			31	ARI		

	JUL		AUG		SEP		OCT		NOV		DEC
3	GEM	2	CAN	3	VIR	2	LIB	1	SCO	2	CAP
5	CAN	4	LEO	5	LIB	4	SCO	3	SAG	4	AQU
8	LEO	6	VIR	7	SCO	7	SAG	5	CAP	6	PIS
10	VIR	9	LIB	9	SAG	9	CAP	7	AQU	9	ARI
12	LIB	11	SCO	11	CAP	11	AQU	9	PIS	11	TAU
15	SCO	13	SAG	14	AQU	13	PIS	11	ARI	14	GEM
17	SAG	15	CAP	16	PIS	15	ARI	14	TAU	16	CAN
19	CAP	17	AQU	18	ARI	18	TAU	16	GEM	19	LEO
21	AQU	19	PIS	20	TAU	20	GEM	19	CAN	21	VIR
23	PIS	22	ARI	23	GEM	23	CAN	21	LEO	24	LIB
25	ARI	24	TAU	25	CAN	25	LEO	24	VIR	26	SCO
28	TAU	26	GEM	28	LEO	27	VIR	26	LIB	28	SAG
30	GEM	29	CAN	30	VIR	30	LIB	28	SCO	30	CAP
		31	LEO					30	SAG		

1987

	JAN		FEB		MAR		APR		MAY		JUN
1	AQU	1	ARI	1	ARI	2	GEM	2	CAN	3	VIR
3	PIS	4	TAU	3	TAU	4	CAN	4	LEO	5	LIB
5	ARI	6	GEM	5	GEM	7	LEO	7	VIR	8	SCO
7	TAU	9	CAN	8	CAN	9	VIR	9	LIB	10	SAG
10	GEM	11	LEO	10	LEO	12	LIB	11	SCO	12	CAP
12	CAN	14	VIR	13	VIR	14	SCO	13	SAG	14	AQU
15	LEO	16	LIB	15	LIB	16	SAG	15	CAP	16	PIS
17	VIR	18	SCO	18	SCO	18	CAP	17	AQU	18	ARI
20	LIB	21	SAG	20	SAG	20	AQU	20	PIS	20	TAU
22	SCO	23	CAP	22	CAP	22	PIS	22	ARI	23	GEM
24	SAG	25	AQU	24	AQU	25	ARI	24	TAU	25	CAN
26	CAP	27	PIS	26	PIS	27	TAU	26	GEM	28	LEO
28	AQU			28	ARI	29	GEM	29	CAN	30	VIR
30	PIS			30	TAU			31	LEO		

	JUL		AUG		SEP		OCT		NOV		DEC
3	LIB	1	SCO	2	CAP	1	AQU	2	ARI	1	TAU
5	SCO	4	SAG	4	AQU	3	PIS	4	TAU	4	GEM
7	SAG	6	CAP	6	PIS	6	ARI	6	GEM	6	CAN
9	CAP	8	AQU	8	ARI	8	TAU	9	CAN	8	LEO
11	AQU	10	PIS	10	TAU	10	GEM	11	LEO	11	VIR
13	PIS	12	ARI	13	GEM	12	CAN	14	VIR	14	LIB
15	ARI	14	TAU	15	CAN	15	LEO	16	LIB	16	SCO
18	TAU	16	GEM	17	LEO	17	VIR	18	SCO	18	SAG
20	GEM	19	CAN	20	VIR	20	LIB	21	SAG	20	CAP
22	CAN	21	LEO	22	LIB	22	SCO	23	CAP	22	AQU
25	LEO	24	VIR	25	SCO	24	SAG	25	AQU	24	PIS
27	VIR	26	LIB	27	SAG	26	CAP	27	PIS	26	ARI
30	LIB	29	SCO	29	CAP	29	AQU	29	ARI	29	TAU
		31	SAG			31	PIS			31	GEM

1988

	JAN		FEB		MAR		APR		MAY		JUN
2	CAN	1	LEO	2	VIR	1	LIB	3	SAG	1	CAP
5	LEO	4	VIR	4	LIB	3	SCO	5	CAP	3	AQU
7	VIR	6	LIB	7	SCO	5	SAG	7	AQU	5	PIS
10	LIB	9	SCO	9	SAG	8	CAP	9	PIS	8	ARI
12	SCO	11	SAG	11	CAP	10	AQU	11	ARI	10	TAU
15	SAG	13	CAP	14	AQU	12	PIS	13	TAU	12	GEM
17	CAP	15	AQU	16	PIS	14	ARI	16	GEM	14	CAN
19	AQU	17	PIS	18	ARI	16	TAU	18	CAN	17	LEO
21	PIS	19	ARI	20	TAU	18	GEM	20	LEO	19	VIR
23	ARI	21	TAU	22	GEM	20	CAN	23	VIR	22	LIB
25	TAU	23	GEM	24	CAN	23	LEO	25	LIB	24	SCO
27	GEM	26	CAN	27	LEO	25	VIR	28	SCO	26	SAG
30	CAN	28	LEO	29	VIR	28	LIB	30	SAG	29	CAP
						30	SCO				

	JUL		AUG		SEP		OCT		NOV		DEC
1	AQU	1	ARI	2	GEM	1	CAN	2	VIR	2	LIB
3	PIS	3	TAU	4	CAN	4	LEO	5	LIB	5	SCO
5	ARI	5	GEM	6	LEO	6	VIR	7	SCO	7	SAG
7	TAU	8	CAN	9	VIR	9	LIB	10	SAG	9	CAP
9	GEM	10	LEO	11	LIB	11	SCO	12	CAP	12	AQU
11	CAN	13	VIR	14	SCO	14	SAG	14	AQU	14	PIS
14	LEO	15	LIB	16	SAG	16	CAP	17	PIS	16	ARI
16	VIR	18	SCO	19	CAP	18	AQU	19	ARI	18	TAU
19	LIB	20	SAG	21	AQU	20	PIS	21	TAU	20	GEM
21	SCO	22	CAP	23	PIS	22	ARI	23	GEM	22	CAN
24	SAG	24	AQU	25	ARI	24	TAU	25	CAN	25	LEO
26	CAP	26	PIS	27	TAU	26	GEM	27	LEO	27	VIR
28	AQU	28	ARI	29	GEM	29	CAN	30	VIR	30	LIB
30	PIS	30	TAU			31	LEO				

1989

	JAN		FEB		MAR		APR		MAY		JUN
1	SCO	2	CAP	2	CAP	2	PIS	2	ARI	2	GEM
4	SAG	4	AQU	4	AQU	4	ARI	4	TAU	4	CAN
6	CAP	6	PIS	6	PIS	6	TAU	6	GEM	7	LEO
8	AQU	8	ARI	8	ARI	8	GEM	8	CAN	9	VIR
10	PIS	11	TAU	10	TAU	11	CAN	10	LEO	11	LIB
12	ARI	13	GEM	12	GEM	13	LEO	13	VIR	14	SCO
14	TAU	15	CAN	14	CAN	15	VIR	15	LIB	16	SAG
16	GEM	17	LEO	17	LEO	18	LIB	18	SCO	19	CAP
19	CAN	20	VIR	19	VIR	20	SCO	20	SAG	21	AQU
21	LEO	22	LIB	22	LIB	23	SAG	22	CAP	23	PIS
23	VIR	25	SCO	24	SCO	25	CAP	25	AQU	25	ARI
26	LIB	27	SAG	27	SAG	28	AQU	27	PIS	27	TAU
29	SCO			29	CAP	30	PIS	29	ARI	30	GEM
31	SAG			31	AQU			31	TAU		

	JUL		AUG		SEP		OCT		NOV		DEC
2	CAN	3	VIR	1	LIB	1	SCO	2	CAP	2	AQU
4	LEO	5	LIB	4	SCO	4	SAG	5	AQU	4	PIS
6	VIR	8	SCO	6	SAG	6	CAP	7	PIS	7	ARI
9	LIB	10	SAG	9	CAP	9	AQU	9	ARI	9	TAU
11	SCO	12	CAP	11	AQU	11	PIS	11	TAU	11	GEM
14	SAG	15	AQU	13	PIS	13	ARI	13	GEM	13	CAN
16	CAP	17	PIS	15	ARI	15	TAU	15	CAN	15	LEO
18	AQU	19	ARI	17	TAU	17	GEM	17	LEO	17	VIR
20	PIS	21	TAU	19	GEM	19	CAN	20	VIR	19	LIB
23	ARI	23	GEM	21	CAN	21	LEO	22	LIB	22	SCO
25	TAU	25	CAN	24	LEO	23	VIR	25	SCO	24	SAG
27	GEM	28	LEO	26	VIR	26	LIB	27	SAG	27	CAP
29	CAN	30	VIR	29	LIB	28	SCO	30	CAP	29	AQU
31	LEO					31	SAG				

1990

JAN		FEB		MAR		APR		MAY		JUN	
1	PIS	1	TAU	2	GEM	1	CAN	3	VIR	1	LIB
3	ARI	3	GEM	5	CAN	3	LEO	5	LIB	4	SCO
5	TAU	5	CAN	7	LEO	5	VIR	8	SCO	6	SAG
7	GEM	8	LEO	9	VIR	8	LIB	10	SAG	9	CAP
9	CAN	10	VIR	12	LIB	10	SCO	13	CAP	11	AQU
11	LEO	12	LIB	14	SCO	13	SAG	15	AQU	14	PIS
13	VIR	15	SCO	16	SAG	15	CAP	17	PIS	16	ARI
16	LIB	17	SAG	19	CAP	18	AQU	20	ARI	18	TAU
18	SCO	20	CAP	21	AQU	20	PIS	22	TAU	20	GEM
21	SAG	22	AQU	24	PIS	22	ARI	24	GEM	22	CAN
23	CAP	24	PIS	26	ARI	24	TAU	26	CAN	24	LEO
26	AQU	26	ARI	28	TAU	26	GEM	28	LEO	26	VIR
28	PIS	28	TAU	30	GEM	28	CAN	30	VIR	29	LIB
30	ARI					30	LEO				

JUL		AUG		SEP		OCT		NOV		DEC	
1	SCO	2	CAP	1	AQU	1	PIS	2	TAU	1	GEM
4	SAG	5	AQU	3	PIS	3	ARI	4	GEM	3	CAN
6	CAP	7	PIS	6	ARI	5	TAU	6	CAN	5	LEO
9	AQU	9	ARI	9	TAU	7	GEM	8	LEO	7	VIR
11	PIS	12	TAU	10	GEM	9	CAN	10	VIR	9	LIB
13	ARI	14	GEM	12	CAN	11	LEO	12	LIB	12	SCO
15	TAU	16	CAN	14	LEO	14	VIR	15	SCO	14	SAG
17	GEM	18	LEO	16	VIR	16	LIB	17	SAG	17	CAP
19	CAN	20	VIR	19	LIB	18	SCO	20	CAP	19	AQU
21	LEO	22	LIB	21	SCO	21	SAG	22	AQU	22	PIS
24	VIR	25	SCO	24	SAG	23	CAP	25	PIS	24	ARI
26	LIB	27	SAG	26	CAP	26	AQU	27	ARI	26	TAU
28	SCO	30	CAP	29	AQU	28	PIS	29	TAU	28	GEM
31	SAG					30	ARI			30	CAN

1991

JAN		FEB		MAR		APR		MAY		JUN	
1	LEO	2	LIB	2	LIB	3	SAG	2	CAP	1	AQU
4	VIR	4	SCO	4	SCO	5	CAP	5	AQU	4	PIS
6	LIB	7	SAG	6	SAG	8	AQU	7	PIS	6	ARI
8	SCO	9	CAP	9	CAP	10	PIS	10	ARI	8	TAU
11	SAG	12	AQU	11	AQU	12	ARI	12	TAU	10	GEM
13	CAP	14	PIS	14	PIS	15	TAU	14	GEM	12	CAN
16	AQU	17	ARI	16	ARI	17	GEM	16	CAN	14	LEO
18	PIS	19	TAU	18	TAU	19	CAN	18	LEO	16	VIR
20	ARI	21	GEM	20	GEM	21	LEO	20	VIR	19	LIB
23	TAU	23	CAN	22	CAN	23	VIR	22	LIB	21	SCO
25	GEM	25	LEO	25	LEO	25	LIB	25	SCO	23	SAG
27	CAN	27	VIR	27	VIR	28	SCO	27	SAG	26	CAP
29	LEO			29	LIB	30	SAG	30	CAP	29	AQU
31	VIR			31	SCO						

JUL		AUG		SEP		OCT		NOV		DEC	
1	PIS	2	TAU	3	CAN	2	LEO	2	LIB	2	SCO
3	ARI	4	GEM	5	LEO	4	VIR	5	SCO	4	SAG
6	TAU	6	CAN	7	VIR	6	LIB	7	SAG	7	CAP
8	GEM	8	LEO	9	LIB	8	SCO	10	CAP	9	AQU
10	CAN	10	VIR	11	SCO	11	SAG	12	AQU	12	PIS
12	LEO	12	LIB	13	SAG	13	CAP	15	PIS	14	ARI
14	VIR	15	SCO	16	CAP	16	AQU	17	ARI	17	TAU
16	LIB	17	SAG	18	AQU	18	PIS	19	TAU	19	GEM
18	SCO	20	CAP	21	PIS	21	ARI	21	GEM	21	CAN
21	SAG	22	AQU	23	ARI	23	TAU	23	CAN	23	LEO
23	CAP	25	PIS	25	TAU	25	GEM	25	LEO	25	VIR
26	AQU	27	ARI	28	GEM	27	CAN	28	VIR	27	LIB
28	PIS	29	TAU	30	CAN	29	LEO	30	LIB	29	SCO
31	ARI	31	GEM			31	VIR				

1992

	JAN		FEB		MAR		APR		MAY		JUN
1	SAG	2	AQU	3	PIS	1	ARI	1	TAU	2	CAN
3	CAP	4	PIS	5	ARI	4	TAU	3	GEM	4	LEO
6	AQU	7	ARI	8	TAU	6	GEM	5	CAN	6	VIR
8	PIS	9	TAU	10	GEM	8	CAN	8	LEO	8	LIB
11	ARI	12	GEM	12	CAN	10	LEO	10	VIR	10	SCO
13	TAU	14	CAN	14	LEO	12	VIR	12	LIB	13	SAG
15	GEM	16	LEO	16	VIR	15	LIB	14	SCO	15	CAP
17	CAN	18	VIR	18	LIB	17	SCO	16	SAG	17	AQU
19	LEO	20	LIB	20	SCO	19	SAG	19	CAP	20	PIS
21	VIR	22	SCO	23	SAG	21	CAP	21	AQU	22	ARI
23	LIB	24	SAG	25	CAP	24	AQU	24	PIS	25	TAU
25	SCO	27	CAP	27	AQU	26	PIS	26	ARI	27	GEM
28	SAG	29	AQU	30	PIS	29	ARI	28	TAU	29	CAN
30	CAP							31	GEM		

	JUL		AUG		SEP		OCT		NOV		DEC
1	LEO	2	LIB	2	SAG	2	CAP	1	AQU	1	PIS
3	VIR	4	SCO	5	CAP	5	AQU	3	PIS	3	ARI
5	LIB	6	SAG	7	AQU	7	PIS	6	ARI	6	TAU
7	SCO	8	CAP	10	PIS	10	ARI	8	TAU	8	GEM
10	SAG	11	AQU	12	ARI	12	TAU	11	GEM	10	CAN
12	CAP	13	PIS	15	TAU	14	GEM	13	CAN	12	LEO
15	AQU	16	ARI	17	GEM	17	CAN	15	LEO	14	VIR
17	PIS	18	TAU	19	CAN	19	LEO	17	VIR	16	LIB
20	ARI	21	GEM	21	LEO	21	VIR	19	LIB	19	SCO
22	TAU	23	CAN	24	VIR	23	LIB	21	SCO	21	SAG
24	GEM	25	LEO	26	LIB	25	SCO	24	SAG	23	CAP
27	CAN	27	VIR	28	SCO	27	SAG	26	CAP	26	AQU
29	LEO	29	LIB	30	SAG	29	CAP	28	AQU	28	PIS
31	VIR	31	SCO							31	ARI

1993

	JAN		FEB		MAR		APR		MAY		JUN
2	TAU	1	GEM	2	CAN	1	LEO	2	LIB	1	SCO
4	GEM	3	CAN	5	LEO	3	VIR	4	SCO	3	SAG
7	CAN	5	LEO	7	VIR	5	LIB	6	SAG	5	CAP
9	LEO	7	VIR	9	LIB	7	SCO	9	CAP	7	AQU
11	VIR	9	LIB	11	SCO	9	SAG	11	AQU	10	PIS
13	LIB	11	SCO	13	SAG	11	CAP	13	PIS	12	ARI
15	SCO	13	SAG	15	CAP	14	AQU	16	ARI	15	TAU
17	SAG	16	CAP	17	AQU	16	PIS	18	TAU	17	GEM
19	CAP	18	AQU	20	PIS	19	ARI	21	GEM	19	CAN
22	AQU	21	PIS	22	ARI	21	TAU	23	CAN	22	LEO
24	PIS	23	ARI	25	TAU	24	GEM	25	LEO	24	VIR
27	ARI	26	TAU	27	GEM	26	CAN	28	VIR	26	LIB
29	TAU	28	GEM	30	CAN	28	LEO	30	LIB	28	SCO
						30	VIR			30	SAG

	JUL		AUG		SEP		OCT		NOV		DEC
2	CAP	1	AQU	2	ARI	2	TAU	1	GEM	3	LEO
5	AQU	3	PIS	5	TAU	4	GEM	3	CAN	5	VIR
7	PIS	6	ARI	7	GEM	7	CAN	5	LEO	7	LIB
10	ARI	8	TAU	10	CAN	9	LEO	8	VIR	9	SCO
12	TAU	11	GEM	12	LEO	11	VIR	10	LIB	11	SAG
15	GEM	13	CAN	14	VIR	13	LIB	12	SCO	13	CAP
17	CAN	15	LEO	16	LIB	15	SCO	14	SAG	15	AQU
19	LEO	17	VIR	18	SCO	17	SAG	16	CAP	18	PIS
21	VIR	19	LIB	20	SAG	19	CAP	18	AQU	20	ARI
23	LIB	21	SCO	22	CAP	22	AQU	20	PIS	23	TAU
25	SCO	24	SAG	24	AQU	24	PIS	23	ARI	25	GEM
27	SAG	26	CAP	27	PIS	27	ARI	26	TAU	28	CAN
30	CAP	28	AQU	29	ARI	29	TAU	28	GEM	30	LEO
		31	PIS					30	CAN		

Moon Tables

1994

	JAN		FEB		MAR		APR		MAY		JUN
1	VIR	2	SCO	1	SCO	1	CAP	1	AQU	2	ARI
3	LIB	4	SAG	3	SAG	4	AQU	3	PIS	5	TAU
5	SCO	6	CAP	5	CAP	6	PIS	6	ARI	7	GEM
8	SAG	8	AQU	7	AQU	9	ARI	8	TAU	10	CAN
10	CAP	11	PIS	10	PIS	11	TAU	11	GEM	12	LEO
12	AQU	13	ARI	12	ARI	14	GEM	13	CAN	14	VIR
14	PIS	15	TAU	15	TAU	16	CAN	16	LEO	16	LIB
17	ARI	18	GEM	17	GEM	18	LEO	18	VIR	19	SCO
19	TAU	20	CAN	20	CAN	21	VIR	20	LIB	21	SAG
22	GEM	23	LEO	22	LEO	23	LIB	22	SCO	23	CAP
24	CAN	25	VIR	24	VIR	25	SCO	24	SAG	25	AQU
26	LEO	27	LIB	26	LIB	27	SAG	26	CAP	27	PIS
28	VIR			28	SCO	29	CAP	28	AQU	29	ARI
31	LIB			30	SAG			31	PIS		

	JUL		AUG		SEP		OCT		NOV		DEC
2	TAU	1	GEM	2	LEO	2	VIR	2	SCO	2	SAG
4	GEM	3	CAN	4	VIR	4	LIB	4	SAG	4	CAP
7	CAN	6	LEO	6	LIB	6	SCO	6	CAP	6	AQU
9	LEO	8	VIR	8	SCO	8	SAG	8	AQU	8	PIS
11	VIR	10	LIB	10	SAG	10	CAP	11	PIS	10	ARI
14	LIB	12	SCO	13	CAP	12	AQU	13	ARI	13	TAU
16	SCO	14	SAG	15	AQU	14	PIS	15	TAU	15	GEM
18	SAG	16	CAP	17	PIS	17	ARI	18	GEM	18	CAN
20	CAP	18	AQU	19	ARI	19	TAU	20	CAN	20	LEO
22	AQU	21	PIS	22	TAU	22	GEM	23	LEO	23	VIR
24	PIS	23	ARI	24	GEM	24	CAN	25	VIR	25	LIB
27	ARI	26	TAU	27	CAN	27	LEO	28	LIB	27	SCO
29	TAU	28	GEM	29	LEO	29	VIR	30	SCO	29	SAG
		31	CAN			31	LIB			31	CAP

1995

	JAN		FEB		MAR		APR		MAY		JUN
2	AQU	1	PIS	2	ARI	1	TAU	1	GEM	2	LEO
4	PIS	3	ARI	5	TAU	3	GEM	3	CAN	5	VIR
7	ARI	5	TAU	7	GEM	6	CAN	6	LEO	7	LIB
9	TAU	8	GEM	10	CAN	9	LEO	8	VIR	9	SCO
12	GEM	10	CAN	12	LEO	11	VIR	10	LIB	11	SAG
14	CAN	13	LEO	14	VIR	13	LIB	13	SCO	13	CAP
16	LEO	15	VIR	17	LIB	15	SCO	15	SAG	15	AQU
19	VIR	17	LIB	19	SCO	17	SAG	17	CAP	17	PIS
21	LIB	19	SCO	21	SAG	19	CAP	19	AQU	19	ARI
23	SCO	22	SAG	23	CAP	21	AQU	21	PIS	22	TAU
25	SAG	24	CAP	25	AQU	24	PIS	23	ARI	24	GEM
27	CAP	26	AQU	27	PIS	26	ARI	26	TAU	27	CAN
30	AQU	28	PIS	30	ARI	28	TAU	28	GEM	29	LEO
								31	CAN		

	JUL		AUG		SEP		OCT		NOV		DEC
2	VIR	3	SCO	1	SAG	2	AQU	1	PIS	3	TAU
4	LIB	5	SAG	3	CAP	5	PIS	3	ARI	5	GEM
6	SCO	7	CAP	5	AQU	7	ARI	5	TAU	8	CAN
8	SAG	9	AQU	7	PIS	9	TAU	8	GEM	10	LEO
10	CAP	11	PIS	9	ARI	12	GEM	10	CAN	13	VIR
12	AQU	13	ARI	12	TAU	14	CAN	13	LEO	15	LIB
14	PIS	15	TAU	14	GEM	17	LEO	15	VIR	17	SCO
17	ARI	18	GEM	17	CAN	19	VIR	18	LIB	19	SAG
19	TAU	20	CAN	19	LEO	21	LIB	20	SCO	21	CAP
22	GEM	23	LEO	22	VIR	23	SCO	22	SAG	23	AQU
24	CAN	25	VIR	24	LIB	26	SAG	24	CAP	25	PIS
27	LEO	28	LIB	26	SCO	28	CAP	26	AQU	28	ARI
29	VIR	30	SCO	28	SAG	30	AQU	28	PIS	30	TAU
31	LIB			30	CAP			30	ARI		

1996

JAN		FEB		MAR		APR		MAY		JUN	
1	GEM	3	LEO	1	LEO	2	LIB	2	SCO	2	CAP
4	CAN	5	VIR	3	VIR	4	SAG	4	SAG	4	AQU
6	LEO	8	LIB	6	LIB	7	SAG	6	CAP	6	PIS
9	VIR	10	SCO	8	SCO	9	CAP	8	AQU	9	ARI
11	LIB	12	SAG	10	SAG	11	AQU	10	PIS	11	TAU
14	SCO	14	CAP	13	CAP	13	PIS	12	ARI	13	GEM
16	SAG	16	AQU	15	AQU	15	ARI	15	TAU	16	CAN
18	CAP	18	PIS	17	PIS	17	TAU	17	GEM	18	LEO
20	AQU	20	ARI	19	ARI	20	GEM	19	CAN	21	VIR
22	PIS	23	TAU	21	TAU	22	CAN	22	LEO	23	LIB
24	ARI	25	GEM	23	GEM	25	LEO	25	VIR	26	SCO
26	TAU	27	CAN	26	CAN	27	VIR	27	LIB	28	SAG
29	GEM			28	LEO	30	LIB	29	SCO	30	CAP
31	CAN			31	VIR			31	SAG		

JUL		AUG		SEP		OCT		NOV		DEC	
2	AQU	2	ARI	1	TAU	3	CAN	2	LEO	2	VIR
4	PIS	4	TAU	3	GEM	5	LEO	4	VIR	4	LIB
6	ARI	7	GEM	6	CAN	8	VIR	7	LIB	6	SCO
8	TAU	9	CAN	8	LEO	10	LIB	9	SCO	9	SAG
11	GEM	12	LEO	11	VIR	13	SCO	11	SAG	11	CAP
13	CAN	14	VIR	13	LIB	15	SAG	13	CAP	13	AQU
16	LEO	17	LIB	15	SCO	17	CAP	16	AQU	15	PIS
18	VIR	19	SCO	18	SAG	19	AQU	18	PIS	17	ARI
21	LIB	21	SAG	20	CAP	21	PIS	20	ARI	19	TAU
23	SCO	24	CAP	22	AQU	23	ARI	22	TAU	22	GEM
25	SAG	26	AQU	24	PIS	26	TAU	24	GEM	24	CAN
27	CAP	28	PIS	26	ARI	28	GEM	27	CAN	26	LEO
29	AQU	30	ARI	28	TAU	30	CAN	29	LEO	29	VIR
31	PIS			30	GEM					31	LIB

1997

JAN		FEB		MAR		APR		MAY		JUN	
3	SCO	1	SAG	1	AQU	1	AQU	1	PIS	1	TAU
5	SAG	4	CAP	3	CAP	4	PIS	3	ARI	4	GEM
7	CAP	6	AQU	5	AQU	6	ARI	5	TAU	6	CAN
9	AQU	8	PIS	7	PIS	8	TAU	7	GEM	8	LEO
11	PIS	10	ARI	9	ARI	10	GEM	9	CAN	11	VIR
13	ARI	12	TAU	11	TAU	12	CAN	12	LEO	13	LIB
15	TAU	14	GEM	13	GEM	14	LEO	14	VIR	16	SCO
18	GEM	16	CAN	16	CAN	17	VIR	17	LIB	18	SAG
20	CAN	19	LEO	18	LEO	19	LIB	19	SCO	20	CAP
23	LEO	21	VIR	21	VIR	22	SCO	22	SAG	22	AQU
25	VIR	24	LIB	23	LIB	24	SAG	24	CAP	24	PIS
28	LIB	26	SCO	26	SCO	27	CAP	26	AQU	26	ARI
30	SCO			28	SAG	29	AQU	28	PIS	29	TAU
				30	CAP			30	ARI		

JUL		AUG		SEP		OCT		NOV		DEC	
1	GEM	2	LEO	3	LIB	3	SCO	1	SAG	1	CAP
3	CAN	4	VIR	6	SCO	5	SAG	4	CAP	3	AQU
5	LEO	7	LIB	8	SAG	8	CAP	6	AQU	5	PIS
8	VIR	9	SCO	10	CAP	10	AQU	8	PIS	8	ARI
10	LIB	12	SAG	12	AQU	12	PIS	10	ARI	10	TAU
13	SCO	14	CAP	15	PIS	14	ARI	12	TAU	12	GEM
15	SAG	16	AQU	17	ARI	16	TAU	14	GEM	14	CAN
18	CAP	18	PIS	19	TAU	18	GEM	17	CAN	16	LEO
20	AQU	20	ARI	21	GEM	20	CAN	19	LEO	19	VIR
22	PIS	22	TAU	23	CAN	23	LEO	21	VIR	21	LIB
24	ARI	24	GEM	25	LEO	25	VIR	24	LIB	24	SCO
26	TAU	27	CAN	28	VIR	28	LIB	26	SCO	26	SAG
28	GEM	29	LEO	30	LIB	30	SCO	29	SAG	28	CAP
30	CAN	31	VIR							31	AQU

1998

	JAN		FEB		MAR		APR		MAY		JUN
2	PIS	2	TAU	2	TAU	2	CAN	2	LEO	3	LIB
4	ARI	4	GEM	4	GEM	4	LEO	4	VIR	5	SCO
6	TAU	7	CAN	6	CAN	7	VIR	7	LIB	8	SAG
8	GEM	9	LEO	8	LEO	9	LIB	9	SCO	10	CAP
10	cAN	11	VIR	11	VIR	12	SCO	12	SAG	13	AQU
13	LEO	14	LIB	13	LIB	14	SAG	14	CAP	15	PIS
15	VIR	16	SCO	16	SCO	17	CAP	16	AQU	17	ARI
18	LIB	19	SAG	18	SAG	19	AQU	19	PIS	19	TAU
20	SCO	21	CAP	21	CAP	21	PIS	21	ARI	21	GEM
23	SAG	23	AQU	23	AQU	23	ARI	23	TAU	23	CAN
25	CAP	25	PIS	25	PIS	25	TAU	25	GEM	25	LEO
27	AQU	27	ARI	27	ARI	27	GEM	27	CAN	28	VIR
29	PIS			29	TAU	29	CAN	29	LEO	30	LIB
31	ARI			31	GEM			31	VIR		

	JUL		AUG		SEP		OCT		NOV		DEC
3	SCO	2	SAG	3	AQU	2	PIS	1	ARI	2	GEM
5	SAG	4	CAP	5	PIS	4	ARI	3	TAU	4	CAN
8	CAP	6	AQU	7	ARI	6	TAU	5	GEM	6	LEO
10	AQU	8	PIS	9	TAU	8	GEM	7	CAN	9	VIR
12	PIS	11	ARI	11	GEM	10	CAN	9	LEO	11	LIB
14	ARI	13	TAU	13	CAN	13	LEO	11	VIR	14	SCO
16	TAU	15	GEM	15	LEO	15	VIR	14	LIB	16	SAG
18	GEM	17	CAN	18	VIR	17	LIB	16	SCO	19	CAP
21	CAN	19	LEO	20	LIB	20	SCO	19	SAG	21	AQU
23	LEO	21	VIR	23	SCO	23	SAG	21	CAP	23	PIS
25	VIR	24	LIB	25	SAG	25	CAP	24	AQU	25	ARI
28	LIB	26	SCO	28	CAP	27	AQU	26	PIS	28	TAU
30	SCO	29	SAG	30	AQU	30	PIS	28	ARI	30	GEM
		31	CAP					30	TAU		

1999

	JAN		FEB		MAR		APR		MAY		JUN
1	CAN	1	VIR	1	VIR	2	SCO	2	SAG	3	AQU
3	LEO	4	LIB	3	LIB	4	SAG	4	CAP	5	PIS
5	VIR	6	SCO	6	SCO	7	CAP	7	AQU	8	ARI
7	LIB	9	SAG	8	SAG	9	AQU	9	PIS	10	TAU
10	SCO	11	CAP	11	CAP	12	PIS	11	ARI	12	GEM
12	SAG	14	AQU	13	AQU	14	ARI	13	TAU	14	CAN
15	CAP	16	PIS	15	PIS	16	TAU	15	GEM	16	LEO
17	AQU	18	ARI	17	ARI	18	GEM	17	CAN	18	VIR
19	PIS	20	TAU	19	TAU	20	CAN	19	LEO	20	LIB
22	ARI	22	GEM	21	GEM	22	LEO	21	VIR	23	SCO
24	TAU	24	CAN	23	CAN	24	VIR	24	LIB	25	SAG
26	GEM	26	LEO	26	LEO	27	LIB	26	SCO	28	CAP
28	CAN			28	VIR	29	SCO	29	SAG	30	AQU
30	LEO			30	LIB			31	CAP		

	JUL		AUG		SEP		OCT		NOV		DEC
2	PIS	1	ARI	2	GEM	1	CAN	1	VIR	1	LIB
5	ARI	3	TAU	4	CAN	3	LEO	4	LIB	3	SCO
7	TAU	5	GEM	6	LEO	5	VIR	6	SCO	6	SAG
9	GEM	7	CAN	8	VIR	8	LIB	9	SAG	8	CAP
11	CAN	9	LEO	10	LIB	10	SCO	11	CAP	11	AQU
13	LEO	12	VIR	13	SCO	12	SAG	14	AQU	13	PIS
15	VIR	14	LIB	15	SAG	15	CAP	16	PIS	16	ARI
17	LIB	16	SCO	18	CAP	17	AQU	18	ARI	18	TAU
20	SCO	19	SAG	20	AQU	20	PIS	21	TAU	20	GEM
22	SAG	21	CAP	22	PIS	22	ARI	23	GEM	22	CAN
25	CAP	24	AQU	25	ARI	24	TAU	25	CAN	24	LEO
27	AQU	26	PIS	27	TAU	26	GEM	27	LEO	26	VIR
30	PIS	28	ARI	29	GEM	28	CAN	29	VIR	28	LIB
		30	TAU			30	LEO			31	SCO

2000

JAN		FEB		MAR		APR		MAY		JUN	
3	SAG	1	CAP	2	AQU	1	PIS	3	TAU	1	GEM
5	CAP	4	AQU	4	PIS	3	ARI	5	GEM	3	CAN
7	AQU	6	PIS	7	ARI	5	TAU	7	CAN	5	LEO
10	PIS	8	ARI	9	TAU	7	GEM	9	LEO	7	VIR
12	ARI	11	TAU	11	GEM	9	CAN	11	VIR	9	LIB
14	TAU	13	GEM	13	CAN	11	LEO	13	LIB	12	SCO
16	GEM	15	CAN	15	LEO	14	VIR	15	SCO	14	SAG
18	CAN	17	LEO	17	viR	16	LIB	18	SAG	17	CAP
20	LEO	19	VIR	20	LIB	18	SCO	20	CAP	19	AQU
23	VIR	21	LIB	22	SCO	21	SAG	23	AQU	22	PIS
25	LIB	23	SCO	24	SAG	23	CAP	25	PIS	24	ARI
27	SCO	26	SAG	27	CAP	26	AQU	28	ARI	26	TAU
29	SAG	28	CAP	29	AQU	28	PIS	30	TAU	28	GEM
						30	ARI			30	CAN

JUL		AUG		SEP		OCT		NOV		DEC	
2	LEO	1	VIR	2	SCO	1	SAG	3	AQU	2	PIS
4	VIR	3	LIB	4	SAG	4	CAP	5	PIS	5	ARI
7	LIB	5	SCO	6	CAP	6	AQU	8	ARI	7	TAU
9	SCO	8	SAG	9	AQU	9	PIS	10	TAU	9	GEM
11	SAG	10	CAP	11	PIS	11	ARI	12	GEM	11	CAN
14	CAP	13	AQU	14	ARI	13	TAU	14	CAN	13	LEO
16	AQU	15	PIS	16	TAU	16	GEM	16	LEO	15	VIR
19	PIS	18	ARI	18	GEM	18	CAN	18	VIR	18	LIB
21	ARI	20	TAU	20	CAN	20	LEO	20	LIB	20	SCO
24	TAU	22	GEM	23	LEO	22	VIR	23	SCO	22	SAG
26	GEM	24	CAN	25	VIR	24	LIB	25	SAG	25	CAP
28	CAN	26	LEO	27	LIB	26	SCO	27	CAP	27	AQU
30	LEO	28	VIR	29	SCO	29	SAG	30	AQU	30	PIS
		30	LIB			31	CAP				

2001

JAN		FEB		MAR		APR		MAY		JUN	
1	ARI	2	GEM	1	GEM	2	LEO	1	VIR	2	SCO
4	TAU	4	CAN	4	CAN	4	VIR	3	LIB	4	SAG
6	GEM	6	LEO	6	LEO	6	LIB	6	SCO	7	CAP
8	CAN	8	VIR	8	VIR	8	SCO	8	SAG	9	AQU
10	LEO	10	LIB	10	LIB	10	SAG	10	CAP	11	PIS
12	VIR	12	SCO	12	SCO	13	CAP	13	AQU	14	ARI
14	LIB	15	SAG	14	SAG	15	AQU	15	PIS	16	TAU
16	SCO	17	CAP	16	CAP	18	PIS	18	ARI	19	GEM
18	SAG	20	AQU	19	AQU	20	ARI	20	TAU	21	CAN
21	CAP	22	PIS	22	PIS	23	TAU	22	GEM	23	LEO
23	AQU	25	ARI	24	ARI	25	GEM	24	CAN	25	VIR
26	PIS	27	TAU	26	TAU	27	CAN	27	LEO	27	LIB
28	ARI			29	GEM	29	LEO	29	VIR	29	SCO
31	TAU			31	CAN			31	LIB		

JUL		AUG		SEP		OCT		NOV		DEC	
1	SAG	3	AQU	1	PIS	1	ARI	2	GEM	2	CAN
4	CAP	5	PIS	4	ARI	4	TAU	4	CAN	4	LEO
6	AQU	8	ARI	6	TAU	6	GEM	7	LEO	6	VIR
9	PIS	10	TAU	9	GEM	8	CAN	9	VIR	8	LIB
11	ARI	12	GEM	11	CAN	10	LEO	11	LIB	10	SCO
14	TAU	15	CAN	13	LEO	13	VIR	13	SCO	12	SAG
16	GEM	17	LEO	15	VIR	15	LIB	15	SAG	15	CAP
18	CAN	19	VIR	17	LIB	17	SCO	17	CAP	17	AQU
20	LEO	21	LIB	19	SCO	19	SAG	20	AQU	20	PIS
22	VIR	23	SCO	21	SAG	21	CAP	22	PIS	22	ARI
24	LIB	25	SAG	24	CAP	23	AQU	25	ARI	25	TAU
26	SCO	27	CAP	26	AQU	26	PIS	27	TAU	27	GEM
29	SAG	30	AQU	29	PIS	28	ARI	30	GEM	29	CAN
31	CAP					31	TAU			31	LEO

2002

JAN		FEB		MAR		APR		MAY		JUN	
2	VIR	1	LIB	1	SCO	1	SAG	2	AQU	1	PIS
4	LIB	3	SCO	4	SAG	3	CAP	5	PIS	4	ARI
6	SCO	5	SAG	6	CAP	5	AQU	7	ARI	6	TAU
9	SAG	7	CAP	9	AQU	8	PIS	10	TAU	9	GEM
11	CAP	10	AQU	11	PIS	10	ARI	12	GEM	11	CAN
13	AQU	12	PIS	14	ARI	13	TAU	15	CAN	13	LEO
16	PIS	15	ARI	16	TAU	15	GEM	17	LEO	15	VIR
18	ARI	17	TAU	19	GEM	18	CAN	19	VIR	18	LIB
21	TAU	20	GEM	21	CAN	20	LEO	21	LIB	20	SCO
23	GEM	22	CAN	24	LEO	22	VIR	23	SCO	22	SAG
26	CAN	24	LEO	26	VIR	24	LIB	25	SAG	24	CAP
28	LEO	26	VIR	28	LIB	26	SCO	28	CAP	26	AQU
30	VIR	28	LIB	30	SCO	28	SAG	30	AQU	29	PIS
						30	CAP				

JUL		AUG		SEP		OCT		NOV		DEC	
1	ARI	2	GEM	1	CAN	1	LEO	1	LIB	1	SCO
4	TAU	5	CAN	3	LEO	3	VIR	3	SCO	3	SAG
6	GEM	7	LEO	5	VIR	5	LIB	5	SAG	5	CAP
8	CAN	9	VIR	7	LIB	7	SCO	7	CAP	7	AQU
11	LEO	11	LIB	9	SCO	9	SAG	10	AQU	9	PIS
13	VIR	13	SCO	12	SAG	11	CAP	12	PIS	12	ARI
15	LIB	15	SAG	14	CAP	13	AQU	15	ARI	14	TAU
17	SCO	18	CAP	16	AQU	16	PIS	17	TAU	17	GEM
19	SAG	20	AQU	19	PIS	18	ARI	20	GEM	19	CAN
21	CAP	22	PIS	21	ARI	21	TAU	22	CAN	22	LEO
24	AQU	25	ARI	24	TAU	23	GEM	24	LEO	24	VIR
26	PIS	27	TAU	26	GEM	26	CAN	27	VIR	26	LIB
28	ARI	30	GEM	29	CAN	28	LEO	29	LIB	28	SCO
31	TAU					30	VIR			30	SAG

2003

JAN		FEB		MAR		APR		MAY		JUN	
1	CAP	2	PIS	1	PIS	3	TAU	2	GEM	1	CAN
3	AQU	5	ARI	4	ARI	5	GEM	5	CAN	4	LEO
6	PIS	7	TAU	6	TAU	8	CAN	7	LEO	6	VIR
8	ARI	10	GEM	9	GEM	10	LEO	10	VIR	8	LIB
11	TAU	12	CAN	11	CAN	12	VIR	12	LIB	10	SCO
13	GEM	14	LEO	14	LEO	14	LIB	14	SCO	12	SAG
16	CAN	16	VIR	16	VIR	16	SCO	16	SAG	14	CAP
18	LEO	18	LIB	18	LIB	18	SAG	18	CAP	16	AQU
20	VIR	21	SCO	20	SCO	20	CAP	20	AQU	19	PIS
22	LIB	23	SAG	22	SAG	23	AQU	22	PIS	21	ARI
24	SCO	25	CAP	24	CAP	25	PIS	25	ARI	23	TAU
26	SAG	27	AQU	26	AQU	27	ARI	27	TAU	26	GEM
29	CAP			29	PIS	30	TAU	30	GEM	28	CAN
31	AQU			31	ARI						

JUL		AUG		SEP		OCT		NOV		DEC	
1	LEO	2	LIB	2	SAG	1	CAP	2	PIS	2	ARI
3	VIR	4	SCO	4	CAP	4	AQU	5	ARI	4	TAU
5	LIB	6	SAG	6	AQU	6	PIS	7	TAU	7	GEM
7	SCO	8	CAP	9	PIS	8	ARI	10	GEM	9	CAN
10	SAG	10	AQU	11	ARI	11	TAU	12	CAN	12	LEO
12	CAP	12	PIS	13	TAU	13	GEM	15	LEO	14	VIR
14	AQU	15	ARI	16	GEM	16	CAN	17	VIR	16	LIB
16	PIS	17	TAU	18	CAN	18	LEO	19	LIB	19	SCO
18	ARI	20	GEM	21	LEO	21	VIR	21	SCO	21	SAG
21	TAU	22	CAN	23	VIR	23	LIB	23	SAG	23	CAP
23	GEM	24	LEO	25	LIB	25	SCO	25	CAP	25	AQU
26	CAN	27	VIR	27	SCO	27	SAG	27	AQU	27	PIS
28	LEO	29	LIB	29	SAG	29	CAP	29	PIS	29	ARI
30	VIR	31	SCO			31	AQU				

2004

	JAN		FEB		MAR		APR		MAY		JUN
1	TAU	2	CAN	3	LEO	1	VIR	1	LIB	2	SAG
3	GEM	4	LEO	5	VIR	4	LIB	3	SCO	4	CAP
6	CAN	7	VIR	7	LIB	6	SCO	5	SAG	6	AQU
8	LEO	9	LIB	9	SCO	8	SAG	7	CAP	8	PIS
10	VIR	11	SCO	12	SAG	10	CAP	9	AQU	10	ARI
13	LIB	13	SAG	14	CAP	12	AQU	11	PIS	12	TAU
15	SCO	15	CAP	16	AQU	14	PIS	14	ARI	15	GEM
17	SAG	17	AQU	18	PIS	16	ARI	16	TAU	17	CAN
19	CAP	20	PIS	20	ARI	19	TAU	19	GEM	20	LEO
21	AQU	22	ARI	23	TAU	21	GEM	21	CAN	22	VIR
23	PIS	24	TAU	25	GEM	24	CAN	24	LEO	25	LIB
25	ARI	27	GEM	28	CAN	26	LEO	26	VIR	27	SCO
28	TAU	29	CAN	30	LEO	29	VIR	28	LIB	29	SAG
30	GEM							31	SCO		

	JUL		AUG		SEP		OCT		NOV		DEC
1	CAP	1	PIS	2	TAU	2	GEM	1	CAN	1	LEO
3	AQU	4	ARI	5	GEM	5	CAN	3	LEO	3	VIR
5	PIS	6	TAU	7	CAN	7	LEO	6	VIR	6	LIB
7	ARI	8	GEM	10	LEO	10	VIR	8	LIB	8	SCO
10	TAU	11	CAN	12	VIR	12	LIB	10	SCO	10	SAG
12	GEM	13	LEO	14	LIB	14	SCO	13	SAG	12	CAP
15	CAN	16	VIR	17	SCO	16	SAG	15	CAP	14	AQU
17	LEO	18	LIB	19	SAG	18	CAP	17	AQU	16	PIS
20	VIR	20	SCO	21	CAP	20	AQU	19	PIS	18	ARI
22	LIB	23	SAG	23	AQU	23	PIS	21	ARI	21	TAU
24	SCO	25	CAP	25	PIS	25	ARI	23	TAU	23	GEM
26	SAG	27	AQU	27	ARI	27	TAU	26	GEM	25	CAN
28	CAP	29	PIS	30	TAU	29	GEM	28	CAN	28	LEO
30	AQU	31	ARI							31	VIR

2005

	JAN		FEB		MAR		APR		MAY		JUN
2	LIB	1	SCO	2	SAG	3	AQU	2	PIS	3	TAU
4	SCO	3	SAG	4	CAP	5	PIS	4	ARI	5	GEM
6	SAG	5	CAP	6	AQU	7	ARI	6	TAU	7	CAN
8	CAP	7	AQU	8	PIS	9	TAU	9	GEM	10	LEO
10	AQU	9	PIS	10	ARI	11	GEM	11	CAN	12	VIR
12	PIS	11	ARI	13	TAU	14	CAN	14	LEO	15	LIB
15	ARI	13	TAU	15	GEM	16	LEO	16	VIR	17	SCO
17	TAU	16	GEM	17	CAN	19	VIR	18	LIB	19	SAG
19	GEM	18	CAN	20	LEO	21	LIB	21	SCO	21	CAP
22	CAN	21	LEO	22	VIR	23	SCO	23	SAG	23	AQU
24	LEO	23	VIR	25	LIB	26	SAG	25	CAP	25	PIS
27	VIR	25	LIB	27	SCO	28	CAP	27	AQU	28	ARI
29	LIB	28	SCO	29	SAG	30	AQU	29	PIS	30	TAU
				31	CAP			31	ARI		

	JUL		AUG		SEP		OCT		NOV		DEC
2	GEM	1	CAN	2	VIR	2	LIB	1	SCO	2	CAP
5	CAN	3	LEO	5	LIB	4	SCO	3	SAG	4	AQU
7	LEO	6	VIR	7	SCO	7	SAG	5	CAP	7	PIS
10	VIR	8	LIB	9	SAG	9	CAP	7	AQU	9	ARI
12	LIB	11	SCO	12	CAP	11	AQU	9	PIS	11	TAU
15	SCO	13	SAG	14	AQU	13	PIS	11	ARI	13	GEM
17	SAG	15	CAP	16	PIS	15	ARI	14	TAU	15	CAN
19	CAP	17	AQU	18	ARI	17	TAU	16	GEM	18	LEO
21	AQU	19	PIS	20	TAU	19	GEM	18	CAN	20	VIR
23	PIS	21	ARI	22	GEM	22	CAN	21	LEO	23	LIB
25	ARI	23	TAU	24	CAN	24	LEO	23	VIR	25	SCO
27	TAU	26	GEM	27	LEO	27	VIR	26	LIB	28	SAG
29	GEM	28	CAN	29	VIR	29	LIB	28	SCO	30	CAP
		31	LEO					30	SAG		

2006

JAN		FEB		MAR		APR		MAY		JUN	
1	AQU	1	ARI	1	ARI	1	GEM	1	CAN	2	VIR
3	PIS	3	TAU	3	TAU	4	CAN	3	LEO	5	LIB
5	ARI	6	GEM	5	GEM	6	LEO	6	VIR	7	SCO
7	TAU	8	CAN	7	CAN	9	VIR	8	LIB	10	SAG
9	GEM	10	LEO	10	LEO	11	LIB	11	SCO	12	CAP
12	CAN	13	VIR	12	VIR	14	SCO	13	SAG	14	AQU
14	LEO	16	LIB	15	LIB	16	SAG	15	CAP	16	PIS
17	VIR	18	SCO	17	SCO	18	CAP	18	AQU	18	ARI
19	LIB	20	SAG	20	SAG	20	AQU	20	PIS	20	TAU
22	SCO	23	CAP	22	CAP	22	PIS	22	ARI	22	GEM
24	SAG	25	AQU	24	AQU	25	ARI	24	TAU	25	CAN
26	CAP	27	PIS	26	PIS	27	TAU	26	GEM	27	LEO
28	AQU			28	ARI	29	GEM	28	CAN	29	VIR
30	PIS			30	TAU			31	LEO		

JUL		AUG		SEP		OCT		NOV		DEC	
2	LIB	1	SCO	2	CAP	1	AQU	2	ARI	1	TAU
5	SCO	3	SAG	4	AQU	4	PIS	4	TAU	3	GEM
7	SAG	6	CAP	6	PIS	6	ARI	6	GEM	6	CAN
9	CAP	8	AQU	8	ARI	8	TAU	8	CAN	8	LEO
11	AQU	10	PIS	10	TAU	10	GEM	10	LEO	10	VIR
13	PIS	12	ARI	12	GEM	12	CAN	13	VIR	13	LIB
15	ARI	14	TAU	14	CAN	14	LEO	15	LIB	15	SCO
17	TAU	16	GEM	17	LEO	17	VIR	18	SCO	18	SAG
20	GEM	18	CAN	19	VIR	19	LIB	20	SAG	20	CAP
22	CAN	21	LEO	22	LIB	22	SCO	23	CAP	22	AQU
24	LEO	23	VIR	24	SCO	24	SAG	25	AQU	24	PIS
27	VIR	26	LIB	27	SAG	26	CAP	27	PIS	27	ARI
29	LIB	28	SCO	29	CAP	29	AQU	29	ARI	29	TAU
		31	SAG			31	PIS			31	GEM

2007

JAN		FEB		MAR		APR		MAY		JUN	
2	CAN	1	LEO	2	VIR	1	LIB	1	SCO	2	CAP
4	LEO	3	VIR	5	LIB	3	SCO	3	SAG	4	AQU
7	VIR	5	LIB	7	SCO	6	SAG	6	CAP	7	PIS
9	LIB	8	SCO	10	SAG	8	CAP	8	AQU	9	ARI
12	SCO	10	SAG	12	CAP	11	AQU	10	PIS	11	TAU
14	SAG	13	CAP	14	AQU	13	PIS	12	ARI	13	GEM
16	CAP	15	AQU	17	PIS	15	ARI	14	TAU	15	CAN
19	AQU	17	PIS	19	ARI	17	TAU	16	GEM	17	LEO
21	PIS	19	ARI	21	TAU	19	GEM	18	CAN	19	VIR
23	ARI	21	TAU	23	GEM	21	CAN	21	LEO	22	LIB
25	TAU	23	GEM	25	CAN	23	LEO	23	VIR	24	SCO
27	GEM	25	CAN	27	LEO	26	VIR	25	LIB	27	SAG
29	CAN	28	LEO	29	VIR	28	LIB	28	SCO	29	CAP
								31	SAG		

JUL		AUG		SEP		OCT		NOV		DEC	
2	AQU	2	ARI	1	TAU	2	CAN	3	VIR	3	LIB
4	PIS	4	TAU	3	GEM	4	LEO	5	LIB	5	SCO
6	ARI	6	GEM	5	CAN	7	VIR	8	SCO	8	SAG
8	TAU	9	CAN	7	LEO	9	LIB	10	SAG	10	CAP
10	GEM	11	LEO	9	VIR	12	SCO	13	CAP	13	AQU
12	CAN	13	VIR	12	LIB	14	SAG	15	AQU	15	PIS
14	LEO	15	LIB	14	SCO	17	CAP	18	PIS	17	ARI
17	VIR	18	SCO	17	SAG	19	AQU	20	ARI	19	TAU
19	LIB	20	SAG	19	CAP	21	PIS	22	TAU	21	GEM
22	SCO	23	CAP	22	AQU	23	ARI	24	GEM	23	CAN
24	SAG	25	AQU	24	PIS	25	TAU	26	CAN	25	LEO
27	CAP	27	PIS	26	ARI	27	GEM	28	LEO	27	VIR
29	AQU	29	ARI	28	TAU	29	CAN	30	VIR	30	LIB
31	PIS			30	GEM	31	LEO				

2008

JAN		FEB		MAR		APR		MAY		JUN	
1	SCO	3	CAP	1	CAP	2	PIS	2	ARI	2	GEM
4	SAG	5	AQU	3	AQU	4	ARI	4	TAU	4	CAN
6	CAP	7	PIS	6	PIS	6	TAU	6	GEM	6	LEO
9	AQU	10	ARI	8	ARI	8	GEM	8	CAN	8	VIR
11	PIS	12	TAU	10	TAU	10	CAN	10	LEO	11	LIB
13	ARI	14	GEM	12	GEM	13	LEO	12	VIR	13	SCO
15	TAU	16	CAN	14	CAN	15	VIR	14	LIB	16	SAG
18	GEM	18	LEO	16	LEO	17	LIB	17	SCO	18	CAP
20	CAN	20	VIR	19	VIR	20	SCO	19	SAG	21	AQU
22	LEO	23	LIB	21	LIB	22	SAG	22	CAP	23	PIS
24	VIR	25	SCO	23	SCO	25	CAP	24	AQU	25	ARI
26	LIB	28	SAG	26	SAG	27	AQU	27	PIS	28	TAU
29	SCO			28	CAP	30	PIS	29	ARI	30	GEM
31	SAG			31	AQU			31	TAU		

JUL		AUG		SEP		OCT		NOV		DEC	
2	CAN	2	VIR	1	LIB	3	SAG	2	CAP	2	AQU
4	LEO	4	LIB	3	SCO	5	CAP	4	AQU	4	PIS
6	VIR	7	SCO	6	SAG	8	AQU	7	PIS	6	ARI
8	LIB	9	SAG	8	CAP	10	PIS	9	ARI	9	TAU
10	SCO	12	CAP	11	AQU	13	ARI	11	TAU	11	GEM
13	SAG	14	AQU	13	PIS	15	TAU	13	GEM	13	CAN
15	CAP	17	PIS	15	ARI	17	GEM	15	CAN	15	LEO
18	AQU	19	ARI	17	TAU	19	CAN	17	LEO	17	VIR
20	PIS	21	TAU	19	GEM	21	LEO	19	VIR	19	LIB
23	ARI	23	GEM	22	CAN	23	VIR	22	LIB	21	SCO
25	TAU	25	CAN	24	LEO	25	LIB	24	SCO	24	SAG
27	GEM	27	LEO	26	VIR	28	SCO	27	SAG	26	CAP
29	CAN	30	VIR	28	LIB	30	SAG	29	CAP	29	AQU
31	LEO			30	SCO					31	PIS

2009

JAN		FEB		MAR		APR		MAY		JUN	
3	ARI	1	TAU	3	GEM	1	CAN	2	VIR	1	LIB
5	TAU	3	GEM	5	CAN	3	LEO	5	LIB	3	SCO
7	GEM	5	CAN	7	LEO	5	VIR	7	SCO	6	SAG
9	CAN	7	LEO	9	VIR	7	LIB	9	SAG	8	CAP
11	LEO	10	VIR	11	LIB	10	SCO	12	CAP	11	AQU
13	VIR	12	LIB	13	SCO	12	SAG	14	AQU	13	PIS
15	LIB	14	SCO	16	SAG	15	CAP	17	PIS	16	ARI
18	SCO	16	SAG	18	CAP	17	AQU	19	ARI	18	TAU
20	SAG	19	CAP	21	AQU	20	PIS	21	TAU	20	GEM
23	CAP	21	AQU	23	PIS	22	ARI	24	GEM	22	CAN
25	AQU	24	PIS	26	ARI	24	TAU	26	CAN	24	LEO
28	PIS	26	ARI	28	TAU	26	GEM	28	LEO	26	VIR
30	ARI	28	TAU	30	GEM	28	CAN	30	VIR	28	LIB
						30	LEO			30	SCO

JUL		AUG		SEP		OCT		NOV		DEC	
3	SAG	2	CAP	3	PIS	3	ARI	1	TAU	1	GEM
5	CAP	4	AQU	5	ARI	5	TAU	4	GEM	3	CAN
8	AQU	7	PIS	8	TAU	7	GEM	6	CAN	5	LEO
10	PIS	9	ARI	10	GEM	9	CAN	8	LEO	7	VIR
13	ARI	11	TAU	12	CAN	12	LEO	10	VIR	9	LIB
15	TAU	14	GEM	14	LEO	14	VIR	12	LIB	11	SCO
17	GEM	16	CAN	16	VIR	16	LIB	14	SCO	14	SAG
19	CAN	18	LEO	18	LIB	18	SCO	17	SAG	16	CAP
21	LEO	20	VIR	20	SCO	20	SAG	19	CAP	19	AQU
23	VIR	22	LIB	23	SAG	23	CAP	21	AQU	21	PIS
26	LIB	24	SCO	25	CAP	25	AQU	24	PIS	24	ARI
28	SCO	26	SAG	28	AQU	28	PIS	26	ARI	26	TAU
30	SAG	29	CAP	30	PIS	30	ARI	29	TAU	28	GEM
		31	AQU							30	CAN

2010

JAN		FEB		MAR		APR		MAY		JUN	
1	LEO	2	LIB	1	LIB	2	SAG	2	CAP	1	AQU
3	VIR	4	SCO	3	SCO	4	CAP	4	AQU	3	PIS
6	LIB	6	SAG	6	SAG	7	AQU	7	PIS	6	ARI
8	SCO	9	CAP	8	CAP	9	PIS	9	ARI	8	TAU
10	SAG	11	AQU	11	AQU	12	ARI	12	TAU	10	GEM
13	CAP	14	PIS	13	PIS	14	TAU	14	GEM	12	CAN
15	AQU	16	ARI	16	ARI	17	GEM	16	CAN	14	LEO
18	PIS	19	TAU	18	TAU	19	CAN	18	LEO	17	VIR
20	ARI	21	GEM	20	GEM	21	LEO	20	VIR	19	LIB
22	TAU	23	CAN	23	CAN	23	VIR	22	LIB	21	SCO
25	GEM	25	LEO	25	LEO	25	LIB	25	SCO	23	SAG
27	CAN	27	VIR	27	VIR	27	SCO	27	SAG	25	CAP
29	LEO			29	LIB	29	SAG	29	CAP	28	AQU
31	VIR			31	SCO					30	PIS

JUL		AUG		SEP		OCT		NOV		DEC	
3	ARI	2	TAU	3	CAN	2	LEO	3	LIB	2	SCO
5	TAU	4	GEM	5	LEO	4	VIR	5	SCO	4	SAG
8	GEM	6	CAN	7	VIR	6	LIB	7	SAG	6	CAP
10	CAN	8	LEO	9	LIB	8	SCO	9	CAP	9	AQU
12	LEO	10	VIR	11	SCO	10	SAG	11	AQU	11	PIS
14	VIR	12	LIB	13	SAG	12	CAP	14	PIS	14	ARI
16	LIB	14	SCO	15	CAP	15	AQU	16	ARI	16	TAU
18	SCO	17	SAG	18	AQU	17	PIS	19	TAU	18	GEM
20	SAG	19	CAP	20	PIS	20	ARI	21	GEM	21	CAN
23	CAP	21	AQU	23	ARI	22	TAU	23	CAN	23	LEO
25	AQU	24	PIS	25	TAU	25	GEM	26	LEO	25	VIR
28	PIS	26	ARI	28	GEM	27	CAN	28	VIR	27	LIB
30	ARI	29	TAU	30	CAN	29	LEO	30	LIB	29	SCO
		31	GEM			31	VIR			31	SAG

2011

JAN		FEB		MAR		APR		MAY		JUN	
3	CAP	1	AQU	1	AQU	2	ARI	2	TAU	3	CAN
5	AQU	4	PIS	3	PIS	4	TAU	4	GEM	5	LEO
7	PIS	6	ARI	6	ARI	7	GEM	6	CAN	7	VIR
10	ARI	9	TAU	8	TAU	9	CAN	9	LEO	9	LIB
12	TAU	11	GEM	11	GEM	11	LEO	11	VIR	11	SCO
15	GEM	14	CAN	13	CAN	14	VIR	13	LIB	13	SAG
17	CAN	16	LEO	15	LEO	16	LIB	15	SCO	16	CAP
19	LEO	18	VIR	17	VIR	18	SCO	17	SAG	18	AQU
21	VIR	20	LIB	19	LIB	20	SAG	19	CAP	20	PIS
23	LIB	22	SCO	21	SCO	22	CAP	21	AQU	23	ARI
25	SCO	24	SAG	23	SAG	24	AQU	24	PIS	25	TAU
28	SAG	26	CAP	25	CAP	27	PIS	26	ARI	28	GEM
30	CAP			28	AQU	29	ARI	29	TAU	30	CAN
				30	PIS			31	GEM		

JUL		AUG		SEP		OCT		NOV		DEC	
2	LEO	1	VIR	1	SCO	1	SAG	1	AQU	1	PIS
4	VIR	3	LIB	3	SAG	3	CAP	4	PIS	3	ARI
6	LIB	5	SCO	5	CAP	5	AQU	6	ARI	6	TAU
9	SCO	7	SAG	8	AQU	7	PIS	9	TAU	8	GEM
11	SAG	9	CAP	10	PIS	10	ARI	11	GEM	11	CAN
13	CAP	11	AQU	13	ARI	12	TAU	14	CAN	13	LEO
15	AQU	14	PIS	15	TAU	15	GEM	16	LEO	15	VIR
18	PIS	16	ARI	18	GEM	17	CAN	18	VIR	18	LIB
20	ARI	19	TAU	20	CAN	20	LEO	20	LIB	20	SCO
23	TAU	21	GEM	22	LEO	22	VIR	22	SCO	22	SAG
25	GEM	24	CAN	24	VIR	24	LIB	24	SAG	24	CAP
27	CAN	26	LEO	27	LIB	26	SCO	26	CAP	26	AQU
30	LEO	28	VIR	29	SCO	28	SAG	29	AQU	28	PIS
		30	LIB			30	CAP			31	ARI

2012

	JAN		FEB		MAR		APR		MAY		JUN
2	TAU	1	GEM	2	CAN	1	LEO	2	LIB	1	SCO
5	GEM	4	CAN	4	LEO	3	VIR	4	SCO	3	SAG
7	CAN	6	LEO	6	VIR	5	LIB	6	SAG	5	CAP
9	LEO	8	VIR	8	LIB	7	SCO	8	CAP	7	AQU
12	VIR	10	LIB	11	SCO	9	SAG	11	AQU	9	PIS
14	LIB	12	SCO	13	SAG	11	CAP	13	PIS	11	ARI
16	SCO	14	SAG	15	CAP	13	AQU	15	ARI	14	TAU
18	SAG	17	CAP	17	AQU	16	PIS	18	TAU	17	GEM
20	CAP	19	AQU	19	PIS	18	ARI	20	GEM	19	CAN
22	AQU	21	PIS	22	ARI	20	TAU	23	CAN	21	LEO
25	PIS	23	ARI	24	TAU	23	GEM	25	LEO	24	VIR
27	ARI	26	TAU	27	GEM	26	CAN	28	VIR	26	LIB
30	TAU	28	GEM	29	CAN	28	LEO	30	LIB	28	SCO
						30	VIR			30	SAG

	JUL		AUG		SEP		OCT		NOV		DEC
2	CAP	1	AQU	2	ARI	1	TAU	3	CAN	2	LEO
4	AQU	3	PIS	4	TAU	4	GEM	5	LEO	5	VIR
6	PIS	5	ARI	6	GEM	6	CAN	7	VIR	7	LIB
9	ARI	8	TAU	9	CAN	9	LEO	10	LIB	9	SCO
11	TAU	10	GEM	11	LEO	11	VIR	12	SCO	11	SAG
14	GEM	13	CAN	14	VIR	13	LIB	14	SAG	13	CAP
16	CAN	15	LEO	16	LIB	15	SCO	16	CAP	15	AQU
19	LEO	17	VIR	18	SCO	17	SAG	18	AQU	17	PIS
21	VIR	19	LIB	20	SAG	19	CAP	20	PIS	20	ARI
23	LIB	22	SCO	22	CAP	22	AQU	22	ARI	22	TAU
25	SCO	24	SAG	24	AQU	24	PIS	25	TAU	25	GEM
28	SAG	26	CAP	27	PIS	26	ARI	27	GEM	27	CAN
30	CAP	28	AQU	29	ARI	29	TAU	30	CAN	30	LEO
		30	PIS			31	GEM				

2013

	JAN		FEB		MAR		APR		MAY		JUN
1	VIR	2	SCO	1	SCO	2	CAP	1	AQU	2	ARI
3	LIB	4	SAG	3	SAG	4	AQU	3	PIS	4	TAU
6	SCO	6	CAP	5	CAP	6	PIS	5	ARI	6	GEM
8	SAG	8	AQU	7	AQU	8	ARI	8	TAU	9	CAN
10	CAP	10	PIS	10	PIS	10	TAU	10	GEM	12	LEO
12	AQU	12	ARI	12	ARI	13	GEM	13	CAN	14	VIR
14	PIS	15	TAU	14	TAU	15	CAN	15	LEO	16	LIB
16	ARI	17	GEM	17	GEM	18	LEO	18	VIR	19	SCO
18	TAU	20	CAN	19	CAN	20	VIR	20	LIB	21	SAG
21	GEM	22	LEO	22	LEO	23	LIB	22	SCO	23	CAP
23	CAN	25	VIR	24	VIR	25	SCO	24	SAG	25	AQU
26	LEO	27	LIB	26	LIB	27	SAG	26	CAP	27	PIS
28	VIR			28	SCO	29	CAP	28	AQU	29	ARI
31	LIB			30	SAG			30	PIS		

	JUL		AUG		SEP		OCT		NOV		DEC
1	TAU	2	CAN	1	LEO	1	VIR	2	SCO	2	SAG
4	GEM	5	LEO	4	VIR	3	LIB	4	SAG	4	CAP
6	CAN	7	VIR	6	LIB	6	SCO	6	CAP	6	AQU
9	LEO	10	LIB	8	SCO	8	SAG	8	AQU	8	PIS
11	VIR	12	SCO	11	SAG	10	CAP	10	PIS	10	ARI
14	LIB	14	SAG	13	CAP	12	AQU	13	ARI	12	TAU
16	SCO	16	CAP	15	AQU	14	PIS	15	TAU	15	GEM
18	SAG	18	AQU	17	PIS	16	ARI	17	GEM	17	CAN
20	CAP	20	PIS	19	ARI	19	TAU	20	CAN	20	LEO
22	AQU	23	ARI	21	TAU	21	GEM	22	LEO	22	VIR
24	PIS	25	TAU	24	GEM	23	CAN	25	VIR	25	LIB
26	ARI	27	GEM	26	CAN	26	LEO	27	LIB	27	SCO
28	TAU	30	CAN	29	LEO	28	VIR	29	SCO	29	SAG
31	GEM					31	LIB			31	CAP

2014

JAN: 2 AQU, 4 PIS, 6 ARI, 8 TAU, 11 GEM, 13 CAN, 16 LEO, 18 VIR, 21 LIB, 23 SCO, 25 GEM, 28 CAP, 30 AQU

FEB: 1 PIS, 3 ARI, 5 TAU, 7 GEM, 10 CAN, 12 LEO, 15 VIR, 17 LIB, 19 SCO, 22 SAG, 24 CAP, 26 AQU, 28 PIS

MAR: 2 ARI, 4 TAU, 6 GEM, 9 CAN, 11 LEO, 14 VIR, 16 LIB, 19 SCO, 21 SAG, 23 CAP, 25 AQU, 27 PIS, 29 ARI

APR: 1 TAU, 3 GEM, 5 CAN, 8 LEO, 10 VIR, 13 LIB, 15 SCO, 17 SAG, 19 CAP, 21 AQU, 24 PIS, 26 ARI, 28 TAU, 30 GEM

MAY: 3 CAN, 5 LEO, 8 VIR, 10 LIB, 12 SCO, 15 SAG, 17 CAP, 19 AQU, 21 PIS, 23 ARI, 25 TAU, 27 GEM, 30 CAN

JUN: 1 LEO, 4 VIR, 6 LIB, 9 SCO, 11 SAG, 13 CAP, 15 AQU, 17 PIS, 19 ARI, 21 TAU, 24 GEM, 26 CAN, 29 LEO

JUL: 1 VIR, 4 LIB, 6 SCO, 8 SAG, 10 CAP, 12 AQU, 14 PIS, 16 ARI, 19 TAU, 21 GEM, 23 CAN, 26 LEO, 28 VIR, 31 LIB

AUG: 2 SCO, 5 SAG, 7 CAP, 9 AQU, 11 PIS, 13 ARI, 15 TAU, 17 GEM, 20 CAN, 22 LEO, 25 VIR, 27 LIB, 30 SCO

SEP: 1 SAG, 3 CAP, 5 AQU, 7 PIS, 9 ARI, 11 TAU, 14 GEM, 16 CAN, 18 LEO, 21 VIR, 23 LIB, 26 SCO, 28 SAG, 30 CAP

OCT: 3 AQU, 5 PIS, 7 ARI, 9 TAU, 11 GEM, 13 CAN, 16 LEO, 18 VIR, 21 LIB, 23 SCO, 25 SAG, 28 CAP, 30 AQU

NOV: 1 PIS, 3 ARI, 5 TAU, 7 GEM, 10 CAN, 12 LEO, 15 VIR, 17 LIB, 20 SCO, 22 SAG, 24 CAP, 26 AQU, 28 PIS, 30 ARI

DEC: 3 TAU, 5 GEM, 7 CAN, 9 LEO, 12 VIR, 14 LIB, 17 SCO, 19 SAG, 21 CAP, 23 AQU, 25 PIS, 28 ARI, 30 TAU

2015

JAN: 1 GEM, 3 CAN, 6 LEO, 8 VIR, 11 LIB, 13 SCO, 16 SAG, 18 CAP, 20 AQU, 22 PIS, 24 ARI, 26 TAU, 28 GEM, 31 CAN

FEB: 2 LEO, 5 VIR, 7 LIB, 10 SCO, 12 SAG, 14 CAP, 16 AQU, 18 PIS, 20 ARI, 22 TAU, 25 GEM, 27 CAN

MAR: 1 LEO, 4 VIR, 6 LIB, 8 SCO, 11 SAG, 14 CAP, 16 AQU, 18 PIS, 20 ARI, 22 TAU, 24 GEM, 26 CAN, 29 LEO, 31 VIR

APR: 3 LIB, 5 SCO, 8 SAG, 10 CAP, 12 AQU, 14 PIS, 16 ARI, 18 TAU, 20 GEM, 22 CAN, 25 LEO, 27 VIR, 30 LIB

MAY: 2 SCO, 5 SAG, 7 CAP, 9 AQU, 11 PIS, 14 ARI, 16 TAU, 18 GEM, 20 CAN, 22 LEO, 25 VIR, 27 LIB, 30 SCO

JUN: 1 SAG, 3 CAP, 6 AQU, 8 PIS, 10 ARI, 12 TAU, 14 GEM, 16 CAN, 19 LEO, 21 VIR, 24 LIB, 26 SCO, 28 SAG

JUL: 1 CAP, 3 AQU, 5 PIS, 7 ARI, 9 TAU, 11 GEM, 14 CAN, 16 LEO, 18 VIR, 21 LIB, 23 SCO, 26 SAG, 28 CAP, 30 AQU

AUG: 1 PIS, 3 ARI, 5 TAU, 8 GEM, 10 CAN, 12 LEO, 15 VIR, 17 LIB, 20 SCO, 22 SAG, 24 CAP, 27 AQU, 29 PIS, 31 ARI

SEP: 2 TAU, 4 GEM, 6 CAN, 8 LEO, 11 VIR, 13 LIB, 16 SCO, 18 SAG, 21 CAP, 23 AQU, 25 PIS, 27 ARI, 29 TAU

OCT: 1 GEM, 3 CAN, 6 LEO, 8 VIR, 11 LIB, 13 SCO, 16 SAG, 18 CAP, 20 AQU, 23 PIS, 25 ARI, 27 TAU, 29 GEM, 31 CAN

NOV: 2 LEO, 4 VIR, 7 LIB, 9 SCO, 12 SAG, 14 CAP, 17 AQU, 19 PIS, 21 ARI, 23 TAU, 25 GEM, 27 CAN, 29 LEO

DEC: 2 VIR, 4 LIB, 7 SCO, 9 SAG, 12 CAP, 14 AQU, 16 PIS, 18 ARI, 20 TAU, 22 GEM, 25 CAN, 27 LEO, 29 VIR

2016

JAN		FEB		MAR		APR		MAY		JUN	
1	LIB	2	SAG	3	CAP	1	AQU	1	PIS	1	TAU
3	SCO	4	CAP	5	AQU	4	PIS	3	ARI	3	GEM
6	SAG	7	AQU	7	PIS	6	ARI	5	TAU	5	CAN
8	CAP	9	PIS	9	ARI	8	TAU	7	GEM	8	LEO
10	AQU	11	ARI	11	TAU	10	GEM	9	CAN	10	VIR
12	PIS	13	TAU	13	GEM	12	CAN	11	LEO	12	LIB
14	ARI	15	GEM	15	CAN	14	LEO	19	SCO	15	SCO
19	GEM	19	LEO	20	VIR	19	LIB	21	SAG	20	CAP
21	CAN	22	VIR	23	LIB	21	SCO	24	CAP	22	AQU
23	LEO	24	LIB	25	SCO	24	SAG	26	AQU	24	PIS
25	VIR	27	SCO	28	SAG	26	CAP	28	PIS	27	ARI
28	LIB	29	SAG	30	CAP	29	AQU	30	ARI	29	TAU
30	SCO										

JUL		AUG		SEP		OCT		NOV		DEC	
1	GEM	1	LEO	2	LIB	2	SCO	1	SAG	1	CAP
3	CAN	4	VIR	5	SCO	5	SAG	3	CAP	3	AQU
5	LEO	6	LIB	7	SAG	7	CAP	6	AQU	5	PIS
7	VIR	9	SCO	10	CAP	10	AQU	8	PIS	8	ARI
10	LIB	11	SAG	12	AQU	12	PIS	10	ARI	10	TAU
12	SCO	13	CAP	14	PIS	14	ARI	12	TAU	12	GEM
15	SAG	16	AQU	16	ARI	16	TAU	14	GEM	14	CAN
17	CAP	18	PIS	19	TAU	18	GEM	16	CAN	16	LEO
19	AQU	20	ARI	21	GEM	20	CAN	18	LEO	18	VIR
22	PIS	22	TAU	23	CAN	22	LEO	21	VIR	20	LIB
24	ARI	24	GEM	25	LEO	24	VIR	23	LIB	23	SCO
26	TAU	26	CAN	27	VIR	27	LIB	26	SCO	25	SAG
28	GEM	29	LEO	30	LIB	29	SCO	28	SAG	28	CAP
30	CAN	31	VIR							30	AQU

2017

JAN		FEB		MAR		APR		MAY		JUN	
2	PIS	2	TAU	2	TAU	2	CAN	1	LEO	2	LIB
4	ARI	4	GEM	4	GEM	4	LEO	4	VIR	5	SCO
6	TAU	7	CAN	6	CAN	6	VIR	6	LIB	7	SAG
8	GEM	9	LEO	8	LEO	9	LIB	9	SCO	10	CAP
10	CAN	11	VIR	10	VIR	11	SCO	11	SAG	12	AQU
12	LEO	13	LIB	13	LIB	14	SAG	14	CAP	15	PIS
14	VIR	16	SCO	15	SCO	16	CAP	16	AQU	17	ARI
17	LIB	18	SAG	17	SAG	19	AQU	18	PIS	19	TAU
19	SCO	21	CAP	20	CAP	21	PIS	21	ARI	21	GEM
22	SAG	23	AQU	22	AQU	23	ARI	23	TAU	23	CAN
24	CAP	25	PIS	25	PIS	25	TAU	25	GEM	25	LEO
27	AQU	28	ARI	27	ARI	27	GEM	27	CAN	27	VIR
29	PIS			29	TAU	29	CAN	29	LEO	30	LIB
31	ARI			31	GEM			31	VIR		

JUL		AUG		SEP		OCT		NOV		DEC	
2	SCO	1	SAG	2	AQU	2	PIS	1	ARI	2	GEM
5	SAG	3	CAP	5	PIS	4	ARI	3	TAU	4	CAN
7	CAP	6	AQU	7	ARI	6	TAU	5	GEM	6	LEO
10	AQU	8	PIS	9	TAU	8	GEM	7	CAN	8	VIR
12	PIS	11	ARI	11	GEM	10	CAN	9	LEO	11	LIB
14	ARI	13	TAU	13	CAN	13	LEO	11	VIR	13	SCO
17	TAU	15	GEM	15	LEO	15	VIR	13	LIB	15	SAG
19	GEM	17	CAN	18	VIR	17	LIB	16	SCO	18	CAP
21	CAN	19	LEO	20	LIB	19	SCO	18	SAG	20	AQU
23	LEO	21	VIR	22	SCO	22	SAG	21	CAP	23	PIS
25	VIR	23	LIB	24	SAG	24	CAP	23	AQU	25	ARI
27	LIB	26	SCO	27	CAP	27	AQU	26	PIS	28	TAU
29	SCO	28	SAG	29	AQU	29	PIS	28	ARI	30	GEM
		31	CAP					30	TAU		

2018

JAN		FEB		MAR		APR		MAY		JUN	
1	CAN	1	VIR	1	VIR	1	SCO	1	SAG	2	AQU
3	LEO	3	LIB	3	LIB	4	SAG	3	CAP	5	PIS
5	VIR	5	SCO	5	SCO	6	CAP	6	AQU	7	ARI
7	LIB	8	SAG	7	SAG	9	AQU	8	PIS	9	TAU
9	SCO	10	CAP	10	CAP	11	PIS	11	ARI	12	GEM
12	SAG	13	AQU	12	AQU	13	ARI	13	TAU	14	CAN
14	CAP	15	PIS	15	PIS	16	TAU	15	GEM	16	LEO
17	AQU	18	ARI	17	ARI	18	GEM	17	CAN	18	VIR
19	PIS	20	TAU	19	TAU	20	CAN	19	LEO	20	LIB
22	ARI	22	GEM	22	GEM	22	LEO	21	VIR	22	SCO
24	TAU	24	CAN	24	CAN	24	VIR	24	LIB	24	SAG
26	GEM	26	LEO	26	LEO	26	LIB	26	SCO	27	CAP
28	CAN			28	VIR	29	SCO	28	SAG	29	AQU
30	LEO			30	LIB			31	CAP		

JUL		AUG		SEP		OCT		NOV		DEC	
2	PIS	1	ARI	2	GEM	1	CAN	2	VIR	1	LIB
4	ARI	3	TAU	4	CAN	3	LEO	4	LIB	3	SCO
7	TAU	5	GEM	6	LEO	5	VIR	6	SCO	5	SAG
9	GEM	7	CAN	8	VIR	7	LIB	8	SAG	8	CAP
11	CAN	9	LEO	10	LIB	9	SCO	10	CAP	10	AQU
13	LEO	11	VIR	12	SCO	12	SAG	13	AQU	13	PIS
15	VIR	14	LIB	14	SAG	14	CAP	15	PIS	15	ARI
17	LIB	16	SCO	17	CAP	17	AQU	18	ARI	18	TAU
19	SCO	18	SAG	19	AQU	19	PIS	20	TAU	20	GEM
22	SAG	20	CAP	22	PIS	22	ARI	22	GEM	22	CAN
24	CAP	23	AQU	24	ARI	24	TAU	25	CAN	24	LEO
27	AQU	26	PIS	27	TAU	26	GEM	27	LEO	26	VIR
29	PIS	28	ARI	29	GEM	28	CAN	29	VIR	28	LIB
		30	TAU			30	LEO			30	SCO

2019

JAN		FEB		MAR		APR		MAY		JUN	
2	SAG	3	AQU	2	AQU	1	PIS	1	ARI	2	GEM
4	CAP	5	PIS	5	PIS	3	ARI	3	TAU	4	CAN
7	AQU	8	ARI	7	ARI	6	TAU	5	GEM	6	LEO
9	PIS	10	TAU	10	TAU	8	GEM	8	CAN	8	VIR
12	ARI	13	GEM	12	GEM	10	CAN	10	LEO	10	LIB
14	TAU	15	CAN	14	CAN	13	LEO	12	VIR	12	SCO
16	GEM	17	LEO	16	LEO	15	VIR	14	LIB	15	SAG
18	CAN	19	VIR	18	VIR	17	LIB	16	SCO	17	CAP
20	LEO	21	LIB	20	LIB	19	SCO	18	SAG	19	AQU
22	VIR	23	SCO	22	SCO	21	SAG	21	CAP	22	PIS
24	LIB	25	SAG	25	SAG	23	CAP	23	AQU	24	ARI
27	SCO	28	CAP	27	CAP	26	AQU	26	PIS	27	TAU
29	SAG			29	AQU	28	PIS	28	ARI	29	GEM
31	CAP							30	TAU		

JUL		AUG		SEP		OCT		NOV		DEC	
1	CAN	2	VIR	2	SCO	2	SAG	3	AQU	3	PIS
3	LEO	4	LIB	4	SAG	4	CAP	5	PIS	5	ARI
5	VIR	6	SCO	7	CAP	6	AQU	8	ARI	8	TAU
8	LIB	8	SAG	9	AQU	9	PIS	10	TAU	10	GEM
10	SCO	11	CAP	12	PIS	11	ARI	13	GEM	12	CAN
12	SAG	13	AQU	14	ARI	14	TAU	15	CAN	14	LEO
14	CAP	15	PIS	17	TAU	16	GEM	17	LEO	17	VIR
17	AQU	18	ARI	19	GEM	19	CAN	19	VIR	19	LIB
19	PIS	20	TAU	22	CAN	21	LEO	21	LIB	21	SCO
22	ARI	23	GEM	24	LEO	23	VIR	24	SCO	23	SAG
24	TAU	25	CAN	26	VIR	25	LIB	26	SAG	25	CAP
27	GEM	27	LEO	28	LIB	27	SCO	28	CAP	28	AQU
29	CAN	29	VIR	30	SCO	29	SAG	30	AQU	30	PIS
31	LEO	31	LIB			31	CAP				

2020

JAN		FEB		MAR		APR		MAY		JUN	
1	ARI	3	GEM	1	GEM	2	LEO	2	VIR	2	SCO
4	TAU	5	CAN	3	CAN	4	VIR	4	LIB	4	SAG
6	GEM	7	LEO	6	LEO	6	LIB	6	SCO	6	CAP
9	CAN	9	VIR	8	VIR	8	SCO	8	SAG	8	AQU
11	LEO	11	LIB	10	LIB	10	SAG	10	CAP	11	PIS
13	VIR	13	SCO	12	SCO	12	CAP	12	AQU	13	ARI
15	LIB	15	SAG	14	SAG	15	AQU	14	PIS	16	TAU
17	SCO	18	CAP	16	CAP	17	PIS	17	ARI	18	GEM
19	SAG	20	AQU	18	AQU	20	ARI	19	TAU	21	CAN
22	CAP	23	PIS	21	PIS	22	TAU	22	GEM	23	LEO
24	AQU	25	ARI	23	ARI	25	GEM	24	CAN	25	VIR
26	PIS	28	TAU	26	TAU	27	CAN	27	LEO	27	LIB
29	ARI			28	GEM	29	LEO	29	VIR	29	SCO
31	TAU			31	CAN			31	LIB		

JUL		AUG		SEP		OCT		NOV		DEC	
1	SAG	2	AQU	1	PIS	3	TAU	2	GEM	1	CAN
3	CAP	4	PIS	3	ARI	5	GEM	4	CAN	4	LEO
6	AQU	7	ARI	6	TAU	8	CAN	7	LEO	6	VIR
8	PIS	9	TAU	8	GEM	10	LEO	9	VAN	8	LIB
11	ARI	12	GEM	11	CAN	13	VIR	11	LIB	10	SCO
13	TAU	14	CAN	13	LEO	15	LIB	13	SCO	12	SAG
16	GEM	17	LEO	15	VIR	17	SCO	15	SAG	14	CAP
18	CAN	19	VIR	17	LIB	19	SAG	17	CAP	17	AQU
20	LEO	21	LIB	19	SCO	21	CAP	19	AQU	19	PIS
22	VIR	23	SCO	21	SAG	23	AQU	21	PIS	21	ARI
24	LIB	25	SAG	23	CAP	25	PIS	24	ARI	24	TAU
26	SCO	27	CAP	26	AQU	28	ARI	26	TAU	26	GEM
29	SAG	29	AQU	28	PIS	30	TAU	29	GEM	29	CAN
31	CAP			30	ARI					31	LEO

2021

JAN		FEB		MAR		APR		MAY		JUN	
2	VIR	1	LIB	2	SCO	1	SAG	2	AQU	1	PIS
5	LIB	3	SCO	4	SAG	3	CAP	4	PIS	3	ARI
7	SCO	5	SAG	6	CAP	5	AQU	7	ARI	6	TAU
9	SAG	7	CAP	9	AQU	7	PIS	9	TAU	8	GEM
11	CAP	9	AQU	11	PIS	10	ARI	12	GEM	11	CAN
13	AQU	12	PIS	13	ARI	12	TAU	14	CAN	13	LEO
15	PIS	14	ARI	16	TAU	15	GEM	17	LEO	15	VIR
18	ARI	16	TAU	18	GEM	17	CAN	19	VIR	18	LIB
20	TAU	19	GEM	21	CAN	20	LEO	21	LIB	20	SCO
23	GEM	21	CAN	23	LEO	22	VIR	23	SCO	22	SAG
25	CAN	24	LEO	25	VIR	24	LIB	25	SAG	24	CAP
27	LEO	26	VIR	28	LIB	26	SCO	27	CAP	26	AQU
30	VIR	28	LIB	30	SCO	28	SAG	29	AQU	28	PIS
						30	CAP			30	ARI

JUL		AUG		SEP		OCT		NOV		DEC	
3	TAU	2	GEM	1	CAN	3	VIR	1	LIB	1	SCO
5	GEM	4	CAN	3	LEO	5	LIB	3	SCO	3	SAG
8	CAN	7	LEO	5	VIR	7	SCO	5	SAG	5	CAP
10	LEO	9	VIR	7	LIB	9	SAG	7	CAP	7	AQU
13	VIR	11	LIB	10	SCO	11	CAP	9	AQU	9	PIS
15	LIB	13	SCO	12	SAG	13	AQU	12	PIS	11	ARI
17	SCO	15	SAG	14	CAP	15	PIS	14	ARI	14	TAU
19	SAG	18	CAP	16	AQU	18	ARI	16	TAU	16	GEM
21	CAP	20	AQU	18	PIS	20	TAU	19	GEM	19	CAN
23	AQU	22	PIS	20	ARI	23	GEM	21	CAN	21	LEO
25	PIS	24	ARI	23	TAU	25	CAN	24	LEO	24	VIR
28	ARI	26	TAU	25	GEM	28	LEO	26	VIR	26	LIB
30	TAU	29	GEM	28	CAN	30	VIR	29	LIB	28	SCO
				30	LEO					30	SAG

2022

JAN		FEB		MAR		APR		MAY		JUN	
1	CAP	2	PIS	1	PIS	2	TAU	2	GEM	1	CAN
3	AQU	4	ARI	3	ARI	4	GEM	4	CAN	3	LEO
5	PIS	6	TAU	6	TAU	7	CAN	7	LEO	6	VIR
8	ARI	9	GEM	8	GEM	9	LEO	9	VIR	8	LIB
10	TAU	11	CAN	11	CAN	12	VIR	12	LIB	10	SCO
12	GEM	14	LEO	13	LEO	14	LIB	14	SCO	12	SAG
15	CAN	16	VIR	16	VIR	16	SCO	16	SAG	14	CAP
17	LEO	18	LIB	18	LIB	18	SAG	18	CAP	16	AQU
20	VIR	21	SCO	20	SCO	20	CAP	20	AQU	18	PIS
22	LIB	23	SAG	22	SAG	23	AQU	22	PIS	20	ARI
24	SCO	25	CAP	24	CAP	25	PIS	24	ARI	23	TAU
27	SAG	27	AQU	26	AQU	27	ARI	27	TAU	25	GEM
29	CAP			28	PIS	29	TAU	29	GEM	28	CAN
31	AQU			31	ARI					30	LEO

JUL		AUG		SEP		OCT		NOV		DEC	
3	VIR	1	LIB	2	SAG	2	CAP	2	PIS	1	ARI
5	LIB	4	SCO	4	CAP	4	AQU	4	ARI	4	TAU
8	SCO	6	SAG	6	AQU	6	PIS	7	TAU	6	GEM
10	SAG	8	CAP	8	PIS	8	ARI	9	GEM	9	CAN
12	CAP	10	AQU	11	ARI	10	TAU	11	CAN	11	LEO
14	AQU	12	PIS	13	TAU	13	GEM	14	LEO	14	VIR
16	PIS	14	ARI	15	GEM	15	CAN	16	VIR	16	LIB
18	ARI	16	TAU	18	CAN	17	LEO	19	LIB	18	SCO
20	TAU	19	GEM	20	LEO	20	VIR	21	SCO	21	SAG
23	GEM	21	CAN	23	VIR	22	LIB	23	SAG	23	CAP
25	CAN	24	LEO	25	LIB	25	SCO	25	CAP	25	AQU
28	LEO	26	VIR	27	SCO	27	SAG	27	AQU	27	PIS
30	VIR	29	LIB	29	SAG	29	CAP	29	PIS	29	ARI
		31	SCO			31	AQU			31	TAU

2023

JAN		FEB		MAR		APR		MAY		JUN	
2	GEM	1	CAN	3	LEO	2	VIR	2	LIB	3	SAG
5	CAN	4	LEO	5	VIR	4	LIB	4	SCO	5	CAP
7	LEO	6	VIR	8	LIB	7	SCO	6	SAG	7	AQU
10	VIR	9	LIB	10	SCO	9	SAG	8	CAP	9	PIS
12	LIB	11	SCO	13	SAG	11	CAP	10	AQU	11	ARI
15	SCO	13	SAG	15	CAP	13	AQU	12	PIS	13	TAU
17	SAG	16	CAP	17	AQU	15	PIS	15	ARI	15	GEM
19	CAP	18	AQU	19	PIS	17	ARI	17	TAU	18	CAN
21	AQU	20	PIS	21	ARI	19	TAU	19	GEM	20	LEO
23	PIS	22	ARI	23	TAU	22	GEM	21	CAN	23	VIR
25	ARI	24	TAU	25	GEM	24	CAN	24	LEO	25	LIB
27	TAU	26	GEM	28	CAN	27	LEO	26	VIR	28	SCO
30	GEM	28	CAN	30	LEO	29	VIR	29	LIB	30	SAG
								31	SCO		

JUL		AUG		SEP		OCT		NOV		DEC	
2	CAP	2	PIS	1	ARI	3	GEM	1	CAN	1	LEO
4	AQU	4	ARI	3	TAU	5	CAN	4	LEO	3	VIR
6	PIS	7	TAU	5	GEM	7	LEO	6	VIR	6	LIB
8	ARI	9	GEM	8	CAN	10	VIR	9	LIB	8	SCO
10	TAU	11	CAN	10	LEO	12	LIB	11	SCO	11	SAG
13	GEM	14	LEO	13	VIR	15	SCO	13	SAG	13	CAP
15	CAN	16	VIR	15	LIB	17	SAG	16	CAP	15	AQU
17	LEO	19	LIB	18	SCO	19	CAP	18	AQU	17	PIS
20	VIR	21	SCO	20	SAG	22	AQU	20	PIS	19	ARI
23	LIB	24	SAG	22	CAP	24	PIS	22	ARI	21	TAU
25	SCO	26	CAP	24	AQU	26	ARI	24	TAU	24	GEM
27	SAG	28	AQU	26	PIS	28	TAU	26	GEM	26	CAN
29	CAP	30	PIS	28	ARI	30	GEM	29	CAN	28	LEO
31	AQU			30	TAU					31	VIR

2024

JAN		FEB		MAR		APR		MAY		JUN	
2	LIB	1	SCO	2	SAG	3	AQU	2	PIS	3	TAU
5	SCO	4	SAG	4	CAP	5	PIS	4	ARI	5	GEM
7	SAG	6	CAP	6	AQU	7	ARI	6	TAU	7	CAN
9	CAP	8	AQU	8	PIS	9	TAU	8	GEM	9	LEO
11	AQU	10	PIS	10	ARI	11	GEM	10	CAN	12	VIR
13	PIS	12	ARI	12	TAU	13	CAN	13	LEO	14	LIB
16	ARI	14	TAU	14	GEM	15	LEO	15	VIR	17	SCO
18	TAU	16	GEM	17	CAN	18	VIR	18	LIB	19	SAG
20	GEM	18	CAN	19	LEO	20	LIB	20	SCO	21	CAP
22	CAN	21	LEO	22	VIR	23	SCO	23	SAG	23	AQU
25	LEO	23	VIR	24	LIB	25	SAG	25	CAP	26	PIS
27	VIR	26	LIB	27	SCO	28	CAP	27	AQU	28	ARI
30	LIB	28	SCO	29	SAG	30	AQU	29	PIS	30	TAU
				31	CAP			31	ARI		

JUL		AUG		SEP		OCT		NOV		DEC	
2	GEM	3	LEO	1	VIR	1	LIB	3	SAG	2	CAP
4	CAN	5	VIR	4	LIB	4	SCO	5	CAP	4	AQU
6	LEO	8	LIB	7	SCO	6	SAG	7	AQU	7	PIS
9	VIR	10	SCO	9	SAG	9	CAP	9	PIS	9	ARI
11	LIB	13	SAG	11	CAP	11	AQU	12	ARI	11	TAU
14	SCO	15	CAP	14	AQU	13	PIS	14	TAU	13	GEM
16	SAG	17	AQU	16	PIS	15	ARI	16	GEM	15	CAN
19	CAP	19	PIS	18	ARI	17	TAU	18	CAN	17	LEO
21	AQU	21	ARI	20	TAU	19	GEM	20	LEO	20	VIR
23	PIS	23	TAU	22	GEM	21	CAN	22	VIR	22	LIB
25	ARI	25	GEM	24	CAN	24	LEO	25	LIB	25	SCO
27	TAU	28	CAN	26	LEO	26	VIR	27	SCO	27	SAG
29	GEM	30	LEO	29	VIR	28	LIB	30	SAG	29	CAP
31	CAN					31	SCO				

2025

JAN		FEB		MAR		APR		MAY		JUN	
1	AQU	1	ARI	1	ARI	1	GEM	1	CAN	1	VIR
3	PIS	3	TAU	3	TAU	3	CAN	3	LEO	4	LIB
5	ARI	6	GEM	5	GEM	5	LEO	5	VIR	6	SCO
7	TAU	8	CAN	7	CAN	8	VIR	8	LIB	9	SAG
9	GEM	10	LEO	9	LEO	10	LIB	10	SCO	11	CAP
11	CAN	12	VIR	12	VIR	13	SCO	13	SAG	14	AQU
14	LEO	15	LIB	14	LIB	15	SAG	15	CAP	16	PIS
16	VIR	17	SCO	17	SCO	18	CAP	18	AQU	18	ARI
18	LIB	20	SAG	19	SAG	20	AQU	20	PIS	20	TAU
21	SCO	22	CAP	22	CAP	23	PIS	22	ARI	22	GEM
23	SAG	25	AQU	24	AQU	25	ARI	24	TAU	24	CAN
26	CAP	27	PIS	26	PIS	27	TAU	26	GEM	27	LEO
28	AQU			28	ARI	29	GEM	28	CAN	29	VIR
30	PIS			30	TAU			30	LEO		

JUL		AUG		SEP		OCT		NOV		DEC	
1	LIB	3	SAG	1	CAP	1	AQU	2	ARI	1	TAU
4	SCO	5	CAP	4	AQU	3	PIS	4	TAU	3	GEM
6	SAG	7	AQU	6	PIS	6	ARI	6	GEM	5	CAN
9	CAP	10	PIS	8	ARI	8	TAU	8	CAN	7	LEO
11	AQU	12	ARI	10	TAU	10	GEM	10	LEO	10	VIR
13	PIS	14	TAU	12	GEM	12	CAN	12	VIR	12	LIB
15	ARI	16	GEM	14	CAN	14	LEO	15	LIB	14	SCO
18	TAU	18	CAN	17	LEO	16	VIR	17	SCO	17	SAG
20	GEM	20	LEO	19	VIR	18	LIB	20	SAG	20	CAP
22	CAN	23	VIR	21	LIB	21	SCO	22	CAP	22	AQU
24	LEO	25	LIB	24	SCO	23	SAG	25	AQU	24	PIS
26	VIR	27	SCO	26	SAG	26	CAP	27	PIS	27	ARI
29	LIB	30	SAG	29	CAP	28	AQU	29	ARI	29	TAU
31	SCO					31	PIS			31	GEM

Children with Moon in Aries

The Moon in Aries gives the emotional nature an *aggressive, impulsive* way of expressing itself. These children will rush headlong into any relationship or project without first looking things over. They need to be taught to sit back a minute, to count to ten, and think it through. Otherwise, they will find themselves in situations of difficulty before they realize what has happened. In Aries, the emotions are *fiery* and strongly expressed. Their aim tends to be *selfish* because they unconsciously believe their feelings are more important and should come first. Teach them to understand other people have feelings that are just as important. A little understanding can help them curb this self-oriented tendency. In any case, they must be taught to think before they act or speak and not to be so impulsive—otherwise they will have to face the consequences.

They are very courageous and will fight for what to them seems right. They will fight not only for themselves but others as well. They need to understand that their actions are triggered more from an emotional response... if they don't stop and think first they could make many mistakes.

They have a strong desire to learn the truth, and are so concerned with what should be, that they are rarely satisfied with what is. Teach them to work on improving *themselves*, and then all other things will improve automatically. Teach them to sometimes sit still and study the lives, the philosophy of the great people in history so they can expand their understanding of just what is truth.

They will generally try anything once just because it is new and different. They are quite inventive and will come up with many original things to explore. As a toddler they are into *everything*, so be forewarned. And later — Aries goes where angels fear to tread!

When these children are emotionally upset, they are likely to have and be headaches! Aries carries their tension in the head. (Remember? Mars and Aries rules the head part of the body.) This is a tension which must be dealt with throughout life. Two ways to help this challenge are by releasing the tension through some vigorous activity or by talking out their feelings.

Moon in Aries has a *fiery temper*, and like fire, erupts quickly and goes out just as fast. They won't hold a grudge as might other signs. But they need to learn to control themselves because they say things they don't mean and can deeply hurt others. They must be taught that others may be as much or more sensitive than they.

They are idealists and will want to blaze their own trail. Teach them that by learning from the past they will be better equipped to lead into the future.

When you challenge their actions or feelings, you arouse a will of unbelievable strength. This can be a tremendous asset when directed for a productive cause and in a positive manner. Teach them to be the keeper of and to stoke their own fire. Then *they* control it and spread only enough that warms, and not so much that it burns.

The Aries Moon will have trouble with a demanding or controlling mother, father, or teacher. They will be fighting them at every turn whenever they try to restrict them in any way. They have a strong need for *independence* and will continue to fight to maintain it, so give them the lead whenever the opportunity arises. And help them to consciously withhold their need for that independence — or they could waste their lives and energy on acting the rebel.

Children with Moon in Taurus

The Moon is *exalted* in the sign of Taurus. This means that from the beginning the emotions and personality are functioning with a high degree of efficiency. These children will be fairly stable emotionally and will have a good idea of what they want. They want *comfort* and *luxuries* and all the "good things" of the material world. It will be necessary to teach them how to develop values that go beyond possessions. They will be security-oriented and inclined to place their security in not only material things but attachments to people. They must be taught to not place undue emphasis on this kind of security because all material things can be lost, and undue attachments to people cause the negative attribute of over-possessiveness which in later life can lead to heartache.

Moon in the sign of the *Bull* can be quite stubborn with both their ideas and with any need to make changes, especially in their immediate environment. Getting them to change anything may be a challenge. If you can show them how a change (that you want them to make) can be beneficial to *them*, you have a chance. But they are naturally more comfortable with familiarity.

Your child will be a very determined little one with this Moon placement — which, of course, can be a tremendous asset when directed properly. If you direct them in a beneficial, productive manner they will accomplish a great deal. They have great *staying power* and can be a formidable opponent. Teach them the correct use of these attributes. Show them that the overuse of determination is being obstinate. Point out that the world is constantly changing and they would do well not to resist forced changes. They should be encouraged to broaden their scope and expand their values beyond just the immediate and external world. Help them achieve a good self-image, with an attitude of high self-worth... which will bring the benefits of the external world to them.

They will be *conservative* and *cautious* with their possessions and self-indulgent about "the finer things in life." They will love good food, music, art, and anything that represents *comfort*. They are very affectionate and will enjoy both giving and receiving love. They have a lot of charisma and will use it charmingly.

They may not be a self-starter but once you get them in motion they'll generally see things through. They are very patient, sympathetic, and gentle when unprovoked. However, they do have a temper and, if they are prodded long enough, can be furious when angered. Indirect action works best and given time, they will come around on their own. But try always to be gentle with them — for they deeply feel emotional and physical pain. Also, logic doesn't always work, especially when they set their stubborn mind against it and tune you out — something the little Bull is especially proud of doing. If punishment is needed, deny some "goodies" — that should do it.

To these children, values will be very important and they tend to see things as either black or white, right or wrong. Teach them not to limit their knowledge with a narrow frame of reference, but to read about different cultures in order to enhance their attitudes and broaden their values. They may be a little lazy, so give them a gentle nudge.

Since security is so important, teach them inner-security. Teach them to like themselves and to live life with an open heart.

Children with Moon in Gemini

The Moon in Gemini gives the emotions a more *intellectual* approach, because it gives the ability to think the feelings through and the ability to discuss them. In fact, these children enjoy talking about all their feelings and reactions about people and events. They are very adept at expressing themselves. They also are very *articulate* and tell stories well. Short stories, that is — they have a restlessness about them that causes a short attention span. Thus, these children get *bored easily*, especially with routine. Keep them happy by presenting them with new things and diverse experiences. They will be content and easy to handle if you take them places with you and give them plenty of diversions in life. They like to travel with you even if it is only to the grocery store. To them, every outing is a little adventure — and better for their active, curious minds. This insatiable curiosity *must* be properly fed for it is imperative they be learning constantly so that they can more positively use their emotional energy.

Their emotional moods can be quite changeable. When the mood is positive and high, they can be very humorous but when the mood is negative and low, they feel persecuted and filled with self- doubt. At these times they will be nervous and scattered, or they may talk more as well and faster. It should be fairly easy to change their mood to a more positive expression by simply presenting a new experience of some kind.

They do need to learn self-discipline in staying with things long enough to absorb the whole meaning as they have a tendency to skim the surface. Teach them that this leads to being superficial. If they want people to listen to them, they will need to have all their statements backed up by facts. Tell them that they have plenty of time in their lives to have millions of new experiences and still have time to be thorough too.

They should also be made aware that there are a lot of people whose feelings are more sensitive than theirs, and some who are unable to think their feelings through. By understanding this they will be less inclined to hurt others with tactless words and inconsiderate actions.

They have the continual need to receive and dispense knowledge. They are always on the move both physically and mentally. They may even have a nervous stomach. Again, the best remedy is an interesting change in environment, and an occasional quiet period so they can assimilate all their incoming data!

These children are *versatile* and can be good *conversationalists*. When nervous or upset, they can be real chatterboxes. Help them to calm down and you will enjoy their company.

Children with Moon in Cancer

The Moon is in her *natural home* in the sign of Cancer, since the Moon rules Cancer. Here, her influence is unaltered, her characteristics projected in full strength. Your Cancer Moon child will be *sensitive*, responsive, emotional, *intuitive* and possibly psychic. The Moon's monthly cycle will have a strong effect on them and they will be inclined toward *moodiness*. The relationship with mother is most important for strong emotional security. Any insecurity causes an overindulgence, and moderation is one of the keys to success. You would do well to give this child lots of love and affection, to help them feel wanted and accepted. The nurturing principle is very strong. These children need a lot of nurturing and also need to nurture others. They need to feel secure with their emotional energies in order to utilize and give nurturing in a healthy way.

These children will do well with *pets* or younger children because it gives them an opportunity to care for someone or something and will allow this need to nurture develop in a positive manner. They have a lot of compassion and are sympathetic, even empathetic. So much so that you need to teach these children not to be quite so sensitive to those around them and not to respond so much to their environment. Feelings are more important to them than logic, so appeal to their feelings when you need cooperation. Because they may look for security through material possessions and therefore may be disappointed, they must be shown that true security comes from love and faith in themselves and, to a lesser degree, in others. Shower them with love and affection and they will return it in good measure.

Because of such strong emotional reactions and feelings, it will be difficult to reason with them when they are upset or disturbed. For better results, wait until their mood has quieted.

This Moon placement has a tendency for *stressful emotions* to affect the physical body through the stomach. They may not want to eat when upset, or if they do, they may get sick. Bland foods are best and if possible have them eat only when calm. Don't make them eat if they are upset.

When there is a *full* or *new* Moon, this child may be noticeably more high strung. It would be to their advantage to learn at a young age to become aware when these times occur each month. In this way they can be prepared and can learn to control their feelings more, to understand that this will shortly pass.

Their sensitivities are so well developed that they know things which will amaze you. It is an instinctive tuning in to people and environment. This is marvelous, but once again, teach them not to be such sponges — for the psychic energy they are absorbing could be non-beneficial (as well as beneficial) and could severely affect them emotionally. Strong positive training will help them block out and not let anything negative become a part of them. It would be good to have these children say out loud each morning, "I will block out all negativity today and resist letting it become a part of me." In the evening at bedtime ask if they "felt" any negative "vibes" coming into them that day — and teach your child to throw them out! Cancel them! To say, "Cancel, cancel." They will adore this little game — and it gives them a protective shield against the bad, the hurtful.

Children with Moon in Leo

These children's emotions are *warm* and *strongly affectionate*. They are loving yet need a lot of love in return. Most of all, they need reassurance that they are appreciated. If you can teach them to be proud of themselves, they will have less need to be applauded by others. Otherwise, they will become show-offs who demand attention any way they can get it. They need to feel special and important — and they should learn that this must first be developed from within.

They are *generous* with their time and with their belongings. If this positive trait is overdone, they may become extravagant. They need to learn discipline and to establish a realistic set of values — that generosity makes a fine showing but extravagance is showing off. Too much of anything is not good. They are sensitive, have strong feelings, and can be *easily offended*. This comes partly from an inner insecurity or a strong need for approval. They also like things their way! The better they feel about themselves the more difficult it will become to offend them. They should also learn that as much as they need to be themselves, others need to be themselves too.

The Moon in Leo children can be egotistical, overbearing, arrogant, and stubborn when challenged. Teach these children to control their emotions and to

use self-discipline over these non-productive characteristics. On the positive side, they are noble, honorable,
loyal, and have strong leadership abilities. They try to
be outstanding and usually are. They are outgoing and
need to be with people. They will feel frustrated and
unfulfilled if they are not allowed center stage to get the
attention they need.

These children may have a tendency to *exaggerate*
so this trait should be carefully watched, and mini-
mized so that other people can believe and trust in
them. If they want to be effective leaders, a certain
amount of realism is necessary. But as for outright lies
— never. A true Leo Moon would never stoop to that,
or have so little courage.

Pride runs strongly in these personalities. Self-
esteem is so important to them that it is the basis of how
they experience their lives. Be sure to always keep this
factor in mind. One of the quickest ways to trigger a
bad, negative response in them is to insult their integrity or humiliate them. For best results, try to present
criticism in a considerate way, sandwiched between
two compliments! Show them that by making necessary corrections, they will improve themselves and garner
the approval they so ardently desire!

These children are often attracted to the theater.
Being on stage and playing different parts is a good way
for them to let their *dramatic* feelings flower, plus get
that applause they crave. A Leo Moon loves *luxury* and
glamour. They have a keen appreciation for artistic and

creative talents and are blessed with many themselves. They love to have fun and are usually fun to be with. Give them as much praise and respect as possible and you will be contributing to their emotional security.

Children with Moon in Virgo

Children with the Moon in Virgo will have fewer emotional highs and lows than some of the other place-ments. They are inclined to be both *orderly* and *conser-vative*. These children tend to be nitpicks and place too much importance on minor things. Since they want to be useful and are so good at analyzing (Virgo being a thinking, thoughtful sign), show them how valuable they can be if they expose themselves to new experi-ences. Because their instincts are inclined to be some-what narrow and *critical*, they need to expand, to inves-tigate new situations and people, to accept *other* points of view.

With this Moon placement, they not only set high standards for themselves but will expect others to fol-low the same standards, especially those they consider close to them. They need to understand that all people must do what is best for themselves and that each has different priorities and values. They should also learn to stop being so critical of themselves... and of others. No one is perfect.

These children are compulsive about *health* and *cleanliness*, so you can be assured, they will take good care of themselves and their surroundings. Teach them to relax a bit, stop being so fussy, and most importantly, to let others just *be*. Teach them that *moderation* is the key to success. Just because they need to be busy, sometimes compulsively so, others don't! Teach them to set goals for themselves only. Goal-setting will make them happy because they dislike aimlessness. They will be meticulous workers and like to participate in activities in which they can use both their hands and their minds. Their intellectual abilities are excellent and they are able to learn easily. They also have good memory skills. But teach them the importance of applying *feeling* to their thinking and their knowledge. This, in the long run, will bring more happiness to themselves and others.

It is the nature of these children to want to be helpful, to serve in a meaningful way, to accomplish. Being by their nature rather detached and unemotional, they need to learn about others' feelings and emotions. Since they are concerned with health, they must learn that they will destroy their own through their nervous drive of wanting everything to be perfect. Things and people just aren't that way. Show them that we still need the imperfect in order to know what is perfect... that perfection would be boring because then there would be nothing for them to do!

...ese Moon in Virgo children will be happiest when following some intellectual pursuit and are capable of great dedication. They will admire others who are also dedicated. Show them that these are wonderful attributes, and if everyone in the world were the same it would be a pretty sterile and dull place.

They may not be as loving as you would like, but you can have closeness in other ways. They will be great *verbalizers* and will communicate with you and love sharing ideas. Learn together and become good friends. They may be shy and reserved so *you* should make the first effort. They may not need your hugging as much as they need your reassurance. Show them your appreciation for their efforts. In return, they will appreciate you and give you respect and loyalty.

Children with Moon in Libra

The Moon placement in Libra — ruled by Venus gives these personalities a *gentle, peace-loving* nature. If this trait is carried to extremes, we have children who give in too easily, are too agreeable, and will try to achieve peace at any price. Show them it is a valuable attribute to have understanding, but it must be used without sacrificing values and principles. Harmony at any price will not work.

It is very important for them to be liked by people and to be socially accepted. Because they have such strong needs to interact with people, you will almost never find them doing anything alone. If they are taught a little discretion in their choice of associates, they will be able to achieve balance (Libra is always trying to achieve balance) without giving up their values or abandoning their principles.

They are *affectionate*, warm-hearted, *good-natured*, and generally *make friends easily*. They are apt to see only the good in others and can be taken advantage of by those with selfish motives. Their successes can be so dependent upon and influenced by those around them, that they must be helped in choosing their friends wisely. Teach them that they cannot be all things to all people no matter how they try and that they really don't need to be.

These Moon in Libra children have an appreciation for beauty in all forms — art, music, design, adornment, fashion, and luxury. They are refined and have good taste in all things. Music is an excellent way to soothe these children when they become too sensitive and inclined to brood. Show them that it is impossible to have harmony all the time, that one cannot always control one's environment. Teach them that they can learn to control the peace and balance within themselves with a little practice. Once they learn to be less affected by outside stimuli, they will be able to stabilize and control their reactions, and their emotions.

Family ties are important to these children and they need those close to them to have faith in them.

Moon in Libra has more than an ample amount of charm, and they need to learn the proper use of this talent. Natural charm gives a tremendous advantage for advancement in life and should not be misused by sweet-talking one's way out of chores or *any difficult situation.* Speaking of chores, work or any task — they will not be too eager in this department, especially if they have to do it alone. They work better when others are involved, cooperation is one of their long suits. Just be careful that they don't sweet-talk someone else into doing their share. Teach them that although work can sometimes be unrefined (even getting one's hands dirty!) — it is nevertheless a constructive and positive endeavor. Afterwards, they'll feel good about accomplishing something, especially the glow of group effort.

' One of the more important lessons caregivers must bring to their Moon Libra children, for their very survival in the cold harsh world — is to *self-start!* Too often they seem to need prodding, sometimes even a fire lit under them! So emphasize the value of their *initiating* a task, and carrying it through — whether it's homework or cleaning their room. *Reward them* with something beautiful — one perfect flower, a lovely tune, or just cuddling and reading them a poem or story!

Children with Moon in Scorpio

The Moon in Scorpio indicates a nature very *intense* and *emotional.* These children are often *hypersensitive,* yet they rarely show it to others. This trait is a challenging placement for the Moon as it causes them to have great difficultly in freely expressing their feelings, emotions that are so *internalized* they are sometimes buried too deeply to surface. These children need to learn to recognize and appreciate their emotions. To look at them objectively... and then verbally *express* what they feel. Teach them that by holding in, bottling everything up, they only hurt themselves — and those they love when finally the dam bursts. Many times these internalized feelings may even manifest in real physical illness.

Nothing is lukewarm with these children. When they are happy it is total; when they are sad it is extreme. Everything is intense, everything is all or nothing. They have strong convictions and can be obdurate about changing them. It will be extremely difficult to sway them once they have made up their minds. If you should attempt to, you will have a better chance at succeeding if you re-examine your facts, and then have a very open mind when you converse with them. Because they have the ability to see beyond the surface in situations, and people, you may end by admitting that they are correct.

Since Moon in Scorpio children have keenly developed *intuitive* abilities, they will make wonderful detectives, researchers, and scientists. They will enjoy investigating the secrets of people, nature, and the Universe. They want to know all there is to know about the world around them — and the one within them. They often become psychiatrists.

Although it may be hard for a parent to sit by and watch, these children learn best from experience. They are quite energetic, very self-reliant, and in all probability will *have* to experience and *want* to experience more than most people throughout their lives. It is important that they learn to understand their own complicated feelings, and to stop getting so involved with their own emotions. Teach them to lighten up and not to be quite so *serious* all the time. Show them through your example how to laugh at what life brings, that they can laugh at themselves when something unfortunate happens. Laughing is a better way in which to release their intense emotions.

These Moon in Scorpio children have a tendency to go to extremes in all things, so teach them to discipline themselves and to avoid any excessive indulgence — whether in emotion or food or later, drink. They have strong wills and accomplish whatever they set out to do. With loved ones, they are inclined to be jealous and possessive. Since their mother is a primary love, she may find that these children put many demands on her. They will want her for themselves, entirely.

They are quick to attach and again, want to control. Help them learn that it is selfish to put demands and expectations on others. Show them that if the same demands were put on them, they would NOT tolerate it. Because they have an astonishing ability to be perceptive and see the truth, it is most important for you to avoid any manipulation or deception. But *they* have a tendency to *manipulate*, to control... so it is very important that you teach them to *deal openly* and fairly with others. Teach them to respect the integral being of another as they wish to be respected. Help them become aware of this *need to control* so that they can work at "canceling" that out — or they could lose friends and loved ones!

Children with Moon in Sagittarius

Children with their Moon in Sagittarius will have a great *love of outdoors*, sports, and travel; going places and doing things! They will learn a great deal from traveling — and are fun to travel with. They are naturally interested in foreign places, foreign cultures... and foreign people, often later marrying one. They are immensely curious about everything, and want to learn as much as they can about the world. They love any place that is new to them because it satisfies their need for mental stimulation... which is such an important part of their personality. They also have a great attraction to *animals* and *nature*.

Sagittarian Moon children are very *frank* about their ideas which others sometimes take as being too blunt. They easily speak their minds and will tell you exactly what they feel. This is an admirable characteristic, however too often they are not very diplomatic. Help them to develop tact and understand how other people might react to this *direct* approach... and how easily others might misunderstand their well-intentioned words and get their feelings hurt!

These idealistic and in many ways naive children want the world to be honest, honorable, and pleasant. They try always to act this way themselves and just naturally expect others to do the same. They must be taught to accept people and life as it is or they will continually find disappointments. Because they are constantly adding new information and new thoughts, they often may change their attitudes. They have boundless *energy* and are very *active*, both physically and mentally...but they have a tendency, if not properly guided, to be *disorganized* — both physically and mentally!

Since Sagittarius is a fire sign, these children may be quick to anger, but their sudden blaze is just as quickly doused. They are not inclined to hold a grudge and are generally very good natured. Their values are lofty and most honest in origin. They hate hypocrisy. An important lesson for them to learn is to set their goals more realistically, and to forgive others for falling short.

One of their most desirable traits is their great sense of *humor.* These children seem to be able to laugh at themselves and laugh at whatever happens to them... and even to make others laugh. In the most serious, desperate situations, they somehow come up with the flip side of it. The only caution here is that they need to realize that others with serious natures may not appreciate making light of sober and serious situations. In the long run, their inborn wise judgment and a little self-discipline in touchy situations will make their lives much easier.

In disciplining them, you should be direct and honest. If you can give them the reasons for your actions, you will more likely gain their cooperation. These children are unable to stay sad or unhappy for any length of time. They are the bouncy optimists of the zodiac. They are very curious and may ask many questions about all the facets of life, God, and the Universe. They will expect direct and thoughtful answers, so be prepared. If you don't know, tell them so and you will gain their respect. It can be fun to discover the answers together — an intellectual adventure!

They are natural students and will enjoy studying the lives of men and women who have changed the world. Life will be exciting with these fun-loving children — but be sure to love them with an open hand, and an open honest heart, and especially an open mind. In fact, open can be a key word for these little extroverts. Restricted they are miserable — and eventually will rebel or when older just won't be there!

Children with Moon in Capricorn

The Moon in Capricorn is one of the more challenging placements. These children *need more love*, more nurturing, and more attention in the early part of their lives than any other sign. Their *need for security* is so consuming that you will need to satisfy it in their primary years—if not, it may create emotional problems throughout their lives. On the emotional level, they are filled with *fears* of inadequacy which must be addressed. In whatever they do they want to succeed, be given respect, and be recognized. Because they need to feel in control of any situation, they will do well in positions of authority, and often they are the controlling force behind the front man or woman... in other words, a king maker.

These children are very *strong-minded, determined*, and will work hard at acquiring their needs. In fact, work too often can become an obsession with them — the typical workaholic. Their sense of self-worth is directly related to how important they feel. For these children, the amount of affection, reassurance, nurturing, and time that a parent or caregiver gives will determine how positively their self-worth will develop. They have powerful needs to feel accepted, and to belong as a significant part of the world.

The person who is providing the care for these children in their primary years will have a very important role in creating their very needed emotional security. Many times you find children with a Capricorn Moon will have parents that don't mean to neglect the children and in fact don't . However, if the parents themselves are detached or are emotionally nongregarious, or just too busy — the effect is the same, these children would *feel* neglected. Sometimes a child with this Moon placement has parents who are actually physically absent, living elsewhere or even deceased, in which case some family member must provide them with a strong sense of security. Optimally, their parents should be people whom these children can look up to and respect, and people who give to these children much love and commitment.

Always remember to praise your little Capricorn Moon child because they need a lot of positive reinforcement. Make them feel secure and *wanted*, that they are a necessary part of your life. Help them realize that they have an important purpose, that they are *worthy*. Teach them to like themselves, to release the fear, and to stop building a fence around themselves. This is very important because if they don't learn to like themselves, they will constantly demand affection from others. More than attention, it's a true *nurturing* love and acceptance which is so needed.

Help them to understand their demands often are greater than what other people can understand, greater than what most people are able to give. Therefore, they *must* learn to first love themselves and then to give this love to others unselfishly. Help them to openly express their feelings. Once they feel secure with this love principle, they have a tremendous amount to give to others. Teach them to be happy, accepting the type and amount of love that other people are able to give. They must try to stop strangling everyone close to them with their demands and expectations. To feel accepted and to feel loved — these are the two prime psychological needs for the Capricorn Moon child's emotional security and development. You as parents and guardians have, from their birth to approximately age six (the crucial years), the opportunity to fulfill these basic needs.

Children with Moon in Aquarius

The Moon placed in the sign of Aquarius is one of the *least emotional* placements. Feeling is primarily expressed through the intellect. They think rather than spontaneously react, nor are they influenced through feelings and emotions. In fact, they can be quite *un*comfortable with the emotional displays of others. These children need to understand that other people may be different and have less control over their feelings. They need to develop tolerance and patience for those with a different emotional makeup.

These children are often considered unconventional — they are stimulated by new ideas, unorthodox methods, and original or unusual approaches. They like to have the freedom in which to experiment with any new findings. They want to do what they want to do when they want to do it! They can be quite stubborn when these freedoms are taken away or restricted. Because of their unorthodox approach to life, they often become categorized as eccentrics.

They are *generous* and care about groups and society at large. They are *humanitarians* and have good intentions but don't always have practical applications to support their ideas. They like applause and they like to be patted on the back. Praising them will go a long way. Because they want to be a friend to all the world, approach them intellectually by pointing out how they can benefit the world through their serving it... but in a realistic *practical* way... so as to make the world a better place.

Friends are especially important to children with this Moon placement and they will get pleasure from all sorts of group activities. They will want to join clubs or organizations where they can share ideas, pleasures, and thoughts with others. Since changing the world for the better is one of their great drives, they need to learn to be less rigid, to learn to work with others of possibly less "vision," and learn how to accept criticism.

These children will be fascinated with all facets of space and *space travel.* They enjoy *science fiction* as well as dream interpretation, astrology, and hypnotism, and any New Age subject — for they are the New Age! They are often eager to try anything that is new. Stimulate their natural mental acuity by exposing them to these kinds of experiences. They will love visiting natural history museums, space exhibitions, science fairs, and computer trade shows!

When correcting this child you will receive favorable responses by administering discipline without emotions — with logic, not anger. They almost always block out emotional outbursts and impulsive actions by their parents, so the whole point of the lesson will be lost. Think through any discipline before presenting it. If you should happen to react emotionally or get a bit out of control, the best recovery is to explain that sometimes powerful emotions are difficult for some people to control.

These Aquarian Moon children truly want to help... so teach them to first learn how to help themselves, and then they will be able to help others. They can become a great force for social good; making the world a better place to live will fulfill many of their deepest desires. But be sure to teach them that while they are busy changing the world for the better, they should not neglect their own family! They are unconventional but loving when understood.

Children with Moon in Pisces

Having one's Moon in Pisces is one of the more, if not *the most sensitive* placement of this luminary. For these children, emotions can rule and ruin their lives.

Because they are very *receptive* and *easily influenced* by everyone and everything around them, they take almost everything personally. They cry easily and must be allowed this outlet (boys too!). Perhaps the most important lesson with this Moon placement is to teach them to be realistic — and much more objective. This is necessary because they have a tendency to feel misunderstood, feel sorry for themselves, and over-dramatize life's experiences, whether their own or someone else's. Help them to be less vulnerable and develop thicker skins. This process will surely stand them in good stead as they mature.

Moon in Pisces children also have a tendency to live in a dream world. Their fantasies are for them easier to live with than reality. They need to learn to not only stand up for their own rights, but they also must stop taking the line of least resistance. This lesson will aid in eliminating some of their moodiness and changeability, guiding them to bend with the breezes.

Because emotion is such a major factor with these children, nothing being experienced without feelings, they have tremendous creative potential and a vivid imagination. This is one of the reasons why they are so attuned to music, to poetry of love, and particularly to acting... or any other activity that requires creative expression.

Another area these Piscean Moon children excel is one in which they care for people, especially the injured or ill — but they must be careful not to take in their vibrations — particularly those mentally or physically ill. They are quite gifted with *animals*. These children are so acutely attuned to other creatures that they empathetically "feel" them.

Feeling for others is a marvelous gift but because they are so sensitive, they need to learn more stability in their ideas, feelings, and attitudes. Too often they "go with the flow" of others because it is the path of least resistance — they must be taught confidence in their own beliefs and to stand by them! If not learned, doubt and depression can be their enemy. Worse, they can lose their own sense of identity, their feelings of self. Teach them not to be self-indulgent, to not wallow in their sensitivities.

Moon in Pisces children will be most happy and will function best when their environment is kept positive, peaceful, and pleasant. Any negativity, depression, arguing, or fighting from those close to them may be extremely traumatic and deeply felt. Soothing, soft music and a calm environment help these children feel most content.

Have some fun with these children by asking them to tell you their dreams. Quite often they will be prophetic as well as psychic. Most importantly, teach them to recite this statement every morning: "I will let all negativity pass me by today. I will *push* it out and away from me!"

"...astrology is not to discover what is going to 'happen' to us, it is not to forestall the blows of fate, that we should look to our horoscopes. A chart when properly read should enable one to understand the overall pattern of one's life."

Henry Miller

CHAPTER 6

Mercury —
The Messenger of the Gods
& the Key to Communication Modes

Mercury influences our thinking reaction to our physical environment. *Mercury is thought itself.* It is our mental reaction to our five senses... our thoughts about odors, tastes, sounds, sights and tactile feelings. It is the logical and rational part of the mind that deals with reason. It is by itself void of emotions or feelings. Its purpose is to *think, analyze,* and *understand.*

Mercury is *communication* both given and received. It is how *our* thoughts are expressed, and how the communication from others is received and interpreted. Needless to say, when Mercury is placed in the different signs, it takes on different expressions. Again, *the planet is the energy, the sign that it is in is the way that the energy is expressed.* In some signs, Mercury is able to express itself easily because there is compatibility — other signs are more challenging. Some signs color the logic with emotion and feeling, some are more coolly intellectual; while some will be practical, and others abstract, even mystical. Some think quickly, others slowly. Some probe the depths (and get caught there), others scan a broader surface. Different expression is necessary and important to give us an expanded perspective of all possibilities of the thought process, adding variety to life.

Mercury will also show how your child's learning ability is affected, and since you are their primary teacher, this test is of in-estimable importance. We are all teachers and students simultaneously, therefore we need to communicate well. The Mercury connection is one of our most effective tools at the present time.

How can you communicate well with your children if their thinking is on another channel unless you know what channel it is on... and then switch yours to the same one for a direct connection? We are all naturally drawn to people who think the same as we so there is no strain in communicating. Many times you will even know what the other person means before the thought is completely expressed. This idea is great — but with some people it works just the opposite. Most of the problems in any relationship can be traced to lack of or misunderstood communication.

Everyone wants to express themselves in the way that most easily satisfies their own needs, and everyone wants at the same time to be understood. Too often, this desire is impossible. It is *possible*, however, to change your channel or wavelength in order to understand others. All you need is the necessary knowledge and the desire to apply it. In the case of your child, or others with whom you communicate often, it is well worth the effort. The following interpretations of *Mercury* in the *signs* will help you "change your channels" at will.

This brings me to the question, who is responsible for the understanding in the communication — the one giving or the one receiving? The answer is that *it is always the one who is doing the communicating.* It is the responsibility of the one sending the message to get their meaning across, and be understood... that is, if they want to have unified communication and sharing. If they don't, of course it won't matter, and they might as well talk to a door, then no one else will have to experience the separateness either.

Think of the importance of what we project and say to our children! In the beginning they learn everything from us, including the meanings and attitudes we have about different words and thoughts. They even learn how to develop the *parent* and *adult* parts of their personality from us. We teach them how to interact socially, professionally, and ethically. They develop attitudes about family, one-on-one relationships, the world — and most importantly, they learn how to think and feel about themselves! What kind of a picture has the on-going programming created on their mental computer screen? Is it one of assurance and acceptance, or one of fear and doubt? With this in mind, it is important to start "listening" to *what* we say, *how* we say it, and *whether* it is beneficial or not.

Some things to keep in mind when working with children is that their computer brains are storing new information rapidly, more so than at any other time in their lives. They focus generally on what is happening at the moment. When we get their attention with, "Don't open the door!" their attention will go to the door; the "don't" is heard as a general restriction, if it is even heard at all. What can we expect other than them focusing on the door? Statements like, "Will you help me keep the door closed?" are heard more clearly... or better yet, to get the desired focus on "*close*" and to get attention away from the "*open*" we could say, "We need to keep the door closed, will you help me? Thank you." The child's main drive is to learn, and to get approval and acceptance. Help them to satisfy these drives through better communication with them. After all, learning is a process of taking in information, and of making mistakes and adjustments. Learning from error is an important concept for us all to remember, and particularly for children to understand.

It is always good to validate first. By that I mean, give accepting compliments like, "I can understand why you want to —," or "It is okay for you to feel —." Then add, "*and*" (not "but" because "but" takes away from, "and" adds to) "and we are going to do —." Everyone's computer is built for survival. It will automatically resist when invalidated and will create separation for self-preservation. Obviously the closer we are with our children the better we communicate, and the more effective parents or caregivers we will be.

Mercury Retrograde

Mercury travels in a *retrograde* direction *three times a year for approximately 21 days each time.* This adds up to approximately 63 days out of the entire year, a relatively short amount of time so those born during these periods will be in the minority. Since Mercury symbolically represents the thought processes and communications, any children born at a time when Mercury retrograde occurs will require more understanding with how they express their mental abilities.

When a planet is in a *direct motion* its energy is *flowing* in an open, normal, forward way. Because retrograde means going back over and back into, any *retrograde* planet has its energy *restricted* and turned inward. Since we are talking about mental abilities here, children with this situation at birth will often repeat what they say, and will also ask others to repeat. At times, it may seem like they are trying to be antagonistic or 'sassy.' Have patience with them because it seems to take at least two repetitions for anything to mentally register.

Keep a full supply of erasers on hand because these are the children who will need them! Buy them erasable ink pens. They are the original, "Play it again Sam" types. Somehow, they do most everything over again.

Help these children to understand that the way *they* think and the way their brains work is different — otherwise, they can become quite frustrated, and feel they are out-of-step with the rest of the world. Teach them that different does not equal wrong. It is more important for them to accept their differences than it is for them to try to change themselves to fit the way other people think and act. Explain that there *are* other people who think the same way they do, just not as many.

These children often have difficulty expressing their thoughts and feelings, especially if they feel the slightest rejection to their ideas. This will cause them to withdraw, turn inward, and ultimately give up. It is most important for them to learn to understand and

accept their differences, so that they can feel secure —
and not just "different."

School can be a challenge for these children because they don't learn easily from the conventional
methods of teaching. They are apt to feel that they are
not smart since their thought processes are marching
to a different drummer. They have their own unique
methods of solving problems, and when given the
opportunity to use their own methods, they can solve
problems faster than most. I sometimes wonder if they're
not using more of their 'psychic brain' than the so-
called *normal* Mercury direct people. And I feel very
strongly that if a study were to be done, the results
would show that most *dyslexic* children were born when
Mercury was retrograde.

Comprehension of the written word may be difficult for some, while others will be unusual writers as
well as avid readers. It seems that Mercury retrograde
people are capable of reading entire sentences at a
glance — but are afraid of missing something important! Because of this, they go back and repeat each word
one by one to make sure that nothing is missed. After
they develop their own inner-confidence they can become excellent *speed readers*. They have *superb memories*
because of this special ability to think back and to
retrieve information from their "computers."

These children may be inclined to be nervous
types and may worry or fuss over everything. This is
because they are trying so hard to do everything per-

fectly. Help them learn that although *striving* for perfection is acceptable, the attaining of it is in another dimension — and *accepting* each outcome for what it is, this is realistic and less stressful.

Most importantly, teach these children that just because it sometimes takes them longer to learn through the usual conventional methods, it does not mean they are less intelligent. In most cases they will end up with a better understanding and better retention of what they have learned.

Each year during the times that Mercury is retrograde, these children will think and speak very clearly...because it is *their* time! So it is a good time for them to clear up any prior misunderstandings. They will want to organize and take action with anything left undone. Check the tables to discover when these times occur. Encourage them to make their plans and prepare to *take action* — but not until after *Mercury* goes *direct!*

For best results, it is important for all of us to wait until *Mercury* is in its *direct* motion to take *action* on anything. Watch its forward and backward motion and see what happens in your personal life. Keep notes on it to make your own references.

How To Use Mercury Tables

Find the year of Birth on the following pages. Next locate the month under that year. The dates listed indicate the day Mercury moves into a sign. It stays in that sign until the next date is listed.

Example:In the year 1900 Mercury was in Sagittarius on January 1, and stayed in Sagittarius through January 9. On January 10, it entered Capricorn and stayed in Capricorn through January 28. January 29, it entered Aquarius - and so on.

The D and R after the sign indicates whether Mercury was Direct or Retrograde. When the R appears it means Mercury turned Retrograde on that day and will remain Retrograde until the next date a D appears after the sign.

Example:In the year 1900 Mercury turned Retrograde on March 15, and stayed Retrograde through April 6. On April 7, Mercury turned Direct again.

SIGNS

ARI	Aries	LIB	Libra
TAU	Taurus	SCO	Scorpio
GEM	Gemini	SAG	Sagittarius
CAN	Cancer	CAP	Capricorn
LEO	Leo	AQU	Aquarius
VIR	Virgo	PIS	Pisces

1900	1901	1902	1903	1904	1905
JAN 1 SAG-D	JAN 3 CAP-D	JAN 14 AQU-D	JAN 7 AQU-D	JAN 3 AQU-D	JAN 11 CAP-D
JAN 10 CAP-D	JAN 22 AQU-D	FEB 2 PIC-D	JAN 24 AQU-R	JAN 8 AQU-R	FEB 10 AQU-D
JAN 29 AQU-D	FEB 8 PIC-D	FEB 9 AQU-R	FEB 14 AQU-D	JAN 15 CAP-R	FEB 28 PIC-D
FEB 16 PIC-D	FEB 26 PIC-R	FEB 19 AQU-R	MAR 15 PIC-D	JAN 28 CAP-D	MAR 16 ARI-D
MAR 4 ARI-D	MAR 21 PIC-D	MAR 3 AQU-D	APR 3 ARI-D	FEB 16 AQU-D	APR 2 TAU-D
MAR 15 ARI-R	APR 16 ARI-D	MAR 20 PIC-D	APR 17 TAU-D	MAR 8 PIC-D	APR 13 TAU-R
MAR 30 PIC-R	MAY 4 TAU-D	APR 10 ARI-D	MAY 3 GEM-D	MAR 24 ARI-D	APR 29 ARI-R
APR 7 PIC-D	MAY 18 GEM-D	APR 26 TAU-D	MAY 22 GEM-R	APR 8 TAU-D	MAY 7 ARI-D
APR 18 ARI-D	JUN 2 CAN-D	MAY 10 GEM-D	JUN 15 GEM-D	MAY 2 TAU-R	MAY 16 TAU-D
MAY 12 TAU-D	JUN 30 CAN-R	MAY 30 CAN-D	JUL 11 CAN-D	MAY 26 TAU-D	JUN 9 GEM-D
MAY 27 GEM-D	JUL 24 CAN-D	JUN 11 CAN-R	JUL 26 LEO-D	JUN 15 GEM-D	JUN 24 CAN-D
JUN 10 CAN-D	AUG 11 LEO-D	JUN 27 GEM-R	AUG 10 VIR-D	JUL 2 CAN-D	JUL 8 LEO-D
JUN 28 LEO-D	AUG 26 VIR-D	JUL 5 GEM-D	AUG 30 VIR-D	JUL 17 LEO-D	JUL 28 VIR-D
JUL 18 LEO-R	SEP 12 LIB-D	JUL 14 CAN-D	SEP 20 LIB-R	AUG 2 VIR-D	AUG 16 VIR-R
AUG 11 LEO-D	OCT 2 SCO-D	AUG 3 LEO-D	OCT 12 LIB-D	AUG 29 LIB-D	SEP 8 VIR-D
SEP 4 VIR-D	OCT 24 SCO-R	AUG 18 VIR-D	NOV 5 SCO-D	SEP 3 LIB-R	OCT 2 LIB-D
SEP 19 LIB-D	NOV 13 SCO-D	SEP 5 LIB-D	NOV 23 SAG-D	SEP 8 VIR-R	OCT 20 SCO-D
OCT 8 SCO-D	DEC 7 SAG-D	SEP 29 SCO-D	DEC 13 CAP-D	SEP 25 VIR-D	NOV 9 SAG-D
OCT 31 SAG-D	DEC 27 CAP-D	OCT 7 SCO-R		OCT 10 LIB-D	DEC 3 CAP-D
NOV 9 SAG-R		OCT 16 LIB-R		OCT 27 SCO-D	DEC 6 CAP-R
NOV 19 SCO-R		OCT 28 LIB-D		NOV 15 SAG-D	DEC 11 SAG-R
NOV 29 SCO-D		NOV 11 SCO-D		DEC 5 CAP-D	DEC 26 SAG-D
DEC 13 SAG-D		DEC 1 SAG-D		DEC 22 CAP-R	
		DEC 20 CAP-D			

1906	1907	1908	1909	1910	1911
JAN 13 CAP-D	JAN 8 CAP-D	JAN 1 CAP-D	JAN 11 AQU-D	JAN 4 AQU-D	JAN 1 CAP-R
FEB 3 AQU-D	JAN 27 AQU-D	JAN 19 AQU-D	FEB 3 AQU-R	JAN 17 AQU-R	JAN 21 CAP-D
MAR 9 ARI-D	FEB 13 PIC-D	FEB 20 PIC-R	FEB 24 AQU-D	FEB 1 CAP-R	FEB 14 AQU-D
MAR 26 ARI-R	MAR 4 ARI-D	MAR 13 PIC-D	MAR 18 PIC-D	FEB 7 CAP-D	MAR 5 PIC-D
APR 18 ARI-D	MAR 8 ARI-R	APR 13 ARI-D	APR 7 ARI-D	FEB 16 AQU-D	MAR 22 ARI-D
MAY 16 TAU-D	APR 19 ARI-D	APR 30 TAU-D	APR 22 TAU-D	MAR 12 PIC-D	APR 6 TAU-D
JUN 1 GEM-D	MAR 31 PIC-D	MAY 14 GEM-D	MAY 6 GEM-D	MAR 30 ARI-D	APR 24 TAU-R
JUN 15 CAN-D	MAY 10 TAU-D	MAY 31 CAN-D	JUN 3 GEM-R	APR 14 TAU-D	MAY 18 TAU-D
JUL 1 LEO-D	MAY 24 GEM-D	JUN 21 CAN-R	JUN 26 GEM-D	MAY 1 GEM-D	JUN 14 GEM-D
JUL 29 LEO-R	JUN 7 CAN-D	JUL 16 CAN-D	JUL 14 CAN-D	MAY 14 GEM-R	JUN 29 CAN-D
AUG 22 LEO-D	JUN 28 LEO-D	AUG 7 LEO-D	JUL 31 LEO-D	JUN 2 TAU-R	JUL 14 LEO-D
SEP 8 VIR-D	JUL 12 LEO-R	AUG 23 VIR-D	AUG 14 VIR-D	JUN 13 GEM-D	JUL 31 VIR-D
SEP 25 LIB-D	AUG 4 CAN-D	SEP 8 LIB-D	SEP 2 LIB-D	JUL 8 CAN-D	AUG 27 VIR-R
OCT 12 SCO-D	AUG 13 LEO-D	SEP 29 SCO-D	SEP 30 LIB-R	JUL 22 LEO-D	SEP 18 VIR-D
NOV 2 SAG-D	SEP 1 VIR-D	OCT 17 SCO-R	OCT 21 LIB-D	AUG 7 VIR-D	OCT 7 LIB-D
NOV 20 SAG-R	SEP 17 LIB-D	NOV 2 LIB-R	NOV 8 SCO-D	AUG 28 LIB-D	OCT 25 SCO-D
DEC 7 SCO-R	OCT 6 SCO-D	NOV 6 LIB-D	NOV 27 SAG-D	SEP 13 LIB-R	NOV 13 SAG-D
DEC 9 SCO-D	NOV 3 SCO-R	NOV 12 SCO-D	DEC 16 CAP-D	SEP 29 VIR-R	DEC 4 CAP-D
DEC 13 SAG-D	NOV 23 SCO-D	DEC 4 SAG-D		OCT 5 VIR-D	DEC 16 CAP-R
	FEB 6 PIC-D	DEC 23 CAP-D		OCT 13 LIB-D	DEC 28 SAG-R
	DEC 12 SAG-D			NOV 1 SCO-D	
				NOV 20 SAG-D	
				DEC 9 CAP-D	

1912			1913			1914			1915			1916			1917		
JAN	5	SAG-D	JAN	11	CAP-D	JAN	4	CAP-D	JAN	16	AQU-D	JAN	9	AQU-D	JAN	2	AQU-D
JAN	16	CAP-D	JAN	31	AQU-D	JAN	23	AQU-D	FEB	3	PIC-D	JAN	27	AQU-R	JAN	10	AQU-R
FEB	8	AQU-D	FEB	17	PIC-D	FEB	9	PIC-D	FEB	12	PIC-R	FEB	17	AQU-D	JAN	19	CAP-R
FEB	26	PIC-D	MAR	5	ARI-D	MAR	1	PIC-R	FEB	24	AQU-D	MAR	16	PIC-D	JAN	30	CAP-D
MAR	13	ARI-D	MAR	18	ARI-R	MAR	24	PIC-D	MAR	6	AQU-D	APR	3	ARI-D	FEB	16	AQU-D
APR	5	ARI-R	APR	8	PIC-R	APR	17	ARI-D	MAR	20	PIC-D	APR	18	TAU-D	MAR	9	PIC-D
APR	29	ARI-D	APR	10	PIC-D	MAY	6	TAU-D	APR	11	ARI-D	MAY	3	GEM-D	MAR	26	ARI-D
MAY	17	TAU-D	APR	15	ARI-D	MAY	20	GEM-D	APR	27	TAU-D	MAY	25	GEM-R	APR	10	TAU-D
JUN	6	GEM-D	MAY	13	TAU-D	JUN	4	CAN-D	MAY	11	GEM-D	JUN	18	GEM-D	MAY	5	TAU-R
JUN	20	CAN-D	MAY	29	GEM-D	JUL	3	CAN-R	MAY	30	CAN-D	JUL	11	CAN-D	MAY	29	TAU-D
JUL	5	LEO-D	JUN	11	CAN-D	JUL	27	CAN-D	JUN	14	CAN-R	JUL	27	LEO-D	JUN	15	GEM-D
JUL	27	VIR-D	JUN	29	LEO-D	AUG	12	LEO-D	JUL	8	CAN-D	AUG	11	VIR-D	JUL	4	CAN-D
AUG	8	VIR-R	JUL	21	LEO-R	AUG	28	VIR-D	AUG	5	LEO-D	AUG	30	LIB-D	JUL	18	LEO-D
AUG	22	LEO-R	AUG	14	LEO-D	SEP	13	LIB-D	AUG	20	VIR-D	SEP	22	LIB-R	AUG	3	VIR-D
SEP	2	LEO-D	SEP	5	VIR-D	OCT	3	LIB-D	SEP	6	LIB-D	OCT	14	LIB-D	AUG	27	LIB-D
SEP	11	VIR-D	SEP	21	LIB-D	OCT	27	SCO-R	OCT	10	SCO-R	NOV	5	SCO-D	SEP	5	LIB-R
SEP	29	LIB-D	OCT	9	SCO-D	NOV	16	SCO-D	OCT	22	LIB-R	NOV	24	SAG-D	SEP	15	VIR-R
OCT	16	SCO-D	OCT	31	SAG-D	DEC	9	SAG-D	OCT	31	LIB-D	DEC	13	CAP-D	SEP	28	VIR-D
NOV	5	SAG-D	NOV	12	SAG-R	DEC	28	CAP-D	NOV	12	SCO-D				OCT	11	LIB-D
NOV	29	SAG-R	NOV	24	SCO-R				DEC	2	SAG-D				OCT	29	SCO-D
DEC	18	SAG-D	DEC	2	SCO-D				DEC	21	CAP-D				NOV	16	SAG-D
			DEC	14	SAG-D										DEC	6	CAP-D
															DEC	25	CAP-R

1918			1919			1920			1921			1922			1923		
JAN	14	CAP-D	JAN	14	CAP-D	JAN	9	CAP-D	JAN	1	CAP-D	JAN	12	AQU-D	JAN	5	AQU-D
FEB	11	AQU-D	FEB	4	AQU-D	JAN	28	AQU-D	JAN	20	AQU-D	FEB	2	PIC-D	JAN	20	AQU-R
MAR	2	PIC-D	FEB	22	PIC-D	FEB	14	PIC-D	FEB	6	PIC-D	FEB	5	PIC-R	FEB	7	CAP-R
MAR	18	ARI-D	MAR	10	ARI-D	MAR	3	ARI-D	FEB	21	PIC-R	FEB	10	AQU-R	FEB	10	CAP-D
APR	3	TAU-D	MAR	29	ARI-R	MAR	10	ARI-D	MAR	16	PIC-D	FEB	27	AQU-D	FEB	14	AQU-D
APR	16	TAU-R	APR	21	ARI-D	MAR	20	PIC-R	APR	15	ARI-D	MAR	19	PIC-D	MAR	14	PIC-D
MAY	10	TAU-D	MAY	17	TAU-D	APR	3	PIC-D	MAY	2	TAU-D	APR	8	ARI-D	MAR	31	ARI-D
JUN	11	GEM-D	JUN	3	GEM-D	APR	18	ARI-D	MAY	16	GEM-D	APR	23	TAU-D	APR	15	TAU-D
JUN	25	CAN-D	JUN	17	CAN-D	MAY	9	TAU-D	JUN	1	CAN-D	MAY	8	GEM-D	MAY	2	GEM-D
JUL	10	LEO-D	JUL	3	LEO-D	MAY	25	GEM-D	JUN	25	CAN-R	JUN	2	CAN-D	MAY	17	GEM-R
JUL	29	VIR-D	AUG	2	LEO-R	JUN	8	CAN-D	JUL	19	CAN-D	JUN	5	CAN-R	JUN	10	GEM-D
AUG	19	VIR-R	AUG	25	LEO-D	JUN	27	LEO-D	AUG	9	LEO-D	JUN	11	GEM-R	JUL	9	CAN-D
SEP	12	VIR-D	SEP	10	VIR-D	JUL	13	LEO-R	AUG	24	VIR-D	JUN	29	GEM-D	JUL	24	LEO-D
OCT	4	LIB-D	SEP	26	LIB-D	AUG	3	CAN-R	SEP	10	LIB-D	JUL	14	CAN-D	AUG	8	VIR-D
OCT	21	SCO-D	OCT	14	SCO-D	AUG	6	CAN-D	SEP	30	SCO-D	AUG	1	LEO-D	AUG	28	LIB-D
NOV	9	SAG-D	NOV	3	SAG-D	AUG	11	LEO-D	NOV	9	SCO-D	AUG	16	VIR-D	SEP	16	LIB-R
DEC	2	CAP-D	NOV	22	SAG-R	SEP	1	VIR-D	DEC	6	SAG-D	SEP	3	LIB-D	OCT	5	VIR-R
DEC	9	CAP-R	DEC	12	SAG-D	SEP	17	LIB-D	DEC	25	CAP-D	OCT	2	SCO-D	OCT	8	VIR-D
DEC	16	SAG-R				OCT	6	SCO-D				OCT	3	SCO-R	OCT	12	LIB-D
DEC	28	SAG-D				OCT	31	SAG-D				OCT	6	LIB-R	NOV	3	SCO-D
						NOV	5	SAG-R				OCT	24	LIB-D	NOV	21	SAG-D
						NOV	11	SCO-R				NOV	9	SCO-D	DEC	11	CAP-D
						NOV	25	SCO-D				NOV	28	SAG-D			
						DEC	12	SAG-D				DEC	18	CAP-D			

1924	1925	1926	1927	1928	1929
JAN 4 CAP-R	JAN 1 SAG-R	JAN 12 CAP-D	JAN 6 CAP-D	JAN 17 AQU-D	JAN 9 AQU-D
JAN 24 CAP-D	JAN 6 SAG-D	FEB 1 AQU-D	JAN 25 AQU-D	FEB 4 PIC-D	JAN 29 AQU-R
FEB 15 AQU-D	JAN 15 CAP-D	FEB 18 PIC-D	FEB 11 PIC-D	FEB 15 PIC-R	FEB 19 AQU-D
MAR 6 PIC-D	FEB 8 AQU-D	MAR 7 ARI-D	MAR 4 PIC-R	MAR 1 AQU-D	MAR 17 PIC-D
MAR 22 ARI-D	FEB 26 PIC-D	MAR 21 ARI-R	MAR 27 PIC-D	MAR 8 AQU-D	APR 4 ARI-D
APR 6 TAU-D	MAR 14 ARI-D	APR 13 ARI-D	APR 18 ARI-D	MAR 19 PIC-D	APR 20 TAU-D
APR 27 TAU-R	APR 2 TAU-D	MAY 14 TAU-D	MAY 7 TAU-D	APR 12 ARI-D	MAY 4 GEM-D
MAY 21 TAU-D	APR 8 TAU-R	MAY 30 GEM-D	MAY 22 GEM-D	APR 28 TAU-D	MAY 28 GEM-R
JUN 14 GEM-D	APR 16 ARI-R	JUN 13 CAN-D	JUN 5 CAN-D	MAY 12 GEM-D	JUN 21 GEM-D
JUN 30 CAN-D	MAY 2 ARI-D	JUN 30 LEO-D	JUN 29 LEO-D	MAY 29 CAN-D	JUL 12 CAN-D
JUL 14 LEO-D	MAY 18 TAU-D	JUL 24 LEO-R	JUL 6 LEO-R	JUN 16 CAN-R	JUL 28 LEO-D
JUL 31 VIR-D	JUN 7 GEM-D	AUG 17 LEO-D	JUL 15 CAN-R	JUL 10 CAN-D	AUG 12 VIR-D
AUG 29 VIR-R	JUN 21 CAN-D	SEP 6 VIR-D	JUL 30 CAN-D	AUG 5 LEO-D	AUG 31 LIB-D
SEP 20 VIR-D	JUL 6 LEO-D	SEP 22 LIB-D	AUG 13 LEO-D	AUG 20 VIR-D	SEP 25 LIB-R
OCT 8 LIB-D	JUL 27 VIR-D	OCT 10 SCO-D	AUG 29 VIR-D	SEP 6 LIB-D	OCT 17 LIB-D
OCT 25 SCO-D	AUG 11 VIR-R	NOV 1 SAG-D	SEP 15 LIB-D	SEP 28 SCO-D	NOV 6 SCO-D
NOV 13 SAG-D	AUG 28 LEO-R	NOV 15 SAG-R	OCT 4 SCO-D	OCT 12 SCO-D	NOV 25 SAG-D
DEC 3 CAP-D	SEP 4 LEO-D	NOV 29 SCO-R	OCT 30 SCO-R	OCT 25 LIB-R	DEC 14 CAP-D
	SEP 12 VIR-D	DEC 5 SCO-D	NOV 19 SCO-D	NOV 2 LIB-D	
	SEP 30 LIB-D	DEC 14 SAG-D	DEC 10 SAG-D	NOV 12 SCO-D	
	OCT 18 SCO-D		DEC 30 CAP-D	DEC 2 SAG-D	
	NOV 6 SAG-D			DEC 21 CAP-D	
	DEC 2 SAG-R				
	DEC 21 SAG-D				

1930	1931	1932	1933	1934	1935
JAN 3 AQU-D	JAN 17 CAP-D	JAN 15 CAP-D	JAN 9 CAP-D	JAN 2 CAP-D	JAN 14 AQU-D
JAN 13 AQU-R	FEB 12 AQU-D	FEB 6 AQU-D	JAN 28 AQU-D	JAN 21 AQU-D	FEB 2 PIC-D
JAN 24 CAP-R	MAR 3 PIC-D	FEB 24 PIC-D	FEB 15 PIC-D	FEB 7 PIC-D	FEB 8 PIC-R
FEB 2 CAP-D	MAR 19 ARI-D	MAR 10 ARI-D	MAR 4 ARI-D	FEB 24 PIC-R	FEB 16 AQU-R
FEB 16 AQU-D	APR 4 TAU-D	MAR 31 ARI-R	MAR 13 ARI-R	MAR 19 PIC-D	MAR 2 AQU-D
MAR 10 PIC-D	APR 19 TAU-R	APR 24 ARI-D	MAR 26 PIC-R	APR 16 ARI-D	MAR 19 PIC-D
MAR 27 ARI-D	MAY 13 TAU-D	MAY 16 TAU-D	APR 5 PIC-D	MAY 3 TAU-D	APR 9 ARI-D
APR 11 TAU-D	JUN 12 GEM-D	JUN 17 CAN-D	APR 18 ARI-D	MAY 17 GEM-D	APR 25 TAU-D
MAY 2 GEM-D	JUN 27 CAN-D	JUL 3 LEO-D	MAY 11 TAU-D	JUN 2 CAN-D	MAY 9 GEM-D
MAY 8 GEM-R	JUL 11 LEO-D	JUL 28 VIR-D	JUN 9 CAN-D	JUN 28 CAN-R	MAY 30 CAN-D
MAY 18 TAU-R	JUL 29 VIR-D	AUG 3 VIR-R	JUN 28 LEO-D	JUL 22 CAN-D	JUN 21 GEM-R
JUN 2 TAU-D	AUG 22 VIR-R	AUG 11 LEO-R	JUL 16 LEO-D	AUG 10 LEO-D	JUL 3 GEM-D
JUN 15 GEM-D	SEP 14 VIR-D	SEP 10 VIR-D	AUG 9 LEO-D	AUG 26 VIR-D	JUL 14 CAN-D
JUL 5 CAN-D	OCT 5 LIB-D	SEP 27 LIB-D	SEP 3 VIR-D	SEP 11 LIB-D	AUG 3 LEO-D
JUL 20 LEO-D	OCT 23 SCO-D	OCT 14 SCO-D	SEP 19 LIB-D	OCT 1 SCO-D	AUG 17 VIR-D
AUG 5 VIR-D	NOV 11 SAG-D	NOV 3 SAG-D	OCT 7 SCO-D	OCT 22 SCO-R	SEP 5 LIB-D
AUG 27 LIB-D	DEC 3 CAP-D	NOV 24 SAG-R	OCT 31 SAG-D	NOV 12 SCO-D	SEP 29 SCO-D
SEP 8 LIB-R	DEC 11 CAP-R	DEC 14 SAG-D	NOV 8 SAG-R	DEC 7 SAG-D	OCT 6 SCO-R
SEP 21 VIR-R	DEC 21 SAG-R		NOV 17 SCO-R	DEC 26 CAP-D	OCT 13 LIB-D
SEP 30 VIR-D	DEC 31 SAG-D		NOV 28 SCO-D		OCT 27 LIB-D
OCT 12 LIB-D			DEC 13 SAG-D		NOV 11 SCO-D
OCT 30 SCO-D					NOV 30 SAG-D
NOV 18 SAG-D					DEC 19 CAP-D
DEC 7 CAP-D					
DEC 27 CAP-R					

1936	1937	1938	1939	1940	1941
JAN 7 AQU-D	JAN 2 AQU-D	JAN 7 SAG-R	JAN 13 CAP-D	JAN 7 CAP-D	JAN 17 AQU-D
JAN 23 AQU-R	JAN 5 AQU-R	JAN 9 SAG-D	FEB 2 AQU-D	JAN 26 AQU-D	FEB 4 PIC-D
FEB 13 AQU-D	JAN 26 AQU-D	JAN 13 CAP-D	FEB 20 PIC-D	FEB 12 PIC-D	FEB 17 PIC-R
MAR 14 PIC-D	FEB 15 AQU-D	FEB 9 AQU-D	MAR 8 ARI-D	MAR 5 ARI-D	MAR 8 AQU-D
APR 1 ARI-D	MAR 7 PIC-D	FEB 28 PIC-D	MAR 24 ARI-R	MAR 6 ARI-D	MAR 11 AQU-D
APR 16 TAU-D	MAR 24 ARI-D	MAR 16 ARI-D	APR 16 ARI-D	MAR 9 PIC-R	MAR 17 PIC-D
MAY 2 GEM-D	APR 8 TAU-D	APR 2 TAU-D	MAY 15 TAU-D	MAR 29 PIC-D	APR 13 ARI-D
MAY 19 GEM-R	APR 30 TAU-R	APR 11 TAU-R	JUN 1 GEM-D	APR 18 ARI-D	APR 29 TAU-D
JUN 12 GEM-D	MAY 24 TAU-D	APR 24 ARI-D	JUN 14 CAN-D	MAY 7 TAU-D	MAY 14 GEM-D
JUL 9 CAN-D	JUN 14 GEM-D	MAY 5 ARI-D	JUL 1 LEO-D	MAY 22 GEM-D	MAY 30 CAN-D
JUL 24 LEO-D	JUL 2 CAN-D	MAY 17 TAU-D	JUL 27 LEO-R	JUN 5 CAN-D	JUN 19 CAN-R
AUG 8 VIR-D	JUL 16 LEO-D	JUN 9 GEM-D	AUG 20 LEO-D	JUN 27 LEO-D	JUL 14 CAN-D
AUG 28 LIB-D	AUG 1 VIR-D	JUN 23 CAN-D	SEP 8 VIR-D	JUL 8 LEO-R	AUG 7 LEO-D
SEP 18 LIB-R	SEP 2 VIR-R	JUL 8 LEO-D	SEP 24 LIB-D	JUL 22 CAN-D	AUG 22 VIR-D
OCT 10 LIB-D	SEP 23 VIR-D	JUL 27 VIR-D	OCT 12 SCO-D	AUG 2 CAN-D	SEP 7 LIB-D
NOV 3 SCO-D	OCT 9 LIB-D	AUG 14 VIR-R	NOV 2 SAG-D	AUG 12 LEO-D	SEP 29 SCO-D
NOV 22 SAG-D	OCT 27 SAG-D	SEP 4 LEO-D	NOV 18 SAG-R	AUG 30 VIR-D	OCT 15 SCO-R
DEC 11 CAP-D	NOV 14 SAG-D	SEP 6 LEO-D	DEC 4 SCO-D	SEP 15 LIB-D	OCT 30 LIB-R
	DEC 4 CAP-D	SEP 11 VIR-D	DEC 8 SCO-D	OCT 4 SCO-D	NOV 5 LIB-D
		OCT 2 LIB-D	DEC 14 SAG-D	NOV 2 SCO-D	NOV 12 SCO-D
		OCT 19 SCO-D		NOV 21 SCO-D	DEC 4 SAG-D
		NOV 7 SAG-D		DEC 10 SAG-D	DEC 23 CAP-D
		DEC 4 SAG-R		DEC 30 CAP-D	
		DEC 24 SAG-D			

1942	1943	1944	1945	1946	1947
JAN 10 AQU-D	JAN 4 AQU-D	JAN 19 CAP-D	JAN 15 CAP-D	JAN 10 CAP-D	JAN 4 CAP-D
FEB 1 AQU-D	JAN 15 AQU-R	FEB 13 AQU-D	FEB 6 AQU-D	JAN 30 AQU-D	JAN 22 AQU-D
FEB 22 AQU-D	JAN 28 CAP-R	MAR 4 PIC-D	FEB 24 PIC-D	FEB 16 PIC-D	FEB 9 PIC-D
MAR 18 PIC-D	FEB 5 CAP-D	MAR 20 ARI-D	MAR 12 ARI-D	MAR 5 ARI-D	FEB 27 PIC-R
APR 6 ARI-D	FEB 16 AQU-D	APR 4 TAU-D	APR 3 ARI-R	MAR 16 ARI-R	MAR 22 PIC-D
APR 21 TAU-D	MAR 12 PIC-D	APR 22 TAU-R	APR 27 ARI-D	APR 2 PIC-R	APR 17 ARI-D
MAY 6 GEM-D	MAR 29 ARI-D	MAY 18 TAU-D	MAY 17 TAU-D	APR 9 PIC-D	MAY 5 TAU-D
MAY 31 GEM-R	APR 13 TAU-D	JUN 12 GEM-D	JUN 5 GEM-D	APR 17 ARI-D	MAY 19 GEM-D
JUN 24 GEM-D	MAY 1 GEM-D	JUN 28 CAN-D	JUN 19 CAN-D	MAY 12 TAU-D	JUN 3 CAN-D
JUL 13 CAN-D	MAY 12 GEM-R	JUL 12 LEO-D	JUL 4 LEO-D	MAY 28 GEM-D	JUL 2 CAN-R
JUL 30 LEO-D	MAY 27 TAU-R	JUL 29 VIR-D	JUL 28 VIR-D	JUN 11 CAN-D	JUL 25 CAN-D
AUG 14 VIR-D	JUN 5 TAU-D	AUG 24 VIR-R	AUG 6 VIR-R	JUN 28 LEO-D	AUG 11 LEO-D
SEP 1 LIB-D	JUN 15 GEM-D	SEP 16 VIR-D	AUG 18 LEO-R	JUL 19 LEO-R	AUG 27 VIR-D
SEP 28 LIB-R	JUL 7 CAN-D	OCT 23 SCO-D	SEP 11 VIR-D	AUG 12 LEO-D	SEP 12 LIB-D
OCT 20 LIB-D	JUL 21 LEO-D	NOV 11 SAG-D	SEP 28 LIB-D	SEP 4 VIR-D	OCT 2 SCO-D
NOV 8 SCO-D	AUG 6 VIR-D	DEC 2 CAP-D	OCT 16 SCO-D	SEP 20 LIB-D	OCT 25 SCO-R
NOV 26 SAG-D	AUG 28 LIB-D	DEC 13 CAP-R	NOV 4 SAG-D	OCT 8 SCO-D	NOV 15 SCO-D
DEC 15 CAP-D	SEP 11 LIB-R	DEC 24 SAG-R	NOV 27 SAG-R	OCT 31 SAG-D	DEC 8 SAG-D
	SEP 26 VIR-R		DEC 17 SAG-D	NOV 11 SAG-R	DEC 27 CAP-D
	OCT 3 VIR-D			NOV 21 SCO-R	
	OCT 12 LIB-D			DEC 1 SCO-D	
	OCT 31 SCO-D			DEC 14 SAG-D	
	NOV 19 SAG-D				
	DEC 9 CAP-D				
	DEC 30 CAP-R				

1948	1949	1950	1951	1952	1953
JAN 15 AQU-D	JAN 7 AQU-D	JAN 2 AQU-D	JAN 12 CAP-R	JAN 14 CAP-D	JAN 7 CAP-R
FEB 3 PIC-D	JAN 24 AQU-R	JAN 8 AQU-R	FEB 10 AQU-D	FEB 4 AQU-D	JAN 26 AQU-D
FEB 11 PIC-R	FEB 14 AQU-D	JAN 16 CAP-R	MAR 1 PIC-D	FEB 21 PIC-D	FEB 12 PIC-D
FEB 21 AQU-R	MAR 15 PIC-D	FEB 15 AQU-D	MAR 17 ARI-D	MAR 8 ARI-D	MAR 3 ARI-D
MAR 4 AQU-D	APR 17 TAU-D	MAR 8 PIC-D	APR 3 TAU-D	MAR 26 ARI-R	MAR 9 ARI-R
MAR 19 PIC-D	MAY 3 GEM-D	MAR 25 ARI-D	APR 14 TAU-R	APR 19 ARI-D	MAR 16 PIC-R
APR 10 ARI-D	MAY 23 GEM-R	APR 9 TAU-D	MAY 2 ARI-R	MAY 15 TAU-D	APR 1 PIC-D
APR 26 TAU-D	JUN 16 GEM-D	MAY 3 TAU-R	MAY 8 ARI-D	JUN 1 GEM-D	APR 18 ARI-D
MAY 10 GEM-D	JUL 11 CAN-D	MAY 27 TAU-D	MAY 16 TAU-D	JUN 12 CAN-D	MAY 9 TAU-D
MAY 29 CAN-D	JUL 26 LEO-D	JUN 15 GEM-D	JUN 10 GEM-D	JUL 1 LEO-D	MAY 24 GEM-D
JUN 11 CAN-R	AUG 10 VIR-D	JUL 17 LEO-D	JUN 25 CAN-D	JUL 29 LEO-R	JUN 7 CAN-D
JUN 29 GEM-R	AUG 29 LIB-D	AUG 3 VIR-D	JUL 9 LEO-D	AUG 22 LEO-D	JUN 27 LEO-D
JUL 5 GEM-D	SEP 21 LIB-R	AUG 28 LIB-D	JUL 28 VIR-D	SEP 8 VIR-D	JUL 11 LEO-R
JUL 12 CAN-D	SEP 12 LIB-D	SEP 4 LIB-R	AUG 17 VIR-R	SEP 25 LIB-D	JUL 29 CAN-R
AUG 3 LEO-D	NOV 4 SCO-D	SEP 11 VIR-R	SEP 9 VIR-D	OCT 12 SCO-D	AUG 4 CAN-D
AUG 18 VIR-D	NOV 23 SAG-D	SEP 26 VIR-D	OCT 3 LIB-D	NOV 2 SAG-D	AUG 12 LEO-D
SEP 4 LIB-D	DEC 12 CAP-D	OCT 10 LIB-D	OCT 20 SCO-D	NOV 20 SAG-R	AUG 31 VIR-D
SEP 28 SCO-D		OCT 28 SCO-D	NOV 9 SAG-D	DEC 10 SAG-D	SEP 16 LIB-D
OCT 8 SCO-R		NOV 16 SAG-D	DEC 2 CAP-D		OCT 5 SCO-D
OCT 18 LIB-D		DEC 6 CAP-D	DEC 7 CAP-R		NOV 1 SAG-D
NOV 11 SCO-D		DEC 23 CAP-R	DEC 13 SAG-R		NOV 3 SAG-D
NOV 30 SAG-D			DEC 27 SAG-D		NOV 7 SCO-R
DEC 19 CAP-D					NOV 23 SCO-D
					DEC 11 SAG-D
					DEC 31 CAP-D

1954	1955	1956	1957	1958	1959
JAN 19 AQU-D	JAN 11 AQU-D	JAN 5 AQU-D	JAN 2 CAP-R	JAN 5 SAG-D	JAN 11 CAP-D
FEB 5 PIC-D	FEB 3 AQU-R	JAN 18 AQU-R	JAN 21 CAP-D	JAN 15 CAP-D	JAN 31 AQU-D
FEB 20 PIC-R	FEB 25 AQU-D	FEB 3 CAP-R	FEB 13 AQU-D	FEB 7 AQU-D	FEB 18 PIC-D
MAR 14 PIC-D	MAR 18 PIC-D	FEB 8 CAP-D	MAR 5 PIC-D	FEB 25 PIC-D	MAR 6 ARI-D
APR 14 ARI-D	APR 7 ARI-D	FEB 16 AQU-D	MAR 21 ARI-D	MAR 13 ARI-D	MAR 19 ARI-R
MAY 1 TAU-D	APR 23 TAU-D	MAR 12 PIC-D	APR 5 TAU-D	APR 3 TAU-D	APR 12 ARI-D
MAY 15 GEM-D	MAY 7 GEM-D	MAR 29 ARI-D	APR 25 TAU-R	APR 6 TAU-R	MAY 13 TAU-D
MAY 31 CAN-D	JUN 3 GEM-R	APR 13 TAU-D	MAY 19 TAU-D	APR 11 ARI-R	MAY 29 GEM-D
JUN 23 CAN-R	JUN 27 GEM-D	APR 30 GEM-D	JUN 13 GEM-D	APR 30 ARI-D	JUN 12 CAN-D
JUL 17 CAN-D	JUL 14 CAN-D	MAY 14 GEM-R	JUN 29 CAN-D	MAY 18 TAU-D	JUN 29 LEO-D
AUG 8 LEO-D	JUL 31 LEO-D	JUN 7 GEM-D	JUL 13 LEO-D	JUN 6 GEM-D	JUL 22 LEO-R
AUG 23 VIR-D	AUG 15 VIR-D	JUL 7 CAN-D	JUL 31 VIR-D	JUN 21 CAN-D	AUG 15 LEO-D
SEP 9 LIB-D	SEP 2 LIB-D	JUL 22 LEO-D	AUG 27 VIR-R	JUL 5 LEO-D	SEP 6 VIR-D
SEP 30 SCO-D	OCT 2 LIB-R	AUG 6 VIR-D	SEP 19 VIR-D	JUL 27 VIR-D	SEP 22 LIB-D
OCT 18 SCO-R	OCT 22 LIB-D	AUG 27 LIB-D	OCT 7 LIB-D	AUG 9 VIR-R	OCT 10 SCO-D
NOV 12 SCO-D	NOV 9 SCO-D	SEP 13 LIB-R	OCT 24 LIB-D	AUG 24 LEO-R	NOV 1 SAG-D
DEC 5 SAG-D	NOV 28 SAG-D	SEP 30 VIR-R	NOV 12 SAG-D	SEP 2 LEO-D	NOV 14 SAG-R
DEC 24 CAP-D	DEC 17 CAP-D	OCT 5 VIR-D	DEC 3 CAP-D	SEP 12 VIR-D	NOV 26 SCO-R
		OCT 12 LIB-D	DEC 16 CAP-R	SEP 29 LIB-D	DEC 3 SCO-D
		NOV 1 SCO-D	DEC 29 SAG-R	OCT 17 SCO-D	DEC 14 SAG-D
		NOV 19 SAG-D		NOV 6 SAG-D	
		DEC 9 CAP-D		NOV 30 SAG-R	
				DEC 20 SAG-D	

1960	1961	1962	1963	1964	1965
JAN 5 CAP-D	JAN 15 AQU-D	JAN 8 AQU-D	JAN 3 AQU-D	JAN 15 CAP-D	JAN 14 CAP-D
JAN 24 AQU-D	FEB 2 PIC-D	JAN 27 AQU-R	JAN 11 AQU-R	FEB 11 AQU-D	FEB 4 AQU-D
FEB 10 PIC-D	FEB 12 PIC-R	FEB 17 AQU-D	JAN 21 CAP-R	MAR 17 PIC-D	FEB 22 PIC-D
MAR 2 PIC-R	FEB 25 AQU-R	MAR 16 PIC-D	FEB 1 CAP-D	APR 3 ARI-D	MAR 10 ARI-D
MAR 24 PIC-D	MAR 6 AQU-D	APR 4 ARI-D	FEB 16 AQU-D	APR 17 TAU-D	MAR 29 ARI-R
APR 17 ARI-D	MAR 19 PIC-D	APR 19 TAU-D	MAR 10 PIC-D	MAY 10 TAU-D	APR 22 ARI-D
MAY 5 TAU-D	APR 11 ARI-D	MAY 4 GEM-D	MAR 27 ARI-D	JUN 10 GEM-D	MAY 16 TAU-D
MAY 20 GEM-D	APR 27 TAU-D	MAY 26 GEM-R	APR 10 TAU-D	JUN 25 CAN-D	JUN 3 GEM-D
JUN 3 CAN-D	MAY 11 GEM-D	JUN 19 GEM-D	MAY 4 GEM-D	JUL 10 LEO-D	JUN 17 CAN-D
JUL 2 LEO-R	MAY 29 CAN-D	JUL 12 CAN-D	MAY 7 GEM-R	JUL 28 VIR-D	AUG 1 VIR-D
JUL 4 LEO-D	JUN 14 CAN-D	JUL 27 LEO-D	MAY 11 TAU-R	AUG 19 VIR-R	AUG 2 VIR-R
JUL 7 CAN-R	JUL 8 CAN-D	AUG 11 VIR-D	MAY 30 TAU-D	SEP 11 VIR-D	AUG 4 LEO-R
JUL 27 CAN-D	AUG 5 LEO-D	AUG 30 LIB-D	JUN 15 GEM-D	OCT 4 LIB-D	AUG 25 VEO-D
AUG 11 LEO-D	AUG 19 VIR-D	SEP 24 LIB-R	JUL 5 CAN-D	OCT 21 SCO-D	SEP 9 VIR-D
AUG 28 VIR-D	SEP 5 LIB-D	OCT 15 LIB-D	JUL 19 LEO-D	NOV 9 SAG-D	SEP 26 LIB-D
SEP 13 LIB-D	SEP 28 SCO-D	NOV 6 SCO-D	AUG 4 VIR-D	DEC 1 CAP-D	OCT 13 SCO-D
OCT 2 SCO-D	OCT 10 SCO-D	NOV 24 SAG-D	AUG 27 LIB-D	DEC 9 CAP-R	NOV 3 SAG-D
OCT 27 SCO-R	OCT 23 LIB-R	DEC 13 CAP-D	SEP 6 LIB-R	DEC 17 SAG-R	NOV 23 SAG-R
NOV 16 SCO-D	OCT 31 LIB-D		SEP 18 VIR-R	DEC 29 SAG-D	DEC 12 SAG-D
DEC 8 SAG-D	NOV 11 SCO-D		SEP 29 VIR-D		
DEC 28 CAP-D	DEC 1 SAG-D		OCT 11 LIB-D		
	DEC 21 CAP-D		OCT 29 SCO-D		
			NOV 17 SAG-D		
			DEC 7 CAP-D		
			DEC 26 CAP-R		

1966	1967	1968	1969	1970	1971
JAN 8 CAP-D	JAN 2 CAP-D	JAN 13 AQU-D	JAN 5 AQU-D	JAN 4 CAP-R	JAN 3 SAG-R
JAN 29 AQU-D	JAN 20 AQU-D	FEB 2 PIC-D	JAN 20 AQU-R	JAN 24 CAP-D	JAN 8 SAG-R
FEB 14 PIC-D	FEB 7 PIC-D	FEB 6 PIC-R	FEB 10 AQU-D	FEB 14 AQU-D	JAN 15 CAP-D
MAR 4 ARI-D	FEB 24 PIC-R	FEB 12 AQU-R	MAR 13 PIC-D	MAR 6 PIC-D	FEB 8 AQU-D
MAR 12 ARI-R	MAR 17 PIC-D	FEB 28 AQU-D	MAR 31 ARI-D	MAR 23 ARI-D	FEB 27 PIC-D
MAR 23 PIC-R	APR 15 ARI-D	MAR 18 PIC-D	APR 15 TAU-D	APR 7 TAU-D	MAR 15 ARI-D
APR 4 PIC-D	MAY 2 TAU-D	APR 8 ARI-D	MAY 1 GEM-D	APR 28 TAU-R	APR 2 TAU-D
APR 18 ARI-D	MAY 17 GEM-D	APR 23 TAU-D	MAY 17 GEM-R	MAY 22 TAU-D	APR 9 TAU-R
MAY 10 TAU-D	JUN 1 CAN-D	MAY 7 GEM-D	JUN 10 GEM-D	JUN 14 GEM-D	APR 19 ARI-R
MAY 25 GEM-D	JUN 26 CAN-R	MAY 30 CAN-D	JUL 9 CAN-D	JUL 1 CAN-D	MAY 3 ARI-D
JUN 8 CAN-D	JUL 20 CAN-D	JUN 6 CAN-R	JUL 23 LEO-D	JUL 15 LEO-D	MAY 18 TAU-D
JUN 27 LEO-D	AUG 9 LEO-D	JUN 14 GEM-D	AUG 8 VIR-D	AUG 1 VIR-D	JUN 8 GEM-D
JUL 14 LEO-R	AUG 25 VIR-D	JUN 30 GEM-D	AUG 28 LIB-D	AUG 30 VIR-R	JUN 22 CAN-D
AUG 7 LEO-D	SEP 10 LIB-D	JUL 14 CAN-D	SEP 16 LIB-R	SEP 22 VIR-D	JUL 6 LEO-D
SEP 2 VIR-D	OCT 1 SCO-D	AUG 1 LEO-D	OCT 8 SCO-D	OCT 8 LIB-D	JUL 27 VIR-D
SEP 18 LIB-D	OCT 21 SCO-R	AUG 16 VIR-D	OCT 9 SCO-R	OCT 26 SCO-D	AUG 12 VIR-R
OCT 6 SCO-D	NOV 10 SCO-D	SEP 3 LIB-D	OCT 10 LIB-D	NOV 14 SAG-D	AUG 30 LEO-R
OCT 31 SAG-D	DEC 6 SAG-D	SEP 27 SCO-D	NOV 2 SCO-D	DEC 4 CAP-D	SEP 5 LEO-D
NOV 6 SAG-R	DEC 25 CAP-D	OCT 3 SCO-R	NOV 21 SAG-D	DEC 19 CAP-R	SEP 12 VIR-D
NOV 14 SCO-R		OCT 8 LIB-R	DEC 10 CAP-D		OCT 2 LIB-D
NOV 26 SCO-D		OCT 24 LIB-D			OCT 18 SCO-D
DEC 12 SAG-D		NOV 9 SCO-D			NOV 7 SAG-D
		NOV 28 SAG-D			DEC 3 SAG-R
		DEC 17 CAP-D			DEC 22 SAG-D

1972	1973	1974	1975	1976	1977
JAN 12 CAP-D	JAN 5 CAP-D	JAN 17 AQU-D	JAN 9 AQU-D	JAN 3 AQU-D	JAN 17 CAP-D
FEB 1 AQU-D	JAN 24 AQU-D	FEB 3 PIC-D	JAN 30 AQU-R	JAN 14 AQU-R	FEB 11 AQU-D
FEB 19 PIC-D	FEB 10 PIC-D	FEB 15 PIC-R	FEB 20 AQU-D	JAN 26 CAP-R	MAR 3 PIC-D
MAR 6 ARI-D	MAR 4 PIC-R	MAR 3 AQU-D	MAR 17 PIC-D	FEB 3 CAP-D	MAR 19 ARI-D
MAR 21 ARI-D	MAR 27 PIC-D	MAR 9 AQU-D	APR 5 ARI-D	FEB 16 AQU-D	APR 4 TAU-D
APR 13 ARI-D	APR 17 ARI-D	MAR 18 PIC-D	APR 20 TAU-D	MAR 9 PIC-D	APR 20 TAU-R
MAY 13 TAU-D	MAY 7 TAU-D	APR 12 ARI-D	MAY 6 GEM-D	MAR 27 ARI-D	MAY 13 TAU-D
MAY 30 GEM-D	MAY 21 GEM-D	APR 29 TAU-D	MAY 29 GEM-R	APR 11 TAU-D	JUN 11 GEM-D
JUN 13 CAN-D	JUN 5 CAN-D	MAY 13 GEM-D	JUN 22 GEM-D	APR 30 GEM-D	JUN 28 CAN-D
JUN 29 LEO-D	JUN 28 LEO-D	MAY 30 CAN-D	JUL 13 CAN-D	MAY 9 GEM-R	JUL 11 LEO-D
JUL 24 LEO-R	JUL 6 LEO-R	JUN 17 CAN-R	JUL 29 LEO-D	MAY 20 TAU-R	JUL 29 VIR-D
AUG 17 LEO-D	JUL 17 CAN-R	JUL 12 CAN-D	AUG 13 VIR-D	JUN 2 TAU-D	AUG 22 VIR-R
SEP 6 VIR-D	JUL 30 CAN-D	AUG 6 LEO-D	AUG 31 LIB-D	JUN 14 GEM-D	SEP 14 VIR-D
SEP 22 LIB-D	AUG 12 LEO-D	AUG 21 VIR-D	SEP 27 LIB-R	JUL 5 CAN-D	OCT 5 LIB-D
OCT 10 SCO-D	AUG 29 VIR-D	SEP 7 LIB-D	OCT 18 LIB-D	JUL 19 LEO-D	OCT 22 SCO-D
OCT 31 SAG-D	SEP 14 LIB-D	SEP 29 SCO-D	NOV 7 SCO-D	AUG 4 VIR-D	NOV 10 SAG-D
NOV 15 SAG-R	OCT 3 SCO-D	OCT 13 SCO-R	NOV 26 SAG-D	AUG 26 LIB-D	DEC 2 CAP-D
NOV 30 SCO-R	OCT 30 SCO-R	OCT 27 LIB-R	DEC 15 CAP-D	SEP 8 LIB-R	DEC 12 CAP-R
DEC 5 SCO-D	NOV 19 SCO-D	NOV 3 LIB-D		SEP 22 VIR-R	DEC 22 SAG-R
DEC 13 SAG-D	DEC 9 SAG-D	NOV 12 SCO-D		OCT 1 VIR-D	DEC 31 SAG-D
	DEC 29 CAP-D	DEC 3 SAG-D		OCT 11 LIB-D	
		DEC 22 CAP-D		OCT 30 SCO-D	
				NOV 17 SAG-D	
				DEC 7 CAP-D	
				DEC 28 CAP-R	

1978	1979	1980	1981	1982	1983
JAN 14 CAP-D	JAN 9 CAP-D	JAN 3 CAP-D	JAN 13 AQU-D	JAN 6 AQU-D	JAN 2 AQU-D
FEB 5 AQU-D	JAN 29 AQU-D	JAN 22 AQU-D	FEB 1 PIC-D	JAN 23 AQU-R	JAN 7 AQU-R
MAR 11 ARI-D	FEB 15 PIC-D	FEB 8 PIC-D	FEB 8 PIC-R	FEB 13 AQU-D	JAN 13 CAP-R
APR 2 ARI-R	MAR 4 ARI-D	FEB 26 PIC-R	FEB 17 AQU-D	MAR 14 PIC-D	JAN 27 CAP-D
APR 25 ARI-D	MAR 15 ARI-R	MAR 19 PIC-D	MAR 2 AQU-D	APR 1 ARI-D	FEB 15 AQU-D
MAY 17 TAU-D	MAR 29 PIC-R	APR 15 ARI-D	MAR 19 PIC-D	APR 16 TAU-D	MAR 8 PIC-D
JUN 4 GEM-D	APR 7 PIC-D	MAY 17 GEM-D	APR 9 PIC-D	MAY 3 GEM-D	MAR 24 ARI-D
JUN 18 CAN-D	APR 18 ARI-D	JUN 1 CAN-D	APR 25 TAU-D	MAY 21 GEM-R	APR 8 TAU-D
JUL 3 LEO-D	MAY 11 TAU-D	JUN 28 CAN-R	MAY 9 GEM-D	JUN 13 GEM-D	MAY 2 TAU-R
JUL 28 VIR-D	MAY 27 GEM-D	JUL 22 CAN-D	MAY 29 CAN-D	JUL 10 CAN-D	MAY 26 TAU-D
AUG 4 VIR-R	JUN 10 CAN-D	AUG 10 LEO-D	JUN 9 CAN-R	JUL 25 LEO-D	JUN 15 GEM-D
AUG 14 LEO-R	JUN 28 LEO-D	AUG 25 VIR-D	JUN 23 GEM-R	AUG 9 VIR-D	JUL 2 CAN-D
AUG 28 LEO-D	JUL 17 LEO-R	SEP 11 LIB-D	JUL 4 GEM-D	AUG 29 LIB-D	JUL 16 LEO-D
SEP 10 VIR-D	AUG 11 LEO-D	OCT 1 SCO-D	JUL 13 CAN-D	SEP 19 LIB-R	AUG 2 VIR-D
SEP 27 LIB-D	SEP 3 VIR-D	OCT 23 SCO-R	AUG 2 LEO-D	OCT 11 LIB-D	AUG 30 LIB-D
OCT 15 SCO-D	SEP 19 LIB-D	NOV 12 SCO-D	AUG 17 VIR-D	NOV 4 SCO-D	SEP 2 LIB-R
NOV 4 SAG-D	OCT 8 SCO-D	DEC 6 SAG-D	SEP 3 LIB-D	NOV 22 SAG-D	SEP 7 VIR-R
NOV 25 SAG-R	OCT 31 SAG-D	DEC 26 CAP-D	SEP 28 SCO-D	DEC 11 CAP-D	SEP 24 VIR-D
DEC 15 SAG-D	NOV 9 SAG-R		OCT 6 SCO-R		OCT 9 LIB-D
	NOV 19 SCO-R		OCT 15 LIB-R		OCT 27 SCO-D
	NOV 29 SCO-D		OCT 27 LIB-D		NOV 15 SAG-D
	DEC 13 SAG-D		NOV 10 SCO-D		DEC 5 CAP-D
			NOV 29 SAG-D		DEC 22 CAP-R
			DEC 18 CAP-D		

1984	1985	1986	1987	1988	1989
JAN 11 CAP-D	JAN 12 CAP-D	JAN 6 CAP-D	JAN 18 AQU-D	JAN 11 AQU-D	JAN 3 AQU-D
FEB 10 AQU-D	FEB 2 AQU-D	JAN 26 AQU-D	FEB 5 PIC-D	FEB 2 AQU-R	JAN 16 AQU-R
FEB 28 PIC-D	FEB 19 PIC-D	FEB 12 PIC-D	FEB 18 PIC-R	FEB 23 AQU-D	JAN 30 CAP-R
MAR 15 ARI-D	MAR 8 ARI-D	MAR 4 ARI-D	MAR 12 AQU-R	MAR 17 PIC-D	FEB 5 CAP-D
APR 1 TAU-D	MAR 24 ARI-R	MAR 7 ARI-R	MAR 13 AQU-D	APR 5 ARI-D	FEB 15 AQU-D
APR 11 TAU-R	APR 17 ARI-D	MAR 30 PIC-D	MAR 14 PIC-D	APR 21 TAU-D	MAR 11 PIC-D
APR 26 ARI-R	MAY 15 TAU-D	APR 18 ARI-D	APR 12 ARI-D	MAY 5 GEM-D	MAR 29 ARI-D
MAY 6 ARI-D	MAY 31 GEM-D	MAY 8 TAU-D	APR 30 TAU-D	MAY 31 GEM-R	APR 12 TAU-D
MAY 16 TAU-D	JUN 30 LEO-D	MAY 23 GEM-D	MAY 14 GEM-D	JUN 24 GEM-D	APR 30 GEM-D
JUN 8 GEM-D	JUL 28 LEO-R	JUN 6 CAN-D	MAY 31 CAN-D	JUL 13 CAN-D	MAY 12 GEM-R
JUN 23 CAN-D	AUG 20 LEO-D	JUN 27 LEO-D	JUN 21 CAN-R	JUL 29 LEO-D	MAY 29 TAU-R
JUL 7 LEO-D	SEP 7 VIR-D	JUL 9 LEO-R	JUL 15 CAN-D	AUG 13 VIR-D	JUN 5 TAU-D
JUL 27 VIR-D	SEP 23 LIB-D	JUL 24 CAN-R	AUG 7 LEO-D	AUG 31 LIB-D	JUN 13 GEM-D
AUG 14 VIR-R	OCT 11 SCO-D	AUG 3 CAN-D	AUG 22 VIR-D	SEP 28 LIB-R	JUL 7 CAN-D
SEP 7 VIR-D	NOV 1 SAG-D	AUG 12 LEO-D	SEP 9 LIB-D	OCT 20 LIB-D	JUL 21 LEO-D
OCT 1 LIB-D	NOV 18 SAG-R	AUG 31 VIR-D	SEP 30 SCO-D	NOV 7 SCO-D	AUG 6 VIR-D
OCT 19 SCO-D	DEC 5 SCO-R	SEP 16 LIB-D	OCT 16 SCO-R	NOV 26 SAG-D	AUG 27 LIB-D
NOV 7 SAG-D	DEC 8 SCO-D	OCT 5 SCO-D	NOV 2 LIB-R	DEC 15 CAP-D	SEP 11 LIB-R
DEC 2 CAP-D	DEC 13 SAG-D	NOV 2 SCO-R	NOV 6 LIB-D		SEP 27 VIR-R
DEC 4 CAP-R		NOV 22 SCO-D	NOV 12 SCO-D		OCT 4 VIR-D
DEC 8 SAG-R		DEC 11 SAG-D	DEC 4 SAG-D		OCT 12 LIB-D
DEC 24 SAG-D		DEC 30 CAP-D	DEC 23 CAP-D		OCT 31 SCO-D
					NOV 19 SAG-D
					DEC 8 CAP-D
					DEC 30 CAP-R

1990	1991	1992	1993	1994	1995
JAN 20 CAP-D	JAN 4 SAG-D	JAN 11 CAP-D	JAN 3 CAP-D	JAN 15 AQU-D	JAN 7 AQU-D
FEB 13 AQU-D	JAN 15 CAP-D	JAN 30 AQU-D	JAN 22 AQU-D	FEB 2 PIC-D	JAN 26 AQU-R
MAR 4 PIC-D	FEB 6 AQU-D	FEB 17 PIC-D	FEB 8 PIC-D	FEB 11 PIC-R	FEB 16 AQU-D
MAR 21 ARI-D	FEB 25 PIC-D	MAR 4 ARI-D	FEB 27 PIC-R	FEB 22 AQU-R	MAR 15 PIC-D
APR 5 TAU-D	MAR 12 ARI-D	MAR 17 ARI-R	MAR 22 PIC-D	MAR 5 AQU-D	APR 3 ARI-D
APR 23 TAU-R	APR 4 ARI-R	APR 7 PIC-R	APR 16 ARI-D	MAR 19 PIC-D	APR 18 TAU-D
MAY 17 TAU-D	APR 28 ARI-D	APR 9 PIC-D	MAY 4 TAU-D	APR 10 ARI-D	MAY 3 GEM-D
JUN 13 GEM-D	MAY 17 TAU-D	APR 15 ARI-D	MAY 19 GEM-D	APR 26 TAU-D	MAY 24 GEM-R
JUN 28 CAN-D	JUN 6 GEM-D	MAY 12 TAU-D	JUN 3 CAN-D	MAY 10 GEM-D	JUN 17 GEM-D
JUL 12 LEO-D	JUN 20 CAN-D	MAY 27 GEM-D	JUL 2 CAN-R	MAY 29 CAN-D	JUL 11 CAN-D
JUL 30 VIR-D	JUL 5 LEO-D	JUN 10 CAN-D	JUL 25 CAN-D	JUN 12 CAN-R	JUL 26 LEO-D
AUG 25 VIR-D	JUL 27 VIR-D	JUN 28 LEO-D	AUG 11 LEO-D	JUL 3 GEM-D	AUG 11 VIR-D
SEP 17 VIR-D	AUG 7 VIR-R	JUL 20 LEO-R	AUG 27 VIR-D	JUL 6 GEM-D	AUG 30 LIB-D
OCT 6 LIB-D	AUG 20 LEO-D	AUG 13 LEO-D	SEP 12 LIB-D	JUL 11 CAN-D	SEP 22 LIB-R
OCT 24 SCO-D	AUG 31 LEO-D	SEP 4 VIR-D	OCT 2 SCO-D	AUG 4 LEO-D	OCT 14 LIB-D
NOV 12 SAG-D	SEP 11 VIR-D	SEP 20 LIB-D	OCT 25 SCO-R	AUG 19 VIR-D	NOV 5 SCO-D
DEC 3 CAP-D	SEP 29 LIB-D	OCT 8 SCO-D	NOV 15 SCO-D	SEP 5 LIB-D	NOV 23 SAG-D
DEC 14 CAP-R	OCT 16 SCO-D	OCT 30 SAG-D	DEC 8 SAG-D	SEP 28 SCO-D	DEC 13 CAP-D
DEC 26 SAG-R	NOV 5 SAG-D	NOV 11 SAG-R	DEC 27 CAP-D	OCT 9 SCO-R	
	NOV 28 SAG-R	NOV 22 SCO-R		OCT 20 LIB-R	
	DEC 18 SAG-D	DEC 1 SCO-D		OCT 30 LIB-D	
		DEC 13 SAG-D		NOV 11 SCO-D	
				DEC 1 SAG-D	
				DEC 20 CAP-D	

Mercury Tables

1996–2001

1996		1997		1998		1999		2000		2001	
JAN	2 AQU-D	JAN	12 CAP-D	JAN	13 CAP-D	JAN	8 CAP-D	JAN	1 CAP-D	JAN	11 AQU-D
JAN	9 AQU-R	FEB	10 AQU-D	FEB	3 AQU-D	JAN	27 AQU-D	JAN	19 AQU-D	FEB	2 PIC-D
JAN	18 CAP-R	MAR	1 PIC-D	FEB	21 PIC-D	FEB	13 PIC-D	FEB	6 PIC-D	FEB	7 AQU-R
JAN	30 CAP-D	MAR	17 ARI-D	MAR	9 ARI-D	MAR	3 ARI-D	FEB	21 PIC-R	FEB	25 AQU-D
FEB	16 AQU-D	APR	2 TAU-D	MAR	27 ARI-R	MAR	10 ARI-R	MAR	14 PIC-D	MAR	18 PIC-D
MAR	8 PIC-D	APR	14 TAU-R	APR	20 ARI-D	MAR	19 PIC-R	APR	14 ARI-D	APR	7 ARI-D
MAR	25 ARI-D	MAY	6 ARI-R	MAY	16 TAU-D	APR	2 PIC-D	MAY	1 TAU-D	APR	22 TAU-D
APR	9 TAU-D	MAY	8 ARI-D	JUN	2 GEM-D	APR	18 ARI-D	MAY	15 GEM-D	MAY	7 GEM-D
MAY	3 TAU-R	MAY	13 TAU-D	JUN	16 CAN-D	MAY	9 TAU-D	MAY	31 CAN-D	JUN	4 GEM-R
MAY	27 TAU-D	JUN	9 GEM-D	JUL	1 LEO-D	MAY	24 GEM-D	JUN	23 CAN-R	JUN	28 GEM-D
JUN	14 GEM-D	JUN	24 CAN-D	JUL	31 LEO-R	JUN	8 CAN-D	JUL	17 CAN-D	JUL	13 CAN-D
JUL	3 CAN-D	JUL	9 LEO-D	AUG	23 LEO-D	JUN	27 LEO-D	AUG	8 LEO-D	JUL	31 LEO-D
JUL	17 LEO-D	JUL	28 VIR-D	SEP	9 VIR-D	JUL	12 LEO-R	AUG	23 VIR-D	AUG	15 VIR-D
AUG	2 VIR-D	AUG	17 VIR-R	SEP	25 LIB-D	AUG	1 CAN-R	SEP	8 LIB-D	SEP	2 LIB-D
AUG	27 LIB-D	SEP	10 VIR-D	OCT	13 SCO-D	AUG	6 CAN-D	SEP	29 SCO-D	OCT	2 LIB-R
SEP	4 LIB-R	OCT	3 LIB-D	NOV	2 SAG-D	AUG	12 LEO-D	OCT	18 SCO-R	OCT	23 LIB-D
SEP	13 VIR-R	OCT	20 SCO-D	NOV	21 SAG-R	SEP	1 VIR-D	NOV	8 LIB-R	NOV	8 SCO-D
SEP	26 VIR-D	NOV	8 SAG-D	DEC	11 SAG-D	SEP	17 LIB-D	NOV	9 SCO-D	NOV	27 SAG-D
OCT	10 LIB-D	DEC	1 CAP-D			OCT	6 SCO-D	DEC	4 SAG-D	DEC	16 CAP-D
OCT	28 SCO-D	DEC	7 CAP-R			OCT	31 SAG-D	DEC	24 CAP-D		
NOV	15 SAG-D	DEC	14 SAG-R			NOV	5 SAG-R				
DEC	5 CAP-D	DEC	27 SAG-D			NOV	10 SCO-R				
DEC	23 CAP-R					NOV	25 SCO-D				
						DEC	12 SAG-D				

2002–2007

2002		2003		2004		2005		2006		2007	
JAN	4 AQU-D	JAN	14 AQU-D	JAN	6 SAG-D	JAN	11 CAP-D	JAN	4 CAP-D	JAN	16 AQU-D
JAN	18 AQU-R	FEB	6 PIC-D	JAN	15 CAP-D	JAN	31 AQU-D	JAN	23 AQU-D	FEB	3 PIC-D
FEB	5 CAP-R	MAR	22 ARI-D	FEB	8 AQU-D	FEB	17 PIC-D	FEB	10 PIC-D	FEB	14 PIC-R
FEB	8 CAP-D	APR	6 TAU-D	FEB	26 PIC-D	MAR	6 ARI-D	MAR	3 PIC-R	FEB	28 AQU-R
FEB	14 AQU-D	APR	26 TAU-R	MAR	13 ARI-D	MAR	20 ARI-R	MAR	25 PIC-D	MAR	8 AQU-D
MAR	12 PIC-D	MAY	20 TAU-D	APR	2 TAU-D	APR	12 ARI-D	APR	17 ARI-D	MAR	19 PIC-D
MAR	30 ARI-D	JUN	14 GEM-D	APR	6 TAU-R	MAY	13 TAU-D	MAY	6 TAU-D	APR	11 ARI-D
APR	14 TAU-D	JUN	30 CAN-D	APR	14 ARI-R	MAY	29 GEM-D	MAY	20 GEM-D	APR	28 TAU-D
MAY	1 GEM-D	JUL	14 LEO-D	APR	30 ARI-D	JUN	12 CAN-D	JUN	4 CAN-D	MAY	12 GEM-D
MAY	15 GEM-R	JUL	31 VIR-D	MAY	17 TAU-D	JUN	29 LEO-D	JUN	29 LEO-D	MAY	30 CAN-D
JUN	8 GEM-D	AUG	28 VIR-R	JUN	6 GEM-D	JUL	23 LEO-R	JUL	4 LEO-R	JUN	15 CAN-R
JUL	8 CAN-D	SEP	20 VIR-D	JUN	20 CAN-D	AUG	16 LEO-D	JUL	11 CAN-R	JUL	10 CAN-D
JUL	22 LEO-D	OCT	8 LIB-D	JUL	5 LEO-D	SEP	5 VIR-D	JUL	29 CAN-D	AUG	5 LEO-D
AUG	7 VIR-D	OCT	25 SCO-D	JUL	26 VIR-D	SEP	21 LIB-D	AUG	12 LEO-D	AUG	20 VIR-D
AUG	27 LIB-D	NOV	13 SAG-D	AUG	10 VIR-R	OCT	9 SCO-D	AUG	28 VIR-D	SEP	6 LIB-D
SEP	14 LIB-R	DEC	3 CAP-D	AUG	26 LEO-R	OCT	31 SAG-D	SEP	13 LIB-D	SEP	28 SCO-D
OCT	3 VIR-R	DEC	17 CAP-R	SEP	3 LEO-D	NOV	14 SAG-R	OCT	3 SCO-D	OCT	12 SCO-R
OCT	6 VIR-D	DEC	31 SAG-R	SEP	11 VIR-D	NOV	27 SCO-R	OCT	28 SCO-R	OCT	25 LIB-R
OCT	12 LIB-D			SEP	29 LIB-D	DEC	4 SCO-D	NOV	18 SCO-D	NOV	2 LIB-D
NOV	1 SCO-D			OCT	16 SCO-D	DEC	13 SAG-D	DEC	9 SAG-D	NOV	12 SCO-D
NOV	20 SAG-D			NOV	5 SAG-D			DEC	28 CAP-D	DEC	2 SAG-D
DEC	9 CAP-D			NOV	30 SAG-R					DEC	21 CAP-D
DEC	13 CAP-R			DEC	20 SAG-D						
DEC	23 CAP-D										

2008	2009	2010	2011	2012	2013
JAN 9 AQU-D	JAN 2 AQU-D	JAN 15 CAP-D	JAN 14 CAP-D	JAN 9 CAP-D	JAN 1 CAP-D
JAN 28 AQU-R	JAN 11 AQU-R	FEB 11 AQU-D	FEB 4 AQU-D	JAN 28 AQU-D	JAN 20 AQU-D
FEB 19 AQU-D	JAN 22 CAP-R	MAR 2 PIC-D	FEB 22 PIC-D	FEB 15 PIC-D	FEB 6 PIC-D
MAR 15 PIC-D	FEB 1 CAP-D	MAR 18 ARI-D	MAR 10 ARI-D	MAR 2 ARI-D	FEB 23 PIC-R
APR 3 ARI-D	FEB 15 AQU-D	APR 3 TAU-D	MAR 30 ARI-R	MAR 12 ARI-R	MAR 17 PIC-D
APR 18 TAU-R	MAR 9 PIC-D	MAY 11 TAU-D	APR 23 ARI-D	MAR 24 PIC-R	APR 15 ARI-D
MAY 3 GEM-D	MAR 26 ARI-D	JUN 11 GEM-D	MAY 16 TAU-D	APR 4 PIC-D	MAY 2 TAU-D
MAY 26 GEM-R	APR 11 TAU-D	JUN 26 CAN-D	JUN 3 GEM-D	APR 17 ARI-D	MAY 16 GEM-D
JUN 19 GEM-D	MAY 1 GEM-D	JUL 10 LEO-D	JUN 17 CAN-D	MAY 10 TAU-D	JUN 1 CAN-D
JUL 11 CAN-D	MAY 7 GEM-R	JUL 28 VIR-D	JUL 3 LEO-D	JUN 8 CAN-D	JUN 26 CAN-R
JUL 27 LEO-D	MAY 14 TAU-R	AUG 20 VIR-R	JUL 29 VIR-D	JUN 27 LEO-D	JUL 20 CAN-D
AUG 11 VIR-D	MAY 31 TAU-D	SEP 12 LEO-D	AUG 3 VIR-R	JUL 15 LEO-D	AUG 9 LEO-D
AUG 30 LIB-D	JUN 15 GEM-D	OCT 4 LIB-D	AUG 9 LEO-R	AUG 8 LEO-D	AUG 24 VIR-D
SEP 24 LIB-R	JUL 4 CAN-D	OCT 21 SCO-D	AUG 26 LEO-D	SEP 2 VIR-D	SEP 10 LIB-D
OCT 15 LIB-D	JUL 18 LEO-D	NOV 9 SAG-D	SEP 10 VIR-D	SEP 17 LIB-D	SEP 30 SCO-D
NOV 5 SCO-D	AUG 3 VIR-D	DEC 2 CAP-D	SEP 26 LIB-D	OCT 6 SCO-D	OCT 21 SCO-R
NOV 24 SAG-D	AUG 26 LIB-D	DEC 11 CAP-R	OCT 14 SCO-D	OCT 30 SAG-D	NOV 10 SCO-D
DEC 13 CAP-D	SEP 7 LIB-R	DEC 19 SAG-R	NOV 3 SAG-D	NOV 6 SAG-R	DEC 6 SAG-D
	SEP 19 VIR-R	DEC 30 SAG-D	NOV 24 SAG-R	NOV 15 SCO-R	DEC 25 CAP-D
	SEP 29 VIR-D		DEC 14 SAG-D	NOV 26 SCO-D	
	OCT 11 LIB-D			DEC 12 SAG-D	
	OCT 29 SCO-D				
	NOV 17 SAG-D				
	DEC 6 CAP-D				
	DEC 26 CAP-R				

2014	2015	2016	2017	2018	2019
JAN 12 AQU-D	JAN 6 AQU-D	JAN 3 AQU-D	JAN 5 SAG-R	JAN 12 CAP-D	JAN 6 CAP-D
FEB 1 PIC-D	JAN 21 AQU-R	JAN 5 AQU-R	JAN 8 SAG-D	FEB 1 AQU-D	JAN 25 AQU-D
FEB 6 PIC-R	FEB 11 AQU-D	JAN 25 AQU-D	JAN 13 CAP-D	FEB 19 PIC-D	FEB 11 PIC-D
FEB 14 AQU-R	MAR 14 PIC-D	FEB 14 AQU-D	FEB 8 AQU-D	MAR 7 ARI-D	MAR 5 PIC-R
FEB 28 AQU-D	APR 1 ARI-D	MAR 6 PIC-D	FEB 26 PIC-D	MAR 23 ARI-R	MAR 28 PIC-D
MAR 18 PIC-D	APR 15 TAU-D	MAR 23 ARI-D	MAR 14 ARI-D	APR 15 ARI-D	APR 18 ARI-D
APR 8 ARI-D	MAY 2 GEM-D	APR 6 TAU-D	APR 1 TAU-D	MAY 14 TAU-D	MAY 7 TAU-D
APR 24 TAU-D	MAY 19 GEM-R	APR 28 TAU-R	APR 9 TAU-R	MAY 30 GEM-D	MAY 22 GEM-D
MAY 8 GEM-D	JUN 11 GEM-D	MAY 22 TAU-D	APR 21 ARI-R	JUN 13 CAN-D	JUN 5 CAN-D
MAY 30 CAN-D	JUL 9 CAN-D	JUN 13 GEM-D	MAY 3 ARI-D	JUN 30 LEO-D	JUN 28 LEO-D
JUN 7 CAN-R	JUL 24 LEO-D	JUN 30 CAN-D	MAY 17 TAU-D	JUL 26 LEO-R	JUL 7 LEO-R
JUN 18 GEM-R	AUG 8 VIR-D	JUL 15 LEO-D	JUN 7 GEM-D	AUG 19 LEO-D	JUL 20 CAN-R
JUL 2 GEM-D	AUG 28 LIB-D	JUL 31 VIR-D	JUN 22 CAN-D	SEP 7 VIR-D	AUG 2 CAN-D
JUL 14 CAN-D	SEP 17 LIB-R	AUG 30 VIR-R	JUL 7 LEO-D	SEP 23 LIB-D	AUG 12 LEO-D
AUG 1 LEO-D	OCT 9 LIB-D	SEP 22 VIR-D	JUL 26 VIR-D	OCT 11 SCO-D	AUG 30 VIR-D
AUG 16 VIR-D	NOV 3 SCO-D	OCT 8 LIB-D	AUG 13 VIR-R	NOV 1 SAG-D	SEP 15 LIB-D
SEP 3 LIB-D	NOV 21 SAG-D	OCT 25 SCO-D	SEP 1 LEO-R	DEC 2 SCO-R	OCT 4 SCO-D
SEP 28 SCO-D	DEC 11 CAP-D	NOV 13 SAG-D	SEP 5 LEO-D	DEC 6 SCO-D	OCT 31 SCO-R
OCT 4 SCO-R		DEC 3 CAP-D	SEP 11 VIR-D	DEC 13 SAG-D	NOV 20 SCO-D
OCT 11 LIB-R		DEC 19 CAP-R	OCT 1 LIB-D		DEC 10 SAG-D
OCT 25 LIB-D			OCT 18 SCO-D		DEC 30 CAP-D
NOV 9 SCO-D			NOV 6 SAG-D		
NOV 29 SAG-D			DEC 3 SAG-R		
DEC 18 CAP-D			DEC 23 SAG-D		

2020		2021		2022		2023		2024		2025	
JAN	17 AQU-D	JAN	9 AQU-D	JAN	3 AQU-D	JAN	18 CAP-D	JAN	2 SAG-D	JAN	9 CAP-D
FEB	4 PIC-D	JAN	30 AQU-R	JAN	14 AQU-R	FEB	12 AQU-D	JAN	15 CAP-D	JAN	29 AQU-D
FEB	17 PIC-R	FEB	21 AQU-D	JAN	28 CAP-R	MAR	3 PIC-D	FEB	6 AQU-D	FEB	15 PIC-D
MAR	5 AQU-R	MAR	16 PIC-D	FEB	4 CAP-D	MAR	20 ARI-D	FEB	24 PIC-D	MAR	4 ARI-D
MAR	10 AQU-D	APR	5 ARI-D	FEB	15 AQU-D	APR	4 TAU-D	MAR	11 ARI-D	MAR	15 ARI-R
MAR	17 PIC-D	APR	20 TAU-D	MAR	11 PIC-D	APR	21 TAU-R	APR	2 ARI-R	MAR	31 PIC-R
APR	12 ARI-D	MAY	5 GEM-D	MAR	28 ARI-D	MAY	14 TAU-D	APR	25 ARI-D	APR	7 PIC-D
APR	28 TAU-D	MAY	29 GEM-R	APR	12 TAU-D	JUN	12 GEM-D	MAY	16 TAU-D	APR	17 ARI-D
MAY	12 GEM-D	JUN	22 GEM-D	APR	30 GEM-D	JUN	28 CAN-D	JUN	4 GEM-D	MAY	11 TAU-D
MAY	29 CAN-D	JUL	12 CAN-D	MAY	10 GEM-D	JUL	12 LEO-D	JUN	18 CAN-D	MAY	27 GEM-D
JUN	18 CAN-R	AUG	12 VIR-D	MAY	24 TAU-R	JUL	29 VIR-D	JUL	3 LEO-D	JUN	9 CAN-D
JUL	12 CAN-D	AUG	31 LIB-D	JUN	3 TAU-D	AUG	23 VIR-R	JUL	26 VIR-D	JUN	27 LEO-D
AUG	6 LEO-D	SEP	27 LIB-R	JUN	14 GEM-D	SEP	15 VIR-D	AUG	5 VIR-R	JUL	18 LEO-R
AUG	21 VIR-D	OCT	18 LIB-D	JUL	6 CAN-D	OCT	6 LIB-D	AUG	16 LEO-R	AUG	11 LEO-D
SEP	6 LIB-D	NOV	6 SCO-D	JUL	20 LEO-D	OCT	23 SCO-D	AUG	28 LEO-D	SEP	3 VIR-D
SEP	28 SCO-D	NOV	25 SAG-D	AUG	5 VIR-D	NOV	11 SAG-D	SEP	10 VIR-D	SEP	19 LIB-D
OCT	14 SCO-R	DEC	14 CAP-D	AUG	27 LIB-D	DEC	2 CAP-D	SEP	27 LIB-D	OCT	7 SCO-D
OCT	29 LIB-R			SEP	10 LIB-R	DEC	13 CAP-R	OCT	14 SCO-D	OCT	30 SCO-D
NOV	3 LIB-D			SEP	24 VIR-R	DEC	24 SAG-R	NOV	3 SAG-D	NOV	9 SAG-D
NOV	11 SCO-D			OCT	2 VIR-D			NOV	26 SAG-R	NOV	20 SCO-R
DEC	2 SAG-D			OCT	11 LIB-D			DEC	15 SAG-D	NOV	29 SCO-D
DEC	21 CAP-D			OCT	30 SCO-D					DEC	12 SAG-D
				NOV	18 SAG-D						
				DEC	7 CAP-D						
				DEC	29 CAP-R						

Children with Mercury in Aries

Mercury in Aries is an interesting placement. These children will be quick thinking and witty, with inventive minds. They want to be first with their ideas, so they have a tendency to jump to conclusions too quickly. Teach them that making rash, impulsive decisions can cause them many problems, and they need to learn to count to ten before opening their mouths. Help them learn that it's not enough to just come up with original ideas — they have to follow through to get any results! They will be quick on the switch and will love arguments. They will be very good at this and should be encouraged to join the debate team to learn the skill of *constructive* argument. But when they become contentious, it would be wise for you as a parent to say, "Oh it's debate time!" or something similar, and then accept the challenge with a smile. They will often take the opposite viewpoint just for the challenge of the contest. It doesn't mean they always believe what they are saying, they just enjoy the battle of wits!

They are able to express themselves with a fluent, direct approach. But show them the difference between directness and brashness! Teach them to be sensitive to other people's feelings. Being abrasive will not create positive experiences.

These children may become quickly angered at something that is said, and may spout off and say things they don't mean. Fortunately their anger is over as quickly as it started and the experience is forgotten.

They will be very attuned to *sound* (Aries rules the ears as well as eyes) and should be encouraged in developing this ability and understanding music. Pleasant, comfortable sounds in their environment will calm some of their impulsive energy.

They should be excellent students as long as they are allowed enough independence to explore and express their own originality. They must be stimulated with plenty of new material. Teach them it is good to pursue and pioneer the new, but that it is important to complete one thing before moving on to the next! Teach them to discipline themselves with this follow-through. They are anxious to explore any and all new methods of communication and should have no trouble utilizing them. Be sure to put lots of positive action and energy into what you tell them, and you will be able to direct them beneficially.

Key words to use in your communications with Mercury in Aries children are: *courage, pursue, drive, energy, lead, compete, brave, active, initiate, assert, sound, hear, listen and experience.*

Make your communications to the point — stimulating, full of action, and short — they get bored easily and are often way ahead of you! The more dynamic you are, the more Aries will pay attention. Threaten them and they are off to war. Talking things out with them while you both are doing something physical... while walking, biking, playing tennis... works well. Eliminate any form of boredom or confinement; Aries is not interested in the practicality of things, only in the excitement and adventure of them.

Remember! These children born with Mercury in Aries *love mental challenge* — prepare yourself!

Children with Mercury in Taurus

Those of you who have children with Mercury in Taurus will need quite a bit of patience. Their thinking will be *slow and methodical.* They are cautious and will have difficulty in changing their ideas or opinions quickly. They are very *practical* and *determined.* They will appear stubborn and obstinate, and you cannot force or push them to change — they will resist and not cooperate. There are several ways to handle this. *One* is to put out the new information and then back off... give them time to think about it, assimilate it, and change at their own pace. *Two,* present things to them in some way so that they can see things visually through pictures or diagrams... so they can feel or experience them. For example, these children will not respond well or understand if you just verbalize it when you tell them not to touch the fire. Take them to it, hold their hand (safely) close to it so they can feel the heat — they will get the message. They respond best to *visual and sensual* stimuli rather than audible. *Paint them a picture* with your words, and tell them about all the feelings involved, both *emotional and tactile*. They learn readily from travel, movies, and television.

It may appear that they are slow and not too bright, but they are certainly not stupid (Freud, Edison, Brahms, General Grant — to name a few!). Once they have learned something, it sticks. They think about any new information thoroughly and carefully to be sure that it is solid and usable before they accept it. They also are inclined to feel most comfortable holding onto ideas they have, because it is in their nature to feel safer and more secure with holding!

Mathematics can be a problem for them as can any abstract subject. To stimulate interest here, show them the usefulness of these subjects and they will respond. For example, explain that they might be taken advantage of in money situations if they can't add and subtract well.

They also respond well to *common sense*. They are persistent and follow through. You will find yourself delegating responsibility to these children because they will be very dependable. Just be sure to be patient with their inflexibility and slowness in all forms of communication.

Key words to use in your communications with Mercury in Taurus children are: *worth, comfort, quality, ease, increase, stable; value, see, look, visualize, feel, and sense*.

Because physical *comfort* is so important to these children, the best way to put them in a cooperative mood is to make sure they are comfy. For example, give them a plushy chair, put them in their pajamas and make sure the room temperature is just right. If you can physically touch them or stroke them in some way while you are talking, you will tame the natural resistance within them. Reassure them that their comforts and pleasures will still be secure with any changes that you want them to make. Most importantly, show these children the value, benefits, practicality, and usefulness of what you are presenting... and how it will work for them!

Children with Mercury in Gemini

Mercury in Gemini creates very *active thought* processes. They are extremely *quick to assimilate* information and are always looking for more. These children are even capable of absorbing more than one thing at a time. It is important for children with Mercury in Gemini to receive a lot of intellectual stimulation early in their lives. As their parent or caregiver you can show them how to learn by reading. Provide them with the time and the materials to read each day. This is most important. They should also be encouraged to write. Since their need to communicate is so strong, writing out some of their thoughts will cut down on the amount of verbalizing — otherwise, they will chatter incessantly and talk your ear off!

Guide them to discern when they are really saying something or are just babbling. They have the ability to be extremely articulate and express themselves clearly. They will amaze you with a continuous flow of new information. Communicating with these children can be fascinating. And when you communicate with them, using words that concern feeling will fall on deaf ears. It is very important that you *refrain* from using any emotion when conversing with these quick, logical thinkers. Preface your statements with "I think" and ask them what they think. Because they *love games*, you can get them to cooperate by saying, "Let's play a game and see if we can do..." or, "Let's see how fast we can do it."

One problem with this energetic curious mind is that it gets bored too quickly, and too easily. Their mind changes from one thing to another so fast that it often never finishes anything or follows through far enough to completely learn something. Teach them the discipline of steadiness and of staying with it long enough to get the whole picture.

These children are *versatile*, have *high energy*, and *love change*. They can be very nervous. They can scatter themselves in too many directions and burn themselves out. It is important for you to teach them the importance of taking time each day to be quiet, to relax. They also need to keep an orderly environment to have thoughts operate clearly and calmly, so they should learn early to be organized.

Key words to use in your communications with Mercury in Gemini children are: *intelligent, smart, clever, rational, think, look, listen, logical, quick, mental, change, and exciting.*

Your little Mercury in Gemini "computer" will have no problem learning and communicating as long as they are programmed properly and positively. Present information to them with as much variety as possible, making the same point in different ways and citing many different examples. Be sure you approach everything from a logical point of view. Keep the conversation lively and exciting. Add as much *humor* as you can as they are witty creatures and will love the stimulation. Since these children are most comfortable when they have several different activities going on at the same time, it is advisable to approach them with subjects you need to discuss when you are both engaged in some type of activity. Otherwise, if you plan to just sit and talk, be sure to make your discussion very dynamic. And remember, most important of all, always be sure to give them the opportunity to express their own ideas as much as possible!

Children with Mercury in Cancer

Mercury in Cancer creates an *emotionally-based* thought process. That is, they let their emotions rule

how they think. They will always have a feeling con-
nected to every thought and will personalize every communication they experience. They are so *receptive* that
they are influenced too much by what is happening
around them. They can take on the opinions of whomever is close at the moment. They need to learn to step
back and see things more objectively. They have a very
retentive mind and will find it difficult to change habits
and attitudes.

It is important for them to establish beliefs that are
workable for them. They have a tendency to accept
what other people think and feel without thinking
things through. They will be especially vulnerable to
their parents and to the family's projections because
family is so important to them. It is important for them
while they are still very young to learn how *to step
outside of themselves* and look things over. A little objectivity will be very helpful.

These children will be very emotionally responsive and often won't know why they think the way they
do. When they are upset, their thoughts about the
world will be distorted. Teach them to throw away
these thoughts and to become aware of the difference
in how they think when they are calm!

It is not advisable to argue with these children or
ever make a direct attack. This will arouse resistance
and stubbornness. You will get better results by appealing to their sympathy. They have such sensitive feelings
that they always relate to things in a feeling way. Logi-

cal, cold, or harsh communication will be very ineffective with Mercury in Cancer children. Rather than giving them a direct order or making a frontal attack, tell them how *you* feel about it and they will respond. Always remember to ask them how they feel about doing whatever it is you want. *Avoid* using the word "think" — it will not appeal to their emotions.

These children will be very *psychic* and will know things without knowing how. They should be encouraged to rely on their instincts and intuitions. They may have some trouble in school because they *learn best by listening*. It is difficult for them to study, especially factual subject matter. Movies, television, or exposure to travel and people will teach them faster than through reading. Once they have grasped something, they won't forget it. Approach them through their feelings and you will experience much closeness and will grow together.

Key words to use in your communications with Mercury in Cancer children are: *sensitive, support, emotion, intuitive, protect, care, feel, respond, listen, need, sympathetic, and safe.*

Communicate with them from your heart, and preferably choose a very safe, cozy place in which to do it. Tell them how you feel about your subject and *that you care how they feel* about it. Help them to feel secure about changes that are to be made, and let them know that their cooperation is needed. *Feeling needed* is an important part of what makes them feel good inside, so be sure that this is satisfied.

Children with Mercury in Leo

These are the children who will crave center stage, and will have very decisive ideas. The problem is that Mercury in Leo children will identify personally with whatever they think. A challenge to their beliefs or thinking is a direct challenge to them. It is important to teach them that a difference of opinion doesn't make one right and the other wrong... it is simply a different point of view. Show them that contrary ideas shouldn't be taken as a personal insult.

These children try very hard to be sure that they have the truth of anything, and then they are cocksure they do! However, they need to be shown that *truth is in a constant state of change* and they may not have the only valid point of view. They need to learn to be a little more flexible and open to new ideas. It will do no good to try and force the new on them, so try to present the information in a way that is non-threatening and then they will change by themselves. Do teach them to present their ideas with a little humility. They have a tendency to be arrogant which causes others to feel inferior or just annoyed. This of course, will cause an unfavorable response to their ideas and an unwillingness in others to communicate with them.

They will put great energy into *organizing* and *solving problems*. They have the ability to see things on a large scale and as a whole. The bigger the project the better. They need to apply a little discipline so that they pay attention to all the little details to be sure that they do have the complete picture. Their communications are presented with great flair and sometimes with extreme dramatics. They take great pride in what they think, so always treat them with dignity. They will do well in life as long as the flair and dramatics are kept under control.

The comment, "Flattery will get you everywhere," was coined for Leos. The more you compliment them, the better they want to and will do. Sharp criticism can be devastating — to them and to your communicating! They are very warm and loving, and the more you approach them in a loving way the more cooperation you will get. They have strong needs to be accepted and validated, so give them applause and praise often. Since they are *good planners* and can *organize and direct others* well, make them the chief and they will get the Indians to perform!

Key words to use in your communications with Mercury in Leo children are: *creative, entertain, exciting, respect, appreciate, care, talent, noble, dignified, generous, and loving.*

An interesting approach to disciplining these children is to ask them to play your role as the parent, and ask them how they would handle the situation. Do *role playing* — they'll love it! You might be surprised with the creative solution they suggest. When you communicate with them allow them to feel dignified and to *leave their pride intact*. Acknowledge their ideas by saying, "I can appreciate how you might think that way," and then say, "I have a different view point — may I share it with you?" By using this approach, you will eliminate hurt feelings and defensiveness. Most importantly, continue to compliment them on their good ideas and your conversations will always be open and loving.

Children with Mercury in Virgo

Mercury is right at home in the sign of Virgo. These children will have a very *analytical* and *logical* way of receiving and transmitting their communications. Their minds are *quick* and *alert*. They will assimilate and *categorize facts* with ease. They can be very *intolerant of stupidity*. They can be quite *critical* of themselves, not to mention the world in general. You must show them that the world does not run on logic and reason alone. And they need to recognize that their thought processes allow them to function with a high degree of *common sense* but not everyone has this ability. They should learn to be a little more flexible, tolerant... and have more acceptance of life as it is.

They will analyze everything and could do with a little more spontaneity. Teach them to let their heads rest sometimes, to let their feelings develop, and their hearts blossom. Show them that some people think only with their feelings and emotions. *A balance of both heart and mind is best.* Also, show them that by being overly critical of themselves and others they not only damage their own confidence, but their relationship with everyone else. Teach them to see that the world is perfect just as it is and that everything has its own beauty.

They can be *neat*, and *clean*, to the point of per-snickety, and *picky* about their food. They will be interested in learning about nutrition and what is good for the body. *Health* is very important to them. These children are good with their hands and will work well with detail and with great precision. They will especially like to work on things that are practical.

They are good in school and will approach their studies meticulously and methodically. The biggest problem here is that if they can't see the usefulness of a subject they may not apply themselves. Show them what might have no value at the present could be important later. They also may have trouble retaining information that they think is superfluous. Teach them that most facts can be used at one time or other.

Teach them to use their discriminating, analytical skills in a helpful way — by learning to understand the difference between beneficial and non-beneficial. Show them it is more beneficial, when interacting with people, to balance thought with feeling. Help them to look for

the good in others and to add warmth to their communications.

Key *words* to use in your communications with
Mercury in Virgo children: *organize, analyze, order,
discriminate, think, look, specific, proficient, facts, detail,
skill, and practical.*

Be sure that your conversations with these children are organized and realistic. Leave emotions out.
Think of how to get practical responses to your well-
thought-out and coolly-administered disciplinary pro-
cedures. Give them the ABC's of why you are taking
specific actions. Write these actions down or ask the
child to write them down. It helps these children when
they can see what they are dealing with. *Post your rules.*
These children are *list makers* so let them help you
organize. Tell them how capable they are and they will
help you with everything.

Children with Mercury in Libra

When Mercury is in Libra we find children who
are born *diplomats.* They will not like harsh or abrasive
situations. Being natural peacemakers, they will try to
smooth troubled waters for both themselves and others. But because they want both sides to be completely
considered before a decision is made, they may appear
to be argumentative... this is their way of bringing
attention to alternative views. It usually is done in good
taste and with carefully chosen words! This is because

they always want to have harmonious experiences and never to offend anyone. It may even appear that they are vacillating and cannot make up their minds, or that they are unwilling to take a stand — because they want to be fair and keep peace with everyone at the same time. The fact is, they would rather settle for a compromise than to actually take one side or the other. They do have the ability to see validity on both sides of things. Teach them to tune into their hearts, conscience, and souls for answers. When "tuned in," making decisions throughout their lives will become easier.

Also, help these children learn that life can't always be peaceful and harmonious or friendly. They can get really "bent" when people are rude, unfriendly, or — heaven forbid — ill-mannered! Tell them that life is not all sweetness and light, that we need some negative to appreciate the positive. Their rational intellectualizing mind should love that! Also, do help them get over a very serious problem with procrastinating — probably because they can't bear to face unpleasant situations. All of this of course, fits together — they must learn early to "bite the bullet" and do what's necessary, when and with whomever. The operative word here is DO — Libras would rather not.

These children are *sensitive, pliable,* and have *good judgment.* They have a natural proclivity towards all the arts. They are very creative — music and writing and painting may be good ways for them to express themselves. They will like order and beauty, and have excellent taste. They will prefer *quality* to quantity. They also will be very social. They are good speakers and express themselves well. In fact, they will be very convincing when they want you to do something!

These children *love parties* and are very good at planning them. Their creative ideas will make any occasion beautiful, elegant, and in good taste. At the party they will become a social butterfly, flitting from one person to another and making sure that they have given each guest a bit of their time.

Key words to use in your communications with Mercury in Libra are: *cooperate, charm, balance, sociable, tactful, appreciate, diplomatic, look, feel, value, beauty, peace, and harmony.*

Present your conversations to these children diplomatically and tactfully with never any harsh, abrasive, or vulgar expressions. Ask them to *cooperate* with you. Tell them that you will help and work with them... they want to do everything with another person rather than alone. If you offer to work *with* these children you will eliminate a large portion of their resistance. On the other hand, a stern discipline for them is just having to *do* a job, having to do it alone, having to do a dirty job! Have patience with them while they are weighing and evaluating all sides of things before making their decisions — at least you will know that they have given most decisions much thought!

Children with Mercury in Scorpio

Because children with their Mercury in Scorpio have very *penetrating minds*, there is a powerful depth to their thinking. These children will want to investigate and delve into the reasons for everything. They are born asking the question "why?" — discovering the whys of nature, people, life, and death. These great little investigators actually find the solving part of a problem more exciting than the answer itself! Anything that is mysterious or hidden will attract their minds. They have a very keen sense of perception. Listen to them carefully because they will present insights that you might not have even previously considered. They are able to see beyond the obvious. Because their sixth sense is highly developed, they are able to go beneath the surface and get to the real meaning of people and things, cabbages and Kings.

They can be very *secretive* and hard to pin down. It will be difficult to find out what they are thinking unless they want you to know. Sometimes they think so deeply that they won't even have the thoughts sorted out themselves! Be patient, they might let you know what they were thinking when they have it all in order.

They may be critical of themselves and others, and they tend to be *suspicious*... always looking for ulterior motives. Teach them to be nonjudgmental. Also, they can be very sarcastic at times. Show them that most people's feelings are too sensitive to endure their bite. If they want friends, they must learn to control these characteristics. Reassure them that they have a sharp, strong, perceptive mind and that they have no need to belittle or destroy other people's confidence. Some may already feel intimidated by their awareness and penetrating questions.

Always answer their questions directly and honestly. They will see right through lies and manipulation anyway. These children will need to see a good example of truth from you so that they will learn to be truthful themselves. They may ask many questions about sexuality so be prepared. They need to understand the hows and whys, and to learn healthy, even spiritual values about their purpose and usefulness.

Key words to use in your communications with Mercury in Scorpio children are: *purpose, focus, investigate, discover, transform, delve, meaning, feel, sense, power, and empower.*

In your communications with them present any situation objectively. Then ask the Scorpio to help you find a solution and they will turn their thinking to finding the answer. Also, let them help you to determine the conditions of their own discipline. They may be sterner than what you would have suggested. When an action is decided upon, these children will keep their word and follow through once they have made the commitment. If they think you have lied to them, betrayed them, or been unjust to them — they will remem-

ber and have great difficulty ever forgiving you. Teach
these children the transforming power of forgiveness.
You must!

Children with Mercury in Sagittarius

Your child with a Mercury in "Sag" will love communicating on all levels. They are perpetually in search
of the great truth. By that, I mean that they will want
to know all about nature, why humankind thinks and
acts as it does, what makes the Universe as it is, and
how everything fits together! To them it seems important to develop a solid *philosophy of life* and afterlife.
They will be constantly seeking out new information to
enhance this philosophy. They tend to see things as a
whole, in a broad perspective, and will often skim over
or leave out pertinent facts. They need to be taught to
slow down and get all the details before they speak so
they can be sure they have the whole picture.

Because of their lofty thinking and idealism, they
can easily be taken advantage of. Therefore, they should
learn to be more reflective, and look at situations and
people with a bit of skepticism. They seem not to realize
that the whole world is not as truthful as they. These
children are very *direct* in their thinking and in their
communications, sometimes to the point of being blunt.
They need to know that other people may be offended
by this. Teach them to be honest and "tactful" at the

same time; to think a minute and choose their words carefully before speaking.

Mercury in Sagittarius children should be pleasures to be with because they are generally enthusiastic, *upbeat*, and love anything that is new. They will adjust easily and actually welcome change. They love to *travel*, and learn a great deal this way. They will be concerned with people in general rather than those who are close. Remind them to not overlook the importance of those closest and dearest to them. Also — they cannot tolerate deception, so don't lose their respect by telling them untruths.

Their thinking is expansive, and they are basically optimistic. Since they are direct and upfront with everything, you can always count on what you see and hear as being what you get. This will eliminate any doubts about whether you are being appeased, or that they might be pretending in any way.

In dealing with school and academics, teach these children to go back over all tests and assignments. They do them so quickly that they may easily make mistakes. They have a tendency to be careless — and they don't like it either!

Key words to use in your communications with Mercury in Sagittarius children are: *wise, benefit, truth, understand, honest, expand, abundance, optimistic, faith, knowledge, perception, and opportunity.*

When you converse with these children their responses are fiery and quick. Have patience with this because they don't mean to be abrasive. Present your ideas to them with enthusiasm and plenty of excitement. Once again, always communicate with these children directly and honestly. Speak from your heart.

Children with Mercury in Capricorn

Here we find the children who seem old before their time. They are *serious* in their thinking and *cautious* in their actions (sometimes to the point of inaction!). They don't think quickly because they are practical and deliberate. It is difficult for them to change and to accept new ideas — unless they can see the usefulness of what is being presented. These children relate best to things that pertain to the *physical*, material world. Because they are very serious in their thinking, they can take being responsible to an extreme — even sacrificing themselves to their duty, for the job, for another. This can cause them to become dull, and miss out on the joys and excitement in life. Let them know that it is healthy to fantasize and to do lighthearted things from time to time. They should learn to develop a sense of humor. Because they take life so seriously, they need to learn to laugh more. They can be quite moody and at times may seem to be negative and depressing to others. Understand and help them pull out of their moods, or it could affect their health — in mind and body.

These children need to be encouraged to develop faith and to be less attached to the physical and material. They are very earth-oriented and you need to help them create a balance between earth and heaven. This can be very important in their lives. They have the tendency to get caught in the "never enough" syndrome, meaning that they are looking for security by accumulating more and more possessions, and it is never enough. Until they learn to place their security in their own abilities, they will always feel insecure.

They are good organizers and have an instinctive urge to organize everything and everyone they come in contact with. "Messy" thinking, messy anything upsets them — they can be overly fastidious. They will communicate with diplomacy, carefully choosing the way they express themselves. They have great ability to concentrate and will be disciplined in their thinking. They can be taskmasters both for themselves and others — and will demand precision in themselves, and others. Teach them to "lighten up" some and *learn to be more tolerant* of others. These are the children to whom you can delegate responsibility. Let them help you organize and plan — they love it and you will be surprised at how well they do.

Mercury in Capricorn children love to learn and do things that are useful. They think in a very practical way so when you present ideas to them, be sure to show them just how the ideas are useful. Superfluous information or abstract concepts have no value to them.

very good with computers. Their minds enjoy stimulation and excitement — and they may become the inventors creating wonderful new things. They will communicate well with others, and are always willing to listen to new information. Everything is fodder for their creative, inventive minds.

They will choose unusual friends and will usually like anyone who is exciting and different, or has any NEW ideas to offer them. They can become so involved in humanity in general and saving the world that they forget themselves and those who are close to them. Since they naturally are such *space cadets*, they need to plant their feet firmly on the ground and become more practical. Since Aquarians are so adept, they should be taught to have patience with those who are less able to separate out their feelings and leave the pure essence of their thoughts.

They may be *rebellious* and quick to organize protests. They will want to protect and help the abused, to help minorities and the downtrodden gain their rights. They will fight against injustice, especially political injustice. They make very good *lawyers*. They will join the fight for almost any cause — so teach them to carefully choose only those which have real value.

These children will love airplanes and flying and will be curious about subjects such as astronomy, astrology, and anything dealing with space.

Key words to use in your communications with Mercury in Aquarius children are: *unique, unusual,* create, invent, discover, rational, individual, independent, original, experiment, humanitarian, innovative, different, and change.

Try not to be shocked with their progressive ideas, nor try to discourage them from thinking that way. Instead, teach them how to add practicality to their thoughts. If these children develop strong reading habits early, they will always have new information available to them. Also, fill their lives with opportunities to have new experiences... and the need to discipline them will be minimal. Your biggest challenge might be the cost for all these new endeavors, and the fact that the interest in them might be short-lived!

Have fun stimulating these interesting minds.

Children with Mercury in Pisces

This position of Mercury in Pisces causes their thought process to be *emotionally-based*. These children will think with their feelings. They are *very sensitive* and greatly influenced by their environment and the people in it. Other people's beliefs will become their beliefs whether they are beneficial or not. They need to learn to think things out for themselves and to decide what is good for them. Their moods are also influenced by what and whom they are exposed to. Negative people and a negative environment can cause these children to be depressed or even psychically harmed. It is absolutely imperative for them to learn how to insulate themselves from negativity so they will be less affected. Without this awareness their moods will be up and down without knowing why, and possibly without any control. You would do well to encourage them to incorporate some cool-thinking and reason into their character. If they learn to relate to the world that we are living in with a more objective approach, they will benefit greatly.

These children are so imaginative, *poetic*, and sensitive, that they are capable of bringing great beauty into this world. Show them how to create their ideas and visions in some material form. These children are dreamers and visionaries with highly developed psychic abilities. They will love fantasy and romance and may be found *daydreaming* much of the time. Gently, positively help them NOT to dream their way through school! Reading poetry and other literature will aid them in learning how to put their ideas into writing for the world to enjoy.

They need to get in touch with *themselves* — and establish their own values, ideas, and philosophies. When they are able to do this, they will experience more stability in their lives. They are so aware and tuned into other people that they are entirely *too receptive*. They are much like a sponge, absorbing everything. Music is a good way to lift and calm them, even to inspire them.

Subjects that deal with hard cold facts will have no interest to them — yet, they should learn the value of facts, reason, and logic. This could present an interesting challenge for you as a parent or caregiver. Remember, these children have a gentle nature and can be reached through their feelings... so present information or correction to them in a sensitive way. When communicating with them about anything you will get better results if you express it with feeling and sensitivity and use the word "feel" as much as possible. They also think in pictures more than most, so learn to tell stories and paint pictures with your words. They will then more clearly understand.

Key words to use in your communications with Mercury in Pisces children are: *imagine, create, visualize, feel, sensitive, sympathy, intuition, inspire, empathize, service, help, and unify.*

When disciplining them let them know how you "feel" when they do something you don't approve of and you will get a favorable reaction. Also, you can ask them how they would feel if they were in your position. And always remember to be gentle; firm but gentle. If you are the hot-tempered type — *don't* take it out on them.

If these children are given many opportunities to use their rich imaginations and bountiful creativity, they will always be a pleasure to be around — as well as having a great gift for the world.

"Astrology is assured of recognition from psychology without further restrictions because astrology represents the summation of all psychological knowledge of antiquity."

Carl G. Jung

CHAPTER 7

Venus — The Goddess of Love

Venus presents the capacity to *give and receive love and affection*. She represents the appreciation of and need for beauty, harmony, and unity. She relates to relationships, the ability to cooperate, and how one experiences social interaction. These are certainly loaded statements and rightfully so — Venus is an all important consideration for us humans on Earth. Love is what makes the difference between merely existing and truly living. It is one of the most positive and powerful energies we know. This has been demonstrated throughout history and literature, and even more importantly, through the lives of all of our great spiritual leaders who understood love in its total sense. How well and in what manner each one of us expresses this important facet of our being must be understood, nurtured, and developed. Venus is at her best when she is radiating love, and contributing to the happiness and pleasures of others. She is the what, when, where... and how we love.

Venus also shows us how the personal *value system* operates. Her placement in the sign describes not only what is valued but also how it is expressed. Venus describes how each individual feels about possessions, and their attitude toward money and prosperity. She relates to the need for pleasure and creature comforts. The sign in which Venus is placed describes how a person experiences *pleasure* and also how the tactile senses respond... to velvet, to skin, to clay. She shows *artistic abilities* and creative talents. And she depicts the appreciation, awareness, and understanding of all forms of *beauty*... both natural and those which are created. Venus represents the harmony, balance and joy with which we experience our daily life.

Furthermore, the Venus placement shows how an individual will get along with others... how one makes *friends*, how many, and what types they are attracted to (*Venus attracts, pulls, magnetizes. Mars aggresses, pushes, electrifies*). This is the planet which represents relationships and sociability, so important because no one is an island. In fact, relationship may be the single most important process which we experience as human beings. Since other people reflect and ignite our own inner selves, both the strengths and the weaknesses, sociability then becomes our strongest area of growth. Those people who are closest to us — such as parents and other family members, teachers, friends and enemies, partners and mates — are the most intense relationships. These give us the best lessons of both love and hate. Venus shows us where love is within each of us and where it is lacking. Understanding this placement will bring information of how your children will express themselves in all their relationships — and how you can help them grow.

When the Venus energies are restricted or excessive, or out of balance in any way — the expression can manifest itself in vanity, greed, self-indulgence, unhealthy loves or relationship dependencies.

Venus Retrograde

When Venus is retrograde, her energies are somewhat *restricted, internalized, and undemonstrative.* These children have a difficult time believing that they are lovable. They are filled with self-doubt and may lack a true sense of self-worth. Instead of acting in life, they seem to *react* to life. They need a lot of reassurance and, although what you give may be rejected, keep giving it. Venus retrograde children often fears intimacy. Learning to accept love as it is, how and when it is given is an important challenge for these children. They are naturally *suspicious* and *critical of love*... wanting it to be as they idealize it which is often unrealistic or too demanding. This causes many disappointments and just reinforces their problem. Teach them not to expect what they think should be, but to feel good about whatever is given and to receive it joyfully.

Teach them to *trust* love. Experience builds trust so it is very important to give children with retrograde Venus as much love, acceptance, and approval as possible. This positive programming will help them develop their own self-esteem and self-worth. Eventually they will learn to stop evaluating their worth by what others project and will establish self-esteem on their own. Explain to them that self-love is just as important as, and must come before, love from outside. Teach your child that when we love ourselves we automatically have love... help them learn to allow their Venus energies flow.

These children are often uncomfortable in social situations and will attempt to avoid them as often as possible. They have their own value system and refuse to play the usual social games. You will find them wearing whatever suits them rather than dressing for the occasion. They will not be found wasting their time in polite conversations — in fact, they can lack refinement and may even appear crude. Sometimes they become a behind-the-scene troublemaker. Venus retro-

grade children are *non-materialistic*, and are not interested in climbing the social ladder, or winning any
popularity contests.

The most important lesson for these children will
be to learn how to open their hearts to others and to
let the love of others come in, so that they avoid becoming hard, cold, unloving adults.

How To Use Venus Tables

Find the year of Birth on the following pages. Next locate the month under that year. The dates listed indicate the day Venus moves into a sign. It stays in that sign until the next date is listed.

Example: In the year 1900 Venus was in Aquarius on January 1, and stayed in Aquarius through Jan 19th. On January 20, it entered Pisces and stayed in Pisces through Feb 12th. February 13, it entered Aries - and so on.

The D and R after the sign indicates whether Venus was Direct or Retrograde. When the R appears it means Venus turned Retrograde on that day and will remain Retrograde until the next date a D appears after the sign.

Example: In the year 1900 Venus turned Retrograde on June 16, and stayed Retrograde through July 29th. On July 30, Venus turned Direct again.

SIGNS

ARI	Aries	LIB	Libra
TAU	Taurus	SCO	Scorpio
GEM	Gemini	SAG	Sagittarius
CAN	Cancer	CAP	Capricorn
LEO	Leo	AQU	Aquarius
VIR	Virgo	PIS	Pisces

1900			1901			1902			1903		
JAN	1	AQU-D	JAN	16	CAP-D	JAN	11	PIS-D	JAN	11	AQU-D
JAN	20	PIS-D	FEB	9	AQU-D	JAN	25	PIS-R	FEB	5	PIS-D
FEB	13	ARI-D	MAR	5	PIS-D	FEB	7	AQU-R	FEB	28	ARI-D
MAR	10	TAU-D	MAR	29	ARI-D	MAR	7	AQU-D	MAR	24	TAU-D
APR	6	GEM-D	APR	22	TAU-D	APR	4	PIS-D	APR	18	GEM-D
MAY	5	CAN-D	MAY	17	GEM-D	MAY	7	ARI-D	MAY	13	CAN-D
JUN	16	CAN-R	JUN	10	CAN-D	JUN	3	TAU-D	JUN	9	LEO-D
JUL	30	CAN-D	JUL	4	LEO-D	JUL	1	GEM-D	JUL	7	VIR-D
SEP	8	LEO-D	JUL	29	VIR-D	JUL	25	CAN-D	AUG	17	LIB-D
OCT	8	VIR-D	AUG	23	LIB-D	AUG	19	LEO-D	AUG	27	LIB-R
NOV	3	LIB-D	SEP	17	SCO-D	SEP	14	VIR-D	SEP	7	VIR-R
NOV	28	SCO-D	OCT	12	SAG-D	OCT	7	LIB-D	OCT	9	VIR-D
DEC	23	SAG-D	NOV	7	CAP-D	NOV	1	SCO-D	NOV	8	LIB-D
			DEC	5	AQU-D	NOV	24	SAG-D	DEC	9	SCO-D
						DEC	18	CAP-D			

1904			1905			1906			1907		
JAN	5	SAG-D	JAN	7	PIS-D	JAN	1	CAP-D	FEB	6	CAP-D
JAN	30	CAP-D	FEB	4	ARI-D	JAN	25	AQU-D	MAR	6	AQU-D
FEB	24	AQU-D	MAR	6	TAU-D	FEB	18	PIS-D	APR	2	PIS-D
MAR	19	PIS-D	APR	6	TAU-R	MAR	14	ARI-D	APR	27	ARI-D
APR	13	ARI-D	MAY	10	ARI-R	APR	7	TAU-D	MAY	22	TAU-D
MAY	7	TAU-D	MAY	18	ARI-D	MAY	2	GEM-D	JUN	16	GEM-D
JUN	1	GEM-D	MAY	28	TAU-D	MAY	26	CAN-D	JUL	11	CAN-D
JUN	25	CAN-D	JUL	8	GEM-D	JUN	20	LEO-D	AUG	4	LEO-D
JUL	19	LEO-D	AUG	6	CAN-D	JUL	16	VIR-D	AUG	29	VIR-D
AUG	13	VIR-D	SEP	1	LEO-D	AUG	11	LIB-D	SEP	22	LIB-D
SEP	6	LIB-D	SEP	27	VIR-D	SEP	7	SCO-D	OCT	16	SCO-D
OCT	1	SCO-D	OCT	21	LIB-D	OCT	9	SAG-D	NOV	9	SAG-D
OCT	26	SAG-D	NOV	14	SCO-D	NOV	9	SAG-R	DEC	3	CAP-D
NOV	18	CAP-D	DEC	8	SAG-D	DEC	15	SCO-R	DEC	27	AQU-D
DEC	13	AQU-D				DEC	20	SCO-D			
						DEC	26	SAG-D			

1908			1909			1910			1911		
JAN	20	PIS-D	JAN	15	CAP-D	JAN	15	PIS-D	JAN	10	AQU-D
FEB	14	ARI-D	FEB	9	AQU-D	JAN	22	PIS-R	FEB	3	PIS-D
MAR	10	TAU-D	MAR	5	PIS-D	JAN	30	AQU-R	FEB	27	ARI-D
APR	5	GEM-D	MAR	29	ARI-D	MAR	5	AQU-D	MAR	23	TAU-D
MAY	5	CAN-D	APR	22	TAU-D	MAY	7	ARI-D	APR	17	GEM-D
JUN	14	CAN-R	MAY	16	GEM-D	JUN	3	TAU-D	MAY	13	CAN-D
JUL	27	CAN-D	JUN	10	CAN-D	JUN	29	GEM-D	JUN	8	LEO-D
SEP	8	LEO-D	JUL	4	LEO-D	JUL	25	CAN-D	JUL	7	VIR-D
OCT	8	VIR-D	JUL	29	VIR-D	AUG	19	LEO-D	AUG	25	VIR-R
NOV	3	LIB-D	AUG	23	LIB-D	SEP	12	VIR-D	OCT	6	VIR-D
NOV	28	SCO-D	SEP	17	SCO-D	OCT	6	LIB-D	NOV	9	LIB-D
DEC	22	SAG-D	OCT	12	SAG-D	OCT	30	SCO-D	DEC	9	SCO-D
			NOV	7	CAP-D	NOV	23	SAG-D			
			DEC	5	AQU-D	DEC	17	CAP-D			

1912			1913			1914			1915		
JAN	4	SAG-D	JAN	8	PIS-D	JAN	2	CAP-D	FEB	7	CAP-D
JAN	29	CAP-D	FEB	2	ARI-D	JAN	25	AQU-D	MAR	7	AQU-D
FEB	23	AQU-D	MAR	6	TAU-D	FEB	18	PIS-D	APR	2	PIS-D
MAR	19	PIS-D	APR	3	TAU-R	MAR	14	ARI-D	APR	28	ARI-D
APR	12	ARI-D	MAY	3	ARI-R	APR	8	TAU-D	MAY	23	TAU-D
MAY	7	TAU-D	MAY	16	ARI-D	MAY	2	GEM-D	JUN	17	GEM-D
JUN	1	GEM-D	MAY	31	TAU-D	MAY	27	CAN-D	JUL	11	CAN-D
JUN	25	CAN-D	JUL	8	GEM-D	JUN	29	LEO-D	AUG	5	LEO-D
JUL	19	LEO-D	AUG	5	CAN-D	JUL	16	VIR-D	AUG	29	VIR-D
AUG	12	VIR-D	SEP	2	LEO-D	AUG	9	LIB-D	SEP	22	LIB-D
SEP	6	LIB-D	SEP	26	VIR-D	SEP	7	SCO-D	OCT	16	SCO-D
OCT	1	SCO-D	OCT	22	LIB-D	OCT	10	SAG-D	NOV	9	SAG-D
OCT	24	SAG-D	NOV	15	SCO-D	NOV	7	SAG-R	DEC	3	CAP-D
NOV	18	CAP-D	DEC	9	SAG-D	DEC	6	SCO-R	DEC	26	AQU-D
DEC	12	AQU-D				DEC	18	SCO-D			
						DEC	30	SAG-D			

1916			1917			1918			1919		
JAN	21	PIS-D	JAN	16	CAP-D	JAN	20	AQU-R	JAN	11	AQU-D
FEB	13	ARI-D	FEB	9	AQU-D	MAR	2	AQU-D	FEB	3	PIS-D
MAR	9	TAU-D	MAR	5	PIS-D	APR	6	PIS-D	FEB	28	ARI-D
APR	5	GEM-D	MAR	29	ARI-D	MAY	7	ARI-D	MAR	24	TAU-D
MAY	5	CAN-D	APR	22	TAU-D	JUN	4	TAU-D	APR	18	GEM-D
JUN	12	CAN-R	MAY	17	GEM-D	JUN	30	GEM-D	MAY	13	CAN-D
JUL	25	CAN-D	JUN	10	CAN-D	JUL	25	CAN-D	JUN	9	LEO-D
SEP	9	LEO-D	JUL	5	LEO-D	AUG	19	LEO-D	JUL	8	VIR-D
OCT	8	VIR-D	JUL	29	VIR-D	SEP	13	VIR-D	AUG	22	VIR-R
NOV	4	LIB-D	AUG	23	LIB-D	OCT	7	LIB-D	OCT	4	VIR-D
NOV	28	SCO-D	SEP	17	SCO-D	OCT	31	SCO-D	NOV	10	LIB-D
DEC	23	SAG-D	OCT	12	SAG-D	NOV	24	SAG-D	DEC	10	SCO-D
			NOV	8	CAP-D	DEC	18	CAP-D			
			DEC	6	AQU-D						

1920			1921			1922			1923		
JAN	5	SAG-D	JAN	7	PIS-D	JAN	1	CAP-D	JAN	3	SAG-D
JAN	30	CAP-D	FEB	3	ARI-D	JAN	25	AQU-D	FEB	7	CAP-D
FEB	24	AQU-D	MAR	8	TAU-D	FEB	18	PIS-D	MAR	7	AQU-D
MAR	19	PIS-D	APR	1	TAU-R	MAR	14	ARI-D	APR	2	PIS-D
APR	13	ARI-D	APR	26	ARI-R	APR	7	TAU-D	APR	27	ARI-D
MAY	7	TAU-D	MAY	14	ARI-D	MAY	2	GEM-D	MAY	22	TAU-D
JUN	25	CAN-D	JUN	3	TAU-D	MAY	26	CAN-D	JUN	16	GEM-D
JUL	19	LEO-D	JUL	9	GEM-D	JUN	20	LEO-D	JUL	11	CAN-D
AUG	13	VIR-D	AUG	6	CAN-D	JUL	16	VIR-D	AUG	4	LEO-D
SEP	6	LIB-D	SEP	1	LEO-D	AUG	11	LIB-D	AUG	28	VIR-D
SEP	30	SCO-D	SEP	27	VIR-D	SEP	8	SCO-D	SEP	22	LIB-D
OCT	25	SAG-D	OCT	21	LIB-D	OCT	11	SAG-D	OCT	16	SCO-D
NOV	18	CAP-D	NOV	14	SCO-D	NOV	4	SAG-R	NOV	9	SAG-D
DEC	13	AQU-D	DEC	8	SAG-D	NOV	29	SCO-D	DEC	3	CAP-D
						DEC	15	SCO-D	DEC	27	AQU-D

1924			1925			1926			1927		
JAN	20	PIS-D	JAN	15	CAP-D	JAN	17	AQU-R	JAN	10	AQU-D
FEB	14	ARI-D	FEB	8	AQU-D	FEB	28	AQU-D	FEB	3	PIS-D
MAR	10	TAU-D	MAR	6	PIS-D	APR	7	PIS-D	FEB	27	ARI-D
APR	6	GEM-D	MAR	29	ARI-D	MAY	7	ARI-D	MAR	23	TAU-D
MAY	7	CAN-D	APR	22	TAU-D	JUN	3	TAU-D	APR	17	GEM-D
JUN	10	CAN-R	MAY	15	GEM-D	JUN	29	GEM-D	MAY	13	CAN-D
JUL	24	CAN-D	JUN	10	CAN-D	JUL	25	CAN-D	JUN	9	LEO-D
SEP	9	LEO-D	JUL	4	LEO-D	AUG	19	LEO-D	JUL	8	VIR-D
OCT	8	VIR-D	JUL	29	VIR-D	SEP	12	VIR-D	AUG	20	VIR-R
NOV	3	LIB-D	AUG	23	LIB-D	OCT	6	LIB-D	OCT	2	VIR-D
NOV	28	SCO-D	SEP	17	SCO-D	OCT	30	SCO-D	NOV	10	LIB-D
DEC	22	SAG-D	OCT	12	SAG-D	NOV	23	SAG-D	DEC	10	SCO-D
			NOV	7	CAP-D	DEC	17	CAP-D			
			DEC	6	AQU-D						

1928			1929			1930			1931		
JAN	5	SAG-D	JAN	7	PIS-D	JAN	25	AQU-D	JAN	4	SAG-D
JAN	30	CAP-D	FEB	3	ARI-D	FEB	17	PIS-D	FEB	7	CAP-D
FEB	23	AQU-D	MAR	9	TAU-D	MAR	13	ARI-D	MAR	6	AQU-D
MAR	19	PIS-D	MAR	30	TAU-R	APR	6	TAU-D	APR	1	PIS-D
APR	12	ARI-D	APR	21	ARI-R	MAY	1	GEM-D	APR	26	ARI-D
MAY	7	TAU-D	MAY	11	ARI-D	MAY	25	CAN-D	MAY	21	TAU-D
MAY	31	GEM-D	JUN	4	TAU-D	JUN	19	LEO-D	JUN	15	GEM-D
JUN	24	CAN-D	JUL	9	GEM-D	AUG	10	LIB-D	JUL	10	CAN-D
JUL	19	LEO-D	AUG	6	CAN-D	SEP	7	SCO-D	AUG	3	LEO-D
AUG	12	VIR-D	SEP	1	LEO-D	OCT	12	SAG-D	AUG	28	VIR-D
SEP	5	LIB-D	SEP	26	VIR-D	NOV	3	SAG-R	SEP	21	LIB-D
SEP	30	SCO-D	OCT	21	LIB-D	NOV	23	SCO-R	OCT	15	SCO-D
OCT	24	SAG-D	NOV	14	SCO-D	DEC	14	SCO-D	NOV	8	SAG-D
NOV	18	CAP-D	DEC	8	SAG-D				DEC	2	CAP-D
DEC	13	AQU-D							DEC	26	AQU-D

1932			1933			1934			1935		
	JAN 19	PIS-D		JAN 15	CAP-D		JAN 15	AQU-R		JAN 9	AQU-D
	FEB 13	ARI-D		FEB 8	AQU-D		FEB 25	AQU-D		FEB 2	PIS-D
	MAR 9	TAU-D		MAR 4	PIS-D		APR 7	PIS-D		FEB 26	ARI-D
	APR 5	GEM-D		MAR 28	ARI-D		MAY 7	ARI-D		MAR 23	TAU-D
	MAY 7	CAN-D		APR 21	TAU-D		JUN 3	TAU-D		APR 17	GEM-D
	JUN 7	CAN-R		MAY 15	GEM-D		JUN 29	GEM-D		MAY 12	CAN-D
	JUL 14	GEM-R		JUN 9	CAN-D		JUL 24	CAN-D		JUN 8	LEO-D
	JUL 20	GEM-D		JUL 3	LEO-D		AUG 18	LEO-D		JUL 8	VIR-D
	JUL 29	CAN-D		JUL 28	VIR-D		OCT 6	LIB-D		AUG 18	VIR-R
	SEP 9	LEO-D		AUG 21	LIB-D		OCT 30	SCO-D		SEP 29	VIR-D
	OCT 8	VIR-D		SEP 16	SCO-D		NOV 22	SAG-D		NOV 10	LIB-D
	NOV 2	LIB-D		OCT 11	SAG-D		DEC 16	CAP-D		DEC 9	SCO-D
	NOV 27	SCO-D		NOV 7	CAP-D						
	DEC 22	SAG-D		DEC 6	AQU-D						

1936			1937			1938			1939		
	JAN 4	SAG-D		JAN 6	PIS-D		JAN 24	AQU-D		JAN 5	SAG-D
	JAN 29	CAP-D		FEB 3	ARI-D		FEB 17	PIS-D		FEB 7	CAP-D
	FEB 22	AQU-D		MAR 10	TAU-R		MAR 13	ARI-D		MAR 6	AQU-D
	MAR 18	PIS-D		MAR 27	TAU-R		APR 6	TAU-D		APR 1	PIS-D
	APR 11	ARI-D		APR 15	ARI-R		APR 30	GEM-D		APR 26	ARI-D
	MAY 6	TAU-D		MAY 9	ARI-D		MAY 25	CAN-D		MAY 21	TAU-D
	MAY 30	GEM-D		JUN 5	TAU-D		JUN 19	LEO-D		JUN 15	GEM-D
	JUN 24	CAN-D		JUL 8	GEM-D		JUL 15	VIR-D		JUL 9	CAN-D
	JUL 18	LEO-D		AUG 5	CAN-D		AUG 10	LIB-D		AUG 3	LEO-D
	AUG 11	VIR-D		AUG 31	LEO-D		SEP 7	SCO-D		AUG 27	VIR-D
	SEP 5	LIB-D		SEP 25	VIR-D		OCT 14	SAG-D		SEP 20	LIB-D
	SEP 29	SCO-D		OCT 20	LIB-D		OCT 30	SAG-R		OCT 14	SCO-D
	OCT 23	SAG-D		NOV 13	SCO-D		NOV 16	SCO-R		NOV 7	SAG-D
	NOV 17	CAP-D		DEC 7	SAG-D		DEC 10	SCO-D		DEC 1	CAP-D
	DEC 12	AQU-D		DEC 31	CAP-D					DEC 26	AQU-D

1940			1941			1942			1943		
	JAN 19	PIS-D		JAN 14	CAP-D		JAN 13	AQU-R		JAN 9	AQU-D
	FEB 13	ARI-D		FEB 7	AQU-D		FEB 23	AQU-D		FEB 2	PIS-D
	MAR 9	TAU-D		MAR 3	PIS-D		APR 7	PIS-D		FEB 26	ARI-D
	APR 5	GEM-D		MAR 27	ARI-D		MAY 6	ARI-D		MAR 22	TAU-D
	MAY 7	CAN-D		APR 21	TAU-D		JUN 2	TAU-D		APR 16	GEM-D
	JUN 5	CAN-R		MAY 15	GEM-D		JUN 28	GEM-D		MAY 12	CAN-D
	JUL 6	GEM-R		JUN 8	CAN-D		JUL 24	CAN-D		JUN 8	LEO-D
	JUL 18	GEM-D		JUL 3	LEO-D		AUG 17	LEO-D		JUL 8	VIR-D
	AUG 1	CAN-D		JUL 27	VIR-D		SEP 11	VIR-D		AUG 15	VIR-R
	SEP 9	LEO-D		AUG 21	LIB-D		OCT 5	LIB-D		SEP 27	VIR-D
	OCT 7	VIR-D		SEP 15	SCO-D		OCT 29	SCO-D		NOV 10	LIB-D
	NOV 2	LIB-D		OCT 11	SAG-D		NOV 22	SAG-D		DEC 9	SCO-D
	NOV 27	SCO-D		NOV 7	CAP-D		DEC 16	CAP-D				
	DEC 21	SAG-D		DEC 6	AQU-D						

1944			1945			1946			1947		
	JAN 3	SAG-D		JAN 6	PIS-D		JAN 23	AQU-D		JAN 6	SAG-D
	JAN 28	CAP-D		FEB 3	ARI-D		FEB 16	PIS-D		FEB 7	CAP-D
	FEB 22	AQU-D		MAR 12	TAU-D		MAR 12	ARI-D		MAR 5	AQU-D
	MAR 17	PIS-D		MAR 25	TAU-R		APR 5	TAU-D		MAR 31	PIS-D
	APR 11	ARI-D		APR 8	ARI-R		APR 30	GEM-D		APR 25	ARI-D
	MAY 5	TAU-D		MAY 6	ARI-D		MAY 24	CAN-D		MAY 20	TAU-D
	MAY 30	GEM-D		JUN 5	TAU-D		JUN 18	LEO-D		JUN 14	GEM-D
	JUN 23	CAN-D		JUL 8	GEM-D		JUL 14	VIR-D		JUL 9	CAN-D
	JUL 17	LEO-D		AUG 5	CAN-D		AUG 10	LIB-D		AUG 2	LEO-D
	AUG 11	VIR-D		AUG 31	LEO-D		SEP 7	SCO-D		AUG 27	VIR-D
	SEP 4	LIB-D		OCT 18	LIB-D		OCT 17	SAG-D		SEP 20	LIB-D
	SEP 29	SAG-D		NOV 13	SCO-D		OCT 28	SAG-R		OCT 14	SCO-D
	NOV 17	CAP-D		DEC 7	SAG-D		NOV 9	SCO-R		NOV 7	SAG-D
	DEC 11	AQU-D		DEC 30	CAP-D		DEC 8	SCO-D		DEC 1	CAP-D
										DEC 24	AQU-D

Venus Tables

1948			1949			1950			1951		
JAN	18	PIS-D	JAN	14	CAP-D	JAN	10	AQU-R	JAN	8	AQU-D
FEB	12	ARI-D	FEB	7	AQU-D	FEB	20	AQU-D	FEB	1	PIS-D
MAR	9	TAU-D	MAR	3	PIS-D	APR	7	PIS-D	FEB	25	ARI-D
APR	5	GEM-D	MAR	27	ARI-D	MAY	6	ARI-D	MAR	22	TAU-D
MAY	8	CAN-D	APR	20	TAU-D	JUN	2	TAU-D	APR	16	GEM-D
JUN	3	CAN-R	MAY	14	GEM-D	JUN	28	GEM-D	MAY	11	CAN-D
JUN	30	GEM-R	JUN	8	CAN-D	JUL	23	CAN-D	JUN	8	LEO-D
JUL	16	GEM-D	JUL	2	LEO-D	AUG	17	LEO-D	JUL	8	VIR-D
AUG	3	CAN-D	JUL	27	VIR-D	SEP	10	VIR-D	AUG	13	VIR-R
SEP	9	LEO-D	AUG	21	LIB-D	OCT	5	LIB-D	SEP	25	VIR-D
OCT	7	VIR-D	SEP	15	SCO-D	OCT	29	SCO-D	NOV	10	LIB-D
NOV	2	LIB-D	OCT	11	SAG-D	NOV	21	SAG-D	DEC	8	SCO-D
NOV	26	SCO-D	NOV	6	CAP-D	DEC	15	CAP-D			
DEC	21	SAG-D	DEC	7	AQU-D						

1952			1953			1954			1955		
JAN	3	SAG-D	JAN	6	PIS-D	JAN	23	AQU-D	JAN	7	SAG-D
JAN	28	CAP-D	FEB	3	ARI-D	FEB	16	PIS-D	FEB	6	CAP-D
FEB	21	AQU-D	MAR	15	TAU-D	MAR	12	ARI-D	MAR	5	AQU-D
MAR	17	PIS-D	MAR	23	TAU-D	APR	5	TAU-D	MAR	31	PIS-D
APR	10	ARI-D	APR	1	ARI-D	APR	29	GEM-D	APR	25	ARI-D
MAY	5	TAU-D	JUN	6	TAU-D	MAY	24	CAN-D	MAY	20	TAU-D
MAY	29	GEM-D	JUL	8	GEM-D	JUN	18	LEO-D	JUN	14	GEM-D
JUN	23	CAN-D	AUG	4	CAN-D	JUL	14	VIR-D	JUL	8	CAN-D
JUL	17	LEO-D	AUG	30	LEO-D	AUG	9	LIB-D	AUG	2	LEO-D
AUG	10	VIR-D	SEP	24	VIR-D	SEP	7	SCO-D	AUG	26	VIR-D
SEP	4	LIB-D	OCT	19	LIB-D	OCT	25	SAG-R	SEP	19	LIB-D
SEP	28	SCO-D	NOV	11	SCO-D	OCT	28	SCO-R	OCT	13	SCO-D
OCT	22	SAG-D	DEC	6	SAG-D	DEC	5	SCO-D	NOV	6	SAG-D
NOV	16	CAP-D	DEC	30	CAP-D				NOV	20	CAP-D
DEC	11	AQU-D							DEC	25	AQU-D

1956			1957			1958			1959		
JAN	18	PIS-D	JAN	13	CAP-D	JAN	8	AQU-R	JAN	8	AQU-D
FEB	12	ARI-D	FEB	6	AQU-D	FEB	18	AQU-D	FEB	1	PIS-D
MAR	8	TAU-D	MAR	2	PIS-D	APR	7	PIS-D	FEB	25	ARI-D
APR	5	GEM-D	MAR	26	ARI-D	MAY	6	ARI-D	MAR	21	TAU-D
MAY	9	CAN-D	APR	19	TAU-D	JUN	1	TAU-D	APR	15	GEM-D
MAY	31	CAN-R	MAY	14	GEM-D	JUN	27	GEM-D	MAY	11	CAN-D
JUN	23	GEM-R	JUN	7	CAN-D	JUL	23	CAN-D	JUN	7	LEO-D
JUL	13	GEM-D	JUL	2	LEO-D	AUG	16	LEO-D	JUL	9	VIR-D
AUG	5	CAN-D	JUL	26	VIR-D	SEP	10	VIR-D	AUG	10	VIR-R
SEP	9	LEO-D	AUG	20	LIB-D	OCT	4	LIB-D	SEP	21	LEO-R
OCT	6	VIR-D	SEP	15	SCO-D	OCT	28	SCO-D	SEP	22	LEO-D
NOV	1	LIB-D	OCT	10	SAG-D	NOV	21	SAG-D	SEP	25	VIR-D
NOV	26	SCO-D	NOV	6	CAP-D	DEC	15	CAP-D	NOV	10	LIB-D
DEC	20	SAG-D	DEC	7	AQU-D				DEC	8	SCO-D

1960			1961			1962			1963		
JAN	3	SAG-D	JAN	5	PIS-D	JAN	22	AQU-D	JAN	7	SAG-D
JAN	27	CAP-D	FEB	2	ARI-D	FEB	15	PIS-D	FEB	6	CAP-D
FEB	21	AQU-D	MAR	20	ARI-R	MAR	11	ARI-D	MAR	5	AQU-D
MAR	16	PIS-D	MAY	2	ARI-D	APR	4	TAU-D	MAR	30	PIS-D
APR	10	ARI-D	JUN	6	TAU-D	APR	29	GEM-D	APR	24	ARI-D
MAY	4	TAU-D	JUL	7	GEM-D	MAY	23	CAN-D	MAY	19	TAU-D
MAY	29	GEM-D	AUG	4	CAN-D	JUN	18	LEO-D	JUN	13	GEM-D
JUN	22	CAN-D	AUG	29	LEO-D	JUL	13	VIR-D	JUL	8	CAN-D
JUL	16	LEO-D	OCT	18	LIB-D	AUG	9	LIB-D	AUG	1	LEO-D
AUG	10	VIR-D	NOV	12	SCO-D	SEP	6	SCO-D	AUG	26	VIR-D
SEP	3	LIB-D	DEC	5	SAG-D	OCT	23	SCO-R	SEP	19	LIB-D
SEP	27	SCO-D	DEC	29	CAP-D	DEC	3	SCO-D	OCT	13	SCO-D
OCT	22	SAG-D							NOV	6	SAG-D
NOV	15	CAP-D							NOV	30	CAP-D
DEC	10	AQU-D							DEC	24	AQU-D

1964			1965			1966			1967		
JAN	17	PIS-D	JAN	13	CAP-D	JAN	5	AQU-R	JAN	7	AQU-D
FEB	11	ARI-D	FEB	6	AQU-D	JAN	15	CAP-R	JAN	31	PIS-D
MAR	8	TAU-D	MAR	2	PIS-D	FEB	7	CAP-D	FEB	24	ARI-D
APR	4	GEM-D	MAR	26	ARI-D	FEB	26	AQU-D	MAR	21	TAU-D
MAY	9	CAN-D	APR	19	TAU-D	APR	7	PIS-D	APR	15	GEM-D
MAY	29	CAN-R	MAY	13	GEM-D	MAY	5	ARI-D	MAY	11	CAN-D
JUN	18	GEM-R	JUN	7	CAN-D	JUN	1	TAU-D	JUN	7	LEO-D
JUL	11	GEM-D	JUL	1	LEO-D	JUN	27	GEM-D	JUL	9	VIR-D
AUG	6	CAN-D	JUL	26	VIR-D	JUL	22	CAN-D	AUG	8	VIR-R
SEP	8	LEO-D	AUG	20	LIB-D	AUG	16	LEO-D	SEP	9	LEO-R
OCT	6	VIR-D	SEP	14	SCO-D	SEP	9	VIR-D	SEP	21	LEO-D
NOV	1	LIB-D	OCT	10	SAG-D	OCT	3	LIB-D	OCT	2	LIB-D
NOV	25	SCO-D	NOV	6	CAP-D	OCT	27	SCO-D	NOV	10	LIB-D
DEC	20	SAG-D	DEC	7	AQU-D	NOV	20	SAG-D	DEC	8	SCO-D
						DEC	14	CAP-D			

1968			1969			1970			1971		
JAN	2	SAG-D	JAN	5	PIS-D	JAN	22	AQU-D	JAN	7	SAG-D
JAN	27	CAP-D	FEB	2	ARI-D	FEB	14	PIS-D	FEB	6	CAP-D
FEB	20	AQU-D	MAR	18	ARI-R	MAR	11	ARI-D	MAR	4	AQU-D
MAR	16	PIS-D	APR	29	ARI-D	APR	4	TAU-D	MAR	30	PIS-D
APR	9	ARI-D	JUN	6	TAU-D	APR	28	GEM-D	APR	24	ARI-D
MAY	4	TAU-D	JUL	7	GEM-D	MAY	23	CAN-D	MAY	19	TAU-D
MAY	28	GEM-D	AUG	4	CAN-D	JUN	17	LEO-D	JUN	13	GEM-D
JUN	21	CAN-D	AUG	29	LEO-D	JUL	13	VIR-D	JUL	7	CAN-D
JUL	16	LEO-D	SEP	23	VIR-D	AUG	9	LIB-D	AUG	1	LEO-D
AUG	9	VIR-D	OCT	18	LIB-D	SEP	7	SCO-D	AUG	25	VIR-D
SEP	3	LIB-D	NOV	11	SCO-D	OCT	20	SCO-R	SEP	18	LIB-D
SEP	27	SCO-D	DEC	5	SAG-D	DEC	2	SCO-D	OCT	12	SCO-D
OCT	22	SAG-D	DEC	29	CAP-D				NOV	5	SAG-D
NOV	15	CAP-D							NOV	29	CAP-D
DEC	10	AQU-D							DEC	24	AQU-D

1972			1973			1974			1975		
JAN	17	PIS-D	JAN	12	CAP-D	JAN	3	AQU-R	JAN	7	AQU-D
FEB	11	ARI-D	FEB	5	AQU-D	JAN	30	CAP-R	JAN	31	PIS-D
MAR	7	TAU-D	MAR	1	PIS-D	FEB	13	CAP-D	FEB	24	ARI-D
APR	4	GEM-D	MAR	25	ARI-D	MAR	1	AQU-D	MAR	20	TAU-D
MAY	10	CAN-D	APR	18	TAU-D	APR	7	PIS-D	APR	14	GEM-D
MAY	27	CAN-R	MAY	13	GEM-D	MAY	5	ARI-D	MAY	10	CAN-D
JUN	12	GEM-R	JUN	6	CAN-D	JUN	1	TAU-D	JUN	7	LEO-D
JUL	9	GEM-D	JUL	1	LEO-D	JUN	26	GEM-D	JUL	10	VIR-D
AUG	6	CAN-D	JUL	25	VIR-D	JUL	21	CAN-D	AUG	6	VIR-R
SEP	8	LEO-D	AUG	19	LIB-D	AUG	15	LEO-D	SEP	3	LEO-R
OCT	6	VIR-D	SEP	14	SCO-D	SEP	9	VIR-D	SEP	18	LEO-D
OCT	31	LIB-D	OCT	10	SAG-D	OCT	3	LIB-D	OCT	5	VIR-D
NOV	25	SCO-D	NOV	6	CAP-D	OCT	27	SCO-D	NOV	10	LIB-D
DEC	19	SAG-D	DEC	7	AQU-D	NOV	20	SAG-D	DEC	7	SCO-D
						DEC	14	CAP-D			

1976			1977			1978			1979		
JAN	2	SAG-D	JAN	5	PIS-D	JAN	21	AQU-D	JAN	8	SAG-D
JAN	27	CAP-D	FEB	3	ARI-D	FEB	14	PIS-D	FEB	6	CAP-D
FEB	20	AQU-D	MAR	16	ARI-R	MAR	10	ARI-D	MAR	4	AQU-D
MAR	15	PIS-D	APR	27	ARI-D	APR	3	TAU-D	MAR	29	PIS-D
APR	9	ARI-D	JUN	7	TAU-D	APR	28	GEM-D	APR	23	ARI-D
MAY	3	TAU-D	JUL	7	GEM-D	MAY	22	CAN-D	MAY	18	TAU-D
MAY	27	GEM-D	AUG	3	CAN-D	JUN	17	LEO-D	JUN	12	GEM-D
JUN	21	CAN-D	AUG	29	LEO-D	JUL	12	VIR-D	JUL	7	CAN-D
JUL	14	LEO-D	SEP	23	VIR-D	AUG	8	LIB-D	JUL	31	LEO-D
AUG	9	VIR-D	OCT	17	LIB-D	SEP	8	SCO-D	AUG	24	VIR-D
SEP	2	LIB-D	NOV	10	SCO-D	OCT	18	SCO-R	SEP	18	LIB-D
OCT	21	SAG-D	DEC	4	SAG-D	NOV	28	SCO-D	OCT	12	SCO-D
NOV	15	CAP-D	DEC	28	CAP-D				NOV	5	SAG-D
DEC	10	AQU-D							NOV	29	CAP-D
									DEC	23	AQU-D

Venus Tables

1980		1981		1982		1983	
JAN 16	PIS-D	JAN 11	CAP-D	JAN 24	CAP-R	JAN 6	AQU-D
FEB 10	ARI-D	FEB 5	AQU-D	FEB 10	CAP-D	JAN 30	PIS-D
MAR 7	TAU-D	MAR 1	PIS-D	MAR 3	AQU-D	FEB 23	ARI-D
APR 4	GEM-D	MAR 25	ARI-D	APR 7	PIS-D	MAR 20	TAU-D
MAY 13	CAN-D	APR 18	TAU-D	MAY 5	ARI-D	APR 14	GEM-D
MAY 24	CAN-R	MAY 12	GEM-D	MAY 31	TAU-D	MAY 10	CAN-D
JUN 6	GEM-R	JUN 6	CAN-D	JUN 26	GEM-D	JUN 7	LEO-D
JUL 6	GEM-D	JUN 30	LEO-D	JUL 21	CAN-D	JUL 11	VIR-D
AUG 7	CAN-D	JUL 25	VIR-D	AUG 15	LEO-D	AUG 3	VIR-R
SEP 8	LEO-D	AUG 19	LIB-D	SEP 8	VIR-D	AUG 27	LEO-R
OCT 5	VIR-D	SEP 13	SCO-D	OCT 2	LIB-D	SEP 15	LEO-D
OCT 31	LIB-D	OCT 9	SAG-D	NOV 19	SAG-D	OCT 6	VIR-D
NOV 24	SCO-D	NOV 6	CAP-D	DEC 13	CAP-D	NOV 10	LIB-D
DEC 19	SAG-D	DEC 9	AQU-D			DEC 7	SCO-D
		DEC 31	AQU-R				

1984		1985		1986		1987	
JAN 1	SAG-D	JAN 5	PIS-D	JAN 21	AQU-D	JAN 8	SAG-D
JAN 26	CAP-D	FEB 3	ARI-D	FEB 13	PIS-D	FEB 5	CAP-D
FEB 19	AQU-D	MAR 13	ARI-R	MAR 9	ARI-D	MAR 4	AQU-D
MAR 15	PIS-D	APR 25	ARI-D	APR 3	TAU-D	MAR 29	PIS-D
APR 8	ARI-D	JUN 7	TAU-D	APR 27	GEM-D	APR 23	ARI-D
MAY 2	TAU-D	JUL 7	GEM-D	MAY 21	CAN-D	MAY 18	TAU-D
MAY 27	GEM-D	AUG 3	CAN-D	JUN 16	LEO-D	JUN 12	GEM-D
JUN 20	CAN-D	AUG 28	LEO-D	JUL 12	VIR-D	JUL 6	CAN-D
JUL 15	LEO-D	SEP 22	VIR-D	AUG 8	LIB-D	JUL 31	LEO-D
AUG 8	VIR-D	OCT 17	LIB-D	SEP 8	VIR-D	AUG 24	VIR-D
SEP 1	LIB-D	NOV 10	SCO-D	OCT 15	SCO-R	SEP 17	LIB-D
SEP 26	SCO-D	DEC 4	SAG-D	NOV 26	SCO-D	OCT 11	SCO-D
OCT 21	SAG-D	DEC 28	CAP-D			NOV 4	SAG-D
NOV 14	CAP-D					NOV 28	CAP-D
DEC 9	AQU-D					DEC 23	AQU-D

1988		1989		1990		1991	
JAN 16	PIS-D	JAN 11	CAP-D	JAN 17	CAP-R	JAN 5	AQU-D
FEB 10	ARI-D	FEB 4	AQU-D	FEB 8	CAP-D	JAN 29	PIS-D
MAR 7	TAU-D	FEB 28	PIS-D	MAR 4	AQU-D	FEB 23	ARI-D
APR 4	GEM-D	MAR 24	ARI-D	APR 7	PIS-D	MAR 19	TAU-D
MAY 18	CAN-D	APR 17	TAU-D	MAY 4	ARI-D	APR 13	GEM-D
MAY 22	CAN-R	MAY 12	GEM-D	MAY 31	TAU-D	MAY 9	CAN-D
MAY 28	GEM-R	JUN 5	CAN-D	JUN 25	GEM-D	JUN 6	LEO-D
JUL 4	GEM-D	JUN 30	LEO-D	JUL 20	CAN-D	JUL 12	VIR-D
AUG 7	CAN-D	JUL 24	VIR-D	AUG 14	LEO-D	AUG 1	VIR-R
SEP 8	LEO-D	AUG 18	LIB-D	SEP 8	VIR-D	AUG 22	LEO-R
OCT 5	VIR-D	SEP 13	SCO-D	OCT 2	LIB-D	SEP 13	LEO-D
OCT 30	LIB-D	OCT 9	SAG-D	OCT 26	SCO-D	OCT 7	VIR-D
NOV 24	SCO-D	NOV 6	CAP-D	NOV 19	SAG-D	NOV 10	LIB-D
DEC 18	SAG-D	DEC 10	AQU-D	DEC 13	CAP-D	DEC 7	SCO-D
		DEC 29	AQU-R				

1992		1993		1994		1995	
JAN 1	SAG-D	JAN 4	PIS-D	JAN 20	AQU-D	JAN 8	SAG-D
JAN 26	CAP-D	FEB 3	ARI-D	FEB 13	PIS-D	FEB 5	CAP-D
FEB 19	AQU-D	MAR 11	ARI-R	MAR 9	ARI-D	MAR 3	AQU-D
MAR 14	PIS-D	APR 22	ARI-D	APR 2	TAU-D	MAR 29	PIS-D
APR 8	ARI-D	JUN 6	TAU-D	APR 27	GEM-D	APR 22	ARI-D
MAY 2	TAU-D	JUL 6	GEM-D	MAY 21	CAN-D	MAY 17	TAU-D
MAY 26	GEM-D	AUG 2	CAN-D	JUN 16	LEO-D	JUN 11	GEM-D
JUN 20	CAN-D	AUG 28	LEO-D	JUL 12	VIR-D	JUL 6	CAN-D
JUL 14	LEO-D	SEP 22	VIR-D	AUG 8	LIB-D	JUL 30	LEO-D
AUG 8	VIR-D	OCT 16	LIB-D	SEP 8	SCO-D	AUG 23	VIR-D
SEP 1	LIB-D	NOV 9	SCO-D	OCT 13	SCO-R	SEP 16	LIB-D
SEP 25	SCO-D	DEC 3	SAG-D	NOV 23	SCO-D	OCT 11	SCO-D
OCT 20	SAG-D	DEC 27	CAP-D			NOV 4	SAG-D
NOV 14	CAP-D					NOV 28	CAP-D
DEC 9	AQU-D					DEC 22	AQU-D

1996			1997			1998			1999		
JAN	15	PIS-D	JAN	11	CAP-D	JAN	10	CAP-R	JAN	5	AQU-D
FEB	9	ARI-D	FEB	3	AQU-D	FEB	5	CAP-D	JAN	29	PIS-D
MAR	6	TAU-D	FEB	27	PIS-D	MAR	5	AQU-D	FEB	22	ARI-D
APR	4	GEM-D	MAR	24	ARI-D	APR	7	PIS-D	MAR	19	TAU-D
MAY	20	GEM-D	APR	17	TAU-D	MAY	4	ARI-D	APR	13	GEM-D
JUL	2	GEM-D	MAY	11	GEM-D	MAY	30	TAU-D	MAY	9	CAN-D
AUG	8	CAN-D	JUN	4	CAN-D	JUN	25	GEM-D	JUN	6	LEO-D
SEP	7	LEO-D	JUN	29	LEO-D	JUL	20	CAN-D	JUL	13	VIR-D
OCT	4	VIR-D	JUL	24	VIR-D	AUG	14	LEO-D	JUL	30	VIR-R
OCT	30	LIB-D	AUG	18	LIB-D	SEP	7	VIR-D	AUG	16	LEO-R
NOV	23	SCO-D	SEP	12	SCO-D	OCT	1	LIB-D	SEP	11	LEO-D
DEC	18	SAG-D	OCT	9	SAG-D	OCT	25	SCO-D	OCT	8	VIR-D
			NOV	6	CAP-D	NOV	18	SAG-D	NOV	9	LIB-D
			DEC	12	AQU-D	DEC	12	CAP-D	DEC	6	SCO-D
			DEC	26	AQU-R				DEC	31	SAG-D

2000			2001			2002			2003		
JAN	25	CAP-D	JAN	4	PIS-D	JAN	19	AQU-D	JAN	8	SAG-D
FEB	18	AQU-D	FEB	3	ARI-D	FEB	12	PIS-D	FEB	5	CAP-D
MAR	14	PIS-D	MAR	9	ARI-R	MAR	8	ARI-D	MAR	3	AQU-D
APR	7	ARI-D	APR	20	ARI-D	APR	2	TAU-D	MAR	28	PIS-D
MAY	1	TAU-D	JUN	7	TAU-D	APR	26	GEM-D	APR	22	ARI-D
MAY	26	GEM-D	JUL	6	GEM-D	MAY	21	CAN-D	MAY	17	TAU-D
JUN	19	CAN-D	AUG	2	CAN-D	JUN	15	LEO-D	JUN	10	GEM-D
JUL	14	LEO-D	AUG	27	LEO-D	JUL	11	VIR-D	JUL	5	CAN-D
AUG	7	VIR-D	SEP	21	VIR-D	AUG	8	LIB-D	JUL	29	LEO-D
AUG	31	LIB-D	OCT	16	LIB-D	SEP	8	SCO-D	UG	23	VIR-D
SEP	25	SCO-D	NOV	9	SCO-D	OCT	10	SCO-R	SEP	16	LIB-D
OCT	20	SAG-D	DEC	3	SAG-D	NOV	21	SCO-D	OCT	10	SCO-D
NOV	13	CAP-D	DEC	27	CAP-D				NOV	3	SAG-D
DEC	9	AQU-D							NOV	27	CAP-D
									DEC	22	AQU-D

2004			2005			2006			2007		
JAN	15	PIS-D	JAN	10	CAP-D	JAN	2	CAP-R	JAN	4	AQU-D
FEB	9	ARI-D	FEB	3	AQU-D	FEB	3	CAP-D	JAN	28	PIS-D
MAR	6	TAU-D	FEB	27	PIS-D	MAR	6	AQU-D	FEB	22	ARI-D
APR	4	GEM-D	MAR	23	ARI-D	APR	6	PIS-D	MAR	18	TAU-D
MAY	17	GEM-R	APR	16	TAU-D	MAY	4	ARI-D	APR	12	GEM-D
JUN	29	GEM-D	MAY	10	GEM-D	MAY	30	TAU-D	MAY	9	CAN-D
AUG	8	CAN-D	JUN	4	CAN-D	JUN	24	GEM-D	JUN	6	LEO-D
SEP	7	LEO-D	JUN	29	LEO-D	JUL	19	CAN-D	JUL	15	VIR-D
OCT	4	VIR-D	JUL	23	vIR-D	AUG	13	LEO-D	JUL	27	VIR-R
OCT	29	LIB-D	AUG	17	LIB-D	SEP	7	VIR-D	AUG	9	LEO-R
NOV	23	SCO-D	SEP	12	SCO-D	OCT	1	LIB-D	SEP	8	LEO-D
DEC	17	SAG-D	OCT	8	SAG-D	OCT	25	SCO-D	OCT	9	VIR-D
			NOV	6	CAP-D	NOV	18	SAG-D	NOV	9	LIB-D
			DEC	15	AQU-D	DEC	12	cAP-D	DEC	6	SCO-D
			DEC	24	AQU-R				DEC	31	SAG-D

2008			2009			2010			2011		
JAN	25	CAP-D	JAN	4	PIS-D	JAN	19	AQU-D	JAN	8	SAG-D
FEB	18	AQU-D	FEB	3	ARI-D	FEB	12	PIS-D	FEB	5	CAP-D
MAR	13	PIS-D	MAR	6	ARI-R	MAR	8	ARI-D	MAR	2	AQU-D
APR	7	ARI-D	APR	12	PIS-R	APR	1	TAU-D	MAR	28	PIS-D
MAY	1	TAU-D	APR	17	PIS-D	APR	25	GEM-D	APR	21	ARI-D
MAY	25	GEM-D	APR	25	ARI-D	MAY	20	CAN-D	MAY	15	TAU-D
JUN	19	CAN-D	JUN	7	TAU-D	JUN	15	LEO-D	JUN	10	GEM-D
JUL	13	LEO-D	JUL	6	GEM-D	JUL	11	VIR-D	JUL	4	CAN-D
AUG	6	VIR-D	AUG	1	CAN-D	AUG	7	LIB-D	JUL	29	LEO-D
AUG	31	LIB-D	AUG	27	LEO-D	SEP	9	SCO-D	AUG	22	VIR-D
SEP	24	SCO-D	SEP	21	VIR-D	OCT	8	SCO-R	SEP	15	LIB-D
OCT	19	SAG-D	OCT	15	LIB-D	NOV	8	LIB-R	OCT	10	SCO-D
NOV	13	CAP-D	NOV	8	SCO-D	NOV	18	LIB-D	NOV	3	SAG-D
DEC	8	AQU-D	DEC	2	SAG-D	NOV	30	SCO-D	NOV	27	CAP-D
			DEC	26	CAP-D				DEC	21	AQU-D

2012			2013			2014			2015		
JAN	15	PIS-D	JAN	9	CAP-D	JAN	31	CAP-D	JAN	4	AQU-D
FEB	9	ARI-D	FEB	2	AQU-D	MAR	6	AQU-D	JAN	28	PIS-D
MAR	6	TAU-D	FEB	26	PIS-D	APR	6	PIS-D	FEB	21	ARI-D
APR	4	GEM-D	MAR	22	ARI-D	MAY	3	ARI-D	MAR	18	TAU-D
MAY	15	GEM-R	APR	16	TAU-D	MAY	29	TAU-D	APR	12	GEM-D
JUN	27	GEM-D	MAY	10	GEM-D	JUN	24	GEM-D	MAY	8	CAN-D
AUG	8	CAN-D	JUN	3	CAN-D	JUL	19	CAN-D	JUN	6	LEO-D
SEP	7	LEO-D	JUN	28	LEO-D	AUG	13	LEO-D	JUL	19	VIR-D
OCT	4	VIR-D	JUL	23	VIR-D	SEP	6	VIR-D	JUL	25	VIR-R
OCT	29	LIB-D	AUG	17	LIB-D	SEP	30	LIB-D	AUG	1	LEO-R
NOV	22	SCO-D	SEP	12	SCO-D	OCT	24	SCO-D	SEP	6	LEO-D
DEC	16	SAG-D	OCT	8	SAG-D	NOV	17	SAG-D	OCT	9	VIR-D
			NOV	6	CAP-D	DEC	11	CAP-D	NOV	9	LIB-D
			DEC	21	CAP-R				DEC	5	SCO-D
									DEC	31	SAG-D

2016			2017			2018			2019		
JAN	24	CAP-D	JAN	4	PIS-D	JAN	18	AQU-D	JAN	8	SAG-D
FEB	17	AQU-D	FEB	4	ARI-D	FEB	11	PIS-D	FEB	4	CAP-D
MAR	13	PIS-D	MAR	4	ARI-R	MAR	7	ARI-D	MAR	2	AQU-D
APR	6	ARI-D	APR	3	PIS-R	MAR	31	TAU-D	MAR	27	PIS-D
APR	30	TAU-D	APR	15	PIS-D	APR	25	GEM-D	APR	21	ARI-D
MAY	25	GEM-D	APR	29	ARI-D	MAY	20	CAN-D	MAY	16	TAU-D
JUN	18	CAN-D	JUN	7	TAU-D	JUN	14	LEO-D	JUN	9	GEM-D
JUL	13	LEO-D	JUL	5	GEM-D	JUL	10	VIR-D	JUL	4	CAN-D
AUG	6	VIR-D	AUG	1	CAN-D	AUG	7	LIB-D	JUL	28	LEO-D
AUG	30	LIB-D	AUG	26	LEO-D	SEP	10	SCO-D	AUG	22	VIR-D
SEP	24	SCO-D	SEP	20	VIR-D	OCT	5	SCO-R	SEP	15	LIB-D
OCT	19	SAG-D	OCT	15	LIB-D	NOV	1	LIB-R	OCT	9	SCO-D
NOV	12	CAP-D	NOV	8	SCO-D	NOV	16	LIB-D	NOV	2	SAG-D
DEC	8	AQU-D	DEC	2	SAG-D	DEC	3	SCO-D	NOV	26	CAP-D
			DEC	26	CAP-D				DEC	21	AQU-D

2020			2021			2022			2023		
JAN	14	PIS-D	JAN	9	CAP-D	JAN	30	CAP-D	JAN	3	AQU-D
FEB	8	ARI-D	FEB	2	AQU-D	MAR	7	AQU-D	JAN	27	PIS-D
MAR	5	TAU-D	FEB	26	PIS-D	APR	6	PIS-D	FEB	21	ARI-D
APR	4	GEM-D	MAR	22	ARI-D	MAY	3	ARI-D	MAR	17	TAU-D
MAY	13	GEM-R	APR	15	TAU-D	MAY	29	TAU-D	APR	11	GEM-D
JUN	25	GEM-D	MAY	9	GEM-D	JUN	23	GEM-D	MAY	8	CAN-D
AUG	8	cAN-D	JUN	3	CAN-D	JUL	18	CAN-D	JUN	6	LEO-D
SEP	7	LEO-D	JUN	27	LEO-D	AUG	12	LEO-D	JUL	23	LEO-R
OCT	3	VIR-D	JUL	22	VIR-D	SEP	5	VIR-D	SEP	4	LEO-D
OCT	28	LIB-D	AUG	16	LIB-D	SEP	30	LIB-D	OCT	9	VIR-D
NOV	22	SCO-D	SEP	11	SCO-D	OCT	24	SCO-D	NOV	9	LIB-D
DEC	16	SAG-D	OCT	8	SAG-D	NOV	17	SAG-D	DEC	5	SCO-D
			NOV	6	CAP-D	DEC	10	CAP-D	DEC	30	SAG-D
			DEC	19	CAP-R						

2024			2025		
JAN	24	CAP-D	JAN	3	PIS-D
FEB	17	AQU-D	FEB	5	ARI-D
MAR	12	PIS-D	MAR	2	ARI-R
APR	5	ARI-D	MAR	28	PIS-R
APR	30	TAU-D	APR	13	PIS-D
MAY	24	GEM-D	MAY	1	ARI-D
JUN	18	CAN-D	JUN	6	TAU-D
JUL	12	LEO-D	JUL	5	GEM-D
AUG	5	VIR-D	JUL	31	CAN-D
AUG	30	LIB-D	AUG	26	LEO-D
SEP	23	SCO-D	SEP	20	VIR-D
OCT	18	SAG-D	OCT	14	LIB-D
NOV	12	CAP-D	NOV	7	SCO-D
DEC	8	AQU-D	DEC	1	SAG-D
			DEC	25	CAP-D

Children with Venus in A

Aries represents the sign of self—it is number one, so when Venus is placed here the individual tends to think more about their own satisfaction. They are inclined to be more into receiving than giving in almost everything, including love and affection. Lessons for these natives to learn are cooperation, compromise, and how to put themselves in the other person's place! They tend to want things their own way. If you teach them early to share more, they will become less abrasive to others.

The nature of Aries is *fiery* and *aggressive*, not blending well with the gentle, passive, and receptive nature of Venus. This is easy to understand when you remember that Mars is the natural ruler of Aries as Venus is of Libra—and that these two signs *oppose* each other in the zodiac just as Mars and Venus naturally oppose each other. Therefore, this placement creates an interesting challenge — to learn to balance between these conflicting forces!

These children sometimes put too little effort into making friends, and those they do make may be hard to keep. They can be quite touchy, easily offended, and often inconsiderate. Help them to think of other people's feelings and what *others* might need or want. Socially they may have the same problem as they make little effort to be popular and can sometimes be even rude.

They value their independence and will dislike being tied down by any person or situation. If they feel uncomfortable they simply leave. Some people will consider them unstable because they are so impulsive and changeable in their relationships — unless there is something else in their chart to compensate, or they learn to understand this tendency and choose to change it.

Like all fire signs, Aries has lots of energy and can be *passionate* when motivated. These children are dynamic and experimental. They like the *color red* and music which has high energy, like marches, or classical Rachmaninoff — who was Aries Sun! In art they like anything with action, such as mobiles. They won't value money for security reasons only for how it can serve them to get what they want. Also, the value of any possession is short-lived as they will move quickly on to something else they will want. As you can see, this is not an easy placement to contend with and these natives will need much guidance. Consider these children as a crude stone... and you are going to help them smooth their rough edges and polish themselves to a warm and loving glow.

Children with Venus in Taurus

Since Venus rules Taurus, she is now at home. Her energy is expressed here in a very earthly manner. These natives have a natural love of Mother Earth.

These are the children who will stop and smell the flowers. Although they are passive and somewhat *shy*, they generally won't seek out others to love. When it does come to them as it usually does, they give their *love easily*. Actually they crave all forms of touching, caressing, hugging, and kissing. They are extremely *affectionate*, sensual, and require physical contact. Don't be surprised if when young, they will toddle over to anyone.

These children are fond of *comfort* and enjoy *luxury*. An excessive focus on the same can create overindulgence or even laziness. They have an innate sense of what makes "value." They seem to be magnets for prosperity and good fortune. *Possessions* are important to them, especially those which contribute to their comfort and pleasure. They like money and the luxury that it can provide. They are usually socially adept and will want to participate in functions which provide entertainment and which gratify their pleasure principle. They are *loyal* in both love relationships and in friendships. They may have a tendency to hold onto or become overly attached to people which could cause problems. Help them to become aware and to overcome this tendency by teaching them to love with an open hand.

These Venus in Taurus natives are creative in the fields of finance and real estate and also in any area which has to do with luxury — such as jewelry, furs, fine restaurants, or entertainment. Their appreciation for beauty and art is usually with items which are useful or have value. They have a need for and a great love of music, usually romantic. They are stubbornly steadfast in their pursuit of their needs and usually acquire more than most. This is a good placement for Venus, as she is able to express all of her benefits in a physical earthly manner.

Children with Venus in Gemini

Children who have Venus placed in Gemini will express their love verbally and in a light, airy manner. They are able to share with a large number of people as long as they can keep the exchange on a surface level. They find it *difficult to become involved* with deep emotional intensity or to form strong attachments. The responsibility and also the restriction which go along with getting close to others is not comfortable for them. These children do not display a great deal of emotion and will not appreciate it when others do. They are common-sense oriented and logical, and will respect actions that are based on the same. As their parent or caregiver or teacher, you will accomplish most by staying cool and logical, in control of yourself. When you use this approach, you will create a cooperative admirer.

Venus in Gemini is the bright, witty social butterfly. These children flit from flower to flower blessing each one with their charm... and the more the better. The motto here is — "Variety is the spice of life." These natives make friends easily and are attracted to a multitude of types. They seem to understand and tolerate the differences in people because they enjoy *diversity*. The mundane is boring to them and won't be tolerated long. Since these children have such a strong need for people and social interaction, they are happiest and at their best when in contact with others.

You will find Venus in mercurial Gemini delightfully *humorous* and very entertaining. All mental stimulation gives them great pleasure and they will know a little bit about a lot of things. They love to communicate because their interests are unlimited. They value words and the way they are used, respecting and appreciating articulate expression in all forms. They are lively, entertaining, and make great companions as long as the other person doesn't want or need attachment. These children will enjoy traveling from place to place, and from thing to thing, both literally and figuratively. A change of surroundings is always refreshing to them. *Their lessons are to learn steadfastness, as well as to develop loyalty and dependability.* Their simple creative abilities could be well utilized as writers, teachers, actors, and public speakers. Make sure that they avoid long periods of isolation as this may cause some form of repression, even depression. Finally, have fun exposing your Venus in Gemini child to new types of social activities, new ways of learning, and all forms of artistic pursuit.

Children with Venus in Cancer

As with all water signs, there is great sensitivity when Venus is placed in Cancer. The need for love and affection is strong. These children *need parental affection* more than most, especially from their mother. They are very demonstrative and will need to have affection returned. They are good at giving emotional support to others and will require great amounts for themselves. These natives require large doses of reassurance because if they feel unloved or insecure they can become timid and withdrawn. Sometimes this may result from and lead to sibling rivalry. These children are too dependent on others for their security, especially their parents, and later their mate. Be sure to show your love for them often, and teach them to learn to be less needy and more emotionally self-reliant.

Individuals with this placement are naturals at mothering others, sometimes even to the extent that they may be smothering. (If immature at *any age*, they could have a selfish need for the flip side of that — to be always babied.) They have a tendency to hold on to relationships long after it would have been better to let go. These children do not need a large number of friends; they will be happy with a few good ones. Generally Venus in Cancer are good friends to have be-cause they are sensitive to other people's needs and will not hurt others, unless hurt first — but since they are hurt too easily themselves, they won't want to hurt anyone.

Socially these children are apt to be a little shy and retiring. In fact, they may not want to participate in social activities at all. They are more comfortable in their own home. They feel more secure when sur-rounded by their own belongings. Don't be surprised if these children resist leaving home to go to school. For these young ones, be sure to familiarize them with the school they will be attending before the first day.

These children are inclined to use their creative abilities in domestic areas such as *home decorating* and *gourmet cooking*. They are attracted to art work which activates sentiment within themselves. They will want their environments to be cozy and safe like the shell of the crab. Sometimes these natives become excellent business people (often preferring to operate a business out of their homes), because they value money for the security it can bring. This security is important to them — if they don't receive enough love as a child, they could later hold on too *tightly* to money. Teach them that security lies in the heart, not in the pocket.

Nurture well the children with this Venus in Can-cer placement... to encourage them to shed their pro-tective shell and to love more open-heartedly... to be-come as they develop, more adventuresome about life.

Children with Venus in Leo

Venus expresses her love and affections with great gusto and flair in the fiery sign of Leo. These natives are truly the *lovers of life*. These children are gregarious, demonstrative types, having no difficulty expressing how they feel or in lavishing others with affection. They are dramatic and are born *romantics*. They are warm-hearted and *loyal* in close relationships and also in friendships. They will have many friends as they are the actors who need a large audience. They want to be, and usually are, very popular wherever they go. They also have a tendency to choose people for associates who will make them look good. They prefer to give and attend social events which are glamorous and theatrical, expensive and lavish... befitting any king of the jungle! They often become the entertainment at these gatherings as they are always ready to be on stage and in the spotlight. It will be obvious that they take great pride in all that they do, both personally and socially.

Children with Venus placed in Leo *value money for the luxury and glamour it can provide*. Their choice of possessions runs to the expensive, often extravagant, and they will want to have them in abundance. They will appreciate all of *your grand gestures* to them with money — and, they will be willing to work for anything they might want, and are usually quite capable of doing whatever is necessary to acquire it.

These children are blessed with many creative talents expressed in numerous areas and in a royal fashion! One of their finest attributes is the ability to inspire others. They are *masters at stimulating enthusiasm,* and are gifted at helping others to become their very best. They enjoy being around children and can become great motivators when working with them. These children are outgoing, warm, entertaining personalities who will undoubtedly bring great sparkle to your days.

Children with Venus in Virgo

This is a challenging place for Venus because her energies have difficulty integrating with the mental, analytical characteristics of Virgo. Since Virgo, ruled by Mercury, *thinks* everything and the energy of Venus is *feeling,* there is difficulty in expressing her Venusian characteristics well. This combination interferes with and hinders spontaneous loving and giving. These natives may not even understand love, or at the very least will have trouble expressing it. *To learn how to give and receive, plus eventually feel love, is the most important lesson for this placement.* They are inclined to show their love and friendship by doing things for others because they have a strong desire to serve. These children also need to learn to love themselves as they often feel undeserving, and they underestimate their own worth. Help them with this as early as possible.

This is the placement of the *perfectionist*. These children can be quite critical. Occasionally we find one that is not neat, clean, and orderly — but not often. These natives have such high standards, they are apt to face many disappointments. They need to learn that by having impossible expectations they put themselves and others through unnecessary frustration. Teach them that imperfection is part of being human — and is all in the way one looks at it — that everything has its own beauty just the way it is. Have them learn the saying, "Don't try to change the world — change the way you look at it."

These children are *shy* and retiring personalities and have difficulty making friends easily. They *lack confidence* and are uneasy in social situations. You will help them immensely if you will teach them the social graces and prepare them adequately for any social occasion they may be required to experience. This will strengthen their confidence and help them to find more pleasure at any gathering. If they don't learn to lovingly relate to *people* early in their lives, they may repress their affections completely, expending these affections on animals, or using this energy in their work. These children do *like to work* as they can avoid personal contact with other people this way. (They can develop into touch-me-nots!) In fact they can become all work and no play. Help them to have fun and enjoy the pleasures of life and the stimulation of other people.

Venus in Virgo children may have di[...]
seeing art and beauty as a whole because the[...] ....
each part individually and analyze it. *They are born
critics.* They have a natural ability to express themselves
in words. Some of our most famous literary and social
critics have had this placement. Any craft or artistic
project they undertake will be done to perfection as
they are good with their hands. They may become *good
seamstresses or fashion designers, woodworkers, or food
planners* because of their interest in health and the
body.

Basically most of their lessons can be learned by
developing humbleness, tolerance, and forgiveness of
others for their human failings — and by accepting
themselves for being just slightly less than perfect.
Remember to praise them for whatever they do!

Children with Venus in Libra

Since Libra is one of the two signs that Venus
rules, her energy is expressed most naturally and com-
fortably when placed here. These children possess all
of the refinement and charm for which Venus is noted,
and they are easily offended by any coarseness and
uncouth behavior.

Since Libra is an air sign, they are stimulated
through mental activity as are all air signs. They are
especially adept at communicating in one-to-one situations. They make wonderful *counselors* because they

see both sides of situations and will present ways to resolve differences and create harmony. They also have the ability to say things in a way that is pleasing and comfortable for others; never offensive or intimidating, which makes what they say easier to accept.

This sign placement represents the masters of cooperation, for they are definitely *people-oriented*. For these children, *sharing* love is second nature, wishing to please others and to be pleasing themselves. They are usually very attractive and present themselves with classic style.

Relationship is a primary goal for all Libra placements, and with Venus here it is accentuated. These natives do not like to be alone. They must have others around them most of the time. They thrive on the feedback from others, needing to reflect off of others in order to know themselves. This is an area to watch carefully because this need is so strong they have a tendency to become too dependent on other people. They also may attract people who will use, to their own advantage, Venus in Libras' willingness to openly share.

There is an eternal naivete and trust about them which can lead to heartache. It is important these overly-pleasing children learn to be themselves in all friendships as well as in all close relationships. They need to be sure that they are receiving as much as they are giving in all of their personal exchanges. Too often they want to avoid conflict at all costs because discord can sometimes affect their health, and they have a horror of being rude or offensive to anyone. Remind them that the extreme people-pleaser can become a sick door mat. Venus Librans, when they have reached their breaking point with someone, never say a word — they just close the door and disappear.

As well as harmonious relationships, these children value a pleasant active social life, and a beautiful peaceful environment. They will choose friends who are intellectually stimulating and who have good social manners. They place high priority on social know-how, which therefore, makes them excellent hosts and hostesses. They have a good aesthetical sense with a natural instinct for color and design, and are talented in many areas which include: art, literature (poetry!), music, fashion, entertainment, and counseling. *They make good caterers, restaurant owners, home decorators, social directors, and ambassadors.* Encourage these adaptable, loving children to eliminate the tendency for indecision and settle on a direction that will benefit themselves as well as others.

Children with Venus in Scorpio

The love of Venus placed in the sign of Scorpio is expressed with extreme intensity. These children have *powerful and deep feelings*, penetrating to the core of their beings. There is nothing lukewarm or moderate about these natives; it is always all or nothing. In the few close relationships which they form, they will be warmly affectionate, and must feel trust and loyalty for that other person, and visa versa. They are not good at speaking their feelings which may appear as if they are secretive and calculating about them. This is not always true. Sometimes the feelings are too deep for words, and sometimes they haven't yet figured out what they feel — they just know they *have* these strong feelings.

There may be some challenges in their relationships because they have a *need to control*. Some natives with this placement are very possessive. Any relationships which these children have, including friendships, will always be intense...never superficial. They either like someone very much or not at all.

In social situations they like to stay in the background so they can observe everyone, quietly studying the behavior of others like a master sleuth looking for clues. They also have a tendency to ignore and dismiss people with whom they are not involved, or who seem too bland or uninteresting. They can be quite abrupt and rude about this — and do not suffer as fools if they can help it!

These Venus in Scorpio children *value the honor and power which comes with financial success, which in turn motivates them to accomplish and achieve a great deal.* They have strong personal pride and conduct themselves with dignity. They are shrewd and reserved and make excellent business people.

These natives have a dramatic taste in art, loving black and whites, red and blacks, and artwork which has sharp design. In their environment they prefer decor with clean, angular lines. They may have a flair for modern art if they choose to use these creative abilities. Some of these natives have been powerful *writers*, others great *composers*. Whatever they do, it's done intensely — but be careful it doesn't become obsessive!

You can help these children by becoming aware of their deep sensitivity and by teaching them to be less suspicious, to not always look for a dark motive. Also watch for a cruel side and *teach them to treat others as they would like to be treated.* They are intensely magnetic... they can draw both good and bad into their lives. Teach them to discriminate — and not just plunge into a relationship with something or someone who intrigues them. If properly guided, these children can bring much benefit to the world.

Children with Venus in Sagittarius

Since Sagittarius is a fire sign, Venus placed here is outgoing and friendly. There is always a certain amount of gusto with all of the fire signs and Sagittarius is no exception. These children have no difficulty expressing their affections and will *love spontaneous giving and receiving.* They are very outspoken about telling you how they feel, being direct and honest... and will appreciate others who also are to the point. In fact they *value honesty* so much that they will end any friendship or relationship in which there is deceit.

They also will have difficulty with people who try to restrict them in any way, as they have no tolerance for possessive types. They place a *high value on their freedom* and cannot be forced or pressured into commitments of any kind. The result of any attempt is that they will bolt — they need a wide berth to decide for themselves.

The friends these Venus in Sagittarius children choose most likely will have similar religious or philosophical beliefs... or will need to have an open mind about these beliefs. There is a strong need for associates with whom they can have lively discussions and share their hypotheses, since they are very sociable and enjoy the interaction with others.

In matters of art and creativity, these natives appreciate natural art forms and in bigger-than-life sizes. They love anything which is done in grand style or with flamboyant colors — their tastes may be *extravagant*, and they are sometimes called the *gamblers*. They are often attracted to art which relates to religion or pieces from Greek or Roman history. These children take pleasure participating in almost all sports and particularly those which are individualistic such as horseback riding, tennis, skiing, mountain climbing, and hiking. They handle their money and their possessions with an easy-come-easy-go manner, being generous and impulsive with regards to giving and spending. You could teach them a little discipline in both these areas. Basically you should have great fun with Venus in Sagittarius children — especially if you remember to give them their freedom.

Children with Venus in Capricorn

This is another challenging sign placement for Venus. In the cautious, conservative sign of Capricorn, the love and affection expressions of Venus are restricted and withheld for Capricorns are very reserved when it comes to expressing their feelings. They are *not demonstrative* and are not fond of gregarious excessive-type personalities. They keep their feelings under control because they have a fear of being hurt. Since Capricorn is an earth sign, these natives need tangible assurance from others to trust or believe that it is safe for them to open their hearts and minds. They exercise great control over their desires, and simply won't allow themselves to become self-indulgent. However, when they do feel safe they will enjoy the pleasure of tactile exchanges.

These children *value prestige and status*. Socially they will do whatever is required to obtain positions of authority and recognition. They may even use their friends to get ahead, and will usually choose those individuals who will be helpful. You will not find them associating with frivolous or irresponsible people, or

attending a gathering just for the fun of a party; they
have a secondary agenda in mind. They are often attracted to older, more mature people because they not
only want to draw on their experience and wisdom,
they also seem to feel more comfortable with them.
When they do establish a close friendship it will last,
as they are *loyal and willing to take on personal responsibility.*

These Venus in Capricorn children *value money
because they want the control* that it brings to them. They
may not appreciate art for its own sake because they
value only that which is useful... unless, of course, the
object brings them recognition and prestige! They respect and have creative abilities which produce beauty
in practical, useful results such as carpentry, furniture-
making, or metal-working. They enjoy the world of
business and are greatly attracted to *politics*, with many
becoming very successful in these arenas.

*The most needed lesson for these natives is to learn
how to extend themselves to others more readily and to
allow themselves to experience the joys and pleasures of life
just for its own sake.*

Children with Venus in Aquarius

This is not one of the most comfortable placements for Venus because the Aquarian instincts are to
be impersonal and aloof. This causes these children to
have *trouble with loving and forming close ties.* Their

loving is usually expressed in the form of detached friendships and for humanity in general. This, of course, does not mean that they are incapable of loving — just that the intensity of a one-to-one involvement is not their natural mode.

These natives *value freedom and independence* to the point that when any relationship becomes restrictive or confining they will drop it. Also, when an association loses its excitement they will look elsewhere, making them rather unpredictable in relationships. In social situations they tend to be themselves, the nonconformist of the group. Their mottoes are: "Take me as I am or not at all," and "What you see is what you get." The good side to this is that they are unique, interesting, and exciting... plus you always know where you stand!

These Venus in Aquarius children are not emotional, sentimental, or interested in tactile touching. They are not the romantics of the zodiac, so don't take it personally if they appear detached. Their stimulation is usually mental and comes from the excitement of learning or experiencing something new and different. *Originality* is one of their strong points and they will demonstrate plenty of it. This placement can be drawn to modern art, and they are *entrepreneurs* who pursue originality to create new means and methods. Their minds are quick, inventive, and unconventional in style. They are apt to find their pleasures in the act of discovery, so be prepared. Help them direct their search in areas that will be useful to humanity, and do be patient with their idiosyncrasies.

Children with Venus in Pisces

Venus in Pisces children are filled with love and empathy which they are quite willing to share with the world. They have no difficulty expressing how they feel or giving what they have. They feel so much tenderness and compassion for all, that one lesson which they *need to learn is to be more discerning about whom they choose to love*. Sometimes they are too interested in "saving" someone, regardless of that person's desire to change. And they are so willing to serve others that they could find themselves the victim of abusive types — whether mental, emotional, or worse. Help them to guard against any of this by becoming *selective* — to feel a little less and think a little more before "falling" in love.

These children are truly the *romantics* and *poets*. They are inspired by all artistic creativity. They are very talented in this area as they have vision and a very creative imagination. They visualize easily and need to be motivated to put their ideas into concrete form, so encourage them to take action! — to write the poem or book, to paint the picture.

These natives are *supersensitive*, both for others and for themselves. They can be easily hurt emotionally and can have difficulty coping with that pain, so they need much reassurance and a sensitive ear. They appreciate touching and caressing in all forms, and they are big huggers and kissers! They usually make friends easily even though they may be a little shy at first, and they are pleasant and amiable. They are not likely to rock the boat or take control in any situation, including their relationships.

Children with this Venus in Pisces placement have values and ideals not geared to this Earth — and sometimes they may feel that they don't even belong here! They have very little use for money, rich people, or material possessions... being more interested in the "real" person and in feelings. These children have a beautiful spiritual nature which will be a pleasure to experience. Help them learn how to protect themselves from less sensitive types so they can safely and freely express the very beautiful side of themselves.

"Nature has given us astrology as an adjunct and ally to astronomy."
Johannes Kepler, 17th century astronomer

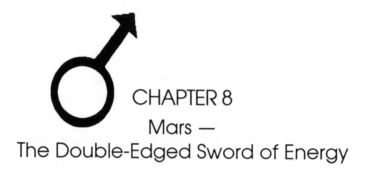

CHAPTER 8
Mars —
The Double-Edged Sword of Energy

*M*ars is energy! It is masculine, physical en ergy... it is assertive energy... it is creative energy. His energy is the fuel supply for the Sun. It might be said that Mars is the Sun's right-hand man. Mars stimulates "action" which causes reaction, which stimulates growth. He represents the ability to express individuality, telling us about an individual's get-up-and-go. Mars also represents deepest conflicts and greatest challenges... what turns us on, and what mo-tivates us. He assists in expressing where the greatest drive and ambition will be focused in the self... where each one will take initiative and lead. The sign that Mars is in tells "how" the energy is expressed.

Like everything else in this world there is a beneficial and a non-beneficial expression. Mars is a two-edged sword — he is the warrior able to attack and/or to defend. His energy is like fire... it can either warm or burn... and it needs to be used constructively or it can cause much destruction. Some words used to describe Mars are — *aggressive, protective, restless, initiative, combative, courageous and, of course, impatience, action, and energy. Patience is the biggest lesson of Mars.* If your child has a strong Mars placement, to help them learn this lesson will be one of your greatest tasks.

Another important factor which will be helpful — since Mars rules anger, don't be too upset if your child expresses this anger, just be happy that they are able to get it out. Do teach them not to be destructive or abusive with it. *Mars also rules sex and sports, and its placement shows how that energy will be expended or controlled. Children with high energy levels need to be encouraged to participate in competitive sports.* Contact sports are especially good because they seem to satisfy the need for physical encounters which might otherwise lead to early sexual activities. A serious interest in a sport can often satisfy these early strong sexual drives. And for all sign placements in Mars, some sports should be encouraged — for the health of mind and body, to learn fair play, and to understand the value of teamwork.

Mars is the planet which tells us about our physical world, and the placement tells the what and why's as well as how action will be taken. Mars is the need to express oneself unconditionally, without restriction. Only the non-beneficial or uncontrolled expressions of Mars should have to be moderated or redirected, for there is *always* a positive outlet for this energy. Guide your child into using their Mars energy constructively.

Mars Retrograde

When Mars is retrograde at birth, its energy is restricted and turned inward, causing a lack of spontaneous expression. The energy of Mars may be just as strong but it is short-circuited in its output. Since Mars deals with anger, if it can't be expressed outwardly, it will be turned inwardly. We all know that pent-up anger is dangerous and unpredictable. It can cause not only frustration, but an inability to defend oneself (necessary for survival!), and can cause depression, physical illness, even accidents. There is also a fear of letting go that can build to a point where there is no control — the energy is stuffed and then explodes. It will be very important as a parent or caregiver to teach retrograde Mars children how to express this energy in a positive way and as soon as it is felt — so that it doesn't internalize or build. This can be done by providing these children with creative projects, or healthy physical activities.

The biggest problem you will have is that retrograde Mars children usually won't have the necessary motivation, and you will have to supply the stimulation using your creative imagination. This lack of motivation can stem from a physical source — the adrenalin production may be slow, or the oxidation and metabolic process sluggish — as well as from a psychological cause. Mars retrogrades are lacking in initiative and are not inclined to be competitive, since these children are filled with self- doubt and they fear taking risks. They will need to hear statements such as: "It's not the "winning" that is so important, it's the "doing" that counts," and that, "Winners are just those who are willing to risks because they are *not afraid of failure.*"

Most of their battles take place on an internal level — constantly competing with themselves, and becoming angry to boot! They need to know that anger is a normal human function which can be acknowledged and handled. It is not healthy to self-inflict or repress these feelings, so get these children to write about what they are thinking and feeling inside, to alleviate a build-up of negative energy.

Teach these children that they will have to put a little more extra effort into using their Mars than most people, and to *not feel defeated* before they start. They need to know that every living person has their own personal difficulties to deal with. Once they are able to handle and express energy constructively, it will no longer be a point of concern.

How To Use Mars Tables

Find the year of Birth on the following pages. Next locate the month under that year. The dates listed indicate the day Mars moves into a sign. It stays in that sign until the next date is listed.

Example: In the year 1900 Mars was in Capricorn on January 1, and stayed in Capricorn through January 20. On January 21, it entered Aquarius and stayed in Aquarius through February 28. March 1, it entered Pisces - and so on.

The D and R after the sign indicates whether Mars was Direct or Retrograde. When the R appears it means Mars turned Retrograde on that day and will remain Retrograde until the next date a D appears after the sign.

Example: In the year 1901 Mars turned Retrograde on January 13, and stayed Retrograde through March 1. On March 2, Mars turned Direct again.

SIGNS

ARI	Aries	LIB	Libra
TAU	Taurus	SCO	Scorpio
GEM	Gemini	SAG	Sagittarius
CAN	Cancer	CAP	Capricorn
LEO	Leo	AQU	Aquarius
VIR	Virgo	PIS	Pisces

Mars Tables

1900–1905

1900	1901	1902	1903	1904	1905
JAN 1 CAP-D	JAN 13 VIR-R	JAN 2 AQU-D	JAN 17 LIB-R	JAN 20 PIS-D	JAN 14 SCO-D
JAN 21 AQU-D	MAR 2 LEO-D	FEB 9 PIS-D	APR 20 VIR-R	FEB 28 ARI-D	APR 1 SCO-R
MAR 1 PIS-D	APR 3 LEO-D	MAR 20 ARI-D	MAY 8 VIR-D	APR 7 TAU-D	JUN 16 SCO-D
APR 8 ARI-D	MAY 12 VIR-D	APR 28 TAU-D	MAY 31 LIB-D	MAY 19 GEM-D	AUG 22 SAG-D
MAY 17 TAU-D	JUL 14 LIB-D	JUN 8 GEM-D	AUG 7 SCO-D	JUL 1 CAN-D	OCT 9 CAP-D
JUN 27 GEM-D	AUG 31 SCO-D	JUL 21 CAN-D	SEP 23 SAG-D	AUG 16 LEO-D	NOV 19 AQU-D
AUG 10 CAN-D	OCT 15 SAG-D	SEP 5 LEO-D	NOV 4 CAP-D	OCT 2 VIR-D	DEC 28 PIS-D
SEP 26 LEO-D	NOV 25 CAP-D	OCT 24 VIR-D	DEC 13 AQU-D	NOV 21 LIB-D	
NOV 23 VIR-D		DEC 21 LIB-D			

1906–1911

1906	1907	1908	1909	1910	1911
FEB 5 ARI-D	FEB 6 SAG-D	JAN 12 ARI-D	JAN 11 SAG-D	JAN 24 TAU-D	FEB 1 CAP-D
MAR 18 TAU-D	APR 2 CAP-D	FEB 24 TAU-D	FEB 25 CAP-D	MAR 15 GEM-D	MAR 15 AQU-D
APR 29 GEM-D	JUN 4 CAP-R	APR 8 GEM-D	APR 10 AQU-D	MAY 2 CAN-D	APR 24 PIS-D
JUN 12 CAN-D	AUG 8 CAP-D	MAY 23 CAN-D	MAY 26 PIS-D	JUN 20 LEO-D	JUN 3 ARI-D
JUL 28 LEO-D	OCT 14 AQU-D	JUL 9 LEO-D	JUL 22 ARI-D	AUG 7 VIR-D	JUL 16 TAU-D
SEP 13 VIR-D	NOV 30 PIS-D	AUG 25 VIR-D	AUG 22 ARI-R	SEP 23 LIB-D	SEP 6 GEM-D
OCT 31 LIB-D		OCT 11 LIB-D	SEP 27 PIS-R	NOV 7 SCO-D	OCT 16 GEM-R
DEC 18 SCO-D		NOV 26 SCO-D	OCT 23 PIS-D	DEC 21 SAG-D	DEC 1 TAU-R
			NOV 21 ARI-D		DEC 28 TAU-D

1912–1917

1912	1913	1914	1915	1916	1917
JAN 31 GEM-D	JAN 11 CAP-D	FEB 11 CAN-D	JAN 31 AQU-D	MAR 20 LEO-D	JAN 10 AQU-D
APR 6 CAN-D	FEB 20 AQU-D	MAY 2 LEO-D	MAR 10 PIS-D	MAY 29 VIR-D	FEB 17 PIS-D
MAY 29 LEO-D	MAR 31 PIS-D	JUN 27 VIR-D	APR 17 ARI-D	JUL 24 LIB-D	MAR 27 ARI-D
JUL 18 VIR-D	MAY 9 ARI-D	AUG 15 LIB-D	MAY 27 TAU-D	SEP 9 SCO-D	MAY 5 TAU-D
SEP 3 LIB-D	JUN 18 TAU-D	SEP 30 SCO-D	JUL 7 GEM-D	OCT 23 SAG-D	JUN 15 GEM-D
OCT 19 SCO-D	JUL 30 GEM-D	NOV 12 SAG-D	AUG 20 CAN-D	DEC 2 CAP-D	JUL 29 CAN-D
DEC 1 SAG-D	SEP 16 CAN-D	DEC 23 CAP-D	OCT 8 LEO-D		SEP 13 LEO-D
	NOV 25 CAN-R		DEC 30 LEO-R		NOV 3 VIR-D

1918–1923

1918	1919	1920	1921	1922	1923
JAN 12 LIB-D	JAN 28 PIS-D	FEB 1 SCO-D	JAN 6 PIS-D	FEB 19 SAG-D	JAN 22 ARI-D
FEB 2 LIB-R	MAR 7 ARI-D	MAR 14 SCO-R	FEB 14 ARI-D	MAY 7 SAG-R	MAR 5 TAU-D
FEB 25 VIR-R	APR 16 TAU-D	APR 24 LIB-R	MAR 26 TAU-D	JUL 16 SAG-D	APR 17 GEM-D
APR 24 VIR-D	MAY 27 GEM-D	MAY 30 LIB-D	MAY 7 GEM-D	SEP 14 CAP-D	MAY 31 CAN-D
JUN 24 LIB-D	JUL 9 CAN-D	JUL 11 SCO-D	JUN 19 CAN-D	OCT 31 AQU-D	JUL 17 LEO-D
AUG 18 SCO-D	AUG 24 LEO-D	SEP 5 SAG-D	AUG 4 LEO-D	DEC 12 PIS-D	SEP 2 VIR-D
OCT 2 SAG-D	OCT 11 VIR-D	OCT 19 CAP-D	SEP 20 VIR-D		OCT 19 LIB-D
NOV 12 CAP-D	DEC 1 LIB-D	NOV 28 AQU-D	NOV 7 LIB-D		DEC 5 SCO-D
DEC 21 AQU-D			DEC 27 SCO-D		

1924–1929

1924	1925	1926	1927	1928	1929
JAN 20 SAG-D	FEB 6 TAU-D	FEB 10 CAP-D	FEB 23 GEM-D	JAN 20 CAP-D	JAN 26 GEM-D
MAR 7 CAP-D	MAR 25 GEM-D	MAR 24 AQU-D	APR 18 CAN-D	MAR 1 AQU-D	MAR 10 CAN-D
APR 25 AQU-D	MAY 10 CAN-D	MAY 4 PIS-D	JUN 7 LEO-D	APR 8 PIS-D	MAY 14 LEO-D
JUN 25 PIS-D	JUN 27 LEO-D	JUN 16 ARI-D	JUL 26 VIR-D	MAY 17 ARI-D	JUL 5 VIR-D
JUL 23 PIS-D	AUG 13 VIR-D	AUG 2 TAU-D	SEP 11 LIB-D	JUN 27 TAU-D	AUG 22 LIB-D
AUG 24 AQU-R	SEP 29 LIB-D	SEP 28 TAU-R	OCT 27 SCO-D	AUG 10 GEM-D	OCT 7 SCO-D
SEP 21 AQU-D	NOV 14 SCO-D	DEC 6 TAU-D	DEC 9 SAG-D	OCT 4 CAN-D	NOV 19 SAG-D
OCT 20 PIS-D	DEC 29 SAG-D			NOV 11 CAN-R	DEC 30 CAP-D
DEC 20 ARI-D				DEC 21 GEM-R	

1930		1931		1932		1933		1934		1935	
FEB 7	AQU-D	FEB 17	CAN-R	JAN 19	AQU-D	JAN 20	VIR-R	FEB 5	PIS-D	FEB 26	LIB-R
MAR 18	PIS-D	MAR 7	CAN-D	FEB 26	PIS-D	APR 11	VIR-D	MAR 15	ARI-D	MAY 17	LIB-D
APR 25	ARI-D	MAR 31	LEO-D	APR 4	ARI-D	JUL 7	LIB-D	APR 23	TAU-D	JUL 30	SCO-D
JUN 4	TAU-D	JUN 11	VIR-D	MAY 13	TAU-D	AUG 27	SCO-D	JUN 3	GEM-D	SEP 17	SAG-D
JUL 15	GEM-D	AUG 2	LIB-D	JUN 23	GEM-D	OCT 10	SAG-D	JUL 16	CAN-D	OCT 29	CAP-D
AUG 29	CAN-D	SEP 18	SCO-D	AUG 5	CAN-D	NOV 20	CAP-D	AUG 31	LEO-D	DEC 8	AQU-D
OCT 21	LEO-D	OCT 31	SAG-D	SEP 21	LEO-D	DEC 29	AQU-D	OCT 19	VIR-D		
DEC 17	LEO-R	DEC 11	CAP-D	NOV 14	VIR-D			DEC 12	LIB-D		

1936		1937		1938		1939		1940		1941	
JAN 15	PIS-D	JAN 6	SCO-D	JAN 31	ARI-D	JAN 30	SAG-D	JAN 5	ARI-D	JAN 5	SAG-D
FEB 23	ARI-D	MAR 14	SAG-D	MAR 13	TAU-D	MAR 22	CAP-D	FEB 18	TAU-D	FEB 18	CAP-D
MAY 14	GEM-D	APR 13	SAG-R	APR 24	GEM-D	MAY 26	AQU-D	APR 2	GEM-D	APR 3	AQU-D
JUN 26	CAN-D	MAY 15	SCO-R	JUN 8	CAN-D	JUN 21	AQU-R	MAY 18	CAN-D	MAY 17	PIS-D
AUG 11	LEO-D	JUN 26	SCO-D	JUL 23	LEO-D	JUL 22	CAP-D	JUL 4	LEO-D	JUL 3	ARI-D
SEP 27	VIR-D	AUG 9	SAG-D	SEP 8	VIR-D	AUG 22	CAP-D	AUG 20	VIR-D	SEP 5	ARI-R
NOV 15	LIB-D	OCT 1	CAP-D	OCT 26	LIB-D	SEP 25	AQU-D	OCT 6	LIB-D	NOV 9	ARI-D
		NOV 12	AQU-D	DEC 12	SCO-D	NOV 20	PIS-D	NOV 21	SCO-D		
		DEC 22	PIS-D								

1942		1943		1944		1945		1946		1947	
JAN 12	TAU-D	JAN 27	CAP-D	JAN 9	GEM-D	JAN 6	CAP-D	FEB 21	CAN-D	JAN 26	AQU-D
MAR 8	GEM-D	MAR 9	AQU-D	MAR 29	CAN-D	FEB 15	AQU-D	APR 23	LEO-D	MAR 5	PIS-D
APR 27	CAN-D	APR 18	PIS-D	MAY 23	LEO-D	MAR 26	PIS-D	JUN 21	VIR-D	APR 12	ARI-D
JUN 15	LEO-D	MAY 28	ARI-D	JUL 13	VIR-D	MAY 3	ARI-D	AUG 10	LIB-D	MAY 22	TAU-D
AUG 2	VIR-D	JUL 8	TAU-D	AUG 30	LIB-D	JUN 12	TAU-D	SEP 25	SCO-D	JUL 2	GEM-D
SEP 18	LIB-D	AUG 24	GEM-D	OCT 14	SCO-D	JUL 24	GEM-D	NOV 7	SAG-D	AUG 14	CAN-D
NOV 2	SCO-D	OCT 27	GEM-R	NOV 26	SAG-D	SEP 8	CAN-D	DEC 18	CAP-D	OCT 2	LEO-D
DEC 16	SAG-D					NOV 12	LEO-D			DEC 2	VIR-D
						DEC 3	LEO-R				
						DEC 27	CAN-R				

1948		1949		1950		1951		1952		1953	
JAN 7	VIR-R	JAN 5	AQU-D	FEB 11	LIB-R	JAN 23	PIS-D	JAN 21	SCO-D	FEB 9	ARI-D
FEB 13	LEO-R	FEB 12	PIS-D	MAR 29	VIR-R	MAR 2	ARI-D	MAR 24	SCO-R	MAR 21	TAU-D
MAR 28	LEO-D	MAR 22	ARI-D	MAY 2	VIR-D	APR 11	TAU-D	JUN 9	SCO-D	MAY 2	GEM-D
MAY 19	VIR-D	MAY 1	TAU-D	JUN 12	LIB-D	MAY 22	GEM-D	AUG 28	SAG-D	JUN 15	CAN-D
JUL 18	LIB-D	JUN 11	GEM-D	AUG 11	SCO-D	JUL 4	CAN-D	OCT 13	CAP-D	JUL 30	LEO-D
SEP 4	SCO-D	JUL 24	CAN-D	SEP 26	SAG-D	AUG 19	LEO-D	NOV 22	AQU-D	SEP 15	VIR-D
OCT 18	SAG-D	SEP 8	LEO-D	NOV 7	CAP-D	OCT 6	VIR-D	DEC 31	PIS-D	NOV 2	LIB-D
NOV 27	CAP-D	OCT 28	VIR-D	DEC 16	AQU-D	NOV 25	LIB-D			DEC 21	SCO-D
		DEC 27	LIB-D								

1954		1955		1956		1957		1958		1959	
FEB 10	SAG-D	JAN 16	ARI-D	JAN 15	SAG-D	JAN 29	TAU-D	FEB 4	CAP-D	FEB 11	GEM-D
APR 13	CAP-D	FEB 27	TAU-D	MAR 1	CAP-D	MAR 18	GEM-D	MAR 18	AQU-D	APR 11	CAN-D
MAY 22	CAP-R	APR 11	GEM-D	APR 15	AQU-D	MAY 5	CAN-D	APR 28	PIS-D	JUN 2	LEO-D
JUL 4	SAG-R	MAY 27	CAN-D	JUN 4	PIS-D	JUN 22	LEO-D	JUN 8	ARI-D	JUL 21	VIR-D
JUL 28	SAG-D	JUL 12	LEO-D	AUG 9	PIS-R	AUG 9	VIR-D	JUL 22	TAU-D	SEP 6	LIB-D
AUG 25	CAP-D	AUG 28	VIR-D	OCT 9	PIS-D	SEP 25	LIB-D	SEP 22	GEM-D	OCT 22	SCO-D
OCT 22	AQU-D	OCT 14	LIB-D	DEC 7	ARI-D	NOV 9	SCO-D	OCT 9	GEM-R	DEC 4	SAG-D
DEC 5	PIS-D	NOV 30	SCO-D			DEC 24	SAG-D	OCT 30	TAU-R		
								DEC 19	TAU-D		

Mars Tables

1960–1965

1960	1961	1962	1963	1964	1965
JAN 15 CAP-D	FEB 5 GEM-R	FEB 2 AQU-D	MAR 15 LEO-D	JAN 14 AQU-D	JAN 27 VIR-R
FEB 24 AQU-D	FEB 6 GEM-D	MAR 13 PIS-D	JUN 4 VIR-D	FEB 21 PIS-D	APR 18 VIR-D
APR 3 PIS-D	FEB 8 CAN-D	APR 20 ARI-D	JUL 28 LIB-D	MAR 30 ARI-D	JUN 30 LIB-D
MAY 12 ARI-D	MAY 7 LEO-D	MAY 29 TAU-D	SEP 13 SCO-D	MAY 8 TAU-D	AUG 21 SCO-D
JUN 21 TAU-D	JUN 29 VIR-D	JUL 10 GEM-D	OCT 26 SAG-D	JUN 18 GEM-D	OCT 5 SAG-D
AUG 3 GEM-D	AUG 18 LIB-D	AUG 23 CAN-D	DEC 6 CAP-D	JUL 31 CAN-D	NOV 15 CAP-D
SEP 22 CAN-D	OCT 2 SCO-D	OCT 12 LEO-D		SEP 16 LEO-D	DEC 24 AQU-D
NOV 19 CAN-R	NOV 14 SAG-D	DEC 25 LEO-R		NOV 7 VIR-D	
	DEC 25 CAPD				

1966–1971

1966	1967	1968	1969	1970	1971
JAN 31 PIS-D	FEB 13 SCO-D	JAN 10 PIS-D	FEB 26 SAG-D	JAN 25 ARI-D	JAN 24 SAG-D
MAR 10 ARI-D	MAR 7 SCO-R	FEB 18 ARI-D	APR 26 SAG-R	MAR 8 TAU-D	MAR 13 CAP-D
APR 18 TAU-D	APR 1 LIB-R	MAR 28 TAU-D	JUL 7 SAG-D	APR 19 GEM-D	MAY 4 AQU-D
MAY 29 GEM-D	MAY 27 LIB-D	MAY 9 GEM-D	SEP 22 CAP-D	JUN 3 CAN-D	JUL 10 AQU-R
JUL 12 CAN-D	JUL 20 SCO-D	JUN 22 CAN-D	NOV 5 AQU-D	JUL 19 LEO-D	SEP 8 AQU-D
AUG 26 LEO-D	SEP 11 SAG-D	AUG 6 LEO-D	DEC 16 PIS-D	SEP 4 VIR-D	NOV 7 PIS-D
OCT 13 VIR-D	OCT 24 CAP-D	SEP 22 VIR-D		OCT 21 LIB-D	DEC 27 ARI-D
DEC 5 LIB-D	DEC 2 AQU-D	NOV 10 LIB-D		DEC 7 SCO-D	
		DEC 30 SCO-D			

1972–1977

1972	1973	1974	1975	1976	1977
FEB 11 TAU-D	FEB 13 CAP-D	FEB 28 GEM-D	JAN 22 CAP-D	JAN 19 GEM-D	JAN 2 CAP-D
MAR 28 GEM-D	MAR 27 AQU-D	APR 21 CAN-D	MAR 4 AQU-D	MAR 19 CAN-D	FEB 10 AQU-D
MAY 12 CAN-D	MAY 9 PIS-D	JUN 10 LEO-D	APR 12 PIS-D	MAY 17 LEO-D	MAR 21 PIS-D
JUN 29 LEO-D	JUN 21 ARI-D	JUL 28 VIR-D	MAY 22 ARI-D	JUL 7 VIR-D	APR 28 ARI-D
AUG 16 VIR-D	AUG 13 TAU-D	SEP 13 LIB-D	JUL 2 TAU-D	AUG 25 LIB-D	JUN 7 TAU-D
OCT 1 LIB-D	SEP 18 TAU-R	OCT 29 SCO-D	AUG 14 GEM-D	OCT 9 SCO-D	JUL 18 GEM-D
NOV 16 SCO-D	OCT 30 ARI-R	DEC 11 SAG-D	OCT 18 CAN-D	NOV 21 SAG-D	SEP 2 CAN-D
DEC 31 SAG-D	NOV 25 ARI-D		NOV 5 CAN-R		OCT 27 LEO-D
	DEC 25 TAU-D		NOV 26 GEM-R		DEC 11 LEO-R

1978–1983

1978	1979	1980	1981	1982	1983
JAN 27 CAN-R	JAN 21 AQU-D	JAN 15 VIR-R	FEB 7 PIS-D	FEB 19 LIB-R	JAN 18 PIS-D
MAR 1 CAN-D	FEB 28 PIS-D	MAR 12 LEO-R	MAR 18 ARI-D	MAY 10 LIB-D	FEB 26 ARI-D
APR 11 LEO-D	APR 8 ARI-D	APR 5 LEO-D	APR 26 TAU-D	AUG 4 SCO-D	APR 6 TAU-D
JUN 15 VIR-D	MAY 17 TAU-D	MAY 5 VIR-D	JUN 6 GEM-D	SEP 21 SAG-D	MAY 17 GEM-D
AUG 5 LIB-D	JUN 27 GEM-D	JUL 11 LIB-D	JUL 18 CAN-D	NOV 1 CAP-D	JUN 30 CAN-D
SEP 20 SCO-D	AUG 9 CAN-D	AUG 30 SCO-D	SEP 3 LEO-D	DEC 11 AQU-D	AUG 14 LEO-D
NOV 3 SAG-D	SEP 25 LEO-D	OCT 13 SAG-D	OCT 22 VIR-D		OCT 1 VIR-D
DEC 13 CAP-D	NOV 20 VIR-D	NOV 23 CAP-D	DEC 17 LIB-D		NOV 19 LIB-D
		DEC 31 AQU-D			

1984–1989

1984	1985	1986	1987	1988	1989
JAN 12 SCO-D	FEB 3 ARI-D	FEB 3 SAG-D	JAN 9 ARI-D	JAN 9 SAG-D	JAN 20 TAU-D
APR 4 SCO-R	MAR 16 TAU-D	MAR 29 CAP-D	FEB 21 TAU-D	FEB 23 CAP-D	MAR 12 GEM-D
JUN 18 SCO-D	APR 27 GEM-D	JUN 7 CAP-R	APR 6 GEM-D	APR 7 AQU-D	APR 30 CAN-D
AUG 18 SAG-D	JUN 10 CAN-D	AUG 11 CAP-D	MAY 22 CAN-D	MAY 23 PIS-D	JUN 17 LEO-D
OCT 6 CAP-D	JUL 26 LEO-D	OCT 10 AQU-D	JUL 7 LEO-D	JUL 14 ARI-D	AUG 4 VIR-D
NOV 16 AQU-D	SEP 11 VIR-D	NOV 27 PIS-D	AUG 23 VIR-D	AUG 25 ARI-R	SEP 20 LIB-D
DEC 26 PIS-D	OCT 28 LIB-D		OCT 9 LIB-D	OCT 24 PIS-R	NOV 5 SCO-D
	DEC 15 SCO-D		NOV 25 SCO-D	OCT 27 PIS-D	DEC 19 SAG-D
				NOV 2 ARI-D	

1990	1991	1992	1993	1994	1995
JAN 30 CAP-D	JAN 1 TAU-D	JAN 10 CAP-D	FEB 14 CAN-D	JAN 29 AQU-D	JAN 1 VIR-R
MAR 12 AQU-D	JAN 21 GEM-D	FEB 19 AQU-D	APR 28 LEO-D	MAR 8 PIS-D	JAN 23 LEO-R
APR 21 PIS-D	APR 4 CAN-D	MAR 29 PIS-D	JUN 24 VIR-D	APR 15 ARI-D	MAR 23 LEO-D
JUN 1 ARI-D	MAY 27 LEO-D	MAY 6 ARI-D	AUG 13 LIB-D	MAY 24 TAU-D	MAY 26 VIR-D
JUL 14 TAU-D	JUL 16 VIR-D	JUN 15 TAU-D	SEP 28 SCO-D	JUL 4 GEM-D	JUL 22 LIB-D
SEP 1 GEM-D	SEP 2 LIB-D	JUL 27 GEM-D	NOV 10 SAG-D	AUG 17 CAN-D	SEP 8 SCO-D
OCT 19 GEM-R	OCT 17 SCO-D	SEP 13 CAN-D	DEC 21 CAP-D	OCT 5 LEO-D	OCT 21 SAG-D
DEC 15 TAU-R	NOV 30 SAG-D	NOV 28 CAN-R		DEC 13 VIR-D	DEC 1 CAP-D

1996	1997	1998	1999	2000	2001
JAN 9 AQU-D	JAN 4 LIB-D	JAN 26 PIS-D	JAN 27 SCO-D	JAN 5 PIS-D	FEB 14 SAG-D
FEB 16 PIS-D	FEB 5 LIB-R	MAR 5 ARI-D	MAR 17 SCO-R	FEB 13 ARI-D	JUL 18 SAG-D
MAR 25 ARI-D	MAR 9 VIR-R	APR 14 TAU-D	MAY 6 LIB-R	MAR 24 TAU-D	SEP 8 CAP-D
MAY 3 TAU-D	APR 26 VIR-D	MAY 25 GEM-D	JUN 3 LIB-D	MAY 4 GEM-D	OCT 27 AQU-D
JUN 13 GEM-D	JUN 20 LIB-D	JUL 7 CAN-D	JUL 6 SCO-D	JUN 17 CAN-D	DEC 8 PIS-D
JUL 26 CAN-D	AUG 15 SCO-D	AUG 21 LEO-D	SEP 3 SAG-D	AUG 2 LEO-D	
SEP 10 LEO-D	SEP 29 SAG-D	OCT 8 VIR-D	OCT 18 CAP-D	SEP 18 VIR-D	
OCT 31 VIR-D	NOV 10 CAP-D	NOV 28 LIB-D	NOV 27 AQU-D	NOV 5 LIB-D	
	DEC 19 AQU-D			DEC 24 SCO-D	

2002	2003	2004	2005	2006	2007
JAN 18 ARI-D	JAN 16 SAG-D	FEB 3 TAU-D	FEB 6 CAP-D	FEB 17 GEM-D	JAN 16 CAP-D
MAR 2 TAU-D	MAR 4 CAP-D	MAR 21 GEM-D	MAR 20 AQU-D	APR 13 CAN-D	FEB 25 AQU-D
APR 13 GEM-D	APR 21 AQU-D	MAY 7 CAN-D	APR 30 PIS-D	JUN 3 LEO-D	APR 6 PIS-D
MAY 28 CAN-D	JUN 16 PIS-D	JUN 23 LEO-D	JUN 11 ARI-D	JUL 22 VIR-D	MAY 15 ARI-D
JUL 13 LEO-D	JUL 29 PIS-R	AUG 10 VIR-D	JUL 27 TAU-D	SEP 7 LIB-D	JUN 24 TAU-D
AUG 29 VIR-D	SEP 27 PIS-D	SEP 26 LIB-D	OCT 1 TAU-R	OCT 23 SCO-D	AUG 7 GEM-D
OCT 15 LIB-D	DEC 16 ARI-D	NOV 10 SCO-D	DEC 9 TAU-D	DEC 5 SAG-D	SEP 28 CAN-D
DEC 1 SCO-D		DEC 25 SAG-D			NOV 14 CAN-R
					DEC 31 GEM-R

2008	2009	2010	2011	2012	2013
JAN 30 GEM-D	FEB 4 AQU-D	MAR 9 LEO-D	JAN 15 AQU-D	JAN 23 VIR-R	FEB 1 PIS-D
MAR 4 CAN-D	MAR 14 PIS-D	JUN 7 VIR-D	FEB 22 PIS-D	APR 13 VIR-D	MAR 12 ARI-D
MAY 9 LEO-D	APR 22 ARI-D	JUL 29 LIB-D	APR 1 ARI-D	JUL 3 LIB-D	APR 31 GEM-D
JUL 1 VIR-D	MAY 31 TAU-D	SEP 14 SCO-D	MAY 11 TAU-D	AUG 23 SCO-D	JUL 13 CAN-D
AUG 19 LIB-D	JUL 11 GEM-D	OCT 28 SAG-D	JUN 20 GEM-D	OCT 6 SAG-D	AUG 27 LEO-D
OCT 3 SCO-D	AUG 25 CAN-D	DEC 7 CAP-D	AUG 3 CAN-D	NOV 16 CAP-D	OCT 15 VIR-D
NOV 16 SAG-D	OCT 16 LEO-D		SEP 18 LEO-D	DEC 25 AQU-D	DEC 7 LIB-D
DEC 31 CAP-D	DEC 19 LEO-R		NOV 10 VIR-D		

2014	2015	2016	2017	2018	2019
MAR 1 LIB-R	JAN 12 PIS-D	JAN 3 SCO-D	JAN 28 ARI-D	JAN 26 SAG-D	FEB 14 TAU-D
MAY 19 LIB-D	FEB 19 ARI-D	MAR 6 SAG-D	MAR 9 TAU-D	MAR 17 CAP-D	MAR 31 GEM-D
JUL 25 SCO-D	MAR 31 TAU-D	APR 16 SAG-R	APR 21 GEM-D	MAY 15 AQU-D	MAY 15 CAN-D
SEP 13 SAG-D	MAY 11 GEM-D	MAY 27 SCO-R	JUN 4 CAN-D	JUN 25 AQU-R	JUL 1 LEO-D
OCT 26 CAP-D	JUN 24 CAN-D	JUN 28 SCO-D	JUL 20 LEO-D	AUG 12 CAP-D	AUG 17 VIR-D
DEC 4 AQU-D	AUG 8 LEO-D	AUG 2 SAG-D	SEP 5 VIR-D	AUG 27 CAP-D	OCT 3 LIB-D
	SEP 24 VIR-D	SEP 27 CAP-D	OCT 22 LIB-D	SEP 10 AQU-D	NOV 19 SCO-D
	NOV 12 LIB-D	NOV 9 AQU-D	DEC 9 SCO-D	NOV 15 PIS-D	
		DEC 19 PIS-D		DEC 31 ARI-D	

Mars Tables

	2020		2021		2022		2023		2024		2025
JAN	3 SAG-D	JAN	6 TAU-D	JAN	24 CAP-D	JAN	11 GEM-D	JAN	4 CAP-D	JAN	6 CAN-R
FEB	16 CAP-D	MAR	3 GEM-D	MAR	6 AQU-D	MAR	25 CAN-D	FEB	13 AQU-D	FEB	23 CAN-D
MAR	30 AQU-D	APR	23 CAN-D	APR	14 PIS-D	MAY	20 LEO-D	MAR	22 PIS-D	APR	17 LEO-D
MAY	12 PIS-D	JUN	11 LEO-D	MAY	24 ARI-D	JUL	10 VIR-D	APR	30 ARI-D	JUN	17 VIR-D
JUN	27 ARI-D	JUL	29 VIR-D	JUL	5 TAU-D	AUG	27 LIB-D	JUN	8 TAU-D	AUG	6 LIB-D
SEP	8 ARI-R	SEP	14 LIB-D	AUG	20 GEM-D	OCT	11 SCO-D	JUL	20 GEM-D	SEP	22 SCO-D
NOV	14 ARI-D	OCT	30 SCO-D	OCT	29 GEM-R	NOV	24 SAG-D	SEP	4 CAN-D	NOV	4 SAG-D
		DEC	13 SAG-D					NOV	3 LEO-D	DEC	15 CAP-D
								DEC	5 LEO-R		

Children with Mars in Aries

This is the most comfortable placement for Mars, since it rules Aries; it is at home, so to speak. It enables Mars to express its energy in the most natural and direct way. Mars in Aries is *highly energetic, powerful and has spontaneous physical energy* — sometimes leaping into action before looking or thinking. This placement makes good starters and poor finishers, so they will need to learn perseverance. Inclined to have hot tempers, these children should be taught to take a deep breath and count to ten before reacting and saying anything that might be harmful. Their anger, although quickly ignited, is usually short in duration.

These natives can be easily directed when *motivated by challenge*. As parents, caregivers, or therapists choose wisely and carefully in which direction you send them. They are courageous and forceful, and they like to be first in anything, whether in the classroom, in business, in driving a car! Mars in Aries is a strong and very personalized placement, so they can be consumed with self-importance. For these children, self-preservation levels are extremely high.

In relationships, these children will want to *dominate*, although they usually will choose those who are also strong, as well as interesting as friends and associates. But sometimes they come on too strong, causing others to back away. They will tend to be direct, so teach them how to do it with less force and more diplomacy. A little modification in their desire to dominate is also a good idea... they need to learn cooperation. If others refuse to do what they want, they should go do it themselves! Teach them about balance... give and take... and equality.

These children can *make good leaders*. They like to be in charge and they *make good executives*. In school, career, or anything else the important factor is "challenge." They are very assertive, love competition, and dislike repetition or anything and anyone boring! Use this information as your tool for motivating them wisely.

Children with Mars in Taurus

Mars is uncomfortable in Taurus because it is restricted in this Venusian earth sign — the physical energy being low and slow to move. These natives are motivated on a sensual level by things which bring them comfort, and on a practical level by accumulating material possessions. These children need to express their assertiveness through solid achievements and in endeavors that require patience, persistence, and efficiency. One of the most positive assets of this position is *perseverance*. Once they are motivated, they will work very hard and follow through to get what they want. They also will do a better-than-average job with whatever they undertake.

These natives are stubborn and cannot be pushed, resisting any efforts to change them or to make them move more quickly. Since their *drive is to accumulate material possessions and to receive physical comfort,* as parent or caregiver, you will do best by stimulating these children with rewards that bring them comfort and pleasure. They love affection so lots of hugs and kisses can be a wonderful way to motivate and reward them.

Children with this placement find it difficult to express anger naturally because they hold it in, causing it to build up and then explode! — usually out of proportion and at inappropriate times. Sometimes they will even get a sore throat as a result of holding back or of having too much anxiety. (Taurus rules the throat, and having Mars in a sign shows where to expect physical problems.) Their patience is enduring — in fact, so enduring that they are sometimes taken advantage of by others. On the surface they are controlled, and inside they may be steaming. Teach these children to *verbalize* the way they feel to avoid any emotional or physical repercussions.

Any problems that may occur in relationships stem from *jealousy* and *possessiveness.* These natives tend to treat people the way they do their possessions, preferring to own them! The old adage that states, "If you set something free and it comes back, then it belongs with you," is a good thought for these children to learn and keep in mind. If they hear it often enough from you it will become a part of them.

Children with Mars in Gemini

Children with Mars placed in Gemini are *motivated by intellectual stimulation*. They will use a great deal of their energy in *mental pursuits*; having very active minds they thrive on learning. All information, especially anything new, will be attractive and exciting to them. They excel in areas that require mental activity, from school to quiz games. Their major downfalls in school will be their lack of follow-through, and diminished concentration when they are bored. If you find that they are slacking off in a particular study, check for monotony and help them to find a way to make it more mentally challenging. They are very resourceful so most times, once you direct them along this line, they will find their own solution. As for the follow-through, they simply *need to learn the importance and the discipline of perseverance*. They will start many things (sometimes simultaneously!), and will need to learn the significance of finishing them.

These children are *gifted with manual dexterity* and will be able to work very quickly. They need to use this Mars energy both mentally and physically by using their hands; otherwise, it will manifest as nervousness. Computers are a great way to use both. Often these

children have a talent for writing and *make good report-
ers and critics.* They are quick-witted — and when misdi-
rected their wit can be taken as sarcastic and abrupt.
Help them to use their quickness in beneficial ways.
For optimum results, keep them active with fresh, stimulating information and many *challenging discussions.*
Silence is not golden, and will be next to impossible
with these children! Teach them to "edit" what they
want to say, beforehand — so it doesn't come out as a
garrulous stream!

Children with Mars in Cancer

This is not one of the more comfortable places for
Mars. The fiery Martian's aggressive physical nature
gets water-logged in Cancer. Mars represents assertion
but Cancer, like the crab, withdraws and goes within
their own protective shell, when they feel in the least
threatened. Since these children have difficulty being
assertive, and rarely use a *direct* approach to gaining
what they desire, they can be very devious. Sometimes
they will use guilt as a method of *manipulation* to get
their results. It is very important to help them *see* this
manipulative nature, and to help them be more direct!

These children are *super-sensitive* and can become
very hurt and angry inside when they feel offended,
bitter, or put- upon — and, of course, they usually will
not express this anger openly. Repressed hostility can

make them seem moody and worrisome... and can be the cause of many physical illnesses, even ulcers. Teach them to express and discuss their angry feelings, bringing these feelings out in the open to avoid much of the emotional frustration so typical of this placement. Have a little session every night and ask them if anything is bothering them, help them express the resentment and rage.

The *key motivation for these children is to gain security.* Cancer is a sign that has strong *protective drives,* both for themselves and toward others. In fact, sometimes they are so protective of those they care about they can be smothering. They are very good at *nurturing* others and will want to take care of those in need. This characteristic, when overdone or indiscriminative, can make them slaves to those who may take advantage. Teach them to serve only those people who will appreciate *them,* and to nourish in ways that will bring benefits to each. They have good instincts and *strong intuition,* which they should learn to use more and use "self-feelings" less.

These natives will put huge amounts of energy into domestic issues, building safety for home and family. At the same time they can *make excellent business people* — often doing best operating their own business and preferably from home! Many are very good at home repairs too. These children are conservative, so they usually stay out of troubles caused by the usual Mars impulsive actions. Help them to release all fears about security and especially their pent-up ings about people... thereby eliminating most of t ... problems.

Children with Mars in Leo

Leo is a fire sign so this is a *powerful* position for Mars as it provides *tremendous vitality*. Children with this placement will be *forceful, impulsive, dynamic, dramatic, restless, enthusiastic, creative, and very ambitious.* These natives are best motivated with applause and by the recognition they will gain. They are driven to develop their own talents, which are numerous, because they want to achieve something of great importance in the world. These natives are *loaded with personal magnetism and passion* — passion for people, passion for the deed. Their *enthusiasm* and *self-confidence* which inspire others are characteristics which make this personality so attractive. Teach them that nothing is exciting or glamorous all the time, and that they will be stronger and happier and accomplish more if they don't let their enthusiasm dwindle too much when things slow down or become routine.

Pride is another strong characteristic inherent in Mars in Leo children. This is a fine trait which is necessary for accomplishment — however, excessive pride can lead to arrogance. Teach them the advantage of this trait and the disadvantage of its misuse. Point out that humility is also necessary for advancement and for getting along with people... this is a very important quality for these children to develop. Sometimes they feel that they are better than others, so help them to see the difference between liking themselves and feeling confident... and looking down on others from their lofty heights.

These natives have a great deal of *courage*, and will often become leaders. Show them that the great leaders were not dictators — they earned their positions through respect and admiration... and for their deeds done. These children will not take kindly to being dictated to, so this presents a useful way to show them how others feel!

They are not afraid of work, and will want to show you that you can rely on them. They want you to think of them as being *physically and emotionally strong* at all times. With all this high energy they are usually *good at sports*, and are naturally drawn to physical activities of all kinds. They have a quick temper, though usually not dangerous. They have *strong will power* and can be defiant or authoritative. Teach them to modify these forces within themselves. They like center stage and will cooperate best when you appeal to their sense of the dramatic, as well as to their sense of fairness. Help these children to channel their powerful energy into constructive directions... and you will be amazed at all they can accomplish.

Children with Mars in Virgo

Mars in Virgo children are motivated to *put their energy into achieving perfection* in all aspects of their lives. It is their main drive. These are the children who plan their activities before taking action, as they want to do everything as perfectly as possible. Since Virgo is an earth sign, they are inclined to only take action in areas which will bring practical results... producing material value and gain. They will not want to use their energy on anything unproductive. These natives focus on details and are good not just with their heads but with their hands. This makes them *excellent crafts people.* They put their efforts into keeping *organization* in their lives, and in their environment as well. The force and energy of Mars is carefully directed with this placement — they systematically become skilled in any area they choose. These children will do well in all areas of the *medical field especially as surgeons. Computer programming* is another good option.

The challenging side of this placement is that these natives may also expect other people to adhere to the same perfectionistic standards which they set for themselves. They can be very *critical and picky*, finding fault in others and in their work, which will cause much dissension in their lives. People won't like it! Teach them to lighten up a little, especially on others. If they look to the larger plan they will become aware that all might already be in the right order.

Children with Mars in Libra

Children with Mars placed in Libra may have some challenges as to how they express their energy. (Mars rules the sign Aries — opposite Libra!) Since Mars is self-oriented and Libra is other-oriented, you can see the conflict. One part of them wants to be partners focusing on cooperation, and another part of them is very competitive. The competitive side wants to take action, and the other side is afraid to because they need approval so desperately. Oh, what a see-saw they're on!

With this placement we see the fire of Mars expressed through the mental mode of Libra, the air sign. These children can be motivated and will take physical action only through mental stimulation. They do not like hard or dirty physical work; menial tasks have little appeal. They also don't take orders very well, so you will need to *ask for their cooperation.* For best results, work along with them.

These are the natives who like to use their energy working very hard creating social events and initiating parties. They also are very skilled at inspiring others to cooperate and contribute to their projects. (They're great at fund-raising!) *Socializing and relationships are their prime motivators. Keep this in mind with your disciplines and rewards.*

These children will be the ones who will want to have a girlfriend or boyfriend at an early age. Teach them how to be discriminating with those they choose. Sometimes they can be taken advantage of because of their strong need for a partner, their willingness to do whatever is necessary to make it work, and their trusting naivete. Often they jeopardize their own needs and priorities. If the relationship doesn't work out, they can feel like a failure. This dependency on others may cause them many problems.

Children with Mars placed in Libra can become real warriors, and will fight vigorously when justice is violated. When "fairness" is the question, they will exhibit anger and display courage to make corrections, whether they are involved personally or not. Again, discrimination is the key to assure that their efforts are not wasted or misplaced. Sometimes they seem to have a tendency to tilt at windmills! Help these children to use their energy so that they will not become the eternal people-pleasers, and will become decisive individuals who can stand on their own feet... as they go about in life, creating social benefit.

Children with Mars in Scorpio

Mars placed in the sign of Scorpio creates a powerful, combustible combination. The fiery forceful nature of Mars is coupled with the *intensity, endurance, and power* of Scorpio! These natives are motivated by the desire for power and control. These children are very determined, persistent types who must be motivated and guided to use their strong power in beneficial ways. Otherwise, it can cause great destruction, as these natives are quite capable of accomplishing whatever they decide — for or against.

These children have very *strong physical and emotional desires*, and their intensity can be overwhelming. (They are also inclined to be very sensual.) They have *deep feelings* and are unable to experience anything in a moderate manner. When they are angry it is usually internalized and the pressure continues to build. Holding on to their anger in this fashion causes them to hold grudges and to think about revenge. You can tell when they are angry because they will become sarcastic and make biting remarks. Teach them to release all hostility, so they can channel their energy into productive causes. This negativity serves no beneficial purpose, and can be detrimental to any relationship, whether personal or business.

The physical energy of these children is high and enduring. They are active and forceful, and you may find them challenging to keep up with. Their energy is applied in a steady, persistent manner... they are not likely to give up when the going gets tough. In fact, this will activate their courage, and oblige them to apply all of their energy. They are quite willing to fight for what they want. These children, more than others, will need to learn about the win-win concept. Teach them to use their power to benefit others just as they benefit themselves in their endeavors. *The main lesson to teach them is to always choose the high road.* Since they have such great power, this will cause them to become the catalyst for many great accomplishments. They are motivated to succeed and do well in the world, and they make excellent business people.

Children with Mars in Sagittarius

Natives with this placement will expend large amounts of their Mars energy *rebelling against any form of restriction.* You can motivate these natives by showing them how they can gain more freedom. As their parent, caregiver or teacher, I would advise loosening the reins and giving these children some elbowroom — this will eliminate wasting a lot of time and energy for both of you. They have strong needs for *freedom* and *spontaneity.* If you use your creativity to guide them into using their own judgment wisely, restricting them won't be as necessary.

These children *love being outdoors. Sports, especially* those which are played outside and require lots of physical energy, are particularly appealing. They also *love travel and adventure.* Motivate them with rewards along these lines. They are *open and direct people (sometimes too much so!), and you will obtain your best results by being the same.*

The lessons these children *need to learn are endurance and discrimination.* They can spread themselves too thin, and scatter their energy, resulting in sloppy work and unfinished projects. Also, they seem to be careless with material objects, because their minds are racing ahead.

They tend to act without thinking and need to slow down. Teach them to count to ten. Their lack of follow-through can create problems with deadlines, so you will need to redirect their energy into matters which need completing.

These children are the *crusaders who have lofty goals.* They will fight for the good of the country, the world, humankind, and God. Teach them to discriminate, so they will use their energy appropriately to best serve these ideals. Your challenge is great... but the rewards can be greater.

Children with Mars in Capricorn

Mars is well placed in the sign of Capricorn because the caution of Capricorn slows, modifies, and brings practicality and discrimination to the impulsiveness of Mars. These natives are motivated by ways to gain positions of authority and respect from others. These children are not reckless. *When they take action it is well planned.* They use their physical energy carefully in *disciplined* ways. They will want to put their energy into work which brings them concrete results.

They are not afraid of hard work and will *demonstrate great perseverance*. Be careful they don't become work-alcoholics. They are so *ambitious* that they are often planning their career at a very early age — and are strongly motivated by professional ambitions, and to achieve positions which have prestige or bring recognition. They have a compelling drive to get ahead materially, as they take seriously their *duty* to take care of and fulfill their responsibilities. Sometimes they can become too calculating or seem cold with this strong drive for success. They will take active leadership roles, but may be inclined to step on others on their way up. Be sure to teach them the value of caring about people so they won't lose sight of the humanistic side of life. These natives *make good executives, politicians, and military personnel*.

When these children become angry, they exhibit control over their actions. However, you will know when they are angry because they will act aloof and become as cold as ice. Sometimes their hostility comes from the fact that they have no tolerance for, and in fact, will vehemently disrespect laziness. They will not associate with people who have no ambition. Whenever they are exposed to these types it becomes very distressing for them... because they simply cannot understand it! Help them to learn to apply their standards to themselves only, and to tolerate people who have other priorities. Oddly enough this placement can be thin-skinned (Capricorn rules the skin). It might be that their sense of dignity has been breached, and their feeling of self-worth sullied. So help them build another top layer!

Children with Mars in Aquarius

With this placement we find the raw physical energy which Mars represents frustrated, because it is expected to express itself through the mental channel of the air sign Aquarius. This may not be one of the better placements for Mars as it can cause *low physical energy.* When blocked, this Mars energy may build up and cause nervous tension. However, these children will gladly use their physical energy when motivated by any "cause" or exciting mental pursuit.

Their natural instinct is to *use their energy to obtain freedom and avoid restriction.* They require the room to be independent and to find their own way, using their own originality. As a parent or teacher, you need to know that these are the children who... the more you try to control them... the more they fight to get free. They remind one of a song entitled *(I Did It) My Way.* For best results, keep their need for independence in mind. You will also see a practical side to these children, so direct them toward productive causes where they can expend their Mars energy for the benefit of many. The Aquarians are naturally inclined to have goals which will benefit others as well as themselves, so this should be easy.

In relationships, these gregarious and friendly children are not comfortable with and have no need for displays of emotion. The Aquarians do not usually form deep attachments to others, and do not understand nor tolerate well the possessiveness of some signs. They like and enjoy many friends. The *best approach* to Mars in Aquarian children is *through logical, intelligent, and practical means.*

Since these children have an inability to follow orders very well, you will get better results by suggesting, rather than telling. Then, as a parent, caregiver or teacher, try to stay open to experiencing a new way of doing things!

Too often these children are inclined to resist any kind of authority, or form of restriction. If they grow up with lightly held reins, and are made aware of this anti-authority tendency in a friendly and logical way — it could cause much fewer problems when they are adults! In fact, these children, who can be so rebellious and impatient, can always be reached by your cool-headed logic. Since basically they are inspired by intelligence, they shouldn't go too far for too long — unless, of course, those reins were held too tightly. *The key to working with them is to lighten the control, and motivate them through their intellect.*

These children are naturally very enterprising and original. Appeal to that side of them. Some of the world's *great inventors and thinkers* have had this placement. They love to do and think new things and have new experiences. So be willing to also — and your life with them can be an adventurous joy!

Children with Mars in Pisces

This is not one of the more advantageous places for fiery aggressive Mars to reside. Motivate these natives to use their creativity and fertile imaginations to benefit others. In the sensitive watery sign of Pisces, its expression is dampened and somewhat stifled. This is what might be considered a weak placement. They tend to *lack courage* and have a tendency to buckle under pressure; not being forceful, assertive types. These children *live in a world of feelings and imagination* rather than in the world of action. They are not likely to set goals as they prefer to wander through life based on how they feel. They are *always motivated by feelings* rather than thoughts — a very important point for you to remember.

These children are apt to have *low physical energy* and will not expend what they do have on strenuous activities. A thoughtless parent or teacher might call them "lazy" — a harmful label that they will remember for years. If you ask them, they'll say they're waiting to be "inspired" — be clever and think of a way to do just that! It is very difficult for them to come up from their imaginings and become self-starters, even harder to follow through. See if you can turn their task into a story of some kind. Train them to do this, and they can play this little game on all their work — and they might eventually use their fertile imaginations to create something important!

Too often their energy is used on their emotional sensitivity and over-responsiveness to just about everything. Sometimes these natives have *low levels of self-confidence*... this, plus their low levels of energy, may be what inhibits their ability to take decisive action. They tend to be shy, timid, and apologetic. However, they do *make good listeners and would make excellent psychologists.*

These children need help in releasing their anger. They tend to suppress it, many times feeling they are to blame. Help them to develop strong self-esteem — and to eliminate all feelings of internalized guilt, which can cause many illnesses. These feelings of guilt can actually be a wallowing in emotion instead of coldly looking at something and taking responsibility for it! Again, less guilt — more action.

Sometimes individuals with this Mars in Pisces placement put much energy into their own weaknesses, and project that out on others, whom they then dominate with their helplessness and their dependency! Help them to learn self-responsibility by *praising* what they do... and in the beginning, every little effort! Don't criticize if it isn't done just the way you want it. Appreciate their efforts, and help them appreciate themselves. Get their focus away from their inner-imaginings and out to where it can serve others. *Service and sacrifice (within healthy limits!) are two of the noblest traits of this placement.*

"Divine being has permitted me to learn from the revolution of the stars."

Nostradamus

4 CHAPTER 9
Jupiter —
The Point of Expansion,
Opportunity and Luck

Jupiter is considered one of the good guys in the zodiac; that is, if there were truly good and bad guys. Obviously, each planet has its own best use and highest manifestation, as well as its excessiveness and misuse. Although Jupiter is called *the great benefactor*, he also has his extremes and inappropriate expressions.

Jupiter's placement in the chart is considered the lucky spot. He represents the area of ease, where one receives the little benefits of life. He is our optimism, our expansion point, where we feel unlimited. Jupiter symbolizes our abundance. He is the planet which puts us in search of higher knowledge and broader horizons. With Jupiter, we seek our own truths and philosophies. This planet always sees the "big picture"— the overall plan.

We all have a Jupiter in our chart. However, where he is placed and how he Aspects the other planets depicts how his influence is felt. For example, he is restrained when Aspected by Saturn and energized when Aspected by Mars. Jupiter's energies, like Saturn's, are only felt on a personal level when he is in close Aspect to the Sun, Moon, Mercury, Venus, Mars or the angle's of the chart. He is in each sign for approximately one year. Therefore, all who are born during that particular year have Jupiter in the same sign. We will not describe Jupiter through the twelve signs. It is really necessary to have a chart cast to discover how he affects individual personality traits.

Key words which describe Jupiter are: *expansion, opportunity, luck, optimism, abundance, enhancement, idealism, benevolence, humor, honesty, truth, education, knowledge, understanding, wisdom, philosophy, exploration, adventure, travel, freedom, exuberance, carefree, happy and positive.* Negative expressions are: overconfident, careless, gullible, flippant, cocky, tactless, procrastination, reckless, undisciplined, presumptuous, wasteful and foolhardy.

"The admirable harmony of the creation could be seen in the influence of the stars upon herbs and body of man."

Nicholas Culpeper

CHAPTER 10

Saturn —
The Taskmaster

Saturn is the guy with the bad reputation. He has been called the *taskmaster* of the zodiac, and probably was the originator of the "bread and water" treatment for punishment. One thing for sure — *Saturn is the planet of discipline!* Even more, he will discipline us until we learn to discipline ourselves. It is true he does catch a lot of flack, yet ultimately, he can become our greatest strength.

Saturn represents how we build our structures, and how we utilize self-discipline. Saturn's placement in the chart depicts life's lessons. Saturn's placement by sign and house, along with his aspects in a birth chart, show the areas of life which (once mastered) will become our foundations and strengths. These same areas also can be the source of difficulty, denial and challenge in life.

With this planet in the signs, there is a forced opportunity to develop discipline through the particular sign in which Saturn is placed. We are forced to blend and utilize Saturn's qualities with the qualities of the sign. The Aspects show how Saturn affects personality traits, and the houses show the areas of life involved. Saturn and discipline are synonymous. He challenges us with the weaknesses inherent in the sign in which he is placed, and forces us to develop the strengths of that sign.

In broad terms, Saturn symbolizes the structure of the world. All the laws apply, both naturally such as gravity and time, and man-made such as beaucracy and culture. He symbolizes the father and authority; he is truly a serious consideration in life. He always demands we earn what we receive. When we apply the necessary discipline, we become the master, and then the lesson brings joy. Resisting or avoiding the lesson brings unpleasant experiences which cause feelings of being restrained, limited, resentful, angry, depressed, lacking in energy and even illness. These are manifestations of Saturn's misuse, or our failure to take responsibility.

Knowing what the lessons are and how to develop them is paramount.

It takes Saturn twenty-nine years to complete his cycle through the zodiac, which means he is in each sign approximately 2 ½ years. All people born within this time frame will have Saturn placed in the same sign. This occurrence means the sign placement tends to be generational and describes the characteristics of entire groups of people. Unless Saturn makes a strong aspect to the luminaries, the personal planets, or the chart angles, you will not (personally) experience his influence. For a complete understanding of how Saturn operates in any person's life, a comprehensive astrological chart must be cast.

Key words which describe Saturn are: *caution, practicality, seriousness, reservation, dependability, reliability, responsibility, discipline, maturity, self-control, restraint, integrity, authority, status, recognition, stability, tradition, perseverance, persistence, diligence, endurance and structure.* Negative expressions are: fearfulness, limitation, restriction, deprivation, denial, inhibition, selfishness, solitary, cruelness, rigidity, coldness and pessimism.

SIGNS

ARI	Aries	LIB	Libra
TAU	Taurus	SCO	Scorpio
GEM	Gemini	SAG	Sagittarius
CAN	Cancer	CAP	Capricorn
LEO	Leo	AQU	Aquarius
VIR	Virgo	PIS	Pisces

Saturn Tables

Year	Mon	Day	Sign		Year	Mon	Day	Sign		Year	Mon	Day	Sign
1900	JAN	1	SAG		1939	MAR	21	TAU		1982	NOV	30	SCO
	JAN	21	CAP			SEP	23	ARI		1983	MAY	7	LIB
	JUL	19	SAG		1940	MAR	21	TAU			AUG	25	SCO
	OCT	18	CAP		1941			TAU		1984			SCO
1901			CAP		1942	MAY	9	GEM		1985	NOV	17	SAG
1902			CAP		1943			GEM		1986			SAG
1903	JAN	20	AQU		1944	JAN	21	CAN		1987			SAG
1904			AQU		1945			CAN		1988	FEB	14	CAP
1905	APR	14	PIS		1946	AUG	3	LEO			JUN	11	SAG
	AUG	18	AQU		1947			LEO			NOV	13	CAP
1906	JAN	9	PIS		1948	SEP	20	VIR		1989			CAP
1907			PIS		1949	APR	4	LEO		1990			CAP
1908	MAR	20	ARI			MAY	30	VIR		1991	FEB	7	AQU
1909			ARI		1950	NOV	21	LIB		1992			AQU
1910	MAY	18	TAU		1951	MAR	8	VIR		1993	MAY	22	PIS
	DEC	15	ARI			AUG	14	LIB			JUL	1	AQU
1911	JAN	21	TAU		1952			LIB		1994	JAN	29	PIS
1912	JUL	8	GEM		1953	OCT	23	SCO		1995			PIS
	DEC	1	TAU		1954			SCO		1996	APR	8	ARI
1913	MAR	27	GEM		1955			SCO		1997			ARI
1914	AUG	25	CAN		1956	JAN	13	SAG		1998	JUN	10	TAU
	DEC	8	GEM			MAY	15	SCO			OCT	26	ARI
1915	MAY	12	CAN			OCT	11	SAG		1999	MAR	2	TAU
1916	OCT	18	LEO		1957			SAG		2000			TAU
	DEC	8	CAN		1958			SAG		2001	APR	21	GEM
1917	JUN	25	LEO		1959	JAN	6	CAP		2002			GEM
1918			LEO		1960			CAP		2003	JUN	5	CAN
1919	AUG	13	VIR		1961			CAP		2004			CAN
1920			VIR		1962	JAN	4	AQU		2005	JUL	17	LEO
1921	OCT	8	LIB		1963			AQU		2006			LEO
1922			LIB		1964	MAR	25	PIS		2007	SEP	3	VIR
1923	DEC	21	SCO			SEP	17	AQU		2008			VIR
1924	APR	7	LIB			DEC	17	PIS		2009	OCT	30	LIB
	SEP	14	SCO		1965			PIS		2010	APR	8	VIR
1925			SCO		1966			PIS			JUL	22	LIB
1926	DEC	3	SAG		1967	MAR	4	ARI		2011			LIB
1927			SAG		1968			ARI		2012	OCT	6	SCO
1928			SAG		1969	APR	30	TAU		2013			SCO
1929	MAR	16	CAP		1970			TAU		2014	DEC	24	SAG
	MAY	6	SAG		1971	JUN	19	GEM		2015	JUN	15	SCO
	DEC	1	CAP		1972	JAN	10	TAU			SEP	19	SAG
1930			CAP			FEB	22	GEM		2016			SAG
1931			CAP		1973	AUG	2	CAN		2017	DEC	20	CAP
1932	FEB	25	AQU		1974	JAN	8	GEM		2018			CAP
	AUG	14	CAP			APR	19	CAN		2019			CAP
	NOV	21	AQU		1975	SEP	18	LEO		2020	MAR	22	AQU
1933			AQU		1976	JAN	15	CAN			JUL	2	CAP
1934			AQU			JUN	6	LEO			DEC	18	AQU
1935	FEB	15	PIS		1977	NOV	18	VIR		2021			AQU
1936			PIS		1978	JAN	6	LEO		2022			AQU
1937	APR	26	ARI			JUL	27	VIR		2023	MAR	8	PIS
	OCT	19	PIS		1979			VIR		2024			PIS
1938	JAN	15	ARI		1980	SEP	22	LIB		2025	MAY	25	ARI
					1981			LIB			SEP	1	PIS

Children with Saturn in Aries

FEAR — of being inhibited or restrained by others, of outside control, of identity loss.

CHALLENGE — with patience, other people's priorities.

LESSONS — to learn responsible action and consideration.

NEEDS TO ELIMINATE — selfishness, hastiness.

BENEFICIALLY APPLIED — brings a enduring competitor, disciplined leader.

Children with Saturn in Taurus

FEAR — of not having enough, of deprivation and denial, loss of comfort and possessions.

CHALLENGE — with stubbornness and possessiveness.

LESSON — to learn moderate indulgence and non-attachment.

NEEDS TO ELIMINATE – greed, indulgence, inflexibility.

BENEFICIALLY APPLIED – displays responsible values, financial benefactor.

Children with Saturn in Gemini

FEAR – of boredom and inactivity, loss of mental stimulation.

CHALLENGE – with consistency, endurance, dedication.

LESSON – to learn disciplined intellectual pursuit and application, perseverance and practical learning.

NEEDS TO ELIMINATE – scattering self, becoming the know-it-all.

BENEFICIALLY APPLIED – provides solid authoritative information, production of material resources, persevering useful study.

Children with Saturn in Cancer

FEAR – of not being taken care of, loss of security, safety and protection.

CHALLENGE — with moodiness, ability to feel secure within self.

LESSON — to develop self-confidence and mature emotional responses.

NEEDS TO ELIMINATE — insecurity, hiding feelings, hoarding belongings.

BENEFICIALLY APPLIED — provides protection for others, disciplined feelings.

Children with Saturn in Leo

FEAR — of not being or having love, loss of praise and admiration, dignity and approval.

CHALLENGE — with humility and being of service to others.

LESSON — to learn to applaud self inwardly.

NEEDS TO ELIMINATE — arrogance and the need to dominate others.

BENEFICIALLY APPLIED — inspires responsibility in others, organized leader, respectable status.

Children with Saturn in Virgo

FEAR — of being criticized, loss of appreciation.

CHALLENGE — with imperfection and lack of order.

LESSON — to learn productive discrimination and acceptance of current reality.

NEEDS TO ELIMINATE — judgment and intolerance.

BENEFICIALLY APPLIED — brings skillful creation of form, mastery in health areas.

Children with Saturn in Libra

FEAR — of rejection and loneliness, loss of unity.

CHALLENGE — with relationships, indecisiveness, vacillation.

LESSON — to learn responsible cooperation, confidence and independence.

NEEDS TO ELIMINATE — inconsistency and being a people-pleaser.

BENEFICIALLY APPLIED — provides an enduring peacemaker, justice based on integrity.

Children with Saturn in Scorpio

FEAR — of becoming vulnerable, loss of control.

CHALLENGE — with exposing self, being secretive.

LESSON — to learn to trust and to place importance on control of the self.

NEEDS TO ELIMINATE — harmful manipulation, need for revenge.

BENEFICIALLY APPLIED — displays empowering others, responsible perceptions, teaching others self-control.

Children with Saturn in Sagittarius

FEAR — of being limited or restricted, loss of movement and space.

CHALLENGE—with confinement and commitment.

LESSON—to develop practical philosophies, master wisdom.

NEEDS TO ELIMINATE—tactlessness and bluntness, dissipating resources and energies.

BENEFICIALLY APPLIED—provides organized adventures, reliable enduring truths.

Children with Saturn in Capricorn

FEAR – of being in a subservient position, loss of respect, and authority.

CHALLENGE—with experiencing warmth, learning to lighten-up.

LESSON – to develop humor and compassionate administration.

NEEDS TO ELIMINATE – being overly structured, rigid and isolated.

BENEFICIALLY APPLIED – displays administrative responsibility, diplomatic ambassador.

Children with Saturn in Aquarius

FEAR — of having to conform or of becoming attached, loss of freedom.

CHALLENGE — with authority and tradition, making commitments.

LESSON — to learn reasonable limitations, stable changes and reconstruction.

NEEDS TO ELIMINATE — detachment, irresponsible rebellion.

BENEFICIALLY APPLIED — shows practical innovation, reform with integrity.

Children with Saturn in Pisces

FEAR — of having a routine mundane existence, loss of imagination and fantasy.

CHALLENGE — with physical reality, depression.

LESSON — to learn stability, bring spirituality to earth.

NEEDS TO ELIMINATE — over sensitivity, escapisms.

BENEFICIALLY APPLIED — provides practical spiritual application, creative artistic structures.

*"The current popularity of astrology
is not a threat to religion but an opportunity,
a chance to show searching minds how they can
combine all the world's wisdom into one coherent,
living faith in our Creator."*

Jeane Dixon

CONCLUSION

In the great dance of relationship, the material in this book is but a first step toward understanding the complexities of human behavior as they relate to the role of parenting, caregiving, teaching, and counseling. Also, keep in mind there may be other factors in a chart which can modify the descriptions given here. Sometimes there is so much strength in an opposite characteristic, it may weaken a placement so that it is almost unnoticed. A complete chart drawn up by a professional astrologer will present more facets of one's life, purpose, and movement. It will present a more complete personality profile plus the *timing* of developments throughout the individual's life!

Please realize that each description presented here, of a planet in a sign, will also apply to any adult with that placement. After all, we all had to be children some time, didn't we? From a broader perspective, *we are all still children in the process of becoming!* So apply this understanding and use these guidelines for all of your relationships, as well as for understanding yourself. The astrological approach provides us with the opportunity to look at ourselves from a *detached viewpoint,* and in an objective manner. I believe that all people are capable of changing their reactions and behavior... and this becomes possible once they understand *what* to change, and *when* they will have a strong enough desire. The desire is the *motivation,* it then becomes a matter of *persistence.* The more times we repeat a behavior, the more it becomes automatic — an ingrained habit.

Start thinking of all of us here on the planet as a sprinkling of diamonds. As we touch one another through our contact in our relationships, we reflect our different facets. We are all made of the same substance, each with the potential to shine. It is our gift to help one another — love is the way!

"The whole universe is one whole; there is an interaction between all things, but not determinism."
Plotinus (204 - 270 AD)

ABOUT THE AUTHOR

Samantha Davis has been on a personal quest to discover the "whys" as well as the hows on living a more productive, beneficial, and enjoyable life. This quest, beginning quite young, has led her to become an educator, lecturer, and writer.

In 1972, Samantha co-founded The Arizona Society for Astrologers, and became widely recognized as the dynamic director of Programs and Education. Samantha practiced professionally in Arizona and developed a large national counseling practice, along with her teaching, and lecturing. She found time to author many articles in nationally recognized astrology magazines. Additionally, you may have read Ms. Davis' weekly astrological newspaper column.

In 1979, Samantha Davis became a certified lecturer for Silv: Method of Mind Development International. With this additional expertise, she became proficient in teaching controlled relaxation, stress management, and self-improvement to hundreds of people.

She is a favorite on national TV and radio talk shows, and is a consultant for many business and professional organizations. Ms. Davis now spends her time between her homes in Arizona and California, plus travels the world. Her practice today is at such a point where she does not accept any new clients, with rare exceptions.

Samantha says that, *"This book, my labor of love, is committed to helping parents, caregivers, teachers, and therapists gain added insights into our children's personalities. And to assist them in learning new effective tools and methods for raising, guiding, and understanding the children of our world."*

"And God said, Let there be lights in the firmament of the heaven to divide the day from the night; and let them be for signs, and for seasons, and for days, and years."

Genesis 1:14

GLOSSARY

ASCENDANT — The constellation or sign that was on the horizon at the exact time and from the exact location where the individual was born.

ASPECTS — Angular relationships between two or more planets.

MAJOR "SOFT" ASPECTS or benefics:
Trine — 120 degrees apart, an aspect between planets in the same element... as Sun in Taurus trine Mars in Virgo. Considered very favorable.
Grand Trine — all three signs of an element... such as the *air* signs Gemini, Libra, Aquarius... all trining. Considered tops!

Sextile — 60 degrees apart, an aspect between compatible elements, like Venus in *earth* Taurus sextiling Moon in *water* Cancer — or Sun in *air* Gemini sextiling Mars in *fire* Leo. Considered favorable, but you have to help it. It just won't fall in your lap like a happy trine.

MAJOR "HARD" ASPECTS of non-benefics!

Square — 90 degrees apart, a challenge, a difficulty. Sometimes seems to hold you in a vise, or you swing from one to the other.

Grand Square or *Grand Cross* — when all four of the MODE OF ACTION signs square each other, or form a cross. A CARDINAL CROSS involves Aries, Cancer, Libra, Capricorn, a MUTABLE CROSS all four mutables signs, etc. Such a chart is said to be a *karmic* one, with many obstacles to work out (or lessons to learn) in this life. Children with such a configuration should be helped to understand this challenge so that they can learn to *use* it to accomplish... rather than allow it to have a non-beneficial effect. Help them to look at and accept each challenge as a very special *opportunity*.

In general, one needs challenging "hard" aspects — to get tossed out of the hammock — to get going! People who accomplish much, whether in the world or within themselves, usually have many hard aspects.

To know these aspects you should consult a professional astrologer, and then undertake to learn more about astrology yourself... to watch the TRANSITS and the to guide your children, and your own life for the better! The more you know your charts, the more you are able to work *with* them beneficially, the more forewarned you are — the more you can take appropriate action.

Also, it should be said that when your *trine* is contacted by a transiting benefic planet — good things will happen! Welcome them, and *use* them!

Conjunction — planets within 8-12 degrees of each other. They can be in the same sign or at the end of one and the beginning of the next — such as Moon 28 degrees Gemini and Venus 4 degrees Cancer. A conjunction can be harmonious or inharmonious, according to the nature of the planets involved: For example, Mars conjunct Moon, not so good, because fiery Mars is incompatible with watery Moon.

ELEMENTS — FIRE, EARTH, AIR, and WATER. There are three signs in each element. The signs in the same element are compatible. Two different elements can be compatible (sextile): fire and air, earth and water. The less compatible are fire burning earth; earth suffocating air; air bubbling in water; and water putting out fire.

Elements are concerned with tendencies of the *tem perament* — planets in earth will be practical doers — in air, mental and often intellectual — in water, emotional and creative — in fire, action-oriented and inspirational.

MODES OF ACTION (for the elements) — Cardinal, Fixed, Mutable. There are four signs in each mode.

CARDINAL — Aries, Cancer, Libra, Capricorn. Usually considered the "movers and the shakers," the go-for-it signs. Too much cardinal in one person's chart compared to another person's cardinal can be extremely irritating — they both want to be first! To have their own way!

FIXED — Taurus, Leo, Scorpio, Aquarius. Each of these signs are in different elements. They are likened to — Taurus/Earth/Rock, Leo/Fire/Torch, Scorpio/Water/Ice, Aquarius/Air/Tornado. They endure, they persevere, they get the job done. If two charts each have a lot of *fixity*, they tend to butt heads! If you are a cardinal person and want *action*, you will have to develop tremendous patience and tolerance, since these fixed individuals are difficult to bend, change, or move! If you are mostly mutable, you may have a challenge with their obstinacy. However, mutables are very clever, and will probably think of something!

MUTABLE — Gemini, Virgo, Sagittarius, Pisces. The most adaptable of the signs, like reeds that move with the wind... not standing firm and fixed until they break. These natives are like chameleons, they can fit into many different environments. They are flexible, re sourceful, ingenious. Sometimes they also can be nervous, fluttery, too changeable.

CARDINAL – initiates the concept, kicks it off.
FIXED – works persistently to produce a result.
MUTABLE – promotes and sells it.

HOUSES – The *horoscope* or *wheel* of 360 degrees is divided into twelve parts which area called *houses*. Each house represents an area of life.

HOUSE 1 – Self-image, self-expression, personality, appearance, behavior, body.

HOUSE 2 – Money, income, financial source, spending, values, possessions, property, resources, monetary security.

HOUSE 3 – Communication, sense perception, learning, thinking, teaching, writing, commuting, errands.

HOUSE 4 – Home territory, roots, tradition, emotional security, parents, family, parenting.

HOUSE 5 – Creative expression, recreation, romance, entertainment, play, children, pets, speculation.

HOUSE 6 – Work, jobs, skills, productivity, analysis, criticism, correction, health.

HOUSE 7 – Relationships, partnerships, marriage, contracts, agreements, the law, politics, harmony.

HOUSE 8 – Sex, sexuality, crisis, catalytic experiences, death and rebirth, transformation, the occult.

HOUSE 9 — Knowledge, wisdom, philosophy, religion, deep study, higher education, publishing, journeys, exploration.

HOUSE 10 — Career, success, public recognition, ambition, prestige, status, authority, government.

HOUSE 11 — Friends, associates, groups, aspirations, expectations, plans, the future.

HOUSE 12 — Service, inspiration, spirituality, intuition, empathy, illusion, sacrifice, self-undoing, misfortune, tragedy.

LUMINARIES — the Sun, the core of the being, the SELF; the Moon, one's emotional makeup, responsiveness.

PLANETS — The planets symbolically represent the different facets of human makeup.

RULERSHIP — where a planet is at *home* — as Mars in Aries, Mercury in Gemini and Virgo, etc. At home the planet most easily expresses itself. When a planet is placed *opposite* its home — as Mars in Libra, Mercury in Sagittarius or Pisces, etc. — it is considered weaker, impaired, can't work at full power or utilize its true nature.

Sun rules Leo
Moon rules Cancer
Mercury rules both Gemini and Virgo

Venus rules both Taurus and Libra
Mars rules both Aries and Scorpio
Jupiter rules both Sagittarius and Pisces
Saturn rules both Capricorn and Aquarius

SIGNS — and the HOUSES they would naturally influence:

ARIES the Ram (first house) — a *cardinal fire* sign ruled by Mars. Parts of the body ruled are head and face.
TAURUS the Bull (second house) — a *fixed earth* sign ruled by Venus. Parts of the body ruled are the ears, neck, and throat.
GEMINI the Twins (third house) — a *mutable air* sign ruled by Mercury. Parts of the body ruled are lungs (air in them), shoulders, arms, wrists, and fingers.
CANCER the Crab (fourth house) — a *cardinal water* sign ruled by the Moon. Parts of the body ruled are breasts, stomach, and solar plexus.
LEO the Lion (fifth house) — a *fixed fire* sign ruled by the Sun. Parts of the body ruled are heart, back, and spine.
VIRGO the Virgin (sixth house) — a *mutable earth* sign ruled by Mercury. Rules the nervous system and the intestines.
LIBRA the Scales (seventh house) — a *cardinal air* sign ruled by Venus. Parts of the body ruled are the kidneys.

SCORPIO the Scorpion (eighth house) — a *fixed water* sign ruled by Pluto (old ruler is Mars). Rules the reproductive system.

SAGITTARIUS the Centaur (ninth house) — a *mutable fire* sign ruled by Jupiter. Parts of the body ruled are the hips, and thighs.

CAPRICORN the Goat (tenth house) — a *cardinal earth* sign ruled by Saturn. Rules the skin, teeth, skeleton in general, and knees in particular.

AQUARIUS the Water Bearer (eleventh house) — a *fixed air* sign ruled by Uranus (old ruler Saturn). Rules the calves, and ankles.

PISCES the Fish (twelfth house) — a *mutable water* sign ruled by Neptune (old ruler Jupiter). Parts of the body ruled are the feet.

SIGNS are actually constellations, or stars in the sky, arbitrarily considered by the Ancients to be a *group* because they suggested an outline of some animal or mythological being. If you look carefully at the *glyph* of each sign, you can see an outline — of a Ram's head (Aries), a Bull's head (Taurus), the Gemini Twins, the Cancer Crab, the Leo Lion, the Virgo Virgin, the balancing Scales of Libra, the Scorpion stinging tail (Scorpio), the Sagittarius Centaur shooting his arrow into the sky, water flowing from the Aquarian Water-bearer's pitcher, two Pisces Fish swimming.

The *odd* numbered signs, beginning with the first one, Aries, are called "positive" or "masculine;" the *even* numbered signs, beginning with the second one, Taurus, are called "negative" or "feminine"! Think of these old-fashioned terms, "positive" and "negative," as two kinds of psychic current — a force flowing out, a force pulling in. Electric and magnetic; out-going and in-pulling. (In the planets, Mars — pushing out, Venus — pulling in.)

In the elements, the "masculine" signs are *fire* and *air*, the "feminine" are *earth* and *water*. Both natures are, of course, needed in a chart for proper balance of being.

ZODIAC, Horoscope, or wheel — an imaginary belt in the Heavens, with the apparent path of the Sun, the Moon, and the planets of the Solar System. The zodiac is divided into twelve *signs*; the wheel, into twelve *houses*.

Index

ESP FOR KIDS
How to Develop Your Child's Psychic Ability
by Dr. Tag Powell and Carol Howell Mills

An unequaled, one-of-a-kind approach to psychic development and children. It is based upon over 25-years of research and psychic development classes taught worldwide. Learn about the special dilemmas and unique talents found among children like yours. Experience the challenges being met by gifted youths and learn how to help your child develop his or her own special abilities. Written using step-by-step techniques, this book is easy-to-read and includes fun games designed to nurture and improve your child's psychic talents. Children will delight in activities such as spoon bending, psychometry and psychic healing.

What makes this book an unprecedented work for you and your child?

☞ the experiences discussed are ACTUAL case studies
☞ the "FUN GAMES" are tested and proven psychic development techniques.

An astounding work for any parent curious about the versatile and wonderful minds of children.

ISBN 0-914295-98-5, Quality Paperback, 192 pages, Photos, $12.95 + $3.00 s/h

NUMEROLOGY:
A Number Of Your Friends Are Animals
by Jackie Suggs, Ph.D.

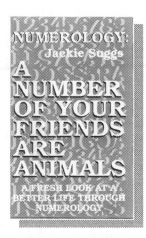

At last... a fresh and bold NEW look at better living through the age-old Science of Numerology. *"This book is humorous, the illustrations are unique, the techniques are exciting, useful, and the customized information is fascinating."* The Amazing Kreskin. Covering traditional Numerology - Name Path and Life Path Numbers — Dr. Suggs in a unique approach, compares animal characteristics with human personality traits. A perfect company with *Understanding Children Through Astrology*.

256 pages illustrated, $9.95 + $3.00 s/h

Numerology Chart Reading (computer generated). Learn how not only your birth date but also your birth name tells a lot about you and where you are headed in your life. Send your entire birthdate and the name as it appears on the birth certificate.

$9.95 includes s/h; Two names to the same address $15.95 includes s/h printout.

**SPECIAL: Both Numerology book and chart only US $17.95 + $3.00 s/h
Make Check to: POWELL PRODUCTIONS**

ASTROLOGY TABLES
FOUND IN THIS BOOK
AVAILABLE ON DISK (Pagemaker4.0)
Either 3.5 or 5.25 diskettes
$29.95 + $4.00 s/h

GIVE THE GIFT OF POETRY
12 SUN SIGN BIRTHDAY POEMS

Understanding Children Through Astrology's 12 birthday poems. A very uplifting gift for friends, family and the like. **Set of 12 Sun Sign Birthday Poems** each with Sun sign picture on 8½ x 11"parchment paper. Suitable for framing.

$9.95 per set of 12, includes s/h.
Individual Poem, Specify month
$3.00 each, includes s/h.

12 SUN SIGNS AT A GLANCE

Two 8½ x 11" sheets in clear vinyl sleeve for added protection and long life. This work concisely lists all twelve signs along with their characteristics: best day of the week, harmonious music, best color, best foods, various health concerns, etc... many areas of insight for each sign. $9.95 includes s/h.